מילין חביבין

BELOVED WORDS

Milin Havivin

An Annual Devoted to
Torah, Society and the Rabbinate

Published by
Yeshivat Chovevei Torah Rabbinical School

Volume Three
December 2007 – Tevet 5768

Editors:	Benjamin Shiller
	Akiva Dovid Weiss
Editorial Staff:	Yehuda Hausman
	Drew Kaplan
	Michael Katzman
	Devin Villarreal
	Seth Winberg
	David Wolkenfeld
YCT Faculty Advisor:	Rabbi Nathaniel Helfgot

Milin Havivin
YCT Rabbinical School
212-666-0036 | 212-666-5633 (fax) | milinhavivin@yctorah.org

We welcome comments, submissions and requests for additional copies of this journal from the general public. Please contact us via fax, telephone or electronic mail, using the information above.

ISBN: 1-934730-50-5
ISBN13: 978-1-934730-50-8

ישיבת | YCT
חובבי | RABBINICAL
תורה | SCHOOL

Where Open Orthodoxy Begins

YCT Rabbinical School's
Mission Statement and Core Values

YCT Rabbinical School's mission is to professionally train Orthodox rabbis who will lead the Jewish community and shape its spiritual and intellectual character in consonance with modern and open Orthodox values and commitments.

We are deeply committed to:

Inspiring a passionate commitment to the study of Torah in all its rich forms, the belief in *ikarei ha'emunah*, and the scrupulous observance of *halakha*.

Cultivating *yir'at shamayim* – i.e. spirituality, God-consciousness, piety, and ethical sensitivity - and integrating it into all learning, religious practice, and worldly pursuits.

Encouraging intellectual openness, questioning, and critical thinking as important components of one's full service to God (*avodat Hashem*).

Affirming the shared covenantal bond between all Jews. Promoting love of all Jews (*ahavat Yisrael*) and actively pursuing the positive and respectful interaction of all Jewish movements.

Recognizing the need to enhance and expand the role of women in *Talmud Torah*, the halakhic process, religious life and communal leadership within the bounds of *halakha*.

Recognizing *Eretz Yisrael* as our homeland and affirming the religious and historical significance of the State of Israel for all Jews in Israel and the Diaspora.

Affirming the shared divine image (*tzelem Elokim*) of all people, our responsibility to improve the world, to relieve suffering and to engage in acts of loving kindness towards all persons

Living our personal, family and public lives guided by the highest ethical standards, reflective of moral rectitude and sanctification of God's name (*kiddush shem shamayim*).

לזכר נשמת דליה נעמי חי ז"ל

בת שלמה דוד ז"ל ותבדל לחיים ארוכים שושנה הלפגוט

The editors of **Milin Havivin-"Beloved Words"**
decided, in an act of love and tribute,
to dedicate this year's edition to
the memory of my beloved sister,

Dalia Naomi Hai *z"l,*

who passed away this past year after a lengthy battle
with brain cancer. My family and I are exceedingly
touched by this gesture and may God grant you
good health and success in all your future endeavors.

My sister, Dalia, was a beloved woman, wife, mother,
teacher and friend. She was truly an *Isha Havivah*
whose loss still affects all who knew her. My sister had
a love of life and a zest for life that was overflowing
in all her work. She was a dedicated teacher at the
Solomon Schecter Day School of Bergen County for
close to a decade and a half, with legions of students
who loved and cherished their time with *Morah Dalia.*
Her devotion to her students was only surpassed by
her love, caring and dedication to her family.

May the words of Torah and reflection that appear
in this volume be a merit to her precious soul and
may she be bound up in the bonds of eternity in
the bosom of God's everlasting embrace.

Rabbi Nathaniel Helfgot

Editors' Foreword

"And a thrice-bound cord is not easily broken."   *Kohelet*, 4:12

In Halakha, an event's third instance establishes its *hazakah*, its presumptive status. For example, the notion of *"shor mu'ad,"* suggests that after goring three consecutive times an ox has effectively altered its own halakhic status, revealing an underlying reality that only now demands its owner's recognition. Additionally, the Talmud (*Masekhet Bava Batra*, Ch. 3) determines that land held in possession for three years establishes a *hazakah*, a basis of ownership. At times, a court of law must acknowledge and yield to the *hazakah's* strength as a reality of established property ownership. Aside from establishing such precedent and presumptive reality, the notion of a thrice-repeated action or event can also be viewed as having strength and power in its own right. It is this notion that is reflected in the words of King Solomon quoted above—that what has been bound three-times over cannot easily be taken apart.

For *Milin Havivin*, our third volume suggests both our vision and potential as well as the strength of our accomplishments. *Milin Havivin's* continued sharing of Torah, ideas, and analysis suggests the future of our beloved yeshiva as a whole. Our *rabbanim*, faculty, administration, staff, and students have already demonstrated dedication to our mission and will continue to inspire religious commitment and growth both within the walls of our yeshiva, as well as throughout the greater Jewish community and entire world.

Just as it takes time and effort to establish a *hazakah*, the publication of Volume Three was an endeavor that owes its completion to the efforts of numerous individuals who contributed in many different ways. There are several people who must be mentioned by name, but first and foremost we must thank Rav Nati Helfgot. Rav Nati's constant guidance and encouragement were instrumental and extraordinary, and his insights and suggestions proved essential. We are grateful to our entire dedicated student editorial staff, as well as Charlie Friedman who assisted in Hebrew translations. Our Rosh Yeshiva, Rabbi Dov Linzer, in addition to providing daily inspiration, provided tremendous support and understanding throughout the academic year. Last but not least, Yoram Bitton's diligent efforts reviewing and editing the Hebrew section of our journal proved invaluable.

Our hope is that these pages, the Torah and ideas herein, will continue to articulate, share, and contribute to the collective vision of *le-taken olam be-malkhut Shakai*, to help transform our world with the highest values and ideals.

Be-Ahavat ha-Torah,

Benjamin Shiller
Akiva Dovid Weiss

Yeshivat Chovevei Torah Rabbinical School
December 2007 – Tevet 5768

TABLE OF CONTENTS

(See also Rabbi Dov Linzer's "Marriage and Torah: Navigating the Tension" in the Hebrew section)

Concepts in *Pesak* Halakha

Tanakh Insights

Jewish Thought and Liturgy

Hebrew Section

(Hebrew table of contents is at the back of this volume)

Dear Editors:

Avidan Freedman is to be congratulated for translating and Milin Havivin is to be congratulated for publishing the important letter of Professor Nehama Leibowitz, z"l, to Rabbi Yehudah Ansbacher z"l ("Accept the Truth from Wherever it Comes," *Milin Havivin* 1 [2005]:108-110). The letter is a perfect example of open Orthodoxy at its best. I would just like to correct one error in Freedman's otherwise excellent translation, where he was misled by what is clearly a typo or error in transcription in the published version of the original Hebrew.

The letter in English translation reads, "Rosenzweig's intention was to parallel the rise of Moshe and *Ha-Kadosh Barukh Hu.*" This makes no sense. The published version of the Hebrew letter in *Pirkei Nehama*, p.657, reads "*Kavanat Rosenzweig le-hakbil aliyat Moshe / aliyat Ha-Kadosh Barukh Hu.*" This, as I just stated, is clearly a typo or error in transcription, and what Professor Leibowitz indubitably wrote was "*Kavanat Rosenzweig le-hakbil ASIYAT Moshe\ ASIYAT Ha-Kadosh Barukh Hu,*" that is, "Rosenzweig's intention was to parallel the making of Moshe and the making of *Ha-Kadosh Barukh Hu.*" This correction is obvious and no confirmation is needed, but, if such confirmation is requested, note that in her essay "*Ve-Asu Li Mikdash ve-Shakhanti be-Tokham*" in *Iyyunim be-Sefer Shemot*, pp.344-354, Professor Leibowitz in a extended note on p. 348 writes, "*Rosenzweig medaber al... mashma'ut kol ha-perakim ha-eleh [pirkei ha-mishkan] she-nose'am hu asiyah enoshit be-ma'aseh ha-mishkan asher takhbil le-asiyah ha-E-lohit be-ma'aseh bereshit.*" Also note the chart on pp. 351-352 listing the parallel uses of "*asah*" in connection with God in the creation chapters in Genesis and its uses in connection with Moshe in the mishkan chapters in Exodus.

I look forward to further translations from Freedman's pen.

Lawrence Kaplan
Department of Jewish Studies
McGill University
Montreal, Quebec

Rabbi Dov Weiss serves as Yeshivat Chovevei
Torah Rabbinical School's Director of
Admissions and is currently pursuing
a doctorate in rabbinic theology at the
University of Chicago.

BETWEEN VALUES AND THEOLOGY:
THE CASE OF SALVATION THROUGH CHILDREN IN
RABBINIC THOUGHT–PART I[1]
Rabbi Dov Weiss

I. Introduction

Christianity is not the only religion that professes a salvation theology, achieved through a righteous and suffering son. Judaism, although with considerably less emphasis and not as well known, does so as well. But whereas classical Christianity believes in the crucified and completely righteous child of God, Jesus, as the *exclusive* method by which every person can escape eternal damnation, rabbinic Judaism affirms the saving power of the children of *sinners*—either through their premature death or righteous deeds—as one of *many ways* in which sinning parents can be saved from spending twelve months, if not eternity, in hell.[2]

This paper will attempt to explicate rabbinic child-salvation theology by answering three fundamental questions. The first revolves around its *exegetical* basis. Since all rabbinic theology, as Michael Fishbane points out, is rooted in exegesis,[3] how did the rabbis living between the second and tenth centuries extrapolate a salvation theology of this kind from the *Tanakh*, where there is no direct mention of the after-life? Through examining the multiple exegetical maneuvers used by different textual voices, we will discover a consistent rabbinic method: interpretive inversions. This approach allows the interpreter to affirm a theology by exploiting its textual opposite. Thus, we will see how the rabbis transform, amongst other things, punishment into salvation, this world into the next, fear of death into hope for death, and human responsibilities into divine ones—in order to build a case for child-salvation theology. Moreover,

---

[1] I hope to publish Part II of this paper in a future volume of *Milin Havivin*. My thinking about the interplay between values and theology has been influenced by Moshe Halbertal's important work, *Mahapekhot Parshaniyot be-Hithavutan* (Jerusalem: Magnes Press, 1997).

[2] For varying views on the duration of *Gehinom*, see *Eduyot* 2:10, *Shabbat* 33b, *J.T. Sanhedrin* 10:2, *Lam. Rabah* 1:40, *Seder Olam Rabah* ch. 3, *Gen. Rabah* ch. 6, and *Masekhet Semakhot* (*Hibut ha-Kever* 1:8).

[3] M. Fishbane, *The Exegetical Imagination: on Jewish Thought and Theology* (Cambridge: Ha‑vard University Press, 1998).

we will also highlight the various textual genres in which these interpretive reversals take place. These not only include biblical statements of theology, but legal passages and narratives as well[4].

Second, we will investigate the *hermeneutical* justifications for these interpretive reversals. How did a particular rabbinic text defend these radical exegetical moves? In this regard, we will focus on the often decisive role that *values* play—as a criterion of interpretation—in the formation of child salvation theology. Moreover, we will expose not only *if* a rabbinic exegete draws on values, but how much *weight* he grants it. Some rabbinic texts are only prepared to use value-laden considerations to generate *new* theologies that are not embedded in biblical passages and can only be logically extrapolated from them, while other more bold rabbinic texts are prepared to grant values the power to consciously re-interpret and even supplant straightforward biblical passages. Other rabbinic texts will also be presented that either implicitly or explicitly deny the power that values play in the determination of theology, and we will attempt to show what alternatives they offer to justify these interpretive reversals as well.

The third and final critical question surrounding child-salvation theology concerns its *conceptual* justification. In short, is this theology—in both of its forms—merited or unmerited? In the Christian tradition, this issue dominates any discussion of salvation, and we can present the same dilemma concerning Jewish forms of salvation in general and rabbinic child-salvation in particular.[5] That is, are rabbinic forms of salvation achieved because one deserves it—either by actively performing good deeds or through personally suffering and thereby paying for the sins of one's past—or does salvation occur essentially through events that take place outside of the self—either through the medium of others or the arbitrary grace of God? Put differently, can rabbinic salvation be rationally justified or is its efficacy beyond the confines of logic? Of course, the answer may be more complex than just a yes or no response. Each salvation theology could operate in a unique way—some more merited (and rationally based) than others. Moreover, within each salvation theology, different texts may profess different points of view. While we will give a brief conceptual overview of rabbinic salvation in general, our primary goal will be to illuminate this issue in the context of child-salvation theology.

Before we begin exploring specific texts regarding child-salvation theology and its exegetical and conceptual justifications however, we need to present an overview of how the rabbis conceived of hell in general and the myriad of

---

4 Part 1 of this article will deal exclusively with how *Hazal* ground child salvation theology in Biblical theological texts. The other methods used to anchor rabbinic theology will be explored in Part 2.

5 See Meir Soloveichik, "Redemption and the Power of Man," *Azure* 16 (Winter 2004), 51-76. Soloveichik denies the existence of unmerited salvation in the Jewish tradition. This paper will challenge this read of the rabbinic tradition.

ways in which humans—and in particular Jews—can achieve salvation from its flames.

II. Salvation from Hell: Overview

Although numerous Jewish apologists have tried to deny it, rabbinic literature makes thousands of references, albeit in an unsystematic fashion, to *Gehinom* (hell), a fiery place where people are tortured for sins committed during their lifetime.[6] Some texts vaguely state that people who live "average religious lives" receive a twelve-month sentence in *Gehinom* to cleanse them of their sins, while the truly wicked are destined for eternal damnation.[7] Other texts, however, are more exact and reserve *Gehinom* for those whose sins outweigh his/her merits.[8] There are also hundreds of rabbinic texts that cite one specific sin as sufficient cause for one to "inherit" the fires of *Gehinom*. Yet given the radical nature of these later voices, it is hard to know whether these texts should be taken literally, or whether they function as hyperbolic exhortations whose goal is to ensure compliance with a specific law.

Although the majority of rabbinic texts mentioning *Gehinom* are preoccupied with either listing those who are destined to go there, debating the duration of one's stay, or even with supplying actual images of what *Gehinom* looks like, a fair number of rabbinic texts concentrate on presenting methods for one's deliverance from hell. These rabbinic salvation texts can be divided into two categories.[9] The first group describes people solely saved through their own merit; for example: those performing certain religious rituals,[10] embodying proper faith,[11] or observing proper ethical behavior.[12] The second group delineates people saved from sources outside of themselves. These include: salvation through the medium of patriarchs,[13] family members (parents[14] and children), being born into a certain religious group (ex. being a Jew),[15] experiencing suffering,[16] or

---

[6] See D. Cohn-Sherbock, *Rabbinic Perspectives on the New Testament* (New York: Mellen Press, 1990), p. 1 who cites many modern Jewish apologists who attempt to deny the important role that *Gehinom* plays in the rabbinic tradition.

[7] *Tosefta Sanhedrin* 13:3-5.

[8] *Masekhet Semakhot of Rabbi Hiyah* (1:6), JT *Pe'ah* 1:1.

[9] As just mentioned regarding what actions brings a person to hell, here too, one can question the literalness of many of these statements. Our approach in this paper will be to take them seriously.

[10] Such as keeping the Sabbath (*Shabbat* 118a), offering sacrifices (*Gen. Rabah* 44:2), fasting (*Bava Metzia* 85a), and maintaining the laws of family purity (*Otzar Midrashim* pg. 398).

[11] Through prayer (*Berakhot* 15b), repentance (*Ecc. Rabah* 7:21), and belief in God and Abraham his servant (*Otzar Midrashim* "*Avraham Avinu*").

[12] Such as visiting the sick (*Nedarim* 40a), giving charity (*Gitin* 7a), or refraining from slander (*Midrash Tehilim* (ed. Buber, n. 52)).

[13] e.g. *Song of Songs Rabah Parshah* 8.

[14] e.g. *Sotah* 10b.

[15] e.g. *Num. Rabah* 2:13.

[16] *Bava Batra* 10a; *Song of Songs Rabah* 2:3; *Eruvin* 41b; *Yevamot* 102b; *Lev. Rabah* 32:1;

through *mitzvot* being performed on them by others such as circumcision[17] or burial in the Land of Israel.[18] While each of these categories deserves research in their own right, our focus in this article will be on explicating one of these methods from the latter group—that of child salvation.[19]

III. Child-Salvation Theology

Rabbinic texts describe two types of children who "save" their parents. The first are young children who die while they are still young, and the second are righteous children who, through their good deeds, cause their parents to escape *Gehinom*. The primary rabbinic work that presents us with an anthology of voices with regard to child salvation is the *Mishnat Rabbi Eliezer*.[20] In chapter five of this work, an anonymous voice draws a distinction between these two forms of salvation. Whereas salvation through the death of a child only saves that child's parents, righteous children can retroactively save their ancestors for up to four generations:[21]

> So too the saving of adult [righteous] children is greater than the saving of the minor children [who die young]. For the saving of the adult [righteous] children saves until three or four generations, but the saving of the minor children [who die young]only saves the actual father alone.[22]

In order to properly explicate these two forms of child salvation, we will

---

Pesikta Zutrata, Shemot 21.

[17] e.g. *Eruvin* 19a; *Midrash Tanhuma* section 6.

[18] *Pesikta Rabati Parshah* 1; *Yalkut Shimoni*, Psalms 874.

[19] We should also note that sometimes this "saving" is depicted by rabbinic texts as a method to guard against *entering* hell, while other texts describe it as an escape *out of* hell.

[20] Most scholars maintain that *Mishnat Rabbi Eliezer* was composed during the 8th c. in Eretz Yisrael. It does, however, preserve (as in our case) precious older *Tanaitic* material that has no analogues in the rest of the rabbinic corpus. The *midrash* is most well-known for its first two chapters, in which the 32 hermeneutical principles to explicate *Agadah* are listed. Sa'adiah Gaon was first to cite this *midrash* in the 10th c. The *midrash* was first published using multiple manuscripts obtained in Yemen in 1933 by Hillel Gershom Enelow, a brilliant scholar, writer, and prominent Reform Rabbi. The *midrash* was reprinted twice in the last 5 years by different Orthodox printing presses and, while both recent editions rely heavily on Enelow's first printing and on his capacious notes, neither of them cites Rabbi Enelow by name. For more on this *midrash* see H.G. Enelow, "The Midrash of Thirty-Two Rules of Interpretation," *Jewish Quarterly Review* 23:4 (1933), 357-367.

[21] Other rabbinic texts, though, that profess a righteous–child salvation theology do not make this claim.

[22] H.G. Enelow, *Mishnat Rabbi Eliezer* (New York: Bloch Publishing, 1933), p. 95. This section of the *midrash* was erroneously cited as forming part of *Midrash Hashkem* in *Otzar Midrashim*, ed. JD Eisenstein (New York: Jewish Writers Guild Cooperative Press, 1915), p. 138. For more on this mistake, see Enelow, *Mishnat Rabbi Eliezer*, p. 95, notes to line 3.

examine the proof-texts provided by these rabbinic voices. This approach will not only isolate the various interpretive and hermeneutical justifications, but will also, at times, help us unravel the conceptual justifications as well. For in what proof-text a rabbinic interpreter chooses to anchor his theology, often influences or is reflective of a specific understanding of that theology.

As we have mentioned, although some rabbinic texts creatively anchor their afterlife theologies using re-interpretation and extrapolation from *theological* passages found in *Tanakh*—even if on the surface they have nothing to do with issues pertaining to the next world—many voices find biblical support in *non-theological* genres altogether. These include biblical legal passages and narratives, as well as early rabbinic laws and sayings. Thus, in these latter instances, the author of a specific afterlife theology not only has the challenge of linking seemingly non-afterlife subjects to the afterlife, but also of making seemingly non-theological texts somehow relevant to theology. We will start our study by looking at proof texts culled from theologically based biblical passages, and then turn our attention to the non-theologically based ones, and then finally to the rabbinic texts.

1. Based on Biblical Theology:
The Shift From Inherited Guilt to Child-Salvation

Inherited Guilt: Background

Four rabbinic texts extract a child-salvation theology from biblical passages that, on a simple read, maintain a theology that children will be *punished* for the sins of parents. Before embarking on an analysis of these rabbinic voices, however, we need to explicate the theology of inherited guilt as it appears in *Tanakh*. In Exodus 34:6-7, God, as a consequence of Israel's sin of the Golden Calf, articulates His attribute formulary to Moses as a method of obtaining Divine mercy. The passages state:

> 6) The Lord passed before him and proclaimed: "The Lord! The Lord! A God compassionate and gracious, slow to anger, abounding in kindness and faithfulness, 7) extending kindness to the thousandth generation, forgiving iniquity, transgression and sin; yet He does not remit all punishment, but visits the iniquity of parents upon children and children's children, upon the third and fourth generations."[23]

In these verses, God declares His kindness and mercy with his attendant compassionate qualities that characterize his providence. The perplexing element of the attribute formulary is the notion that "[God] visits the iniquity of parents upon children" (v. 7). This theological doctrine of divine wrath and

---

[23] All biblical translations, except where otherwise noted, are taken from *JPS Hebrew-English Tanakh* (Philadelphia: Jewish Publication Society, Philadelphia, 1999).

harsh punishment does not square with God's other attributes which accentuate His mercy. Yochanan Muffs, due to the aforementioned consideration, as well as from other biblical texts, argues that this passage is really an expression of God's mercy—not wrath. For him, the import of the verse is not that children *also* suffer for the sins of their parents, but that God does not punish sinners immediately. Instead, God compassionately delays punishment until the time of their children or grandchildren.[24]

Although Exodus 34 presents trans-generational punishment as a symbol of God's forgiving quality by delaying punishment, Exodus 20:5-6 reflects a different approach to the theology, as seen by its context:

> 5) You shall not bow down to them or serve them. For I the Lord your God am an impassioned God, visiting the guilt of the parents upon the children, upon the third and upon the fourth generations of those who reject Me, 6) but showing kindness to the thousandth generation of those who love Me and keep My commandments.[25]

Here, the passage appears in the context of the Decalogue, and the doctrine of inherited guilt is used as a motivating and even threatening device to exhort Israel into complying with the prohibition of idolatry by stressing the awful consequences of sin. Not only will sinners suffer for their transgressions, but their progeny will be punished as well. The purport of "visiting the guilt of the parents upon the children" (v.5) is seen here—as opposed to Exodus 34:7—not as *delaying* punishment, but as an *extension* of guilt and responsibility. Though later prophets, most notably Ezekiel and Jeremiah, forcefully and explicitly reject the concept of inherited guilt, whether in its extended or delayed form, some remnants of this older tradition still manage to find their way into prophetic texts.[26]

A. Righteous–Child Salvation Replaces Inherited Guilt

Many rabbinic texts have sought, in different ways, to solve the ethical and literary (relating to both context and consistency) problems that inhere in these passages.[27] The first anonymous voice in the *Mishnat Rabbi Eliezer* solves both

---

[24] Yochanan Muffs, *Love and Joy: Law, Language and Religion in Ancient Israel* (Cambridge: Harvard University Press, 1992), 16-22.

[25] The same formulation appears in the text of Deut. 5:9.

[26] One such example is Jer. 32:18 which states: "And who recompenseth the iniquity of the fathers into the bosom of their children."

[27] See *Mekhilta de-Rabbi Yishmael*, ed. Horovitz—Rabin (Jerusalem: Shalem Press, 1998), p. 226, *Ba-Hodesh*, #7; *Midrash Tanaim*, ed. Hoffman (Berlin: Poppelier Press, 1908), p. 160; *Mekhilta de-Rabbi Shimon ben Yohai*, ed. Epstein and Melamed (Jerusalem: Gates of Mercy Press, 1979), p. 148, #20; *Midrash Tanhuma*, (Jerusalem: Levin Epstein Press, 1962), p. 114, #19; *Makot* 24a; *Num. Rabah*, (Jerusalem: Vagshal Publishing, 2001), p. 479, #33. Also see S. Schechter, *Aspects of Rabbinic Theology* (New York: Schoken Books, 1961), 185-189.

of these challenges by re-interpreting and transforming the meaning of these passages from espousing a theology of inherited guilt into one promoting child-salvation. He writes:

> And where do we know that saving adults occurs until the fourth generation? As it says 'visiting the guilt of parents upon the children' (*poked avon avot*) (Ex. 20:5). You cannot say that if the father was a wicked man and the children were righteous that He (God) inflicts the wickedness of the father on them because this does not comport with [God's] attribute of Justice (*midat ha-Din*). You can also not say that he (the child) is inflicted with his [parents'] obligation because this doesn't comport with [God's] attribute of Mercy (*midat ha-Rahamim*). So what is [God's] attribute of Mercy? He (God) suspends [the sins of] the father until four generations. If one of the children is found to be righteous then the father is saved. If none of the children are found to be righteous than everyone gets punished according to what he deserves. You may say that "Visiting the iniquity of the parents upon the children" is a language of anger. Go and study the thirteen principles of mercy (Ex. 34): 'Lord, Oh Lord, God of mercy etc'. So even when He says '*poked avon avot*' it has language of mercy—that He suspends [the sins of] the fathers for four generations—that if one of the generations is righteous it saves [the father] from the judgment of hell. Furthermore, at the time that Moses our teacher came and requested mercy, what did he say? (Num. 14:12-18) 'And now...'—and if (*poked*) is language of anger—he wouldn't have said this.[28]

This remarkable *midrash* openly declares its re-interpretation to be driven, primarily, by moral sensibilities. The author denies a literal read of Exodus 20 since vicarious guilt is neither merciful nor just, and God, who governs the world through these values, would never command that children be punished for the sins of parents. Moreover, this *midrash* argues that the doctrine of inherited guilt would never have been listed in the context of Exodus 34, which contains a list of God's compassionate qualities.[29]

The first voice of the *Mishnat Rabbi Eliezer* text, therefore, re-interprets the passage to mean that if a person sins and is worthy of death, his meritorious children or grandchildren (up to four generations) can save him from hell. The *midrash* explicates the phrase: "visiting the guilt of the parents upon the

---

[28] *Mishnat Rabbi Eliezer,* p. 95.

[29] See Y. Muffs, *Love and Joy,* 16-22, who makes the same point. Interestingly, both Y. Muffs and the author of *Mishnat Rabbi Eliezer,* although living hundreds of years apart, use Numbers 14 to confirm their theses.

children" to mean that the parents' sins could be atoned for by the children, and not—the way it is usually understood—that the children will suffer for the sins of the parents. Instead of parents harming their children (according to a literal read of Exodus 20), this *midrash* declares—through its bold re-interpretation—that righteous children (and grandchildren) can rescue their parents (and grandparents) from the pains of hell.

B. Righteous–Child Salvation Extrapolated from Inherited Guilt – Two Versions

Version 1:

Rabbi Joshua, the second voice in the *Mishnat Rabbi Eliezer* text, also derives a theology of righteous–child salvation from Exodus 20, but accomplishes this task through a different exegetical technique:

> Rabbi Joshua says: what attribute is greater – attribute of the good or attribute of punishment? And if [regarding] the at-tribute of punishment, which is less, the children are drawn after the fathers in the sin of the fathers, then [regarding] the attribute of goodness, which is greater, should it not be the case that fathers are drawn after the children in the world to come?[30]

Whereas the first anonymous voice of *Mishnat Rabbi Eliezer* radically re-interprets Exodus 20 and thereby replaces a theology of inherited guilt with a theology of righteous–child salvation, Rabbi Joshua maintains the straight-forward read of Exodus 20, thereby adopting a theology of inherited guilt. He uses, however, this theology to build a case through an *a fortiori* argument (*kal ve-homer*) for righteous–child salvation. He argues that if God *punishes* family members for the sins of other family members (inherited guilt) then He should certainly (given that God's attribute of "goodness" outweighs His attribute of "punishment") *reward* family members for the righteous actions of other family members (righteous–child salvation). In short, in order to justify righteous–child salvation, the first voice of *Mishnat Rabbi Eliezer* re-interprets Exodus 20, while Rabbi Joshua (the second voice) merely extrapolates from it.

We should note though, that by emphasizing God's benevolent qualities, both voices ultimately use value-laden considerations, not formal exegetical ones, as the decisive factor in their interpretations.[31] Yet, the key difference between them is that Rabbi Joshua's more moderate justification, using extrapolation and not substitution, does not undermine the simple read of Exodus 20 which reflects God's wrath. We can suggest two reasons why Rabbi Joshua adopts this less radical approach: either Rabbi Joshua does not share the assumption that inherited guilt is unjust, and therefore does not feel compelled to re-interpret,

---

[30] *Mishnat Rabbi Eliezer*, p. 97

[31] I see Rabbi Joshua's *a fortiori* argument as based on the value of God's goodness.

or, more plausibly, he agrees that inherited guilt is unjust and is compelled to re-interpret, but is unable to do so because he gives value-laden considerations less weight as factors of interpretation. Rabbi Joshua, according to the second possibility, may be prepared to use values as a criterion of interpretation so long as it does not supplant the logical read of the biblical verse.

Yet, putting aside this crucial hermeneutical difference, both voices share an interpretive commonality: they both exploit a theology that professes punishment and transform it into its inverse—a theology of salvation! Moreover, these two voices not only share a similar hermeneutical approach, but they both maintain an *unmerited* conceptual approach to righteous–child salvation. The *merited* approach to righteous–child salvation would argue that the parents of a righteous child are saved because they (the parents) played a critical role in educating the child. Thus, righteous–child salvation theology would be both rational and equitable, for the deeds performed by a child would be directly connected with the actions of the parents. Since the parents taught their child right from wrong, they can take credit for their child's virtuous behavior and thereby merit salvation. A medieval Jewish text, *Sefer Hasidim* (13th c. Germany), explicitly adopts this approach:

> But thus said the Holy One, blessed be He: A son merits his father, for example, where the father sins and gives his child to learn Torah, and to do good deeds. Since through the father the son merited, the son merits the father, and if the father commands the children to do [good] things after their death, behold when the son does them it is as if the father does them.[32]

This rational explanation would not fit according to the two previous rabbinic voices due to the potential generational distance (up to four generations) between the saver and the one who is being saved. How could the actions of someone living four generations earlier meaningfully influence the actions of later descendants? These rabbinic voices would most likely agree with the unmerited approach, which would argue that the father or grandparents are not deserving of salvation based on their own actions. This approach would either claim that the theology of righteous–child salvation is an inscrutable mystery, a gift from God to the *child* for the child's good behavior, or is based on the principle of extension, articulated below by the influential medieval Talmudist, R. Solomon Ibn Aderet, known as Rashba (Spain 14th c):

> The child is a part of the father in flesh: The flesh, sinews and bones... And when a person dies, the Holy One blessed be He takes what is His, and leaves to the father and mother their portion, as it says: *"And the dust returns to the earth as it was; and the spirit returns to God who gave it"* (Ecc. 12:7). And therefore,

---

[32] *Sefer Hasidim Siman* 1171 (Margoliyot)

[the] reward of this world is physical—fathers are extended to their children... And that [is]—because the son—since his body alone is part of the father's and not his soul, as we have said, nevertheless behold he is extended (or born) from the father. And therefore, the son is obligated in the honor of his father and his fear, and the father is not commanded so like the son. For the one extended (born) is always obligated to the extender (bearer)—even though he is born automatically, involuntary [to his actions]—and not voluntary [to his will]. And therefore, when he gives birth to a righteous son, [a] worshipper of God, he [too] appears as if, from his offspring, he is worshipping God... But the father, why shall he be a merit to the soul for the son? The father is not part of the son, and is not born from him—not in body and not in soul. If so, what benefit will the father merit for the son?[33]

Rashba claims that children are the physical extensions of their parents and thus, when the children do righteous actions, it is as if their parents are performing those very same actions. This perspective, Rashba claims, explains why the parents' righteous deeds do not save the child. Children are extensions of their parents since they only exist *on account of* their parents. Parents, however, do not owe their existence to their children, and therefore are not viewed as extensions of them.[34]

Version 2:

Rabbi Joshua (as cited in *Mishnat Rabbi Eliezer*) is not the only rabbinic voice to logically deduce child-salvation theology by building an *a fortiori* argument from a theology of inherited guilt. A text from *Ecclesiastes Rabah* (4:1) does so as well, but with crucial differences:

BUT I RETURNED AND CONSIDERED ALL THE OP-PRESSIONS THAT ARE DONE UNDER THE SUN (4:1)... R. Judah says: It refers to the children who are buried early in life through the sins of their fathers in this world. In the Hereafter they will range themselves with the band of the righteous, while their fathers will be ranged with the band of the wicked. They will speak before Him (God) [saying]: 'Lord

---

[33] Responsa of Solomon Ibn Aderet 5:49

[34] There are a couple of practical differences between the approach of *Sefer Hasidim* and Rashba. First, what would happen in a situation where the child was adopted? According to the *Sefer Hasidim*, this child would still save the parent, whereas according to Rashba—he would not. The second practical difference would be in a situation where the child became righteous without the influence or education of the parent. *Sefer Hasidim* would argue that the child doesn't save the parent, but Rashba would argue that he still does.

of the Universe, did we not die early only because of the sins of our fathers? Let our fathers come over to us through our merits.' He replies to them: 'Your fathers sinned also after your [death], and their wrongdoings accuse them.'

R. Judah bar Ilai said in the name of R. Joshua b. Levi: At that time, Elijah (may he be remembered for good) will be there to suggest a defense. He will say to the children: 'Speak before Him (God) [thus]: "Lord of the Universe, which Attribute of Thine predominates, that of Grace or Punishment? Surely the Attribute of Grace is great and that of Punishment small, yet we died through the sins of our fathers. If then the Attribute of Grace exceeds the other, how much more so should our fathers come over to us!" Therefore He (God) says to them: 'Well have you pleaded; let them come over to you,' as it is written: "*And they shall live with their children, and shall return*" (Zech. 10:9), which means that they returned from the descent to *Gehinom* and were rescued through the merit of their children. Therefore every man is under the obligation to teach his son Torah that he may rescue him from *Gehinom*.

According to Rabbi Judah, when the author of Ecclesiastes speaks of "all the oppressions that are done under the sun" (4:1), he refers to children who die young because of the sins of their parents. They are "oppressed" not only because they have lost their lives due to no fault of their own, but also because they "have no comforter" (*ibid.*) since their fathers are joined with the wicked in hell and the young children (since they never sinned as adults) are counted among the righteous in heaven. Their oppression continues, argues Rabbi Judah, when the children, basing themselves on a death-of-child salvation theology, request that their parents be transferred to heaven. God refuses to grant them their wish since the death of young children only atones for sins committed before the moment of death, and not after.[35]

Rabbi Judah b. Ilai (in the name of Rabbi Joshua b. Levi), who is the second rabbinic voice in this text, then states that Elijah the Prophet will teach these children how to marshal a successful argument that will influence God's seemingly obstinate attitude. Elijah suggests that the children shift their strategy: do not plead for parental salvation due to their own untimely death, but rather

---

[35] I am reading "merit" in this context as "through our deaths." The other way to read this text is that the children were asking to be saved because of righteous–child salvation, and the "merit" refers to the fact that the children never sinned. According to this read, God "misunderstands" and responds as if the children were making a claim of death-of-child theology. The second implication of this alternate read would be that Elijah's contribution, according to Rabbi Judah b. Ilai (second voice in the text), is more stylistic than substantive. There is a tactical shift (evoking God's mercy) rather than a substantive one (shifting salvation theologies).

because of their "righteous" status. The specific argument for righteous–child salvation that the children make with the help of Elijah parallels the *a fortiori* argument articulated by Rabbi Joshua above in the *Mishnat Rabbi Eliezer* text. That is, if God punishes children for the sins of parents (vicarious guilt), then certainly—since God's good attributes surpass his attribute of punishment—God should save parents when their children are deemed "righteous" (vicarious merit). Ultimately, God, according to Rabbi Judah b. Ilai, accepts this argument and the parents are reunited with their children in heaven.

Although Rabbi Joshua in the *Mishnat Rabbi Eliezer* text and Rabbi Judah b. Ilai through the voice of Elijah adopt the same *exegetical* basis for righteous–child salvation theology (i.e. extrapolating from inherited guilt), they maintain radically different *hermeneutical* assumptions. For Rabbi Joshua, as we have noted, rabbinic scholars can use value-laden considerations as factors in their interpretations of specific biblical passages so long as they do not supplant the straightforward meaning of the text.[36] On the other hand, through his depiction of the give-and-take between God and these "righteous" children, Rabbi Judah b. Ilai implicitly argues that humans *cannot* use value-based interpretations of biblical texts without the consent of God who is the author of these biblical texts. In this respect, Rabbi Joshua can be seen as more *radical* than his rabbinic counterpart, for he grants more weight to ideological or value-based interpretations and thus greater flexibility to rabbinic exegetes who no longer need to justify their interpretations through formal hermeneutical rules or divine confirmation.

Yet in two respects, Rabbi Judah b. Ilai can be seen as being even more radical than Rabbi Joshua. First, he bestows greater power to humans who can "convince" God to adopt a certain theology of salvation that He (God) was not committed to initially. Rabbi Judah b. Ilai thus sees humanity as playing critical roles in shaping the way God judges people in the next world. In short, whereas Rabbi Joshua grants humans *interpretive* strength in relation to Scripture, Rabbi Judah b. Ilai bestows upon humanity immense *persuasive* strength in relation to God.

The second radical implication for Rabbi Judah b. Ilai focuses not on humanity's ability to affect God's governance of the world, but rather on our understanding of the open-ended nature of *Tanakh*. Initially, according to Rabbi Judah b. Ilai, the Torah did not profess a theology of righteous–child salvation. Later however, after the logical arguments of these "oppressed children" were made, the Torah came to be interpreted as supporting righteous–child salvation theology. The implication, then, is that the Torah can be interpreted in many different ways and—more importantly—its interpretation could evolve over time.

We should also note that the *Ecclesiastes Rabah* text chooses to dramatize

---

36 As we pointed out, the first voice of *Mishnat Rabbi Eliezer* went even further than this view and allowed values to even undermine the straightforward read of Exodus 20.

the persuasive power of humanity in a highly personal manner. The challenge to God does not come from a detached rabbinic scholar who confronts God's seemingly inconsistent theology, but from *actual children* who suffer for their parents' sins! The protest to God's justice system comes precisely from the very victims of that system. Thus, ironically, this text depicts "righteous" children who die young due to inherited guilt as the ones who establish, with God's ultimate consent, the very theology of righteous–child salvation!

Moreover, the uniqueness of this *Ecclesiastes Rabah* text stems not only from its hermeneutical justification—i.e. the *a fortiori* argument marshaled by suffering children, combined with God's revelatory confirmation—but also from its implied conceptual broadening of the term "righteous." The term may no longer only be limited to those children who *act* righteously, but may even be applied to those children who die *without sin*. Since these children may be viewed as having left the world without having had the opportunity to transgress the will of God (i.e. they died too young to commit a sin or even before the age of 13) they can be considered "righteous." This extension in *Ecclesiastes Rabah* implies then, that like the first voice of *Mishnat Rabbi Eliezer* and Rabbi Joshua, righteous–child salvation is unmerited. In this case, we cannot point to the parents' positive influence as the cause of their children's "righteous" status.

We can also speculate, therefore, that the last line of the *Ecclesiastes Rabah* text which reads: "therefore every man is under the obligation to teach his son Torah that he may rescue him from *Gehinom*," was added by another rabbinic voice. Two reasons can substantiate this theory. The first is that there is a disjunction between this line, which emphasizes the need for *actual* righteous behavior on the part of the child (Torah study), and the rest of the *Ecclesiastes Rabah* text, which, as we have just noted, only requires a formal definition of "righteousness" that would include young children who never studied Torah. The second comes from a *Yalkut Shimoni* text which parallels the *Ecclesiastes Rabah* one, but does not contain this last line.[37]

C. Inherited Guilt Becomes Death-of-Child Salvation

The *Mishnat Rabbi Eliezer* voices and the *Ecclesiastes Rabah* text are not the only texts to anchor a theology of child-salvation in a biblical passage professing inherited guilt. Rabbi Simeon b. Yohai, as quoted by an anonymous elder in *Bavli Berakhot* 5b, does so as well:

A Tanna recited before R. Johanan the following: If a man

---

[37] See *Yalkut Shimoni, Ecclesiastes* #969. We should note that it is unclear whether this last line of *Ecc. Rabah* (4:1) maintains that teaching one's child Torah is the sole way to achieve righteous–child salvation and, thus, advocates a meritorious based view of this theology, or whether it is a statement of advice and expresses just one way for the child to achieve righteousness. If we assume that the later approach is correct, then this voice would not subscribe to a meritorious view of righteous child salvation theology.

busies himself in the study of the Torah or in acts of charity or buries his children, all his sins are forgiven him. R. Johanan said to him: I grant you Torah and acts of charity, for it is written: "*By mercy and truth iniquity is expiated.*" (Prov. 16:6) "Mercy" is acts of charity, for it is said: He that followeth after righteousness and mercy findeth life, prosperity and honour. "Truth" is Torah, for it is said: Buy the truth and sell it not. But how do you know [what you say about] the one who buries his children? A certain Elder [thereupon] recited to him in the name of R. Simeon b. Yohai: It is concluded from the analogy in the use of the word "iniquity". Here it is written: By mercy and truth iniquity is expiated. And elsewhere it is written: "*And who recompenseth the iniquity of the fathers into the bosom of their children.*" (Jer. 32:18)

The anonymous tanna of this pericope posits a view that if one studies Torah, does acts of charity, or buries his children then all of his sins will be forgiven. Thus, implicitly, being free of sin, he/she would be spared from any form of punishment in the afterlife. Rabbi Johanan assumes that the proof–text for all of these teachings is Proverbs 16:6, "By mercy and truth iniquity is expiated." After explaining how one can derive the first two expiatory acts from this passage, Rabbi Johanan questions where the anonymous tanna adduced the last of his claims, i.e. death-of-child salvation theology. At that moment, an anonymous elder in the name of Rabbi Simeon b. Yohai resolved the difficulty by use of a "*gezeirah shaveh*" (often translated as "analogy"). This interpretive rule allows details from one context to be transferred to another context when the same word is used in both places. In our case, the elder (in the name of R. Simeon b. Yohai) points out that the word "iniquity" appears in both Jeremiah 32:18 and Proverbs 16:6, and therefore some content from one passage can be transferred to the other. Jeremiah 32:18 states that sins of the fathers are "paid" onto the children. From this context alone we could only know that "recompenseth" means punishment alone, and perhaps the sins of the fathers have not completely been absolved through the death of their children. Yet, because the word "iniquity" in Proverbs 16:6 is found in the context of atonement, we can posit that the "recompenseth" in Jeremiah 32:18, where the word "iniquity" also appears, includes not only punishment, but atonement (and salvation) as well.

This rabbinic text (*Berakhot* 5b), like the last three we have explicated, anchors its interpretive justification for child salvation in an exegetical inversion! It too exploits a theology of (inherited) *punishment* to build a case for (child) *salvation*. Yet, the *Berakhot* 5b text is hermeneutically unique. For according to all of the texts we have seen up until now, values are appropriated with varying degrees of interpretive weight as criterion of interpretation.[38] Rabbi Simeon b. Yohai, on the other hand, refrains from drawing on values to transform inherited guilt into child salvation, and instead relies on a formal hermeneutical rule of *gezeirah shaveh*. One can conjecture that Rabbi Simeon b. Yohai sought to justify this theology without relying on value-laden interpretive maneuvers.

Although *Berakhot* 5b deviates from the other texts by drawing on formal criterion and not values, in another respect it parallels the view of Rabbi Judah b. Ilai as cited in *Ecclesiastes Rabah*. Both argue that child-salvation theology doesn't derive from exegetically replacing passages that seemingly deal with inherited guilt (view of first anonymous voice in *Mishnat Rabbi Eliezer*), nor through building an abstract *a fortiori* argument from inherited guilt (Rabbi Joshua), but instead stems from an *actual* case of inherited guilt. Yet even given this commonality, these two texts diverge in one key respect in addition to the issues of values: whereas Rabbi Simeon b. Yohai professes a theology of *death-of-child* salvation, Rabbi Judah b. Ilai (as well as the two rabbinic voices in *Mishnat Rabbi Eliezer*) affirms a theology of *righteous–child* salvation.

To summarize: all of our rabbinic texts exegetically transform the biblical theology of inherited guilt to marshal a case for child-salvation theology. For the first voice in *Mishnat Rabbi Eliezer*, child-salvation theology *displaces* inherited punishment; for Rabbi Joshua and Rabbi Judah b. Ilai (*Ecc. Rabah 4:1*), child-salvation theology *builds* upon inherited punishment; for the elder (in the name of Rabbi Simeon b. Yohai), child-salvation theology is an automatic *byproduct* of inherited punishment. Yet, as we have noted, the commonality between all of these approaches is to exegetically invert texts about punishment to profess a theology of salvation.

---

[38] Supplanting a straightforward read of Exodus 20, the first voice in *Mishnat Rabbi Eliezer* grants value considerations extreme power; Rabbi Joshua (second voice in *Mishnat Rabbi Eliezer*) is less radical and only draws on values when building a new theology; and Rabbi Judah bar Ilai (*Ecc. Rabah* 4:1) imbues values with minimal power—for it requires the confirmation of God before its interpretation can be established.

Shmuly Yanklowitz is a rabbinical student at Yeshivat Chovevei Torah Rabbinical School and a Wexner Graduate Fellow. He holds a Masters in Human Development & Psychology from Harvard University and is completing a Masters in Jewish Philosophy at Yeshiva University.

PRISON REFORM:
A TORAH PERSPECTIVE ON THE AMERICAN CRISIS
Shmuly Yanklowitz[1]

Introduction

Shocked and dismayed only months after visiting European concentration camps, I now found myself walking throughout former African slave cells in Ghana where captured civilians were sent to American soil for purchase. I had read Jewish literature on the horrors of slavery and genocide, but on the issue of basic incarceration, I found myself clueless to offer a traditional explanation. Does the Jewish tradition justify or support any type of incarceration? What was the role of prison for our sages?

Having taken on a personal mission to visit prison cells of all sorts from Africa to Philadelphia and from Western Europe to New York City, my eyes have been opened to a new reality of consternation. In my continuing research, I have been greatly disturbed by the unremitting reports that I have read of inhumane conditions and the ineffectiveness of the United States penal system. This current pernicious crisis, in turn, is having a negative impact upon our education system, health care, employment, taxes, and security. All institutions produced within any given culture are generally the result of a broader conception of a social good and of human nature and needs. Thus, these institutions are inevitably deeply interconnected in their intentions and structures since they are embedded in the cultures in which they exist. Any given culture's penal system since antiquity, albeit mostly unconscious to citizens, has also impacted how providently that culture's educational, mental health, and legal systems have operated.

One might understand a primary Jewish mission to be found both in the written and oral Torah as the creating of a society that can balance the con-

---

[1] I would like to thank Devin Villarreal, Mike Schultz, Benjamin Shiller, Akiva Dovid Weiss, and Drew Kaplan for all of their assistance. I would also like to thank Rabbi Melvin Sachs for mentoring me at the Rikers Island Detention Center, and my family for their love and support. Most importantly, I would humbly like to thank the *Ribono Shel Olam* for all blessings and opportunities that I have been granted to allow me to engage in a life of *mitzvot* and *tikun olam*.

stant demands of a passive, faith-based pursuit of peace with a proactive and bold search for justice. By tracing the Jewish tradition's approach to the use of prison, we can learn more effective ways to address the current crisis of the American penal system. As will be demonstrated, the Torah takes a fascinating approach, primarily rejecting prison as a punitive measure. This author appreciates that prison reform is unlikely to rise to our absolute top communal priority because there is an understandable communal and personal fear of criminals that tends to inhibit this discourse. Nevertheless, this is a task in which Americans of conscience, and, *a fortiori*, the American Jewish public must engage. It is my hope that this article will help to further a larger discourse within the American Jewish community around the various positions in the Jewish tradition on punishment, American penal history, moral penal philosophy, and our responsibilities regarding American prison reform. I wish to emphasize at the outset that this article clearly does not serve as an attempt to provide a definitive approach to solving the current prodigious moral predicament. The choice has been made to utilize halakhic (Jewish legal) texts only to advocate Jewish moral imperatives, not by any means to set forth any legal rulings or binding positions upon any individual or our system at large. This will by no means make our discussion irrelevant; to the contrary, it will assist in the holy enterprise of creating a modern, traditional Jewish discourse on values and social justice outside and beyond, yet based upon halakha.

Current Crisis in the United States

The United States has the highest rate of incarceration in the world, currently housing well over 2.3 million inmates and about 7 million in custody of the state (in prison or jail, on probation, or on parole). The rate of incarceration has grown exponentially over the past decade, increasing from one in every 218 U.S. residents in 1990 to one in every 147 U.S. residents in 1999. Prisoners are most often locked within cells that average around 30 square feet (4 ½ by 6 ½ ft.) and are forced to use toilets without privacy right next to their beds. Former Virginia Attorney General Mark Earley testified before the U.S. Congress in 2002 that "anywhere from 250,000 to 600,000" (14,500 of whom are juvenile boys and girls) of America's 2.3 million inmates have been traumatically lambasted and raped behind bars.[2] Additionally, the New York state correctional system has an HIV rate of 8.5 percent, which continues to be spread deleteriously through rape.[3] Over the past few decades, prison as a means of rehabilitation has lost support in favor of retribution, and thus opportunities for education, job training, and drug treatment have become more limited. Sentences have increased for non-violent offenders, and it is increasingly likely for a criminal to serve a life sentence for categorically non-violent crimes, most commonly for a drug charge. Over half of today's inmates are incarcer-

---

[2] Jens Soering, *An Expensive Way To Make Bad People Worse* (NY: Lantern Books, 2004).
[3] *Ibid.*

ated on drug charges, despite evidence that rehabilitation programs are much more effective at preventing future drug offenses than prison. A scholar at the John Jay College of Criminal Justice recently informed me that 70 percent of murders in this country are situational (passion crimes caused by anger, greed, or instantaneous reward). While clearly not justifying crimes, this data has led scholars to conclude that murderers are most often not repeat offenders.

While interning at Rikers Island, New York City detention center, I learned that group punishment is often administered to all inmates when only one inmate breaks a rule. Most often, during a period of collective punishment, criminals there can live in 23-hour-a-day detention with a one-hour optional exercise activity with no library access and silent meals. In addition, the tremendous disparity in arresting among different races should be noted.[4] The complexity of the role of racial dynamics in the penal system however, is well beyond the scope of this essay.

In recent years, there has been a plethora of inmate litigation alleging civil rights violations resulting in prison riots, rapes, torture, deprivation, and physical abuse. Yet the last ten years have also seen enormous increases in rates of crime, drug addiction, and recidivism. Due to increased arrests, lengthy sentences, and ineffective drug prevention, many prisons have become filled beyond capacity. While about 625,000 inmates are released each year, a new batch of about 623,000 enters the US penitentiaries (165,000 are violators, 158,000 are recidivists, and 300,000 are first-time felons). 20 percent (around 440,000) of United States inmates are considered to be mentally ill; 37 percent were under the influence of alcohol when they committed their crime; another 33 percent were under the influence of drugs; 19 percent of prisoners are illiterate, 40 percent are functionally illiterate, convicts on average have an IQ of 8-10 points lower than the general population; and 38 percent of arrests are of young males between the ages of 15-24.[5] Because, in general, prisoners were too drunk, too high, too uneducated, and too young to consider the legal repercussions of their actions, toughening laws is unlikely to serve as a deterrent. Additionally, age is said to be the greatest predictor of criminal behavior, indicating a need for more educational and service opportunities to be offered to 17 to 18-year-old high school students.

Jeremy Travis of the U.S. Department of Justice and the fourth president of John Jay College of Criminal Justice writes that only about 25 percent of the violent crime reduction in the 1990s was due to "incapacitation," showing

---

[4] If the American penal system has been successful at anything, it has been successful at fu - thering a racial divide in American society, as inmates are disproportionately from minority communities. According to the Bureau of Justice Statistics, an estimated 32 percent of black males will enter prison during their lifetime, compared with 17 percent of Hispanic males and 5.9 percent of white males.

[5] Soering

that keeping criminals off of the street is not the solution to crime reduction.[6] Similarly, former New York City Mayor Rudy Giuliani's corrections commissioner Michael Jacobson pointed out that the city's nation-leading decline in street crime in the 1990s coincided with a decline in the use of incarceration as a mechanism for crime control. The same situation occurred in San Diego, which ranked second in the nation in crime reduction between 1993 and 2001, when the state sent fewer people to prison than in previous years.[7] The British government's Justice Office reinforced that research, showing that a 25 percent increase in the number of inmates would only reduce crime by 1 percent.[8] Most criminology researchers agree that the best way to reduce crime is to increase the speed and certainty of arrest for those who break the law, rather than to increase the severity of their sentences.

Rehabilitation efforts have not been wholly effective, perhaps in part, because such programs have been allocated only 6 percent of state penitentiary funds nationally. Inmates often suffer from mental illnesses, drug and/or alcohol addictions, illiteracy, sub-average I.Q.s, inadequate parenting, and a history of physical or sexual abuse, and yet there is too little funding allocated to educational and psychological development and growth. 40 percent of jails and 17 percent of prisons never even make the effort to test the mental health status of their inmates. Perhaps most tragic is that about half of the juvenile prisons in the U.S. do not provide any educational services that meet the state or national legal requirements, and 90 percent of juveniles leave adult prisons without a high school diploma or a GED. Pell grants for ex-convicts were canceled in 1994, even while the statistic is known that leaving the penitentiary with a GED degree reduces the chances of recidivism by over 25 percent, compared to those who leave without a high school diploma.[9] It is reported that only 17.3 percent of rapists and molesters ever commit another sex crime after their release, and according to a study conducted by Canada's Solicitor General, that number can be cut to under 10 percent with the help of modern psychotherapy treatments.[10]

New religious rehabilitation programs have been instituted in many prisons, and prisoners have reported that they impinge upon their religious freedoms. These evangelical programs (many created in Texas under the auspices of George W. Bush serving as governor) explicitly aim to "remove sin" from inmates and to "cure them" of their evil.[11] In a lawsuit in June of 2006, Judge Robert W.

---

[6] Travis, *They All Come Back: Facing the Challenges of Prisoner Reentry* (Washington, DC: Urban Institute Press, 2002).

[7] Soering

[8] *Ibid.*

[9] Larry E. Sullivan, *The Prison Reform Movement: Forlorn Hope* (Boston: Twayne Publishers, 1990).

[10] Soering

[11] Laura Magnani & Harmon L. Wray, *Beyond Prisons: A New Interfaith Paradigm for Our Failed Prison System* (Minneapolis: Fortress Press, 2001).

Pratt, the chief judge of the federal courts in the Southern District of Iowa, determined that this religious rehabilitation system had been an unconstitutional use of taxpayer money, used for religious indoctrination.[12] The Iowa prison program, however, is not unique. Since 2000, courts throughout the U.S. have cited more than a dozen programs for having unconstitutionally used taxpayer money to pay for religious activities or evangelism aimed at prisoners, recovering addicts, job seekers, teenagers, and children.

Yet the evangelical faith programs continue to expand. The Corrections Corporation of America, the nation's largest prison management company, which has 65 facilities and 71,000 inmates under its control, is substantially expanding its religion-based curriculum and now has 22 institutions offering residential programs similar to the one in Iowa.[13] The Federal Bureau of Prisons, which manages at least five multi-faith programs at its facilities, is preparing to seek bids for a single-faith prison program as well. In 2002, the Supreme Court ruled that public money could be used for religious instruction or indoctrination, but only when the intended beneficiaries would make the choice themselves between religious and secular programs. The Supreme Court emphasized the difference between "indirect" financing, in which the money flows through beneficiaries who choose that program, and "direct" funding, where the government chooses the programs that receive money.[14]

Mark L. Earley, the former Attorney General in Virginia, is currently the president and chief executive of Prison Fellowship Ministries, which has almost $56 million a year in revenue and oversees the InnerChange Freedom Initiative, which operates the Iowa prison program. This arrangement provides one example of the private interests of corporations and religious groups surreptitiously blurring the distinction between the separation of church and state.[15] It should be noted, however, that many responsible religious rehabilitation programs have actually been quite effective. A Prison Fellowship program in New York showed that its participants recidivated at a rate of 14 percent where as the control group of non-participants re-offended at a rate of 41 percent.[16]

There have been numerous cases of over-sentencing for elderly inmates, a particularly expensive mistake, as they are the most costly to care for (three times more than that of young inmates) and have the lowest recidivism rates. According to a study done by the Sentencing Project, one out of every eleven penitentiary inmates is serving a life sentence (an 83 percent rise since 1992),[17] yet, according to the Bureau of Justice statistics, only 1.4 percent of ex-cons

---

[12] Diana Henriques and Andrew Lehren, "Religion for Captive Audiences, With Taxpayers Footing the Bill," *New York Times* 10 December 2006, final edition, sec. 1, p. 1.

[13] *Ibid.*

[14] *Ibid.*

[15] *Ibid.*

[16] *Ibid.*

[17] Soering.

over the age of 45 re-offend.[18]

Our penal system has become even stricter due to the vested interests of a number of factions in the industry. Various corporations benefit from the needs created by increasing penitentiary inmates, and politicians benefit in their popularity by increasing the "tough on crime" rhetoric. Yet the number of inmates has increased more quickly than the funding allocated to the penal system, resulting in overcrowding, double-bunking in tiny cells, increased mental illness, and inadequate physical and mental healthcare.

Unfortunately, not only are these conditions alarming, they are ineffective as well. According to the Bureau of Justice Statistics, more than two-thirds of released prisoners are re-arrested within three years.[19] Our streets are made less safe due to more dangerous and unhealthy inmates being released, and thus, the penal system is extraordinarily draining on the American taxpayer while leaving her less safe. According to CBS News, taxpayers are paying an estimated $40 billion a year for prisons.[20] Looking at this data pragmatically, we should learn that prisons do not address the task they are assigned to do. As taxpayers we have a moral responsibility to ensure the government acts justly with our funds. Is the government's penal system improving or exacerbating societal problems? Is it using tax money responsibly or irresponsibly? Are prisoners back on the street in a more stable or a more dangerous state than when they entered? The current state of the system does not respond favorably to these questions.

Punishments lose their potential efficacy when not followed by a proper prisoner-society re-entry program. It has been shown that released offenders view themselves as being "in" but not "of" society,[21] and that some would rather accept a prison sentence than be subjected to loss of all autonomy or hope of living in the community.[22] Victoria Mitrani, Ph.D., Department of Psychiatry and Behavioral Sciences at the University of Miami School of Medicine, wrote that:

> Any crisis represents an opportunity to make important changes in personal and family life as values and priorities are re-evaluated and individuals are more motivated to make changes. Unfortunately, the typical prison experience, which is dehumanizing and not directed at rehabilitation, makes such positive changes all but impossible.[23]

---

18 *Ibid.*
19 *Ibid.*
20 *Ibid.*
21 Robert Johnson, *Hard Time: Understanding and Reforming the Prison*, 3rd ed. (Belmont, California: Wadsworth, 2002).
22 Todd Clear and George Cole, *American Corrections*, 3rd Ed. (Pacific Grove, California: 1994).
23 The Aleph Institute, "Project H.E.L.P.", http://www.aleph-institute.org/help.htm (a -

With little positive reinforcement and limited opportunities for success, reintegration is doomed for failure, while a criminal record makes future employment very difficult. Understandably, one of the major contributors to criminal recidivism has been the lack of hope provided for those released from prison to recreate a life. If one has a prison record, one can lose access to all low-income government-housing programs, employment opportunities, and even the right to vote.[24] As the American system has mostly abandoned an emphasis on rehabilitative work and prison education programs, the prison confines have created a culture conducive to moral decadence. The theory that no rehabilitation works is coming under more scrutiny by scholars studying criminal justice and prison reform. A tremendous amount of literature has begun to reflect programs and interventions that have been found to reduce offender recidivism.[25]

While many injustices remain in the penal system, it should be noted that there are many benefits to prison life as opposed to a free life lived in poverty. In prison, one receives free room and board, meals, and medical attention. Often, even educational and recreational opportunities are available. Yet jail removes a person from most opportunities to strive to fulfill one's own personal meaning of existence and perhaps from any chance to freely serve God and make manifest what is good and holy in society. No matter what amenities are provided, time spent in prison can be one of the most miserable forms of suffering; one makes few decisions for oneself and is usually in constant solitude and under strict surveillance.

---

cessed 5 July 2007).

[24] The Personal Responsibility and Work Opportunity Reconciliation Act in 1996 barred ex-felons with a drug conviction from receiving food stamps, family welfare benefits, and access to federally subsidized housing. In 1998 with the Higher Education Act, former drug offenders began to be excluded from student loans. Over 4 million Americans (over 2 percent of the American adult population) are not allowed to vote even after their incarceration has ended. In response, U.S. Supreme Court Justice Thurgood Marshall wrote: "[Ex-offenders] are as much affected by the actions of government as any other citizen, and have as much of a right to participate in governmental decision-making. Furthermore, the denial of a right to vote to such a person is a hindrance to the efforts of society to rehabilitate former felons and convert them into law-abiding and productive citizens." (*Richardson v. Ramirez*, 418 U.S. 24 (1974))

[25] D.A. Andrews, Ivan Zinger, Robert D. Hoge, James Bonta, Paul Gendreau, & Francis T. Cu - len, "Does Correctional Treatment Work? A Clinically-Relevant and Psychologically-Informed Meta-Analysis," *Criminology* 28 (1990): 369-404; Paul Gendreau, "Offender Rehabilitation: What We Know and What Has To Be Done," Criminal Justice and Behavior 23 (1996): 144-161; M.W. Lipsey & D.B. Wilson, "Effective Intervention for Serious Juvenile Offenders: A Synthesis of Research," in *Serious and Violent Juvenile Offenders: Risk Factors and Successful Interventions*, eds. R. Loeber & D. Farrington (Thousand Oaks: Sage, 1998): 313-345; Lawrence W. Sherman, Denise Gottfredson, Doris MacKenzie, John Eck, Peter Reuter, & Shawn Bushway, "Preventing Crime: What Works, What Doesn't, What's Promising," (Washington, DC: U.S. Department of Justice, National Institute of Justice, 1997).

A Brief History of Prison Reform and
the Philosophical Influence in the U.S.

For thousands of years, penal systems consisted of the death penalty, slavery, intense corporal punishment, maiming, and other brutal forms of punishment. In the modern era, much of the physical punishment of antiquity has been done away with worldwide. William Penn, in the American (British) colonies in 1682, prescribed labor as a punishment for crime in place of physical abuse. Upon his death in 1718, however, the government reauthorized corporal punishment. During the early colonial times in America, religious missionary conceptions of the need to save humans from vice and degradation lead to the creation of a prison that was to be "a benevolent system" founded on behavioral correction and religious affirmation. Advocating solitary confinement and opportunities to reflect on one's sins were expected to be the stimuli for the reformation. The Quakers by the late eighteenth century once again advocated prison reform based on labor. A hierarchy of punishments was to be based on a system of deterrence, not of revenge. John Howard, in England, put into practice this deterrent system calculating punishment not based on the severity of the punishment but on the certainty of the punishment when the criminal was acting. By the eighteenth century, this was the practice in the U.S. as well.

In many ways, moral philosophy has heavily swayed the movement of systems of punishment. Immanuel Kant, the eighteenth-century German philosopher, was a proponent of deontological ethics as opposed to utilitarianism or consequentialism, which is to say that for him moral obligations and duties are necessary and binding in themselves, regardless of any initial assessment of the resulting harm or benefit created to others. Such a conclusion has great implication for a penal system as can be seen in his following remarks:

> The penal law is a categorical imperative; and he is to be pitied who slinks through the tortuous maze of utilitarianism, in search of some (opposing) good which may absolve him from punishment (or even, from the due measure of punishment) where justice requires him to be punished.[26]

Kant's ethical system led him to conclude that the government should only create punitive systems where the punishment matches the crime. In eighteenth-century America, however, optimistic ideas for a "progressive penology" based on reformation and cleansing the soul of sin and evil had taken precedence over Kantian deontological ethics. Utilitarian ethics played a leading role in determining the future of the American system, mostly ignoring the intention of the criminal and focusing upon the crime itself and its effect on society. According to most systems of utilitarian ethics, a good action or good society is one that brings the greatest amount of happiness and least amount of suffering to the

---

26 Immanuel Kant, *Grounding for the Metaphysics of Morals*, trans. James W. Ellington (I - dianapolis: Hackett, 1993).

greatest number of people. It was Jeremy Bentham, a leading eighteenth-century utilitarian thinker, who advocated the famous "Panopticon Prison" where convicts would be placed under constant surveillance from a central control station.[27] However, by the late twentieth century, due to various interconnected social and political forces, the penal system had transitioned from the utilitarian conception of a justice system back to the deontological neo-Kantianism and the usage of the penal system for the sake of retribution.[28]

Alexander Maconochie, the eighteenth and nineteenth-century Scottish prison reformer, invented the concept of indeterminate sentencing, which is an incentive-based system involving early release for hard work and good behavior. Maconochie said, "When a man keeps the key of his own prison, he is soon persuaded to fit it to the lock."[29] He argued for task—not time—sentences where one's term ends based on the completion of a measurable amount of labor. Indeterminate sentencing was used in the U.S. for much of the nineteenth and twentieth centuries, until 1974, when sociologist Robert Martinson published an article arguing that, "with few and isolated exceptions" there was no evidence that any rehabilitation programs successfully reduced recidivism.[30] His article, along with the high crime rates of the 1970s, caused a shift in the emphasis of crime policy from rehabilitation to punishment and just deserts—the revenge theory of getting what one deserves. Later, in 1979, Martinson retracted his

---

[27] There are two important moral paradigms relevant to this discussion: the utilitarian and the absolutist. The utilitarian is primarily concerned with what will happen. Absolutism is primarily concerned with what one is doing. In discussing the legitimacy of our current penal system it seems that we must hold ourselves accountable not only for the future safety of our streets, but also for the moral standard of our current actions. On a practical level, we are clearly very distant from the ramifications if both paradigms were true and accepted.

[28] There has been a moral and legal debate as to whether retributive justice is in fact just and whether one should be punished for the sake of punishment itself and with a punishment "equal" to one's crime. An opposing theory of law would allow other values and purposes to affect the determination of a punishment, such as deterrence, compensation/actual damages, prevention from committing other crimes, and other contributions to the larger social good. But retributive justice and deterrence theory as ultimate grand theories are far too limiting. Deterrence does not have to be carried out to punish one "more than deserved" in order to be effective at deterring. On the other hand, a retributive justice model is interested in giving the unsuccessful murderer the same punishment as the successful one. This seems unjust, as our criminal system should not be concerned simply with the *mens rea* (intention) but also with the consequence of an act. In the end, this offender has not brought actual harm to society and it cannot be justified to inflict harsh punishment without an initial wrong that caused damage. On the other hand, such attempts must also be deterred and do create a society that feels less safe.

[29] Michael Ignatief, "Prisons, the State and the Labour Market, 1820-1842," in *A Just Measure of Pain: The Penitentiary in the Industrial Revolution 1750-1850* (London: Peregrine Books, 1979), 174-206.

[30] Martinson, "What Works? Questions and Answers About Prison Reform," *The Public Inte - est* 35 (1974): 22-54.

argument, acknowledging that some rehabilitation programs actually did have "an appreciable effect." But there was no turning back at that point. In 1977, California became the first state to abandon rehabilitation and indeterminate sentencing in favor of punishment and fixed sentences. States around the country quickly followed suit.[31]

The majority of the U.S. community at this point had, perhaps unconsciously, adopted a retributive justice approach. Moreover, there was a sentiment that the convict simply needed to be removed from society and be virtually disposed of at all costs to solve crime problems. Concomitant to such convictions was an appreciation for the death penalty. Most states in the 1980s abolished parole, instituted a "three strikes and you're out" rule, and lowered the age at which juveniles could be tried as adults from 16 to 14. Additionally in the 1980s, there was a massive prison build-up and an increase in stringency in drug laws. By the 1990s, most discussions about hopeful prison reform for better prisoner treatment and more treatments were abandoned.

In recent years, due to budget crises, about half of U.S. states have begun to take steps such as eliminating mandatory minimum sentences, restoring parole opportunities, and relocating non-violent offenders in treatments from prisons. Now, many of the discussions have moved to address the needs of partnership, moving from a model of a prisoner's responsibility in rehabilitation to the community's responsibility in assisting re-entry.

When George W. Bush became President in 2001, he did not terminate the Clinton-era re-entry programs, and instead adapted them to fit with his faith-based plans. Many see Bush as one of the most pro-prisoner presidents in the history of the nation. In his 2004 State of the Union Address, Bush asked Congress to grant 300 million dollars to prisoner re-entry programs.

Michel Foucault, the twentieth-century French post-modern philosopher, argued extensively that western society during the Enlightenment period embraced the humanistic virtues of reason and justice, which led to fundamental shifts in the use of power and discipline. The penal system had shifted from regulating one's body by means such as torture and corporal punishment, and replaced it with "technologies of punishment" that regulate one's thoughts and behavior by means such as strict surveillance and psychological abuse. This "disciplinary punishment" provides a potential abuse of power on the part of the parole officer, jailer, psychologist, and program facilitator over the prisoner. Foucault does not see the penal system as existing only on the margins of society but rather it manifests itself in many different ways throughout society. He views the prison, the school, the army barracks, and the workshop as completely interconnected in how discipline is administered. Foucault also argues that the disciplinary measures taken within the prison walls perpetuate "criminal factories," convincing the inmates that they are lazy, evil, useless,

---

[31] Sullivan

deviant, failures, and worthless.[32]

The Jewish Penal System and the Biblical Just Society:
Tzelem Elokim & *Kavod Ha-Beriyot*

Before addressing Jewish sources on the ethics of punishment and the legal ramifications, let us turn to the foundational concepts of *tzelem Elokim* and *kavod ha-beriyot* (human dignity).

"And God created man in God's image, in the image of God (*tzelem Elokim*) God created him; male and female God created them." (Gen. 1:27) Maintaining the dignity (*tzelem Elokim*) of all human beings is a foundation for biblical ethics, and is a principle that plays a major role in how social justice is manifested. Due to the infinite dignity held by every human being, the Sages inquired as to how it could possibly be just to detain someone and embarrass them prior to finding them guilty (*Sanhedrin* 7:10). Furthermore, the well-known Jewish legal regard for accurate testimony required the testimony of at least two witnesses, thus severely limiting the frequency of detention.[33]

Furthermore, the dignity of the guilty was taken very seriously, not just descriptively, but prescriptively. Executions were prescribed to only take place immediately after a guilty verdict, so as not to torment a prisoner with extended imprisonment or pillory (*Sanhedrin* 4:1, 11:4). The rabbinic prohibition of *inui ha-din* similarly forbade the prolongation of a case or stalling to carry out a sentence since it adds unwarranted aguish to the punishment.

While the Sages operated under a corporal punishment model, human dignity still remained the top priority. The Mishnah teaches us that if one urinates or excretes while being lashed, all further lashing is ceased because the criminal has been shamed (*Makot* 3:14). The Sages took tremendous care to value the dignity of the criminal and, thus, rejected punishment for its own sake. The ethics of *tzelem Elokim* balanced with general social welfare and security are at the forefront for how the Torah teaches of our criminal systems.[34]

---

[32] Michel Foucault, *Discipline and Punishment: The Birth of the Prison*, trans. Alan Sheridan (New York: Vintage, 1975).

[33] To arrest without proper evidence would be ethically wrong according to the Sages, as a person should never be degraded in public even though he may be suspected of having sinned (*Avot* 3:11; *Menahot* 99b; *Bava Metzia* 58b). Similarly the Sages said that one who shames his fellow in public (*ve-ha-malbin penei haveiro be-rabim*), even if he has Torah knowledge and good deeds, has no portion in the world to come (*Sanhedrin* 99a). Additionally, the Midrash (*Genesis Rabah* 24:7) teaches that to embarrass another person is to diminish God. It is even possible, based on this midrash, that in the world-to-come, the legislators, judges, and prison staff could get a harsher punishment than the murderer inmate himself! A murderer, according to the Sages, does not lose his share in the world to come, whereas one guilty of embarrassing another could lose his eternal reward (*Avot* 3:11; Rambam *Hilkhot Hovel U-Mazik* 3:7, 5:9).

[34] In this moral reasoning, one might apply the biblical command "*ve-ahavtah le-rei'akha kamokha*" (Leviticus 19:18), the imperative to treat others as we ourselves want to be treated (Rambam *Hilkhot De'ot* 6:3; *Avot* 2:10) and the Kantian categorical imperative, or Rawls' "veil

The Talmud even goes so far as to say that *kavod ha-beriyot* (human dignity) is so important that it can push off a Torah prohibition (*Berakhot* 19b). The medieval commentator Meiri commented on this text, calling human dignity the most dear and beloved quality in all of Judaism.[35] The Sages taught that even embarrassment of the "lowest" poor person must be compensated (*Bava Kama* 90b). *Tzelem Elokim* can be seen as a foundation of the Torah, creating a culture of people who strive to no lower a moral standard than that of God's. That each human is created with such dignity automatically grants them infinite rights and impresses upon all others infinite obligations to them.

It is true that some values were considered great enough that they permitted the shame of another. For example, the Sages taught that a father could be shamed to force him to feed his children (*Ketubot* 49b). However, these cases seem to have been generally limited to situations where one who is not officially obligated must be influenced to live to a higher moral standard since the risks for another helpless individual were too severe.

One might argue that prisoners who have broken the social contract with the nation have forfeited their rights and protections and have potentially even lost their *tzelem Elokim*. The moral imperatives set forth throughout the Torah, however, seem to indicate the opposite—that even the unjust deserve just treatment.[36] In sum, it is clear that the tradition did not regard incarceration as a time of ethical anarchy.

Biblical Times

Prison was not emphasized in biblical Jewish culture, and it seems that it was generally instituted more within surrounding cultures than in the Jewish society. Prison was certainly widespread among the ancient Egyptians (Gen. 39:20; 42:16-19; Ex. 12:29), the Philistines (Judges 16:21, 25), the Assyrians (2 Kings 17:4), and the Persians (Ezra 7:26). It is hard to tell though what conditions were like in such prisons. The jail may have been a place of repentance and growth for Joseph: "for out of prison, one came forth to reign." (Ecc. 4:14) Although the Egyptian problem didn't have a program set in place, incarceration was a place where Joseph may have had the space to manage on his own to learn and grow.

For the Hebrews, we also find imprisonment, or custody (*"mishmar"*) used within the Torah for the blasphemer (Lev. 24:12) and for the Sabbath violator

of ignorance" device, and one might ask oneself how one would want their own punishment (or one's child's punishment to be) if they missed the mark. Holding on to the tension of securing our streets and preventing crime on the one hand with showing the necessary mercy for the criminal on the other hand is a challenging moral task laid upon us.

[35] See also *Megilah* 3b, *Sotah* 32b, *Bikurim* 3:7, *Mo'ed Katan* 27a, and *Ta'anit* 31a.

[36] R. Naftali Tzvi Yehudah Berlin mentions honoring the dignity of an enemy in his introduction to Genesis (*Ha-Emek Davar*) where he notes that the prophets refer to the Book of Genesis as *Sefer Ha-Yashar*—"The Book of the Just," because the Patriarchs were called *"yashar."* (*Avodah Zara* 25a)

(Num. 15:34). This jailing, however, only served the purpose of keeping the felon under custody until a verdict could be reached. In both cases, Moses went to God to decide the punishment and the incarceration was not considered part of the penalty. Joshua also told Moses to incarcerate (*kela'em*) Eldad and Medad (Num. 11:28). However, in these cases, the imprisonment seems to have served as a temporary detention pending trial rather than as a punitive measure. There is no source in the Torah for incarceration as punishment.

The clear exception to biblical practice, which utilized incarceration strictly for temporary detention, can be found within the powers of the king. Both the kings of Judah and of Israel maintained prisons (1 Kings 22:27; Isa. 24:22; Jer. 37:4, 15-16, 18, 21; 38:6-7, 9-13, 28), and prophets who spoke against the king in power often found themselves in prison. It appears that the kings were entitled to inflict imprisonment and corporal punishment outside the controls of a formal judicial system. The king's decisions, however, are not viewed traditionally as the legal or moral norms of the Torah, but rather as a supra-legal institution created to address larger social issues.

Much can be learned about the Torah's stance on punishment from the two very pragmatic and creative solutions that it offered for criminals: the institutions of *ir ha-miklat* (city of refuge) and the *eved ivri* (indentured servitude).

The *eved ivri* is most often a thief sold by the court to make retribution to his victims. This indentured servant worked under secure, humane, and autonomous conditions, while perhaps even focusing on his rehabilitation. In the case of the *eved ivri*, the Talmud (*Pesahim* 88b) teaches us that "he who acquires a servant, has really acquired a master."[37] It may be cogently argued that the servant is treated with the highest ethical standards because the purpose of this servitude is not pure retribution, but also deterrence, rectitude, and rehabilitation. In fact, if the servant was not happy with his living conditions and decided to run away from his mentor/owner, he had the right to asylum (Deut. 23:15-16).[38] The servants were, however, still bound by Torah commandments throughout their service. Also, if a slave became sick or incapacitated, his master still had to support him, and this nevertheless counted toward his years of service for up to three years. When the slave received his freedom, he received a severance gift (Deut. 15:13-14). If the slave had a wife and children, his master was also obligated to provide for their livelihood as well. The servant, very significantly, cannot be given humiliating work, nor can he be overworked (Lev. 25:39-43). The Talmud teaches that slaves would leave their servitude with crowns on their heads and in states of joy (*Rosh Hashanah* 8b). It was vital that they not be disgraced upon re-entry into society. This paradigm has much to teach as a model for a just and constructive penal system.

The second solution offered criminals, *ir ha-miklat,* while not a perfect comparison to prison since it was reserved only for the *rotzeah be-shogeg* (unin-

---

[37] "*Kanah eved, kanah rav.*"

[38] See also *Mishneh Torah, Hilkhot Avadim* 8:10.

tentional murderer) and was not necessarily even a means of punishment, can, nonetheless, shed tremendous light upon our current subject, as it provided a new community and asylum for the unintentional murderer to live in autonomously while free from victim vengeance. In modern times, one may argue that the majority of prisoners may, in fact, be viewed as not fully intentional criminals according to traditional standards. This possibility needs to be explored given the fact that so many of the current prisoners are in their situation due to being uninformed, underage, or under the influence. This model of *ir ha-miklat* can thus shed tremendous light upon our modern situation. The Talmud proves, at great length, that the purpose of the *ir ha-miklat* is to provide protection from the *go'el ha-dam*, the relative of the victim seeking to redeem the deceased by killing the accidental murderer. This system suggests that there is also a punishment involved for negligence. Much of the personal moral war of conscience in life is fought within the *be-shogeg* moments, since one should be accountable for not being careful and avoiding unintended negligence. Yet the goal is still not the punishment of the killer himself. Rejecting retributive justice in favor of a mediated deterrence theory, while combined with pragmatic concerns, the Torah's laws of punishment served as a way to protect society at large and to preserve the dignity of the criminal by protecting him from the family of the murdered.

Perhaps most profoundly, the Levites (those whose lives have been dedicated to a life of religious service) were the ones chosen to be present with the murderers. Moshe Greenberg, describing the *ir ha-miklat*, wrote:

> The humanitarian purpose of these laws is obvious, and their aspiration to control vengeance by making it possible for public justice to intervene between the slayer and the avenger has long been recognized as an advance over the prior custom of regarding homicide as a purely private matter to be settled between the families of the two parties.[39]

In other words, the institution of the city of refuge is an attempt to bring vengeance into the control of the civil system, and thus protect the *rotzeah be-shogeg* from the *go'el ha-dam*. The city of refuge was neither to be overpopulated nor deserted (*Sifrei Bamidbar* 159), but should be like a city which has marketplaces and proper living conditions (*Makot* 3:8). The Mishnah appears to describe life as a comfortable one within the city of refuge (*Makot* 3:6). Prisoners in such a system had the right and opportunity to live normal lives within the city and to make a living. By virtue of the Torah verse "and that he may live" (Deut. 4:42, 19:5), it is ensured that the dignity of prisoners could be maintained and that they could remain productive. If the prisoner was a scholar, he could take his school with him to the city of refuge, and if he was a

---

[39] Moshe Greenberg, "The Biblical Conception of Asylum," *Journal of Biblical Literature* 78, no. 2 (June 1959), 125.

student, he could have his teacher brought to him (*Makot* 10a). Not only did the Torah mandate that the prisoner work and live freely, but that he should have full access to all learning possibilities, even if it meant bringing a whole school into the auspices of the city.

Most astounding are the procedures that were put in place by the Sages to ensure a proper re-entry into society if and when one was released from a city of refuge. There is a very important dispute between Rabbi Yehudah and Rabbi Meir over whether the freed accidental murderer may return to a position of authority after being released (*Makot* 2:8, *Sifrei Bamidbar* 160). Rabbi Meir believes that the punishment will have relieved the family's anger. The law concludes that the former prisoner who was released should be returned to his former office or position (*Makot* 2:8). Rabbi Meir essentially argued that felons should not be prevented from receiving work, but should rather return to their former status in order to maintain the convict's honor and increase his chances of success in social re-entry. Commenting on the cities of refuge, the Sages said that if divine law provided "paths and ways for homicides to save themselves, how much more must the right of refuge be accorded to the righteous?" (*Numbers Rabah* 23:13)

Ir ha-miklat, as explained above, is based on a system of unintentional crime. The Jewish legal system requires warnings before certain crimes in order for one to be held accountable. Maimonides claimed that, "transgressions can be divided into four classes: involuntary transgressions, sins committed in ignorance, sins done knowingly, and sins done spitefully."[40] The American system, on the other hand, hardly allows for the negligence of law to be claimed. We have witnessed a failure of society to teach the proper expectations, and have a criminal justice system that shows little mercy to the uneducated transgressor. In comparison, while it is true that Jewish courts could administer *malkot* (lashes) and other forms of corporal punishment, such punishments had very strict requirements to convict, including *hatra'ah* (a warning perfectly timed and accepted).

Both of the Torah's criminal institutions limited the criminal's freedom, yet provided pragmatic theories to address the bereaved or damaged. It likewise protected the criminal and avoided harsh punishment for its own sake. The Bible did not even imagine utilizing prisons, but when necessary, provided temporary loss of liberties to address the situation pragmatically. Yet, even in these cases, a tremendous amount of protection and rights were provided for the criminal.

Talmudic Times

The Talmud further developed procedures of justice based pragmatically on the Torah's rejection of prisons as a punitive measure, yet expanded its role for temporary detention. Early on, Ezra began to empower the courts to

---

[40] Moses Maimonides, *Guide of the Perplexed* III:41.

begin applying imprisonment within Jewish law (*Mo'ed Katan* 16a). Although there is no record that it was ever actually utilized, one example in Talmudic law where incarceration was applicable was the temporary incarceration of the *zaken mamre* (rebellious elder) during the pending inquiries of three courts (*Sanhedrin* 11:2-4). Another example of Talmudic incarceration was pre-trial detention for one who wounds another and must wait to see if the wound he inflicted was fatal (*Ketubot* 33b).[41] Also, in capital cases, the accused would be detained pending trial (*Sifrei Shelah* 114), yet it was possible at times to be released on bail (*Mekhilta Mishpatim* 6).

Remarkably, only perpetrators—not procurers, nor instigators—could be criminally liable (*Kidushin* 42b). That said, it deserves note that the Sages instituted a form of imprisonment called "*kipah,*" which was essentially a small chamber where those perpetrators found guilty –or very serious criminals who were held under special circumstances – could be detained "for many years,"[42] or at times, imprisoned for life.[43] The Sages employed the verse "and you shall put the evil away from your midst" (Deut. 13:6, 17:7, 19:9) to argue for its use. *Kipah* was most often used for murderers not killed due to legal technicalities or for one who sinned three times punishable by *karet*. *Kipah* was not an internal legal solution but an auxiliary device allowed by halakha, similar to the power of the king to inflict punishment and the death penalty when the system didn't prescribe it. Both the case of *kipah* and the acts of the king were employed temporally in Jewish history to achieve a social good and protection outside of the standard legal requirements. Neither institution, I contend, was created to provide the necessary consequence to the criminal but to maintain the proper social order. There were certain times when an offender would be imprisoned, such as during the waiting period to see if the victim will pass away (*Ketubot* 33b),[44] but imprisonment was never a punishment under the primary Torah law.

At a later point in Talmudic history, imprisonment became more standard, used for debtors and the enforcement of divorce orders (*Pesahim* 91a and Rashi ad loc.). Criminals who were repeat offenders but were never able to be executed were "placed in a cell" (*Sanhedrin* 81b); however, the detention was often times still not a punishment but was only preparation for a different solution.

Talmudic law allowed many benefits for prisoners (*Pesahim* 8:6; *Sotah* 4:5; *Yevamot* 12:5; *Mo'ed Katan* 3:1). The law also provided provisions for those being released from prison and for those escaping from prison, such as that

---

41 See also *Mekhilta Nezikin* 6, *Sanhedrin* 78b, and *Pesahim* 91a.

42 *Mishneh Torah, Hilkhot Rotzeah* 2:5.

43 Often, these prisoners were kept on a brutal barley diet leading to death (*Sanhedrin* 9:5 and 12:8) This harsher penal theory seems to be an anomaly and has not been proven, as far as this author is aware, to have ever been actualized. This treatment must, of course, be seen within its cultural context.

44 See also Rashi, Ex. 21:19, s.v. *ve-nikah ha-makeh.*

recorded in *Yevamot* 106a: "If a man escaping from prison beheld a ferryboat and said [to the ferryman], 'Take a *dinar* and lead me across,' the boat provider can only claim his ordinary fare."[45] There is even a special prayer that one who is released from prison recites upon celebration of the cessation of the injustice of capture (*Berakhot* 54b).

Similarly, the *mitzvah* of *pidyon shevuyim*, the redeeming of Jewish prisoners, is greatly emphasized within Talmudic law. While such a commandment would rarely, if ever, apply to the U.S. criminal system, halakha does teach that a Jew does not belong in non-Jewish captivity. The Kantian ethic demanding that we honor this same code for non-Jews can be expressed in Jewish law through the principle of *"mipnei darkhei shalom,"* which obligates that non-Jewish prisoners be treated equally to Jewish prisoners in such a case. The Torah's anti-captivity stance is so strong that if a Jew is captured, it is even viewed as a pressing *mitzvah* to rescue him or her (with the exception of hostages who are ransomed in excess of their worth).[46] While the *mitzvah* of *pidyon shevuyim* does not directly relate to our current system, the values learned from this concept are very telling of the Sages' philosophy of punishment, freedom, and of incarceration by non-Jewish courts.

The Sages, when stating: "The repentance of the absolutely (wicked) blocks punishment," (*Yoma* 86b) also acknowledged that even the most nefarious of criminals can change their ways. Even Jeroboam, accredited to be the greatest sinner of all, and perhaps Elishah ben Abuya (*"Aher"*), were nevertheless, implored to repent (*Sanhedrin* 102a). Certain *midrashim* even claim that at the ends of their lives, both Pharoah and Sanheriv repented and were accepted by heaven. These cases of reformed sinners par excellence might demonstrate how Jewish tradition rejects the modern theory that there are criminals doomed to spend their lives in irredeemable sin. The Sages understood a quasi-prison to be a necessary institution to hold criminals waiting for trial, to deter crime, and to rehabilitate those needed, but never was it used for retributive punishment as vengeance for the crime itself.

The death penalty was another issue that the Sages viewed consequentially and pragmatically. Rabbi Simeon ben Gamliel responded to the claim of Rabbi Tarfon and Rabbi Akiva that no one should ever be put to death, with the observation that such a policy would only multiply the blood shedders in Israel (*Makot* 1:10). The debate whether to ever implement a death penalty was not only based on principles of justice, but also on the efficacy of deterring crime.

Medieval and Modern Times

During medieval times, the role of prison seems to have been expanded.

---

[45] See also *Mishneh Torah, Hilkhot Gezeilah* 12:7.

[46] *"Ein podin et ha-shevuyim yoter al kedei demeihen,"* *Gitin* 4:6.

Imprisonment was extended to sexual offenses,[47] property offenses,[48] religious offenses,[49] nonpayment of community taxes,[50] and other transgressions.[51] Yet along with expanding the role of prisons, new, additional limitations were placed upon the system as well. For example, Maimonides wrote that imprisonment due to debt should be disallowed:

> It is Torah law that when a creditor has sued for the debt due to him, he may satisfy himself out of the debtor's property except such as is exempt from attachment; and if it is found that the debtor has no property, or that all his property is exempt, then let him go his way; *he may not be imprisoned*, nor may he be called upon to prove that he is destitute, nor may an oath of insolvency be administered to him—such is the rule in the law of the gentiles.[52]

The Talmud had already taught the commandment to free a captive (*pidyon shevuyim*) since "no captive can release himself from prison," (*Berakhot* 8b, *Nedarim* 7b, *Sanhedrin* 95a). This idea was probably intended to be employed primarily for psychological distress, but perhaps could be applied all the more so for physical distress involving actual imprisonment as well. It is also considered a "high commandment" to help a prisoner or captive attain his or her liberty (*Bava Batra* 8a-b). Maimonides could not be clearer about this priority when he states that:

> *The release of prisoners takes priority over the maintenance of the poor. There is no greater commandment than the release of prisoners, the prisoner being included in the hungry and thirsty and naked in danger of their lives*; and whoever abstains from ransoming them, transgresses the prohibitions of "thou shall not harden thy heart, nor shut thy hand" (Deut. 15:7), "thou shall not stand against the blood of thy neighbor" (Lev. 19:16), and "the other shall not rule with rigor over him in thy sight" (Lev. 25:53), as well as violates the injunctions of "thou shall open thy hand wide unto him" (Deut. 15:8) and "thou shall love thy neighbor as thyself" (Lev. 19:18), and many other similar exhortations—*and there is no greater obligation for you than this.*[53]

---

[47] Rabbi Isaac ben Sheshet Perfet (late fourteenth-century, Spain), Responsa *Rivash*, #351.

[48] Rabbi Yom Tov Asevilli (early fourteenth-century, Spain), Responsa *Ritva*, #159.

[49] *Ibid.*, #179.

[50] Rabbi Asher ben Yehiel (early fourteenth-century, Spain), Responsa *Rosh*, 7:#11.

[51] Simcha Assaf, *Ha-Onshin Aharei Hatimat ha-Talmud* (Jerusalem, 1922), 25-31.

[52] *Mishneh Torah, Hilkhot Malveh ve-Loveh* 2:1 (emphasis added).

[53] *Mishneh Torah, Hilkhot Matanot Aniyim* 8:10 (emphasis added).

While in the medieval period, prison was expanded in its scope, in more modern times Jewish legal authorities stated that imprisonment for debt was incompatible with the spirit of the Torah law.[54] In fact, Jewish thinkers have rarely advocated punishment for its own sake. This is a Christian idea related to purgatory, external damnation, and suffering in the name of Jesus. Judaism traditionally has affirmed life as the highest value and has viewed punishment as a means of solving a communal problem or as a deterrent concerned with the consequence. Modern civil law often incarcerates a robber as a punishment, without ever requiring him to pay back what he stole if he is unable. Jewish criminal law is about repaying and fixing the wrong. If an individual steals and is not able to pay back what was stolen, the Jewish court evaluates the worth of the individual on the open market and sells his services as an indentured servant to ensure that he can pay back what he stole.

In addition to rectifying financial wrongs, systems like the *eved ivri* were created to help the wrongdoer grow. Rehabilitation does not happen when one is isolated from society. Maimonides wrote that *teshuvah* is done when one finds oneself in a situation they were in previously, yet this time they make the right choice.[55] In this worldview, one needs choice to develop and transform oneself through exposure to real human situations.

The issue of retributive justice addressed earlier can now be revisited in the Jewish context of the medieval and modern eras respectively. Maimonides rejected retributive justice and argued that deterrence is the ultimate purpose of punishment.[56] Punishment is thus not always proportionate to the severity of the crime. One need not accept Maimonides' conclusion though, in order to reject retributive justice. A more nuanced, pragmatic punishment philosophy should allow for various reasons and mitigating factors to contribute to how the system operates beyond only deterrence and retribution.

Rabbi Avraham Yitzchak HaCohen Kook argued that other values and mitigating factors must weigh in on justice decisions in addition to the need for punishment. R. Kook argued that punishment cannot just be *nekamah*—for the sake of revenge.[57]

Rabbi Shalom Carmy has informed me that Rav Aharon Soloveichik argued that while the halakha teaches that *Benei Noah* (non-Jews) are given capital punishment for transgressions, this only means that it is *permissible* to kill them, but not obligatory. Rav Aharon taught that there were many other moral and social factors that must weigh on our penal system in addition to just deserts or retribution for what the law condemns.

Judaism, I submit, advocates restitution in personal injury cases, favoring an

---

54 *Sefer Mitzvot Gadol* 1:93; Responsa *Rosh*, 7:#11, 68:#10; *Shulhan Arukh, Hoshen Mishpat* 97:15.

55 *Mishneh Torah, Hilkhot Teshuvah* 2:1.

56 Maimonides, *Guide for the Perplexed* III:41.

57 *Igeret* 89.

emphasis on retribution. Contemporary thinker David Novak describes concern for the needs of victims as based on two considerations:

> First, we are more concerned with rectification than punishment. In other words, rather than making the criminal suffer physical pain and mutilation similar to the victim's, a procedure that neither helps the victim nor reforms the criminal, we make the criminal compensate the victim as he would have to compensate himself if he had harmed himself. Second, true equality is in practice impossible through a procedure as brutal as reciprocal mutilation. This comes out in three of the arguments the Talmud presents to show that "an eye for an eye" is to be taken symbolically rather than literally.[58]

Certain situations may, in fact, necessitate, according to deterrence theory, that one be punished "more harshly" than the crime deserves, although it should be admitted that such calculations are extremely complex. According to what objective scale are we possibly able to equate a crime with a punishment? There are so many external factors in addition to the crime itself that deserve consideration. For example, should not the psychological damage given to a culture in spreading a culture of violence or law-breaking be weighed into the assessment of the punishment? Such a realization should lead us to conclude that we are in need of a more advanced and complex model for guiding our justice systems. Ultimately, the *ir ha-miklat* rejects retributive justice, as the punishment does not equal the crime due to the mitigating factors. The Torah thus mandates that the unintentional murderer not be punished by any procedures beyond being removed from society.

It is agreed by all philosophers that some level of punishment be justified, as it is assumed that members of society are moral agents with moral responsibility. However, punishment does not need to be given solely for the purpose of revenge or deserts. Cain was given seven times the usual punishment for killing his brother Abel, presumably to serve as deterrence for future potential offenders. It should be noted, however, that just because deterrence may have been an effective tool in biblical times does not necessarily mean that it is as effective today. As the psychology of societies changes, so must the penal systems. There needs to be a reassessment of the effectiveness of rehabilitative theories, deterrence theories, and the needs of our current society. Retribution will always have a minimal weight, and other theories should be adjusted based upon the communal needs and psychology. A midrashic work teaches that humans are not permitted to respond with vengeance in any situation where God has not commanded as such.[59] Theories cannot be based solely on deterrence or retribution or any unified theory for that matter. Rather, a

---

[58] David Novak, *Jewish Social Ethics* (New York: Oxford University Press, 1992), 171.
[59] *Midrash Ha-Gadol, Bereshit 37.*

pragmatic approach should be developed to fix the problem: compensate the loss, prevent the damager from doing any more harm, and facilitate programs for *teshuvah* (repentance) and reformation.

Even the most condemned in the Torah have an opportunity to do *teshuvah* and save themselves. Rabbi Abraham Sachatochover wrote regarding the condemned biblical nation Amalek, "If they (Amalek) repent from their [wicked] ways and accept the Noahide Laws, they no longer continue in the way of their forefathers, and are no longer held responsible for the sins of their forefathers."[60]

Coming out against retribution, Rava said, "Anyone who relinquishes his measures [of retribution, the Heavenly Court] relinquishes his sins for him." (*Rosh Hashanah* 17a) According to Rava, God would look more favorably upon an individual, or a court system, that does not engage in retribution. Additionally, the Talmud says, "Great is repentance, for it tears up a person's [evil] decree." (*Rosh Hashanah* 17b) Should we not create systems that emulate God's ways of tearing up our evil decrees by doing so for those who have changed their ways? Do we even have mechanisms in place that can properly assess growth of those being punished in our system and adjust to their needs?

Potential Future Improvements of the Situation

Today, of course, prisons are needed to maintain social order. No attempt is being made here to do away completely with the penal system, rather we must realize its severe limitations and drawbacks. This author understands issues of crime and punishment as a wild, random beast that can be observed and manipulated but never fully contained or understood, and no grand theory or solution will be provided to "solve" this crisis. Evil seems to be a fundamental element in human society which cannot be solved, merely mitigated through a more secure and sophisticated system of punishment.

The 2007 Congress has been discussing The Second Chance Act, a bill that authorizes close to $100 million over two years to address the significant problem of about 700,000 ex-offenders who will leave prison in 2007 (two-thirds of whom are likely to be rearrested within three years). The bill would provide states with grants to develop model programs for prisoners returning to society. However, this bill still has many shortcomings not adequately addressing the recidivism rate, which is increasing due to the breaking of technical parole violations. However, this bill would still serve as a great victory for prison reformers and would mark the first time in decades that legislation has attempted to ease the lives of prisoners rather than make them stricter. For example, in the 1990s, Congress ended the Pell Grant program for prisoners, restricted drug offenders from receiving federal student loans, and cut highway money for states that did not revoke or suspend a drug felon's driver's license. Yet in the campaign document for House Democrats recently elected to of-

---

[60] Responsa *Avnei Nezer, Orah Hayim* 2:508.

fice called "A New Direction for America," prison reform was not one of the issues that made the priorities. In 1994, issues of crime were one of the top priorities of American voters, but in 2003, only 1 percent of voters found it to be a top priority.

Many new types of prison therapy are proving to be quite successful. It has been shown that the Functional Family Therapy program has saved almost $15,000 per child per year and has reduced recidivism rates by 30 percent.[61] Multidimensional Treatment Foster Care saved over $20,000 and resulted in 60 percent fewer days of incarceration. Multi-systemic Therapy saved over $30,000 with to 25-70 percent lower long-term recidivism rates.[62] These therapies involve experts administering comprehensive, consistent therapy that engages multiple involved parties (such as family members) and not just the criminal. Religious rehab with academically rigorous psychological standards and legal checks maintaining religious freedom is needed. In addition to therapy for the prisoner, it is important that the children and spouses of prisoners be prepared for the re-entry process. Counseling for couples and for orphans is also imperative to create a just and safe society.

The time has come to reconsider more progressive options for mentoring programs based on our biblical notion of the *eved ivri*, our biblical concept of deportation to private colonies in the *ir ha-miklat* model, a use of house arrest and half-way houses, a return to a focus on victim restitution, and maintenance of human rights within prison walls. An increase in rehabilitation, education, job training, family involvement, employment readiness, discharge planning, and community justice partnerships must also be considered. One of the most important changes needed in our correction systems is the improvement of the offender re–entry programs, which prepare inmates to re-enter society. More post-release supervision and support must also be provided to allow for growth sustainability. Currently, about 20 percent of released inmates do not receive any kind of supervision or support.[63] Through attempts to improve literacy, giving inmates citizenship responsibilities, and improving vocational skills, inmates can be more properly prepared to re-enter as socially conscious and trained citizens. Additionally, sex offenders and many violent criminals require cognitive-behavioral therapy and empathy training. By repairing their cognitive distortions and by listening to the narratives of victims, learning can be a successful rehabilitative tool. There have been many successful treatment programs that are rebuilding empathy for victims by reading painful accounts of crimes committed and learning to take the perspective of the victim.[64] While

---

61 Diana Henriques and Andrew Lehren, "Religion for Captive Audiences, With Taxpayers Footing the Bill," *New York Times* 10 December 2006, final edition, sec. 1, p. 1.

62 *Ibid.*

63 Joan Petersilia & Jeremy Travis, "Reentry Reconsidered: A New Look at an Old Question," *Crime & Delinquency* 47, no. 3 (2001): 291-313.

64 Goleman, 107.

I was a rabbinic intern at the Rikers Island Prison for detention in New York City, Rabbinic Chaplain Rabbi Melvin Sachs informed me that while New York State does provide some drug therapy, it does not provide any therapy for sex criminals and that the religious chaplains on staff are not generally trained to deal with these matters. There can also be a deleterious lack of coordination between the mental health workers and the religious chaplains, which can exacerbate prisoner frustrations.

Something similar to the *eved ivri* model has been implemented in some community supervision programs, where criminals remain within society as opposed to being jailed. For example, North Carolina put their model into practice in 1994, immediately reducing arrests from 42 to 20 percent, and resulting in tremendous savings ($23,800 per prisoner, compared to $668 for a regular supervision program and $4,187 for the strictest enforcement and supervision).[65] In a poll of police chiefs from around the U.S., 59 percent considered court-supervised treatment more effective than sending offenders to prison or jail.[66] California's state government has found that every dollar spent on substance abuse therapy will generate seven dollars of savings through reduced hospitalization and reduced crime rates.[67]

At this point, readers may still be skeptical. Who in their right mind wants to be more lenient or merciful on criminals? Yet an ABC News poll recently showed that 75 percent of Americans agree that first-time (and even second-time) offenders should be sent to therapeutic programs instead of jail. The Prison Fellowship Ministries Program in Detroit has achieved re-offense rates of 1 percent in cases where a church "adopts" a felon.[68] Other cities have tried using full-time social workers that assist parolees and probationers to find employment, which, in Brooklyn for example, has decreased recidivism rates of participants by 60 percent.[69] There are many programs like this throughout the country.

One of the most appropriate forms of rehabilitation could be conducted through more elaborate and meaningful community service work. Prisoners could be used more extensively, if willing, to assist during flood or tornado disasters. This could be very beneficial to society and could greatly improve the morale of inmates. Prisoners have also been known to successfully talk to students about the dangers of drugs and crime. Recently, a group of about thirty Colorado prison inmates devised a program to help handicapped children. The inmates were successful in training wild horses to be able to give rides to handicapped children providing a phenomenal developmental opportunity for

---

65 Petersilia & Travis.

66 *Ibid.*

67 *Ibid.*

68 Magnani.

69 *Ibid.*

the inmates and an additional communal good.[70] Of course, certain ethical standards should be maintained in administering work to prisoners. Rehabilitative labor should be non-humiliating (i.e., prisoners should not "bust rocks" to make gravel in an age where this is done by machine). It should be useful to society, not merely to a private interest, as this will allow some prisoners to see this labor as a way to successfully "pay a debt" that they may "owe."

Additionally, the labor should be useful to the prisoner in some way. If the prisoner acquires some job skill, he may learn to take his ability to be productive more seriously, and have the confidence to seek gainful employment after prison. In addition, since taking the benefit of his labor under compulsion may rest on somewhat shaky ground morally, ensuring that the prisoner gets something tangible (cash, or a shorter sentence) out of the exchange should be a priority as well.

Prison staff members should be better educated to the psychological trauma experienced by inmates and should understand well that seclusion from modern society is already an immense punishment and should not be exacerbated with further abuse. Prison staff should be hired to assist the prison reformation process, not to increase punishment or stricter surveillance. Salaries for prison staff should be raised to a living wage ensuring that the staff is well enough prepared to take care of their own families and live a healthy life. Anger, resentment, and improper compensation has led countless prison staff members to abuse inmates. In addition, these employees should be placed under higher surveillance and accountability, attempting to cease all inner-prison harassment. Abuse will never improve reformation but will only delay or remove any hope of psychological progressive healing. Quality prison staff, with more sophisticated training, could feel a great sense of accomplishment working to improve prisoner reform rates.

It must be acknowledged that there are those criminals who face little chance of reform and this author proposes no leniency for these hard-core, pernicious criminals. Psychopaths generally feel no remorse for even the cruelest acts. However, these cases should generally be viewed as the exceptions to the rule. There is no magic ball revealing the potential for change for any given inmate and so we must assume that each criminal has a chance. Even those prisoners who face extended time or life sentences should be deeply involved in the reform process due to the contribution that they can make in creating the prison culture and to their own human needs and dignity. It should be made clear that this author is not advocating all types of rehabilitation with a *carte blanche*. It is clear that many types are ineffective, penurious, and even more are immorally conducted. However, many therapies and programs have great promise for success and are even desired by prisoners. Additionally, there are alternatives that can be applied in place of incarceration, such as various treatment programs.

---

[70] Soering.

Responsibility falls not only upon legislators, prison staff, and government officials; rather, all of society has necessary contributions to make. Some communities have begun to create faith-based advisory councils to try and narrow the prison-community divide. It behooves American Jewish communities, at the very least, to offer more and better support to Jewish criminals released in their own communities. As a bare minimum, Jewish community members can be involved with lobbying and political advocacy for prison reform. Those more inspired can volunteer time to assist the re-entry process for inured and desensitized criminals in one's home community, providing job training, relocation assistance, and other types of mentorship and friendship.

In addition, the Jewish community should continue to reinforce the importance of family life and parental education. Often, beginning in infancy, emotional neglect can leave children permanently scarred and ultimately behind bars. To prevent such situations from increasing, there should be continual reinforcement of the importance of adoption, supporting orphans, improving the educational system and after-school programs, and, of course, most challengingly, improving the quantity and quality of time spent with one's own children. Parents should reinforce the efficacy of teaching and assisting the development of their children as opposed to careless punishment for its own sake without concomitant education.

The Aleph Institute is one of the Jewish organizations that has been doing work in Jewish rehabilitation within prisons—organizing programs with workshops, one-to-one meetings with rabbis, halakha classes, videos, group discussions, mentor sessions, prayer and meditation, anger management, and discussion about communication and interpersonal relationships. They are addressing a great need, yet they still need more partners. Other clergy members, counselors, and more rabbis need the proper training to work with this population during incarceration and thereafter. In addition, our religious community needs programs to aid in the re-entry process.

As a community, let us consider two fundamental psychological inquiries: how do humans learn, grow, and change? and what motivates individuals to act? Much has been written on these questions that can shed incredible light on how we should rethink many of our communal assumptions and institutions, but primarily our penal system.

Conclusion

Fyodor Dostoevsky, the prolific nineteenth-century Russian novelist, argued that the way a society treats its prisoners is indicative of whether or not it is a moral civilization.[71] It seems that the values of *tzelem Elokim*, that all humans are created in the image of God, and *kavod ha-beriyot*, human dignity, should be at the core for how we develop our communal policies and institutions. A sophisticated understanding of the interconnectivity of the influence of various

---

[71] Fyodor Dostoevsky, *The House of the Dead.*

public systems demonstrates that no system can live in isolation from another, nor can it avoid the intellectual underpinnings of the culture in which it is embedded. How we create our prison systems will inevitably affect how we raise our own children, how we view our secular legislation, our views on war theory, torture, rehabilitation and human change, and how we create our educational and health systems. In addition, any given culture's worldview and values will inevitably be remolded by how we have created our public institutions, their efficacy, and their moral standards.

The American system, in the late twentieth century, lost faith or interest in inmate reform and has come to advocate prisons as a form of retribution, revenge, and punishment as an end in itself. However, it has been argued here that the Jewish tradition has taught us that prison, if it must exist, should be used for learning, deterrence, rehabilitation, pragmatic concerns of reducing harm to all involved, and for the general protection of society at large. American Jewish citizens should be at the forefront of prison reform and at shaping American society around the most humane, just, and ethical standards. Should a prisoner endure some form of punishment, our Jewish tradition demands that it be done with standards emphasizing the convict's human dignity and potential for repentance and change.

It may be worth considering how the Torah's models of *ir ha-miklat* and *eved ivri* can inform us of ways to implement new types of home arrest, mentorship programs, and more humane and developed rehabilitation programs. Our justice system should be viewed from a pragmatic, systemic perspective, addressing issues for all involved such as: the victim's needs, the criminal's dignity, the court's authority, potential future criminals, and the security of society at large. In addition, we must become more aware of how our prison systems affect our educational systems, our understanding of human nature, our taxes, and our security. It seems that the concepts of punishment that we apply in our prisons are beginning to be utilized in school disciplining as well. For example, there has been a reported rise in suspensions and expulsions within many Jewish day schools.[72] Also a sign of increased consciousness of punishment, it has been reported that about 80 percent of American parents still spank their children.[73]

Our understanding of repentance within our religious practices may be connected to how we understand our communal corrective systems. A classic example is the ascetic tradition, which, for many Jews, involved engaging in penitential practices such as rolling in the snow and self-flogging so as to improve themselves morally. These actions were somewhat similar to the secular view of punishment at that time. In sixteenth-century Safed they even imposed self-affliction by imitating the four traditional methods of capital punishment.

---

[72] Kwame Anthony Appiah, *The Ethics of Identity* (New Jersey: Princeton University Press, 2004).

[73] *Ibid.*

So too today, our methods of repentance are connected to our perceptions of our prison system. How we have viewed prisons has historically been connected to how we have viewed the mentally ill, having used tranquilizing chairs, water torture, and cages to "cure" the mentally ill with behavioral and mental reconditioning. (During those time periods, we applied these types of reconditioning to our prisoners as well.)

Most of modern, western society has removed torture, capital punishment, corporal punishment, and solitary confinement from the penal system. However, the current American penal system has fallen behind. Our Torah values and moral convictions place responsibility upon the American Jewish community to advocate for better conditions within prisons and for more creative solutions for rehabilitation than are currently being provided. In addition, greater measures need to be taken to ensure the security of prisoners from the great violations of human rights that have been experienced within their cells. The Jewish Nation has a mission to assist the helpless, and those locked away without advocates are calling to us. While our tradition may teach us that prison itself is an undesirable institution, and since we are in no position to imprudently tear down the system as a whole, we will need to think of a more moderate response to our modern situation that fully condemns only the inhumane and ineffective prisons as evil.

A world that minimizes prisons within the justice system is not an aloof messianic ideal but a real and attainable vision. What must be sought is a new western morality and a recognition of empirical facts attesting to how people change. The current American retributive justice system is driven by fear, whereas the ethics of Jewish tradition demand us to create a system based on a balance between concerns for human dignity, communal security, and, above all, peace. It may be that our society fears addressing the real, underlying issues and looking our prisoners in the eye to see his or her humanity and needs. The current system breeds more violence, more racism, more poverty, and deeper hatred. There is a need to move from many of the church's models of religious rehabilitation to one of learning and holistic healing. Every aspect of prison life has a profound impact on the prisoner's long-term psyche and so more care must be taken to create the proper prisoner culture, supervision, and education. It is a move from a fear-based redemptive model to one of healing and development.

The Talmud teaches us that Joseph was released from jail on Rosh Hashanah (*Rosh Hashanah* 11a). The New Year represents a time when repentance is accepted and when one has a chance to recreate one's self. It is our responsibility to grant a "new year" to those released and to imitate God in extricating the captive and supplying them with a chance for a renewal of self. In the coming years, will we heed the call of the Psalmist who declares that we must "hear the cries of the prisoner, to liberate those condemned to die?" (Ps. 102:21)

Ben Greenberg is a rabbinical student at Yeshivat Chovevei Torah Rabbinical School and an alumnus of Interfaith Worker Justice's Seminary Summer program.

The Exodus as the Foundational Paradigm for Social Justice
Ben Greenberg

A recent survey of the American Jewish population determined that more than 70% of American Jews have participated, at least once in their lives, in a Passover ritual.[1] Passover, along with Hanukkah and Yom Kippur, occupies a significant place in the religio-cultural life of American Jewry. What is the reason this holiday is so widely observed amongst Jews from all denominational backgrounds? One could argue that a significant factor in its widespread popularity may be because so many of its central observances and rituals take place outside of the institutional walls of a synagogue (i.e. in the home and family context). However, perhaps there is another reason, one that is more fundamental to the nature of the holiday that compels such a vast percentage of American Jewry, despite its high rates of assimilation and disaffection, to associate with its practice.

Rabban Gamliel is quoted as stating that "in each and every generation, one is obligated to see oneself as having left Egypt" (*Pesahim* 10:5). This particular mishnah occupies a high point in the annual Passover seder, the public feast and set of rituals performed the first two nights of the holiday. The biblical source for the obligation to personalize the liberation from Egypt is a verse in the Book of Exodus, "And you shall tell your child on that day saying: It is because of this that God acted on my behalf when I left Egypt" (13:8). The mishnah places the emphasis in the verse on the word "you," thereby exhorting the reader to view the Exodus not as an event only to be recorded in the annals of history, but rather as a moment living within the consciousness of modern times and within the memory of each living individual. Accordingly, Dr. Ronald Hendel of the University of California at Berkeley describes the Exodus from Egypt quoting a saying by William Faulkner: "The past is never dead. It's not even past."[2]

The biblical saga of the children of Jacob migrating to Egypt, rising to power and affluence, descending into a state of slavery while suffering immense perse-

---

[1] "Surveying the Jewish Population in the United States," *Institute for Jewish and Community Research*, 2003.

[2] "The Exodus in Biblical Memory," *Journal of Biblical Literature* 120, No. 4 (Winter 2001), 601.

cution, and then eventually being redeemed by the mighty and awesome God of their forefathers serves as the main source of authenticity to the eventual covenant formed between the nascent Israelite nation and God. This is alluded to in the biblical commentary of the preeminent medieval scholar Rabbi Abraham Ibn Ezra (1093–1167). Ibn Ezra expounds on the verse in Exodus 13:8 and suggests that the term "this" refers to the biblical commandments to eat *matzah* and the sacrificial Passover offering. Ibn Ezra maintains that the primary motivation for the miraculous redemption of the Israelite nation was to forge a nation that would heed the Divine command. The people would then commit themselves to performing the will of God as embodied in a set of particularistic obligations and thereby become the "treasured" nation of the Divine (Ex. 19:5). The entire covenantal relationship would most likely never have developed if the children of Jacob had not sojourned in Egypt and went through the ordeals and trauma of slavery and then after experienced a divine liberation.[3]

Yet one may question why it was necessary—indeed absolutely critical—for the Israelites to experience the torment of oppression in order to become elevated to the status of a chosen, treasured people? The entire Hebrew biblical tradition relies on the Exodus as a critical cornerstone of the narrative of covenant, as the bedrock of all subsequent commandments, and as the inspiration for much of the later prophetic tradition.[4] Moreover, the holiday of Passover, against all odds, persists in being observed in the modern era despite it being an era of unaffiliation, assimilation, and apathy. The common understanding of the Exodus is that of a prelude to the revelation of the Torah at Horeb and the eventual construction of the building of the Temple in Jerusalem. This perspective is most popularly represented in the liturgical song of the Passover seder "*Dayeinu*," in which the events of the Exodus, the revelation of the Torah, the settlement of the Land of Israel, and the building of the Temple are outlined in a seemingly sequential order, with the most exalted being the construction of the Temple. In other words, the entire liberation seems to serve as a backdrop to future events.

This view, though not the view of Ibn Ezra, nor that of other classic and significant commentators,[5] operates under the assumption that the Exodus from Egypt served as the foundational moment in the formation of the Israelite nation and its election as God's chosen people. Yet a question must be raised as to why there was a necessity to begin the covenantal relationship in the furnace of oppression in Egypt? The Exodus serves as the prime biblical event to be forever commemorated and remembered in the lives of the people of Israel. It

---

[3] The necessity of an experience of servitude was alluded to in Genesis 15:13 at the "Covenant of the Parts" between God and Abraham.

[4] Hendel, "The Exodus in Biblical Memory," 601.

[5] For example, see the commentaries of Rashbam (Rabbi Shmuel ben Meir, 12th century) and Ramban (Rabbi Moshe ben Nahman, 13th century) on the verse in Exodus 13:8 that opine similarly to Ibn Ezra.

forges a common identity amongst a collection of disparate tribes, clans, and families and unites them all into a nation. The children of Abraham, Isaac, and Jacob are only first referred to as a nation in the context of the redemptive experience from Egypt. It is through the collective and shared suffering and commiseration that the children of Jacob are able to leave Egypt as the nation of Israel. Hendel opines that the "memories of shared suffering are potent ingredients in the formation and persistence of ethnic identity," thus, the Pharoah recorded in the narrative of the Exodus is intentionally left nameless in order to remain an "emblem of collective memory."[6] All in all, the beginnings of the Israelite national experience—the major thrust of the biblical narrative and one of the central themes of the Jewish calendrical year—are encapsulated by the experiential depths of oppression and servitude, inversely laced and coupled with an ultimate and climactic redemption and liberation.

The Catholic Church, in a different context, wrestled with its own issues of oppression and redemption in the latter half of the twentieth century during a period of intense political upset and revolt in Latin America.[7] A wave of anti-establishment sentiment swept the continent, which had been historically dominated by colonialist forces. The local Catholic Church responding to the needs of the population began to re-evaluate traditional theological positions of order and hierarchy and developed a theology that would revolutionize Christendom: Liberation Theology. One of the seminal works of this new theology was written in 1972 by the Peruvian priest Gustavo Gutierrez entitled *A Theology of Liberation: Perspectives*. Gutierrez in his work, highlights three steps towards a total liberation. The first step dictates there be a real and practical solution implemented to the situation of the world's poor and oppressed and that there can be no theologizing or any lofty agenda until the immediate temporal needs of the poor are dealt with. The second is that global society must address the systemic biases that "limit their (the oppressed and poor) capacity to develop themselves freely and in dignity."[8] Finally, in order to create a lasting change that profoundly impacts the lives of the downtrodden, humanity's bond to God must be reaffirmed and strengthened. People must pursue a life of continuous introspection and improvement. This last step will ultimately bring about a liberation from what lies at the heart of all oppressions: sinfulness and selfishness.

The Vatican, the seat of authority for the Roman Catholic Church, did not react positively to the developments in Latin America. The new liberation theologians were quickly dismissed as Marxists with a thin guise of religion.[9]

---

6 Hendel, "The Exodus in Biblical Memory," 608.

7 Jean-Pierre Cloutier, "Theologies: Liberation vs. Submission," *The Haiti Times*, (1987).

8 Gustavo Gutierrez, *A Theology of Liberation: History, Politics, and Salvation*, ed. & trans. Sister Caridad Inda & John Eagelson (Maryknoll, NY: Orbis, 1988).

9 H. Mark Roelofs, "Liberation Theology: The Recovery of Biblical Radicalism," *The American Political Science Review* 82, No. 2 (June 1988), 549.

However, widespread popularity of Liberation Theology, particularly amongst the poor, contributed to its success in surviving, despite harsh opposition from the Church establishment. Prior to the formation of Liberation Theology, the Catholic Church in 1962-1965 convened and established the principles of Vatican II under Pope John XXIII and subsequently under Pope Paul VI. At the heart of Vatican II was a struggle with autonomy that preceded the challenge to Church structure that the liberation theologians posed. For centuries the *modus operandi* of the Church could have been summarized in the oft-quoted adage, *"Rome locuta, causa finita* -- Rome has spoken, the case is settled."[10] In other words, the ultimate authority for all matters of theology and religious practice rested not in the Bible, but rather in the halls of the Papal Palace. Indeed, one of the striking features of the Protestant Reformation in sixteenth-century Europe was to disseminate copies of the Bible to the masses and thereby weaken the authority the Pope held in forming a uniform interpretation and reading of the Holy Writ.[11]

Liberation theologians maintained the tradition of Martin Luther and other Protestant reformers, holding that the Bible must be disseminated to as many people as possible and that the Vatican does not possess any particular, special qualities that enable it to interpret the Bible any more definitively than anyone else. They went further and argued that while the Vatican did not possess any privileged perspective to interpret the Bible, the downtrodden and oppressed did. These new theologians contended that:

> The poor, the dispossessed, and the marginalized in society are uniquely placed to read, interpret, and respond to the Bible. The Bible was written by people much like themselves, about people much like themselves, and decisively for people much like themselves. Having no interest or stake or identity in present society, having indeed no interest anywhere beyond their own need for liberation from misery and oppression that is both spiritual and physical without distinction, they alone of society's classes can read the Bible directly.[12]

The current Pope, Benedict XVI, while he was still Monsignor Joseph Alois Ratzinger, argued that Liberation Theology posed a direct threat to Church authority and undermined its influence amongst the laity.[13] Arguably, it still remains the most profound threat to Church authority in the modern era.

The dilemma posed at the outset of this essay as to why the initial formative experience in the creation of the Israelite nation had to occur in the depths of

---

10 Cloutier.

11 Herbet F. Hahn, "The Reformation and Bible Criticism," *Journal of Bible and Religion* 21, No. 4 (October 1953).

12 Roelofs, *Liberation Theology*, 558.

13 Cloutier.

oppression and servitude could possibly find an answer in the ideas similar to those articulated by exponents of Liberation Theology. While Liberation Theology developed in the realm of Christianity and during a specific generation of struggle in Latin America, its message of viewing the Bible through the lens of slavery is as potent for the Jewish community as it is for the Christian one. The covenantal relationship between God and Israel relies in its entirety on the experience of bondage in Egypt. The revelation of the Decalogue was preceded by a reminder that God's relationship to Israel is precisely in the context of "I am the Lord, your God, Who took you out of the Land of Egypt, out of the house of bondage" (Ex. 20:2). Moses, in his last testimony to the nation, addressed the question as to what shall those who witnessed the creation of the covenantal relationship relay to the future generations who were not there. He frames the special relationship Israel enjoys with God in the context of, "You shall say to your child, 'We were slaves to Pharoah in Egypt, and God took us out of Egypt with a strong hand.'" (Deut. 6:21) Nahmanides intimates this idea when he opines that the reason the Book of Exodus begins with the conjoiner word "and" (the Hebrew letter *vav*)—as in "And these are the names of the sons of Israel who came to Egypt" (Ex. 1:1)—is to demonstrate that the Book of Exodus is an immediate continuation of the Book of Genesis.[14] In other words, the narrative of the Creation, the Great Flood, and the Tower of Babel (amongst other meta-events) are directly related to the journeys of Abraham and his family, their eventual sojourn to Egypt, their oppression under the Pharoah, and their ultimate redemption. Not only does the covenantal relationship rely on the experience of slavery in its formation, but indeed, Nahmanides alludes, the entire Torah—including the Creation of the Universe—is profoundly connected to the event of the Exodus.

Furthermore, much of the Hebrew legislative body is guided by the memory of slavery. On four separate occasions major national laws are set forth based on the collective memory of oppression and servitude.[15] The Torah exhorts the Israelites not to oppress because they "know the spirit" (Ex. 23:9) of those that are maligned, marginalized, and, subsequently, persecuted. The mishnah quoted earlier that has become a focal point of the Passover rituals in order to view the Exodus as a personal event and as a memory alive in the minds of Jews in every generation, is at its core a plea to never lose sight of the existential nature of the nascent Israelite experience and to stress how fundamental and primary a role it played in the creation of the Jewish religion.

The Exodus from Egypt was a demonstration of the nature of humanity, of the potential for people to be liberated from the conditions and environments that oppress them, and, through their struggle, change the cultural landscape of human civilization forever. Along these same lines, Gutierrez, the foremost liberation theologist wrote:

---

[14] Nahmanides, Ex. 1:1.

[15] See Ex. 23:20, 23:9; Lev. 19:34; and Deut. 10:19.

To conceive of history as a process of the liberation of man is to consider freedom as a historical conquest; it is to understand that the step from an abstract to a real freedom is not taken without a struggle against all the forces that oppress man, as a struggle full of pitfalls, detours, and temptations to run away. The goal is not only better living conditions, a radical change of structures, or a social revolution; it is more: the continuous creation, never ending, of a new way to be a man—a permanent cultural revolution.[16]

Utilizing this perspective, one might suggest an answer to our opening question. Perhaps the reason the holiday of Passover enjoys such a widespread observance amongst American Jewry in the face of overwhelming assimilation and apathy is because it represents a powerful force in the human condition: the ability to overcome and overthrow the oppressive forces that dominate our lives. It appeals to the social consciousness of those who are troubled by global slavery, human trafficking, and forced labor. More profoundly, perhaps Passover attracts such a wide rate of observance because more than any other holiday it touches on one of the primary narratives of the Jewish religious experience: an experience with oppression, the exaltation and jubilation of liberation, and a commitment to form a national religious culture, legal system, and theology deeply rooted in the slavery experience. It is the slaves who bring the mighty empire of ancient Egypt to a standstill and it is the freed slaves who introduce the Bible and its system of ethics and morals to the world. Our God of the Torah is presented as the God who hears the cries of the oppressed and redeems them. It is no wonder then, why God specifically designates a nation of slaves as the divinely-chosen people.

Additionally, the Exodus also illustrates a life of redemption through action. While in traditional Christianity the grace of God was the salvation of humanity, in Judaism it is an "active existence as experienced, factual life"[17] that motivates and arouses the mind of the Hebrew Bible. The language employed in the Bible connotes action, not just meditative reflection. God redeems the nation of Israel with an "outstretched arm" (Ex. 6:6). The Torah spends a considerable bulk of its space devoted to constructing a system of laws and ethics that are directly concerned with the temporal, immediate, and physical. Rachel Elior, in her work *Exile and Redemption in Jewish Mystical Thought*, states the following:

> Redemption signifies the aspirations for a reversal of existential experience—an alternative mode of existence encompassing vision of freedom, liberty, equality and sovereignty, autonomic power and independent being, promise for continuity, replace-

---

[16] Roelofs, *Liberation Theology*, 558.

[17] *Ibid.*, 552.

ment, an ingathering within national territory, divine providence and an eternal messianic order of justice and liberty.[18]

Only two items in Elior's list reflect a supernatural longing in the Jewish
redemptive vision. The rest are concerned with the ordinary lives of people
in this world who are seeking a world free from the oppressions of tyranny,
inequality, and servitude.

A possible model of a practical application of a Jewish redemptive ethic
can be found in the populist movement developing throughout North and
South America called "Base Communities." These communities of faith began
developing in Latin America at the same time Liberation Theology was first
being articulated. Base Communities, traditionally, are grassroots-organized
groups comprised of people of faith who wish to translate that faith into three
concrete areas: Bible study, communal action, and self-consciousness.[19] The
Jewish community might benefit applying these three areas operating under
the framework of a Jewish Liberation Theology.

While study of Jewish texts is a particularly well developed aspect of at least
the Orthodox Jewish community,[20] a focus on examining the canon through
the perspective of the oppressed and downtrodden is often lacking. A culture of
study within the Jewish community could be encouraged that engages the Jewish textual tradition with questions like: What does it mean to be an American
Jew residing in a country of tremendous wealth and power and yet come from a
religious tradition that demands hearing the cry of the oppressed? If servitude
was the mechanism by which the nation of Israel was formed, yet the Torah
was revealed to freed slaves, how can we, as a community and as individuals,
connect back to that history of slavery? Are there aspects of the modern era
that serve to enslave us today? What ethos is the Torah attempting to convey
by framing mankind's biblical experience of the Divine in the context of oppression? Finally, what are the actions the Torah demands of me with which
to respond to the state of human slavery and suffering today?

The last question posed is a natural catalyst to lead to the second area of a
Base Community: communal action. The areas in which a community could
choose to act are varied and diverse and will reflect the composition of each
group. In the past, Base Communities have acted on issues of health care,
education and affordable housing, and providing assistance to members in
need.[21] Jeannie Appleman, director of the "Rabbinical Leadership for Public
Life" program at the non-profit Jewish Funds for Justice, opined that by creat-

---

18 Rachel Elior, "Exile and Redemption in Jewish Mystical Thought," *Studies in Spirituality*
14 (1991): 1-15.
19 Roelofs, *Liberation Theology*, 559.
20 For example, the March 17th, 2005 edition of *The New York Times* reported the attendance
of more than 26,000 Orthodox Jews at the ceremony marking the completion of the seven-year
cycle of the Daf Yomi program which involves studying a page of Talmud daily.
21 Roelofs, *Liberation Theology*, 559.

ing these communities of shared vision and action we will be working towards building "community, one person and institution at a time," and by "weaving together our shared stories and mutual interests, we provide opportunities for our generation to model the values we cherish, create the communities our families deserve, and work to create a just world."[22] In effect, we transition from a community of study, faith, and prayer to a Jewish community actively transforming the vision of the covenantal relationship to a reality.

The final area of the Base Community revolves around self-consciousness. Base communities hold that real poverty is a "poverty of self-understanding."[23] For a true fulfillment of Liberation Theology, the "poor, oppressed and depressed must be wrenched out of those denigrating self-understandings society imposes upon them and brought to new understandings of themselves as human beings, as proper members of society, and as beings able to love and be loved."[24] At the same time though, there can be no self-delusion as to the actual material state of those who are downtrodden and suffering. Yet, an understanding that each human being is created in "the image of God" (Gen. 1:26) with immeasurable worth, and that this understanding is an overarching principle of the Torah,[25] should never lead to apathy about the state of their existence. On the contrary, the realization that one is created in the likeness of God should lead an individual to a "revolutionary transformation in self-understanding, a genuine social, political, economic and religious self-transcendence."[26]

While the approach outlined in this paper was developed as Liberation Theology within Christendom, its message is most powerfully heard within the Hebrew Bible and the Jewish historical narrative. The central theme of the Passover holiday as stated in the *mishnaic* text that lies at the heart of the seder is to release ourselves from modern-day oppressions and to wrestle with the contemporary biblical Egypts—in whatever guise they may appear. A Jewish community that strives to rid the world of oppression and slavery is strengthened by doing so and will have put into practice the lessons from the biblical account of the Jewish national liberation. As Rabbi Dov Linzer, Rosh HaYeshiva and Academic Dean of Yeshivat Chovevei Torah expressed it:

> What somehow always goes unaddressed is the number of people in our *shuls* who can barely afford to pay the rent or put food on the table for Shabbat. We allow ourselves to pretend that that's not us, maintaining an image of financial affluence. Caring for the orphan and the widow recurs as a theme in the Torah so often because these figures are invisible members of

---

22 Jeannie Appleman, "Developing Rabbinical Leadership: New Ways to Measure Success," *Sh'ma* (January 2007).
23 Roelofs, *Liberation Theology*, 559.
24 *Ibid.*
25 *Sifra, Kedoshim* 2:4.
26 Roelofs, *Liberation Theology*, 559.

society. The rabbi doesn't get the same kudos for spending time addressing their needs as he does with the *shul*'s movers and shakers. This is why it is so crucial that these issues not remain invisible in our own communities.[27]

Indeed, it is critical that these issues and the broader topic of a Jewish Liberation Theology not remain invisible to the Jewish community or we will have neglected a key component of the Jewish tradition.

---

[27] Elizabeth Richman, "Training Rabbis to Lead," *Sh'ma* (January 2007).

Rabbi Dr. Binyamin Lau is the *Rosh Beit Midrash* of Beit Morasha in Jerusalem and is the author of numerous articles and books.

THE TWO OBJECTIVES OF THE INSTITUTION OF MARRIAGE[1]
"For She is Your Companion, and the Wife of Your Covenant." (Malakhi 2:14)
Rabbi Dr. Binyamin Lau

Introduction: Marriage According to Rabbi Joseph B. Soloveitchik

In the beginning of his article on marriage,[2] Rabbi Joseph B. Soloveitchik notes that there are two basic theories about the institution of marriage. The first expresses commitment to the welfare of the group outside the matrimonial union, the partners to the marriage placing themselves at the service of society. The second expresses commitment within the matrimonial union, a commitment rooted in the experience of the joining of two individuals thirsting for love and fellowship. One practical difference between the two theories relates to the place assigned to procreation. According to the first theory, having children is the central element upon which the entire structure of marriage rests. Remove that obligation from marriage, and the institution loses all its meaning. According to the second theory, the significance of marriage is not diminished by the absence of offspring. The very union of the wedded partners is itself the desired creation.

In his typical manner,[3] here too Rabbi Soloveitchik tries to uncover both of these motifs in Scripture. The command to "be fruitful and multiply" (Gen.1:28) expresses the essence and goal of the man created in the first chapter of the book of Genesis. Man's obligation to procreate, which appears in chapter 1, is presented as part of man being God's partner in the continuous process of creation. The sexual act itself that leads to the perpetuation of man's seed is not sanctified, but rather natural and compulsory. A partial reading of the Torah, which limits itself to the first chapter, reveals no difference between man's physical needs and those of a beast. Natural man reacts to the pressures of his own body, and being part of the created world, he too becomes part of

---

[1] This essay originally appeared in *Granot* Vol. 3, (pg. 138-148) published by Beit Morasha of Jerusalem. Our thanks to Rabbi Lau for permission to translate and print his essay.
[2] R. Joseph B. Soloveitchik, *Family Redeemed: Essays on Family Relationships*, ed. David Shatz & Joel Wolowelsky (New York: Toras HaRav Foundation, 2000), 31-72.
[3] I am primarily referring here to R. Soloveitchik's treatment of the redundancy in the account of the creation in the first two chapters of Genesis. See his "Lonely Man of Faith."

the process that perpetuates the creation.

The second chapter of the book of Genesis, which focuses on "It is not good that the man be alone" (2:18), expresses man's longing to live his life together with a partner. Not a word is said in this chapter about man's physical needs; it deals not at all with the obligation of procreation, but only with the oppressive loneliness experienced by the first man. The man and the woman have names; they are not part of nature at large, but rather they have become individual, unique, and singular people. Within such a context, marriage had to assume a different meaning, expressing not only the need of the race but also (and perhaps mainly) the desire of the human individual.[4]

When he moves on to speak of Halakha, Rabbi Soloveitchik argues that it interprets the blessing to "be fruitful and multiply" not only as a biological capability that was given to man and now obligates him, but also as a spiritual-halakhic obligation, in the context of which the meeting between man and woman demands a more exalted experience, the aim of which is the formation of a community:

> Seen from the halakhic viewpoint, matrimonial community is not realized without embracing three personae. At this level, marriage redeems the productive urge from its animal species orientation and turns it into a spiritual tragic longing of man for his origin or source.[5] Sexual activity is redeemed by infusing it with a metaphysical mystery theme—namely, man's desire to give love. One must love not only the real, but the unreal as well, in order to make it real… The central Judaic ethical norm to walk in God's footsteps and to imitate Him obligates man to become a creator.[6]

Marriage embraces both the subjective aspiration to be redeemed from loneliness, and also the objective institution of a covenant between two individuals who wish to form a community together, and for the sake of that end, accept upon themselves a mutual commitment to each other.

In light of what has been said above, I would like to reexamine the rulings found in *Even ha-Ezer*, which constitute the framework for the building of a Jewish marriage, and see what aspects of the two aforementioned theories, or their combination, find their place in practical Halakha.

The Goal of Marriage

At the very beginning of his *Shulhan Arukh, Even ha-Ezer*, Rabbi Yosef Karo describes the goal of marriage as follows:

Every man is obligated to take a wife in order to be fruitful

---

[4] R. Joseph B. Soloveitchik, *Family Redeemed*, 34.

[5] *Ibid.*, 35

[6] *Ibid.*, 39

and multiply. Whoever fails to occupy himself in procreation is regarded as if he sheds blood, diminishes the image, and causes the *Shekhinah* to be removed from Israel.[7]

The Rema (Rabbi Moshe Isserles), in his gloss to this ruling, adds the following:

> Whoever does not have a wife lives without blessing, without Torah, etc., and is not called a man. When a man marries a woman, his sins are stopped off, as it is stated: "He who finds a wife finds a good thing, and obtains favor of the Lord." (Prov. 18:22)

The Rema's formulation is based on the opening passage of the *Tur, Even ha-Ezer*, which in turn is based on the Gemara in the sixth chapter of tractate *Yevamot*. The *Tur*, in his introductory lines, combines the two reasons for marriage:

> God, blessed be His name, who desires the well-being of His creatures, and knew that it is not good that man be alone, therefore, made him a helpmate corresponding to him. And furthermore, since the purpose of man's creation was that he be fruitful and multiply, and this is impossible without a mate, He therefore commanded him to cleave to the mate that He had fashioned for him. Every man is, therefore, obligated to take a wife in order to be fruitful and multiply. For whoever fails to occupy himself in procreation is regarded as if he sheds blood, as it is written: "Whoever sheds man's blood" (Gen. 9:6), and adjacent to it: "And as for you, be fruitful and multiply" (*ibid.*, v. 7). And it is as if he diminishes the image, as it is written: "For in the image of God made He man" (*ibid.*, v. 6), "And as for you, be fruitful and multiply" (*ibid.*, v. 7). And he causes the *Shekhinah* to be removed from Israel. Any man who has no wife lives without goodness, without blessing, without a home, without Torah, without a [protecting] wall, without peace. And Rabbi Elazar said: Any man who has no wife is not a man. When a man marries a woman, his sins are stopped off, as it is stated: "He who finds a wife finds a good thing, and obtains favor of the Lord" (Prov. 18:22).

The *Tur* bases the obligation of marriage on two goals: removing man from his state of loneliness, and realizing the purpose of his creation—serving as God's partner in the act of creation and the perpetuation of the world (through procreation).

---

7 *Shulhan Arukh, Even ha-Ezer* 1:1.

Rabbi Yoel Sirkis, author of the *Bayit Hadash* (the *Bach*) explains the need for a combination of the two goals:

> It may be asked: For what purpose did he [= the *Tur*] open with these words of praise at the beginning of his treatise, they being outside the book's purview, for he comes only to decide practical halakha, and thus he should have opened with: "Every man is obligated, etc."? It seems that [he opened with these words] because there are some people, who owing to their faulty intellect, argue: "Since He fashioned this helpmate for me for my benefit, as it is stated: 'It is not good that the man be alone; I will make him a helpmate corresponding to him' (Gen. 2:18)—I have no desire for this favor, and I do not want it. For in his opinion, it is better for him to live without a wife, and he will find himself a helpmate in a friend or a brother to whose soul his soul is bound. Therefore, in order to remove this error from the heart, he [the *Tur*] said: "God, blessed be His name, etc.," for He, blessed be He, knows who should be his helpmate, and not as man thinks in his heart.[8]

Each of marriage's two goals can, of course, be realized without the other: On the one hand, a man can take a wife in order to escape loneliness – "It is not good that the man be alone." This union is not at all connected to the potential to bring children into the world. It would seem that a good friend might also be able to fill this role of a wife. On the other hand, a man can fulfill the *mitzvah* of procreation without entering into an intimate relationship with his partner. A man who is concerned about the welfare of mankind and the perpetuation of the human species can fill God's world with the seed of Abraham, and they can be fruitful and multiply without the institution of the family.

The novelty in the *Tur's* words, explains the *Bach*, is that the two aspects of the *mitzvah* are interconnected. The purpose of marriage is to cleave to a woman with an exclusive bond in order to fulfill man's mission in the world. Realization of one of the objectives of marriage is possible, but it will always be partial.

Rabbi Yehoshua Falk, author of the *Derishah*, expands on this idea in a different direction. He points out a difficulty in the words of the *Tur*, who records the two objectives of marriage as complementing each other, when in fact they are contradictory: If the goal is to benefit man, then marriage is the ultimate purpose; but if the goal is to realize man's potential for procreation, then marriage is only a means to the next objective.[9]

---

8 *Bayit Hadash, Even ha-Ezer*, 1.

9 *Derishah, Even ha-Ezer* 1:1. There is much room to expand on the difference between marriage as an end and marriage as a means, both according to Jewish thinkers and according to other religions. An initial overview may be found in K. Kahana, *The Theory of Marriage in Jewish Law*,

The *Derishah* reconciles this contradiction: as opposed to animals, man was created male and female together. The separation of man's male and female elements created partiality in man, and this partiality gave rise to man's longing to reunite with his partner. This reunion creates a new whole—the offspring that issues forth from the two of them. Until a person brings a child into the world, he cannot fully restore his own wholeness. Thus, we can understand the verse: "That is why a man leaves his father and his mother, and cleaves to his wife: and they become one flesh." (Gen. 2:24) The cleaving of a man to his wife is the basis for the creation of the new single flesh, which results from their union. Rabbi Falk's understanding raises the concept of marital union above the realm of the social order—the physical connection of the wedded partners gives expression to the wholeness of creation. This approach is well-known in the world of Kabbalah, from the *Igeret ha-Kodesh* (attributed to the Ramban), the *Zohar*, and many other sources. The kabbalists (and in their wake, the great Hasidic thinkers) see the physical connection between man and wife as a symbol of supernal coupling and an expression of the harmony of all the worlds.[10]

We see then that there are three basic positions regarding the purpose of marriage: the functional goal—fulfillment of the *mitzvah* of procreation; the moral goal—removing man from his loneliness; and the spiritual goal – the restoration of the wholeness of man through union with his wife.

The Rambam's Influence on the Paradigm of Marriage in the *Shulhan Arukh*

The *Shulhan Arukh*, in many places, gives expression to the first position. It is quite possible that Rabbi Yosef Karo was influenced by the Rambam's understanding of the goal of marriage. The Rambam expresses his attitude toward the family unit in two places. He dedicates an entire chapter of his *Mishneh Torah* to the *mitzvah* of procreation,[11] and there he clearly implies that the relationship between man and woman exhausts itself in the *mitzvah* of having children.

The following example illustrates this point. The Sages discussed the question whether one is permitted to live a reclusive life: a man without a wife, or a woman without a husband. The mishnah in tractate *Yevamot* states: "A man may not abstain from procreation unless he already has children." (*Yevamot* 6:6) Rabbi Yehoshua adds in a *beraita*: "If he had children in his youth, he should also have children in his old age." (*Yevamot* 62b)

Regarding the first clause of the mishnah, the Gemara proposes two possible understandings. The first possible understanding is that one who has children

---

(Leiden: Brill, 1966). This, however, is not the forum to discuss the issue in greater detail.

[10] See Dr. M. Posen, "*Hayei ha-Nisu'in ve-Hayei ha-Mishpaha be-Aspaklariyat ha-Kabalah*," *Mishpahot Beit Yisrael*, 67-75.

[11] *Mishneh Torah, Hilkhot Ishut* 15.

may abstain from procreation, but may not remove himself from marital life:

> This supports what Rav Nahman said in the name of Shemu'el: Although a man may have many children, he must not remain without a wife, as it is stated: "It is not good that the man be alone."

The second possibility is that one who has already fulfilled the *mitzvah* of procreation is permitted to remove himself altogether from marital life, contrary to the opinion of Shmuel. The Gemara in its conclusion accepts the first possibility. One practical ramification is that a person who has already fulfilled the *mitzvah* of procreation is permitted to marry a woman who is unable to have children.

In the continuation, the Gemara records the position of Rav Matana that the law is in accordance with the view of Rabbi Yehoshua, to which Rav Tanhum bar Hanila'i adds: "Any man who has no wife lives without joy, without blessing, and without goodness. In the West, it was stated: Without Torah and without a [protecting] wall." We see then that the Gemara clearly favors life that is lived together in fellowship with a partner.

In the transition from the Gemara to the Rambam, these rulings undergo a transformation. The Rambam in *Hilkhot Ishut* codifies both the words of the Sages and the words of Rabbi Yehoshua. The position of the Sages is reflected in halakhah 1:

> A woman who after marriage gives her husband permission to withold her conjugal rights from her, is permitted to do so. When does this apply? When he has children, for in that case he has already fulfilled the commandment to be fruitful and multiply. If, however, he has not yet fulfilled it, he is obligated to have sexual intercourse with her according to his schedule until he has children, because this is a positive commandment of the Torah, as it is said: "Be fruitful and multiply." (Gen. 1:28)[12]

The position of Rabbi Yehoshua the Rambam brings in halakhah 16:

> Even if a man has already fulfilled the commandment to be fruitful and multiply, he is still obligated by Scribal enactment not to cease being fruitful and multiplying as long as he has the power to do so, because whosoever adds one soul to Israel has as much as built a whole world. It is also a precept of the Sages that no man should live without a wife, in order that he should not come to unchaste thoughts, nor should a woman live without a husband, in order that she should not become

---

12 *Mishneh Torah, Hilkhot Ishut* 15:1.

subject to suspicion.[13]

The Rambam's concluding words, which explain the rationale for his ruling, are a reworking of what Rav Tanchum says in the Gemara. The Rambam records the bottom line: "No man should live without a wife," but offers the following rationale: "in order that he should not come to unchaste thoughts." In other words, for the Rambam, a wife fulfills two objectives. First, she bears him children, and after he has fulfilled this *mitzvah*, she protects him from sinful thoughts. The Rambam makes no mention of what the Gemara says about the joy, blessing, and goodness of life lived with a partner. The final clause, "nor should a woman live without a husband, in order that she should not become subject to suspicion," is also absent in the Talmudic source. However, the Rambam's source may be a *tosefta* in *Yevamot* which states that: "A man is not permitted to remain without a wife, and a woman is not permitted to remain without a husband."[14]

The Ramban as well understands that Rabbi Yehoshua does not disagree with the Sages, but rather he adds a rabbinic obligation to continue having children, even after the Torah *mitzvah* has been fulfilled. Since it is only ideally (*le-khathila*) that this *mitzvah* must be observed, a person cannot be compelled to do so against his will. The Ramban, however, concludes: "But a man should never be without a wife, for one is forbidden to remain without a wife."[15] He too records the position of Rav Tanchum, but without the Rambam's explanation: that the goal of the relationship is to protect the man from unchaste thoughts.

The *Shulhan Arukh* only records the man's obligation to marry a woman, even if he has already fulfilled the *mitzvah* of procreation, but makes no mention of an obligation falling upon a woman to marry. The Rema, glossing the *Shulhan Arukh's* ruling that a woman is not commanded about procreation, adds the aforementioned words of the Rambam: "Nevertheless, there are those who say that a woman must not remain without a husband, in order that she should not become subject to suspicion."[16]

The obligation to maintain the marital framework even when it will not lead to offspring can be understood in exclusively sexual terms, as we find in the Rambam, but it can also be explained in social terms.

The first approach is found in various *rishonim*, who see marriage as a way

---

13 *Ibid.*, 15:16

14 *Tosefta Yevamot* 8:4. This is the reading found in *Tosefta*, MS Vienna, which R. Saul Lieberman used as the base text. In the printed versions of the *Tosefta*, we find just the opposite: "A woman is permitted to remain without a husband." Based on these variant readings (and the *halakhot* that follow from them), Lieberman tries to reconcile the Rambam's ruling here and his ruling in *Hilkhot Isurei Bi'ah* 21:26, where he permits a woman not to marry. See *Tosefta ki-Peshutah*, *Yevamot*, p. 68.

15 Ramban, *Milhamot ha-Shem* on the Rif, *Yevamot*, chap. 3.

16 *Hagahot ha-Rema* on *Shulhan Arukh*, *Even ha-Ezer* 1:13.

to protect a man from the sin of illicit sexual thoughts and relations. Thus, for example, writes Rabbi David Kokhavi, author of *Sefer ha-Batim*:

> Since the principle objective of marriage is perpetuation of the species, and because one of the goals of marriage is bodily cleanliness and protection from unchaste thoughts, our Rabbis said: A person who lives without a wife lives without goodness.[17]

Rabbi David Kokhavi adapts the source that gives expression to the social framework of the institution of marriage, and uses it as an additional factor to strengthen the man's moral status, to preserve his physical purity, and to prevent sinful thoughts.

A practical difference between these two emphases may be seen in a discussion found in the commentaries to the *Shulhan Arukh*. Rabbi Shemuel Feivish, author of the *Beit Shemu'el*,[18] cites the view of the Rambam that a man is obligated to engage in sexual intercourse according to his schedule until he fulfills the *mitzvah* of procreation, but after he has fulfilled this *mitzvah*, his wife may waive her right to conjugal relations. The *Beit Shemu'el* asks: If the woman's waiver is valid, then it should be accepted even before the man fulfills the *mitzvah* of procreation; and if it lacks validity, then even after he has fulfilled the *mitzvah*, it should not be accepted, because the man is still obligated in the *mitzvah* of "in the evening, do not withhold your hand," the Scribal enactment to continue having children even after a man has fulfilled the *mitzvah* of procreation. The *Beit Shemu'el* is forced to explain that perhaps the man can fulfill his obligation to continue having children with another woman.

Rabbi Chayim Yosef David Azulai (the *Hida*)[19] argues that after a man has fulfilled the *mitzvah* of procreation, his wife is permitted to waive her conjugal rights, but the husband must still engage in marital relations from time to time, in order to fulfill the *mitzvah* of continued procreation. The *Otzar ha-Poskim*[20] brings in the name of the *Beit Moshe* that this requires sexual relations at least once every thirty days, because the husband must maintain a framework of "*derekh eretz*," normal marital life.

The implication is that the *mitzvah* of continued procreation involves not only bringing more and more children into the world, as it would appear from the simple reading of the words of Rabbi Yehoshua in the gemara (*Yevamot* 62b). Rather, a man living with his wife constitutes a value in and of itself, and therefore he should fulfill the *mitzvah* of continued procreation, because that is "*derekh eretz*." Here the *Beit Moshe* (and perhaps also the *Hida*) joins the Rema,

---

17 R. David Kokhavi, *Migdal David*, positive precept 215, 262. For additional sources, see R. David Lau (rabbi of Modi'in), "*Heter Isurim le-Tzorekh Peru u-Revu*," *Techumin* 23 (5763), 231-236.

18 Lived in Poland and Germany, 17th century.

19 Cited in *Pithei Teshuvah*, *Yoreh De'ah* 1, #1.

20 *Otzar ha-Poskim*, letter 3.

who understands that marriage is a value that must be realized irrespective of the *mitzvah* of procreation. Thus, we are returned to the precincts of the *Tur*, who tried to combine both values as the objective of marriage, as opposed to the position represented by the Rambam.

The Rambam's position that the goal of marriage is offspring also finds expression in other *halakhot* in chapter 15 of *Hilkhot Ishut*. In halakhah 3, the Rambam deals with the figure of Ben Azzai as a model for emulation. He writes that if a person yearns to immerse himself in constant Torah study and cleave to it all his life, and, to further that end, he does not take a wife, he commits no sin, provided that his sexual passions are not aroused. If, however, he is repeatedly overcome by his passions, he is obligated to take a wife, even if he already has children. Here, too, it is clear that the reason for marriage is not connected to man's loneliness or his need for companionship, rather a wife's purpose is to save her husband from sin.

In halakhah 7, the Rambam records the law obligating a man to divorce his wife if after ten years of marriage she has still not borne him children. In such a case, divorce is compulsory, and if he does not want to divorce her, the court forces him to do so and flogs him until he is ready to comply. This ruling as well emphasizes the fact that the purpose of marriage is having children and fulfilling the *mitzvah* of procreation. There is no room for an intimate relationship that does not allow for the fulfillment of this *mitzvah*.

At the end of the chapter, the Rambam devotes two *halakhot* to guidelines for the husband and the wife on how they are to treat each other with respect, love, and patience. But, as stated above, the whole relationship is only legitimate when its objective is procreation and fulfillment of the *mitzvah* of having children.

In his *Guide for the Perplexed*, the Rambam describes his attitude toward marital relations as follows:

> By then, he will have detached his thought from, and abolished his desire for, bestial things—I mean the preference for the pleasures of eating, drinking, sexual intercourse, and, in general, of the sense of touch, with regard to which Aristotle gave a clear explanation in the "Ethics," saying that this sense is a disgrace to us. How fine is what he said, and how true it is that it is a disgrace! For we have it in so far as we are animals like the other beasts, and nothing that belongs to the notion of humanity pertains to it. As for the other sensual pleasures—those, for instance, that derive from the sense of smell, from hearing and from seeing—there may be found in them sometimes, though they are corporeal, pleasure for man as man, as Aristotle has explained.[21]

---

[21] *The Guide of the Perplexed*, II:37

Much has been written about the influence of Greek culture on the crystallization of the Rambam's world of values. While it is true that most of the Rambam's rulings have Talmudic sources, his words often betray an underlying outlook, on the basis of which he decides to cite one source and omit the other. All the rabbinic dicta that speak of the loneliness of bachelorhood, the absence of joy among the unmarried, and the like—the Rambam chose to omit.[22]

It seems to me that the rulings of the *Shulhan Arukh* may best be understood in light of the Rambam's *Hilkhot Ishut*, their point of departure being: "In order to engage in procreation." In contrast to the *Shulhan Arukh*, the Rema in various places gives expression to the alternate position, which seeks to include in the motive for marriage the social element of "It is not good that the man be alone."

Delaying the *Mitzvah* of Procreation

There are many practical differences between the two positions regarding the objective of marriage.[23] One of them relates to the issue of delaying the *mitzvah* of procreation. This is one of the questions most frequently asked by young couples, at least in religious Zionist circles, where women enjoy a social status equal to that of men. I am not talking about family planning following the birth of a son and a daughter, but immediately upon entering into marriage.

There are many reasons that a young couple may wish to put off having children: the woman's desire to complete her higher education, a feeling of insecurity during the initial period of married life (personal or economic), and various personal plans. Already thirty years ago, Rabbi Aharon Lichtenstein, Rosh Yeshiva of Yeshivat Har Etzion, noted the frequency of this question: "Almost every halakhic authority, be he a rabbi or a *rosh yeshiva*, who maintains broad contact with young couples, on the threshold of marriage or beyond, can testify to the many queries reaching him in this domain."[24]

---

[22] For an expanded discussion of the Rambam's position regarding the family and its function, see R. Yona Ben Sasson, "*Yesodei Torat ha-Musar shel Hevra u-Mishpaha be-Mishnatam shel Rambam ve-Rihal*," *Mishpahot Beit Yisra'el*, 77-131.

[23] I would like to mention another practical difference between the two objectives of marriage, namely, the permissibility of the husband's offering of assistance to his wife during labor. For many generations, the husband played no role whatsoever in the birthing process. At most, he sat outside the labor room in order to hear the news that a child was born. The birthing woman was assisted by other women—a professional midwife or a female relative. Thus, there was no need to deal with the issue whether it was permissible for a husband to assist his wife during labor. Today, with the strengthening of the personal bond between husband and wife, the birthing woman often requests that her husband remain at her side throughout her labor and childbirth. Thus, we come to the halakhic issue whether the husband may assist his wife during labor, when she is already regarded as a *nidah*. See R. Shelomo Dichovsky, "*Harga'at Yoledet u-Me'uberet*," *Techumin* 23 (5763), 237-240.

[24] R. Aharon Lichtenstein, "*Be-Petah ha-Sha'ar*," in *Tihnun ha-Mishpaha u-Meni'at Hirayon*, ed. R. Elyakim Ellinson (Tel Aviv, 5737), 3.

Rabbi Lichtenstein emphasizes the seriousness and gravity with which one must relate to this question, for it stems not from spiritual laziness or disrespect, but from intense earnestness and a true conflict of values. Against the collective value, which demands concern for the nation, stands the personal value, legitimate from both a human and a Torah perspective: continued Torah study, acquiring a vocation, professional advancement, ensuring emotional stability, preparing for appropriate education of the children, and others.

It is important to emphasize, already at this stage, that the practical confrontation with this question must be conducted on the personal and individual level, and not by issuing general and sweeping guidelines. However, the very opening up of the issue for discussion is important, both halakhically and educationally. From a halakhic perspective, if Halakha embraces possible allowances for a couple to delay the *mitzvah*, these should be made known to every halakhic authority who encounters these questions. From an educational perspective, it is important that serious religious couples struggling with the dilemma be aware of the discussion, so that they may widen the channels of communication with the world of Halakha and its authorities in order to clarify the issue. Ignoring the question, or recycling a sweeping prohibition without discussion, will lead these couples, God forbid, to cut themselves off from the world of Halakha. Many couples who decide on their own to delay the *mitzvah* will live "as the thief is ashamed" (Jer. 2:26), thinking that there is nobody with whom to consult. I wish to contribute to this discussion the distinction between the various positions that we saw with respect to the essence of marriage.

First of all, we must narrow the discussion about delaying the *mitzvah* of procreation, and focus exclusively on the essential question—pushing off the positive precept for a reason that is not clearly a matter of *piku'ah nefesh* (saving a life). Other issues that arise in the responsa literature—with respect to contraceptives—are not unique to our discussion. They appear in every discussion regarding contraception, even when we are dealing with couples who have already fulfilled the *mitzvah* of procreation.[25]

The Rambam[26] rules that a husband is permitted to abstain from his conjugal duty, with the consent of his wife, only after he has already fulfilled the *mitzvah* of procreation. But as long as he has not fulfilled the *mitzvah*, he is obligated to have sexual intercourse with her according to his schedule, because

---

[25] The primary issues are the prohibitions of *hotza'at shikhvat zera le-batalah* (wasted seminal emission) and castration. As for the first prohibition, the use of contraceptives that do not interfere with natural sexual intercourse is accepted by most halakhic authorities as not involving the prohibition of *hotza'at shikhvat zera le-batalah*. See R. Elyakim Ellinson (cited above, note 27), chap. 7: "The Prevalent Means Today." As for the prohibition of castration, most authorities agree that the prohibition only applies to a procedure that is irreversible, but not to a temporary measure. See *Igerot Moshe*, III, no. 15; *Tzitz Eli'ezer*, IX, no. 51, and many other responsa.

[26] *Mishneh Torah, Hilkhot Ishut* 15:1.

procreation is a positive precept by Torah law.

These words of the Rambam constitute the halakhic basis for the sweeping opposition voiced by the halakhic authorities to every question concerning contraception prior to the fulfillment of the *mitzvah*. The *Tur* and the *Shulhan Arukh*[27] cite the words of the Rambam as normative Halakha, as do many contemporary halakhic authorities.[28] Thus, for example, Rabbi Shelomo Aviner addresses the question whether a couple is permitted to space their children if they have not yet fulfilled the *mitzvah* of procreation:

> This question is very complicated. For on the one hand, it is unimaginable to push off and delay fulfillment of the *mitzvah*. On the contrary, one should strive with all one's powers to fulfill it, as the Rambam rules... However, exceedingly difficult family situations do at times present themselves. Sometimes there is a succession of many boys or many girls, and the mother finds herself in a difficult physical or mental state. Sometimes there are women for whom pregnancy, childbirth, and child care are extremely difficult, and starting immediately with a new pregnancy weighs heavily upon them.[29]

In the continuation, Rabbi Aviner emphasizes that any allowance to use contraception prior to the fulfillment of the *mitzvah* of procreation is limited to situations of serious difficulty, but not where the problem is economic or the desire to complete one's studies or the like:

> In such a situation, there is certainly no allowance whatsoever, for people marry for the purpose of procreation, and so there is no possibility of exempting oneself from it, unless there is a situation of danger. Even if one wishes to do this in order to study Torah, there is no allowance.[30]

Rabbi Aviner's words assume what we said above regarding the goal of marriage. According to the Rambam, and in his wake also the *Shulhan Arukh*, the objective of marriage is "in order to engage in procreation." When this is the objective, it is impossible to discuss other values of the type mentioned by Rabbi Lichtenstein. If, however, we take into halakhic consideration the position of the Rema (based on the *Tur*), which includes among the reasons for marriage also the motivation of "it is not good that the man be alone," there is room to discuss the question. If a young man and a young woman fall in love and

---

[27] *Even ha-Ezer* 76:6.

[28] *Minhat Yitzhak*, V, no. 113; *Igerot Moshe, Even ha-Ezer*, I, no. 102, and others. See *Otzar ha-Poskim*, 1, no. 17.

[29] R. Shlomo Aviner, *Banekha ki-Shetilei Zeitim* (Jerusalem, 1984), 36.

[30] R. Aviner joins to his ruling the view of R. Avraham Dov Auerbach, rabbi of Tiberias, who makes the aforementioned distinction.

wish to join themselves in the covenant of marriage, but for reasons that do not constitute *piku'ah nefesh*, but rather a serious personal need, they do not want to have children right away—is it preferable for them to get married and live together, putting off the *mitzvah* of procreation, or is it better that they push off the marriage? This is the question that is currently being asked and we cannot ignore it.

From a halakhic perspective, as long as the couple have not joined in matrimony, the *mitzvah* of procreation does not fall on the woman, and thus from her perspective there is no problem pushing off the wedding until whatever obstacles stand in the way (studies or the like) have been removed. As we have seen, the law that obligates a woman to marry is not at all clear, and the Rambam derives it (apparently based on the *Tosefta*) from the rationale "in order that she should not become subject to suspicion." The question then centers on the man, who is indeed bound by the *mitzvah* of procreation, whether he is permitted to push off the wedding, if he wishes to marry this particular woman. Various responsa imply that one is permitted to push off marriage because of a desire to marry a specific woman.[31] This seems to follow explicitly from a responsum of Rabbi Yosef of Trani, the Maharit. In the course of his answer to a question dealing with an adult man who became engaged to a minor girl and was waiting for her to reach maturity, he deals with the issue whether his waiting involves a nullification of the *mitzvah* of procreation. In the course of his discussion, the Maharit draws a comparison between the man's obligation to the engagement and an oath taken not to fulfill a *mitzvah*, which has no force:

> Perhaps they only said that an oath coming to nullify a *mitzvah* is not valid when the *mitzvah* is totally nullified, as in the case taught in [chapter] *Elu mutarin*: "A *sukah* that I will not build, a *lulav* that I will not take, etc." In the case of oaths it is permitted, for one cannot take an oath to transgress a *mitzvah*. But here, since in the end he will marry and fulfill the *mitzvah* of procreation, it is not called nullification… To summarize, we are not authorized to uproot this oath that it should not be valid, for the reasons that I have explained.[32]

The Maharit means to say that delaying a *mitzvah* is not comparible to its nullification, and so, if a person takes an oath to delay a *mitzvah*, the oath is binding.[33] This being the case, it is possible that if a young man and woman

---

[31] See *Pithei Teshuvah*, *Even ha-Ezer* 1, #5; and see also *Responsa Maharam Schik*, *Even ha-Ezer*, #1.

[32] *Responsa Maharit*, II, *Yoreh De'ah*, no. 47. See the response of Rav Henkin to this article, where he rejects the possibility of relying on the Maharit in our case. He argues that while the Maharit maintains that one who takes an oath to delay the *mitzvah* of procreation is not regarded as one who takes an oath to nullify a *mitzvah* (and so the oath is binding), he nevertheless agrees that putting off the *mitzvah* of procreation involves a transgression.

[33] We also find in an entirely different context the idea of delaying a *mitzvah* in order to fulfill

plan to marry, and they will be putting off the *mitzvah* of procreation because they want to delay their marriage until certain obstacles have been removed, there is no halakha preventing them from pushing off their marriage.

We, however, are being asked a different question: In our social reality, where the couple's relationship is liable to lead to serious complications if they do not get married, is it right to forbid them to delay the *mitzvah* of procreation, or is it preferable to allow them to live together as a married couple and use contraception? In our society, people are marrying at a later age, and we must do everything possible to to help young people enter into marriage. Recognizing that marriage is not just an instrument to facilitate bringing children into the world, but that it constitutes a value in and of itself, in the sense of "it is not good that the man be alone," obligates the halakhic authorities to exert themselves to encourage young people considering marriage. If leniency in the form of an allowance to delay the *mitzvah* of having children is likely to decide the issue in favor of a wedding, this should be given serious consideration. Over against the reasons that forbid a married man (as opposed to a bachelor) to delay the *mitzvah* of procreation,[34] there are reasons to allow a couple to delay fulfillment of the *mitzvah* for a limited period of time, provided that they translate their emotional attachment into a marital bond. In order to encourage marriage, stress should be placed on the words of the Sages that an unmarried person is not whole, that a married person is protected from sinful thoughts, that a man without a wife lives without joy, and the like. Considerations that involve giving preference to a light transgression over a more severe transgression are found in abundance in the halakhic literature. One of the most striking and well known examples is the Rambam's ruling allowing a Jewish man to marry an emancipated slave with whom he is suspected of having had intercourse prior to her emancipation (against an explicit mishnah), as he says:

> We did this so as not to put obstacles in front of penitents. And we said: Better that he eat the gravy, and not the fat itself. And we relied on what the Sages said: "It is time to act for the Lord; they have made void Your Torah" (Ps. 119:126). And we help

it later in a more embellished manner. In *Terumat ha-Deshen*, I, no. 35, R. Yisrael Isserlein was asked about pushing off *Birkat ha-Levanah* to Saturday night, when the blessing can be recited with the entire congregation. In his responsum, R. Isserlein distinguishes between a delay which is liable to bring about its nullification, which is forbidden, and a delay which will bring about its fulfillment in a more embellished manner, which is permitted. There is, of course, a difference between the nullification of *Birkat ha-Levanah*, which is not a positive *mitzvah* but only a blessing of praise, and pushing off procreation which is a positive *mitzvah*.

34 See the letter of R. Shlomo Zalman Auerbach in R. Aviner's article (cited above, note 17), p. 38, which states that the allowance to delay the *mitzvah* does not apply to a married person, but only to a bachelor, for one who lives with his wife and engages in normal marital relations occupies himself with the *mitzvah* of procreation. Here too R. Auerbach relates to marital life strictly from the perspective of procreation, and not from the perspective of "It is not good that the man be alone."

him to marry her with gentleness and tenderness." [35]

Thus far, we have spoken about the need for Halakha and its authorities to be attentive to and help young couples enter into marriage. On the other hand, a sweeping allowance to push off the *mitzvah* of having children places all the weight of marriage on the relationship and on the satisfaction of having escaped the loneliness of bachelorhood. This understanding totally undermines man's obligation to serve as God's partner in the act of creation by establishing a family. The halakhic authority must clarify for the couple struggling with this issue the obligation on nationalistic grounds to build a home and family, at the basis of which lies the obligation to have children. Only a proper presentation of the two objectives of marriage, and their internalization on the part of the couple, can provide the necessary background for a useful and constructive discussion of the issue of family planning. In my opinion, the guidebooks written for brides and grooms must consider the frequency of this question, and allow the couple preparing for marriage to understand that discussing the issue is legitimate. The couple will have to arrive at a practical decision in personal consultation with a rabbi, but in order for the couple to get to the rabbi, they must see that he is ready to listen to them.

An example of this approach may be found in Rabbi Elyashiv Knohl's new book, "*Ish ve-Ishah – Pirkei Hadrakhah le-Hatan ve-Kalah.*"[36] The entire book is based on the author's conscious listening to the many grooms that he had guided and the many couples that he had accompanied to the *hupah* and beyond. Halakhically speaking, there is nothing revolutionary in the book, but it grants legitimacy to the asking of questions. Rabbi Knohl devotes an entire chapter to the issue here under discussion, pointing out the importance of having children and building a family, but he does not recoil from dealing also with the queries of couples wishing to delay having children until after they have overcome certain difficulties in their new path. As an introduction to the discussion, Rabbi Knohl writes: "Many rabbis are sensitive to this issue, and they will make every effort to exploit the power of allowance in order to help the couple find what they are seeking within the framework of Halakha."[37]

In the course of the chapter, Rabbi Knohl outlines the factors that permit a couple to delay the *mitzvah*. At the end of the chapter, he once again invites the couple to find a rabbi with whom they are close and upon whose halakhic judgment they rely, and suggests that they clarify the issue with him and receive halakhic guidance on the matter. Such a voice encourages couples who are struggling between the value of observing Halakha in its plain sense, and the

---

[35] *Responsa Rambam*, ed. Blau, # 211. An analysis of the Rambam's responsum, its novelty and its influence upon later halakhic authorities, may be found in my article: "*Takanat ha-Shavim be-Giyur,*" in *Devarim, Kovetz Ma'amarim le-Tziyun Eser Shanim le-Merkaz Ya'akov Herzog be'Ein Tzurim,* 5760.

[36] Published by *Makhon Shiluvim, Yeshivat ha-Kibbutz ha-Dati Ein Tzurim,* 5763.

[37] Knohl, *Ish ve-Ishah,* 241.

value of developing their individual and joint personalities at different paces, to remain connected to the world of Halakha and build their marriage on its foundations.

Rabbi Yehuda Herzl Henkin, author
of the responsa collection *Benei Banim*
(4 volumes to date), is a leading contemporary modern-Orthodox and
religious-Zionist *posek* (rabbinic decisor)
living in Jerusalem.

Postponement of the *Mitzvah* of Procreation: A Response to Rabbi Dr. Binyamin Lau[1]
Rabbi Yehuda Herzl Henkin

In his article, Rabbi Binyamin Lau seeks to prove from a responsum of the
Maharit (Rabbi Yosef Mi-Trani, 1568-1639) that delaying the fulfillment of a
mitzvah is not akin to its abrogation and that one may, therefore, delay procreation following marriage. Begging his pardon, Rabbi Lau not only quoted
this responsum inaccurately, he did so only partially. In that responsum, the
Maharit discusses a man who swore not to marry a woman—*in addition to a
minor to whom he was already betrothed*—until his current betrothed minor
reached adulthood. (As a child, she was too young to bear him children.) The
following are the relevant parts of the responsum:

> Surely [this is such]! For certainly there is an abrogation of the
> *mitzvah* [of procreation] once a man passes the age of twenty
> years, as they [the Sages] said in the first chapter of [Tractate]
> *Kidushin*: "Up until twenty years, the Holy One, blessed be
> He, sits and waits expectantly...." And the Rambam *z"l* wrote,
> in Chapter 15 of *Hilkhot Ishut*: "Once twenty years have elapsed
> and a man has not taken a wife, he thereby transgresses and
> abrogates a positive commandment."

> Yet there is room for doubt, for perhaps they [the Sages] did not
> say that "An oath made to nullify a *mitzvah* is invalid" except
> where the *mitzvah* in question would be abrogated entirely,
> such as that which we learned in *Elu Mutarin* [concerning]: "A
> *sukah* I [vow that I] will not build, a *lulav* I [vow that I] will
> not take..."—regarding oaths (if sworn as an oath—a *shevu'ah*),
> it is permitted [to still build a *sukah* and to take a *lulav*] be-
> cause "one cannot be bound by an oath taken to transgress

[1]As printed in *Granot* 3 (2003), 149-152, and subsequently in Responsa *Benei Banim* 4:#15.
Our thanks to Rabbi Henkin for permission to translate and print his essay.

the *mitzvot*." But this one, since he will eventually marry and fulfill the commandment of procreation, it is not considered abrogation....

The commandment of procreation remains constant throughout his life-time, yet from the moment he fulfills it [he is] absolved of its obligation, therefore when he delays it, it [constitutes] postponement of the *mitzvah*, but not [its] abrogation; for if he did it in the end, he fulfilled the *mitzvah*. Nevertheless, since he is commanded [in the obligation to procreate] now, he abrogates the [current] fulfillment of the *mitzvah*, as is proven from the language of the Rambam *z"l* who wrote: "Behold this one transgresses and abrogates a positive commandment."[1]

In other words, certainly one who delays the performance of the *mitzvah* transgresses, and, for that reason, the Maharit cited the words of the Rambam. Nonetheless, perhaps one who makes an oath to *delay the mitzvah* is unlike one who takes an oath to *cancel a mitzvah completely*—in which case, his oath is null and void—because, unlike other *mitzvot*, the commandment to be fruitful and multiply is a continuing obligation and, if he does not fulfill it at a certain time, he can fulfill it later on. Therefore, the oath does not entirely cancel the *mitzvah* and, for this reason, the oath takes effect. The entire responsum deals with arguments on both sides of this question—perhaps the oath is binding, perhaps not—and concludes: "The bottom line is that we do not possess the power to uproot this oath (i.e. not to take a second wife) so that it won't be binding upon him, for the reasons we have stated." That is to say, to refrain from action is preferable and he may not marry another wife in addition to his betrothed, lest he violate his oath. But, absent the oath that coerces him, he is forbidden either to do away with the *mitzvah* of procreation completely or even to postpone it.

As R. Elyakim Ellinson *z"l* wrote in an article in *Noam*, citing the aforementioned responsum of the Maharit:

The commandment to procreate is not subject to postponement.... While we have seen that the Sages allowed a man to postpone his marriage up to a certain age and until he finds a fitting partner, one cannot derive permission from this to delay the fulfillment of the *mitzvah* once he is already married, and he is required to fulfill his obligation without additional delay.

It is, therefore, astonishing that in that same year, he published a pamphlet entitled "Family Planning and Contraception" in which he wrote the opposite, permitting contraception after marriage. Moreover, in his above-mentioned

---

[1] *Responsa Maharit, Yoreh De'ah* 2:47

article he made no mention of his pamphlet; and in his pamphlet, he made no mention of his earlier article. I wrote to him at the time to ask about the contradiction. He replied in brief that he had retracted what he had written earlier in the article in *Noam*, but he did not elaborate upon his reasons. At any rate, we are not dependent on him; and even if *he* reversed himself, did the Rambam and the Maharit reverse themselves?

Another point of astonishment is that Rabbi Ellinson wrote in his article in *Noam* that according to the Maharit, if when already betrothed to a minor one takes an oath not to marry another woman, the oath is invalid because it nullifies a *mitzvah*—contrary to what I demonstrated above in Responsa Maharit. Perhaps Rabbi Ellinson based himself on what was written in the *Otzar ha-Poskim* 1:17.[2] But I am even more astonished at the *Otzar ha-Poskim* for reading in the Responsa *Maharit* the opposite of what, in fact, the responsum concluded!

However, Rabbi Tzvi Hirsch ben Yaakov Ashkenazi (known as *Hakham Tzvi*) did understand the Responsa Maharit as I did.[3] It is true that in his responsum, Rabbi Hirsch, himself, disputes the Maharit on this point. But why, then, is his view cited in the *Otzar ha-Poskim* as saying "and thus, too, wrote the *Hakham Tzvi*," as if they agree? At any rate, according to this, all the more so we may not distinguish between delaying fulfillment of the *mitzvah* itself and abrogating it. So, too, *Otzar ha-Poskim* cites a string of *aharonim* who wrote that one who postpones the *mitzvah* of procreation is considered to have abrogated it.

Now, it is said in a *beraita*: "Until he is twenty years, the Holy One, blessed is He, sits and waits expectantly for a man to take a wife. When he reaches twenty and has not yet married, [G-d] says: 'Let his bones swell!'" (*Kidushin* 29b).

Rambam wrote: "From when is the man obligated in this *mitzvah*? [From the age of sixteen years or] from the age of seventeen. And when twenty years have passed, and he has not taken a wife, this one transgresses and abrogates a positive commandment."[4] For Rambam, the phrase of "let his bones swell" is because he did not fulfill the *mitzvah* of procreation. Rabbi Menahem Meiri, on the other hand, explained that one who passes the age of twenty without marrying will never escape licentious thoughts, since he has persisted in them for so long.[5] According to Rambam, then, even if he took a wife prior to age twenty, if he did not then father offspring, he is subsumed under "let his bones swell." While according to Meiri, since he did marry prior to age twenty, in

---

2 *Otzar Ha-Poskim: Systematised Reasoned Digest of All Extant Rabbinic Responsa Bearing Upon Jewish Law and Ritual, Arranged in the Order of the Shulhan Arukh*, ed. Rabbi Isaac Ha-Levi Herzog, vol. 1, *Hilkhot Periyah Ve-reviyah* (*Simanim* 1-6) (Jerusalem: Otzar Ha-Poskim, 1947), 8.

3 Responsa *Hakham Tzvi* #41 (p. 52).

4 *Mishneh Torah, Hilkhot Ishut* 15:2.

5 *Beit ha-Behirah, Kidushin* 29b, s.v. *ve-le'olam yisa*.

the end he will not be subject to sinful thoughts.[6] Rabbi Lau's view is thus opposed to that of Rambam (and even Meiri may disagree with Rambam only as to the applicability of "let his bones swell," while still prohibiting a delay in procreation).

It is, however, true that, in our day, postponing marriage creates great stumbling-blocks, as Rabbi Lau described at length and with good form and reason. It is a *mitzvah* for us to force ourselves, in order to speed up and advance marriage as much as possible. I would almost say, "It is time to act for God, violate Your Torah" in order that couples marry young, even if they wrongly put off procreation for a while. It is preferable (to use the Talmudic idiom) "that they eat the meat of dangerously ill animals that have been properly slaughtered and not eat the meat of animals that have died of illness without having been properly slaughtered" (i.e. the lesser of two evils).

Because of this, I generally permit a couple to use contraceptives for up to six months after the wedding. (Since the man is allowed to choose to be a sailor whose marital obligations to his wife are only once in six months,[7] in such a case, he would, anyways, not be fulfilling the *mitzvah* of procreation during that period of time; even though there is, obviously, room to distinguish between the two cases.) This length of time is sufficient in order to address most of the uncertainties and fears lest the marriage not turn out well, especially on the part of the bride.

The reason for the age of twenty mentioned in the *beraita* in *Kidushin* is not explained, but apparently it follows what Rabbi Yonatan said Isaac would say to God, "…deduct the twenty years that one is not punished for them" (*Shabbat* 89b). We likewise find in a *midrash* that the heavenly court does not punish for sins except from age twenty and up.[8] Prior to that age, they are not penalized for delaying the *mitzvah* of procreation.[9] But even a bachelor who passes the age of twenty and "let his bones swell," nevertheless, when eventually he marries, "his sins are shaken off," as Rabbi Hama ben Hanina said (*Yevamot* 63b), and it is as though he begins anew.

The *Yerushalmi* states that greatness atones for a scholar, a bridegroom, and a *nasi*, learning this about a bridegroom from "Esau went to Yishmael, and he took for a wife Mahlat the daughter of Yishmael" (Gen. 28:9). It queries "But was Mahlat her name? Wasn't her name Basmat? Rather, all his sins were forgiven [*nimhalu*]" (*Yerushalmi Bikurim* 3:3).

Since they learned this from Esau, it might seem that a bridegroom's sins are forgiven even without renunciation and repentance, but I think there is no rationale for saying this. Rather, in my opinion, "all his sins" is imprecise:

---

6 *Ibid.*, s.v. *le'olam yilmod.*

7 See *Shulhan Arukh, Even Ha-Ezer* 76:1, 6, and commentary of *Beit Shmuel* ad loc.

8 See also Responsa *Benei Banim* 2:219, and the note there.

9 See Rabbi Yosef Hazzan's Responsa *Hikrei Lev* (*Even ha-Ezer* #1, end) and Rabbi Yekhiel Mikhel Epstein's *Arukh Ha-Shulhan.*

only those sins that marriage naturally corrects are absolved, such as abrogating procreation, thinking sinful [sexual] thoughts and wasting seed. For this reason, Rabbi Hama ben Hanina said that "*his* sins are shaken off" and "*his* sins are forgiven," in the masculine and referring to the groom, for such sins are not relevant to the bride. This would explain the custom, mentioned by a few *rishonim*, that only the groom fasts on his wedding day and not the bride.[10]

Parallel to the *beraita* in *Kidushin*, we find that Rabbi Yohanan said, "For six months, the Divine Presence waited for the people Israel, perchance they would repent. When they did not repent, He declared, 'Let their bones swell!'" (*Rosh Hashanah* 31a)

It is the same as "let his bones swell!" in the *beraita*, and there certainly must be some source for the six month period in this regard, although it is unknown to us. Both sections discuss the forbearance of the Holy One, blessed is He, before He declares "Let...swell" on the sinners, and it seems that these are the sole places in the Talmud and *midrash* that God uses this language, as it were. Therefore, we can connect the two and learn from one to the other. It emerges that, just as God waits until age twenty before he pronounces upon a man "let his bones swell," if he marries above the age of twenty and his sins are absolved on his wedding day, God waits six more months before proclaiming "let his bones swell." This is somewhat of a source for permitting the postponement of procreation for six months after the wedding, even past the age of twenty.

However, I do not know a basis to delay procreation for a number of years after marriage; only, one should not protest forcefully against [the practice], for the generation is not worthy. And if the bridegroom is less than age twenty-two or twenty-four, following two different versions of a statement of Rava's (*Kidushin* 30a), there are those who wish to rule leniently according to the implication of Rashi's commentary thereon[11] that these time limits were given also regarding taking a wife, but this has not been cited by the *poskim*.[12]

---

10 See Rabbi Yissachar Tamar's comment on this (*Alei Tamar, Yerushalmi Bikurim 3:3*).

11 Rashi, *Kidushin* 30a, s.v. *me–shitasar*.

12 Regarding the issue of calming a woman who is giving birth (mentioned by Rabbi Lau in *Granot*), see my discussion in Responsum *Benei Banim*, 1:#33. Regarding spacing births even prior to the fulfillment of the *mitzvah* of *peru u-revu*, it is well-known that the *ga'on*, my grandfather, *zt"l*, permitted an interlude of two years and more between one pregnancy and the next. See also *Benei Banim* there, #s 30 and 31.

Yitzchak Avi Roness is a doctoral student
in the Talmud department at Bar Ilan University, concurrently studying for *semikhah*
in the Kollel there.

FAMILY PLANNING: THE POSTPONEMENT OF *MITZVAT PERU U-REVU*[1]
Yitzchak Avi Roness

Many newlyweds feel it in their best interests to postpone having children immediately after their marriage due to any or all of the following considerations:

1. They may view their relationship as still relatively undeveloped and wish to more firmly establish it before responsibly enlarging their own family unit. (In a similar vein, they may have feelings of immaturity, perceiving themselves to be too young to undertake the responsibilities of parenthood.)

2. The added pressures and demands of parenthood may interfere with their ability to properly devote themselves to the completion of their studies while one or both spouses are in pursuit of an academic or vocational degree.

3. Their current economic situation causes them to feel that they cannot responsibly afford the added expenditures of a larger and expanding family.

The question that arises, however, is whether or not one may legitimately— by using a halakhically sanctioned form of contraception—choose to postpone the fulfillment of the *mitzvah* of *peru u-revu* for any of these considerations. This article will focus on understanding the halakhic concept of marriage and child-rearing in order to better analyze the tension between the halakhic responsibility of *peru u-revu* and the desire to postpone its performance. We will then evaluate if, for any of the reasons mentioned above, certain considerations may be halakhically sanctioned so as to warrant postponement of this *mitzvah*.

Yet before proceeding any further, an important clarification is in order. The extensive halakhic literature which discusses the status of various means of birth control usually presents an entirely different matter than that which will be discussed in this article. A mere superficial perusal of rabbinic responsa on this topic will reveal a longstanding, stringent tradition stemming from the

---

[1] This article is adapted from a more expansive version in Hebrew, published in *Or Ha-Mizrah*, Vol. 50: 1-2, 2004, 109-123, and Vol. 50:3-4, 2005, 135-151.

problem of *hotza'at zera le-vatalah*—literally, wasting one's seed—which can be inherent in the very notion of certain forms of contraception. Since *hotza'at zera le-vatalah* is considered to be a singularly heinous offense,[2] discussions surrounding matters that concerned it were often considered to be the sole province of the foremost halakhic authorities of the day.[3]

Though the overwhelming majority of halakhic discussions on this topic are preoccupied with the problem of spilling seed so that discussion—or even mention—of the parameters of the *mitzvah* of *peru u-revu* is fully overshadowed, the halakhic reality confronting us today is wholly unlike that addressed by *poskim* of earlier generations. Due to scientific developments of various hormonal contraceptives widely in use today, the halakhic purview of the discussion has been radically redefined.[4] The once fanciful notion of a standardized means of birth control which does not impinge on the *isur* of *hotza'at zera le-vatalah* has today become a commonplace reality.[5]

In order to achieve an appreciation of the true import of this change, one need only consider the following point: under present conditions, with certain available forms of birth control, the decision to postpone the *mitzvah* of *peru u-revu* after marriage is no more halakhically problematic than deferral or postponement of marriage itself.[6] Consequently, any justifications warranting the deferral of marriage from the age of eighteen and onwards should then, likewise, justify the postponement of having children after marriage as well. It is unclear why many do not object to the fact that the serious undertaking one goes through when searching for a spouse is commonly pushed off until one is well into their twenties, yet remarkably, a young married couple is generally not allowed similar leeway in regard to their family planning.[7]

---

2 See the wording of the *Shulhan Arukh*: "*Assur le-hozi shikhvat zera le-vatalah, ve-avon zeh hamur mi-kol aveirot she-ba-Torah.*" *Shulhan Arukh, Even Ha-Ezer* 23:1.

3 See Rabbi Moshe Feinstein *Igerot Moshe, Even Ha-Ezer* 1:64. Note his great caution in dispensing a permitted ruling on this topic.

4 Up until the seventies they were not in widespread use, and they were considered by many to present a serious health hazard.

5 See *Igerot Moshe, Even Ha-Ezer* 2:17, 3:24. One need only compare this directive to his earlier *tshuvot* in order to appreciate the vast difference in tone. For a further elaboration, see R. Shlomo Aviner, *Sefer Asiyah* 4, pp. 171.

6 This fundamental change was forcefully noted by R. Getsel Ellinson (Ellinson, *Procreation in the Light of Halacha: Family Planning and Birth Control* [Jerusalem: World Zionist Organization, Dept. for Torah Education and Culture in the Diaspora, 1977], 9). This last point is based on Rambam, *Hilkhot Ishut,* 15:2. See R. Ellinson, *Procreation in the Light of Halacha,* 33 & 36.

7 See R. Moshe Feinstein's response to R. Ellinson (*Even Ha-Ezer* 4:32) which states that it is better to marry with the intention of postponing parenthood than to postpone marriage itself. Although it is not clear that R. Moshe would have allowed the use of the pill in this instance. It seems that this stems from his understanding that this would constitute "*hit-hakhmot neged ratzon Hashem.*" See *Igerot Moshe, Yoreh De'ah* 3:143 and *Even Ha-Ezer* 4:72. This consideration, however, is strange, since it could just as easily be levelled against all medical or technological

Since in the present reality the unwarranted use of these commonplace means of birth control no longer entails a willful transgression of what is described as one of the severest of the Torah's prohibitions, the general focus of the discussion must be adapted accordingly, assuming the pitch and tone befitting the discussion of a deferral of a *mitzvat aseh*, a positive commandment.[8]

Each of the married couple's considerations enumerated above is surely of great consequence. Indeed, "a decision one way or the other upon so vital an aspect of family life must ultimately affect every facet of human aspiration."[9] Yet the gravity of the halakhic prohibition involved in the use of contraception for those purposes previously left no room for the evaluation of the aforementioned concerns from a broader halakhic perspective. This, then, shall be the express purpose of the following discussion. Though each of these three concerns listed above will be considered and addressed, we shall first start by examining the halakhic legitimacy of the third, which involves establishing a sound financial basis before setting out to enlarge one's family. This principled position bears close resemblance to a rabbinic adage identifying the need to secure financial independence as an elementary prerequisite for marriage.

Marriage and Financial Independence

The Talmudic sages taught that proper "*derekh eretz*" (cultured practice) requires that one first establish a firm financial base before proceeding forward with marriage: "The Torah [has] taught us proper etiquette (*derekh eretz*): one

---

advances, including sperm donations to infertile women which Rav Moshe himself discusses: e.g. wouldn't this same logic lead us to prohibit a married woman to accept a sperm donation? See *Igerot Moshe, Even Ha-Ezer* 1:10, 1:71, 2:11, and 4:32. Similarly, would the acceptance of an epidural be considered *hit-hakhmot* against God's decree of "*be-etzev teiledi banim?*"

[8] The Rambam's wording in *Hilkhot Ishut* 15:2 seems to indicate that the postponement of the *mitzvah* is not merely an issue of "*zerizin makdimin le-mitzvah*," but rather enters into the more serious category of a "*bitul mitzvat aseh*"—annuling a positive commandment. However, as a number of writers have convincingly argued, this simply cannot be Rambam's intention, for he writes in that very same halakhah that one engaged in the study of Torah need not interfere with his studies in order to fulfill this duty, as he is categorized as an "*osek be-mitzvah, patur min ha-mitzvah*" (one engaged in a commandment is excused from performing a commandment). As the Netziv points out, the Rambam's application of this rule to the situation of the Torah scholar implies that we are referring to a case of a *mitzvah she–eino overet*—a commandment where there is no pressing time limit, the postponement of which is not considered to be a *bitul mitzvah*. (On this last point, see *Arukh Ha-Shulhan, Even Ha-Ezer* 1:13, as well as the more recent contributions of R. Shlomo Aviner, R. Avraham Dov Auerbach, and R. Ya'akov Ariel in *Sefer Asiyah* 4, pp. 187. See also the forceful presentation of R. Asher Weiss, *Minhat Asher, Parshat Noah, Mitzvat Periyah ve-Riveyah.*

[9] R. Aharon Lichtenstein, Foreword to *Procreation In the Light of Halacha*, 5. "The true significance of the matters at hand is to be measured by the far reaching consequences involved," as the couple's course of action will greatly affect their "economic prospects, social status and vocational attainments," factors which "will in turn make themselves felt in terms of inner happiness and spiritual wellbeing."

should build a house, plant a vineyard and then marry a wife" (*Sotah* 44a). Rambam codifies this directive in his work *Mishneh Torah* under *Hilkhot De'ot,*[10] describing it as *"derekh baʿalei hokhmah"*—the manner of the wise. He presents this in sharp contrast with the more common practice of *"ha-tipshim"* – the manner of fools. Rambam explains that the future stability of the household will be determined, to a great degree, by one's behavior in this regard. Those who proceed along the rational path—"the manner of the wise"—ensure themselves divine blessing and assistance in the building of their home, whereas those who attempt to establish their home in the contrary order—marrying first and only then beginning the search for a source of income—can expect a shaky future, having chosen a path which will guarantee them a lifetime of financial entanglement and hardship. For Rambam, choosing the latter course of action would effectively be a decision to position oneself within the category of the cursed.[11]

The *Zohar* offers a similar analysis of the importance of following this correct order when establishing one's family, stressing the spiritual consequences of one's actions:

> Rabbi Yohanan [stated]: "With wisdom one builds a house: three things must a man do in the manner of the world (*be-darkhei olam*) and they are: to build his dwelling, to plant a vineyard by which to sustain himself [monetarily], and afterwards, to take for himself a wife and bring forth children [so as] to be sustained by them. And not like the ways of the fools that first take a wife and only after plant a vineyard, and then after build a house. Like that which Rav Simon stated: 'Whoever takes for himself first a wife and does not have at first with what to sustain himself [monetarily]—behold, this is one who is 'free (*hofshi*) from the *mitzvot*' like corpses, which are referred to as 'free'. . .' And why is he called 'free' from the *mitzvot*? Because he is not able to concern himself with the work of his Creator, but rather [only] with the [concern of] work for his wife."

> Rabbi Yehuda says: "It is as if he has taken idols to himself [with which he will then worship]." For Rabbi Yehuda had said: "In the beginning, the wise ones and the pious ones would take for themselves wives and [even if] they did not have enough to sustain themselves [monetarily], they would [subject themselves] with hunger and thirst and let go their worldly concerns [in order to] be involved with Torah, *mitzvot*, and the work of

---

10 5:11.

11 Compare with Rambam's explanation of *"Hashgahah"*—providence—in his work *The Guide to the Perplexed* (III:17), where he demonstrates how both the divine blessing and the divine curse can be the direct result of man's rational or irrational choices.

their Creator. But in our time, when the world is pre-occupied with [sustaining] a livelihood, one must first establish a house and secure his sustenance and [only] after take a wife, [so that he may] be able to worship his Creator and be involved in Torah study. As [the Sages] said: 'If there is no flour, there is no Torah.'"[12]

Since starting a family without having first ensured a proper economic basis will surely force one to engage in a time consuming and desperate pursuit to make ends meet, one can expect to be left without the minimal peace of mind necessary to worship God properly. He who enters such a situation willfully, marrying and having children before he is capable of looking after his family's needs is therefore likened to one who has removed the yoke of the Torah from his shoulders, and is even likened to a worshipper of idols. According to the *Zohar*, financial caution, planning, and foresight when building and establishinging one's home is not only praiseworthy, but is indispensable, and even verily a part of *imitatio dei*.[13]

It is also important to note that the Rabbis' advice regarding the need to prepare a firm financial base is purposefully vague. The expression "to build a house and plant a vineyard" does not convey a clear notion in regard to the size of the home or the size and quality of the vineyard. It is surely true, that generally one must be careful not to overstep the line distinguishing between *"dirah na'eh ve-keilim na'im"*—a nice dwelling and nice utensils—and a completely hedonistic lifestyle. Yet the Rabbis' directive here, is that no matter what the minimal lifestyle one deems necessary for oneself,[14] appropriate steps must be taken to ensure that this standard of living be maintained as one's family and expenses grow, for otherwise domestic strife will surely follow.[15] But far

---

[12] *Zohar Hadash*, Volume 1 (*Torah*), *Bereshit*, 9a

[13] *Ibid*. See the end of the passage there and Rabbi Yehuda's final comments. The fact that God brought man into a complete world equipped with all that was necessary to meet his every need is cited as proof that one must always, in the like manner of God, be concerned first with providing for one's basic needs and only then pursuing other interests. If we wish to construct our home in a similar fashion to reflect how God created the world, we must first prepare all the concrete necessary financial foundations and only then proceed to establish and rear a family.

[14] It is worthy to note, that the Rabbis were aware of the impossibility of setting an objective standard of living applicable to all (see *Mishnah Berurah* 156:1 and *Sha'ar Ha-Tziyun* ad loc., 2). This same understanding is implicit in the halakhic definition of an individual's needs vis-à-vis the *mitzvah* of *tzedakah*. See *Shulhan Arukh, Yoreh De'ah*, 250:1.

[15] Another rabbinic demand that is highly instructive in this regard is the directive that one must ensure that his bride's standard of living does not fall beneath that which she had been accustomed to in her father's home. Marriage in and of itself should not be the cause for lowering one's standard of living. See *Ketuvot* 61a, *Shulhan Arukh, Even Ha-Ezer* 70. The commentators there explain that this refers to one's socio-economic status. One should not expect of his wife to behave in a manner not befitting her previous social milieu. However, if there is a natural distinction between the older, more established generation and the younger generation who

from being some sort of foreign, western notion, a young couple's financial considerations and concerns are fully in accord with the Torah's understanding of the ideal way to set up a household.

Pursuing an Academic Degree—*Osek Be-Mitzvah?*

As mentioned earlier, couples who may have no pressing financial worries may have concerns of a different nature and wish to push off having children in order to first complete their academic studies. Often their studies might require their full attention. Consequently, they may fear that they will not successfully meet the growing demands on their time (as well as the added anxiety on their general frame of mind) as the manifold responsibilities of parenthood begin to take their toll. The notion of a possible conflict between one's scholarly pursuits and the demands of family life is surely not a novel one. *Halakha* explicitly addresses this concern regarding the study of Torah, advising young Torah scholars to delay marriage in order to further their Torah education:

> Always, a man should learn Torah [first] and afterwards marry a woman, for if he marries a woman [first], his mind will not be [untarried] for him to [focus on] learning.[16]

But can the pursuit of an academic degree likewise be compared to the study of Torah in this regard? Or is this halakhah a special dispensation resulting from the unique importance of the *mitzvah* of *talmud Torah*? The Rambam in *Hilkhot Ishut* explains that the justification of the postponement of marriage for the sake of *talmud Torah* is based on the general halakhic principle of "one who is currently involved in a *mitzvah* is exempt from other mitzvot" (*ha-osek be-mitzvah, patur min ha-mitzvah*).[17] This reasoning can be applied equally to similar situations involving other mitzvot as well, and not just to Torah study.[18] Yet may one who pursues an academic degree be regarded as one who is "involved in" a *mitzvah*?

One early rabbinic teaching enumerates a father's responsibilities to his son and couples his duty to teach his son Torah with the additional responsibility to teach him a profession (*Tosefta Kidushin* 1:8). The gemara cites the source of this obligation from the phrase: "Enjoy life with the woman that you love" (Ecc. 9:9), indicating that it is inconceivable for one to live together with his

---

have yet to build up their fortune, then a lowering of one's lifestyle—which is shared by all brides belonging to the same social circle—is decidedly not frowned upon.

16 Tur, *Yoreh De'ah*, 246

17 *Mishneh Torah*, *Hilkhot Ishut* 15:2. Rabbi Naftali Tzvi Yehuda Berlin, *Ha-Emek She'eilah* 103:14 notes that *talmud Torah* does not normally exempt one from all other *mitzvot*. This principle applies here since marriage and parenthood force upon one a myriad of responsibilities which do not allow for a continuation of one's studies in the manner one had been accustomed to previously, thereby frustrating one's ability to acquire an essential knowledge of the Torah. It seems clear that a similar description can be applied to the university student as well.

18 For an elaboration of this last point, see *She'eilot u-Teshuvot Shevet ha-Levi* 6-221.

wife without '*hayim*'—a source of livelihood. Thus, the father's obligation to teach his son Torah and to arrange for his marriage[19] must perforce include an obligation to enable his son to secure a future livelihood as well.

The high regard for one's professional education is also indicated in a *beraita* that says, although the discussion of one's business affairs is prohibited on Shabbat, nevertheless one is allowed to pursue the necessary arrangements for one's son's religious, as well as vocational, education (*Shabbat* 150a).[20] Though these two sources refer to the father's *mitzvah* of taking care of his son, it is clear that when this has not been done it becomes the son's personal responsibility to do so.[21]

Yet another gemara repeats the same theme as above when discussing the general halakhot of the *rotzeakh be-shegagah*—the inadvertent killer. The gemara there teaches us that *galut* (exile) is only required when the inadvertent death resulted from an act which can be categorized as a *devar reshut*—non-obligatory act—while a *rotzeakh be-shegagah* is not exiled if the death resulted from the act of admonishing a sinner, or disciplining a student, since these both fall under the category of *devar mitzvah* (*Makot* 8b). However, the gemara clarifies that the act of disciplining a student is regarded as a *devar mitzvah*, regardless of whether the instructor is a teacher of Torah or a vocational instructor—just so long as the intended act was meant to further the education of the student.[22]

When we consider these sources that equate one's professional schooling to the study of Torah, assuming that an academic degree will serve as a key to one's future livelihood,[23] it seems that the involvement and preoccupation in studies geared towards the acquisition of a profession can indeed be compared to the study of Torah. Both would place one in the category of *osek be-mitzvah*,

---

[19] This is based on the gemara's contention that the word "*ishah*" may be best understood metaphorically as a reference to *talmud Torah*—*Am Yisrael*'s spiritual bride.

[20] The gemara there explains that while the discussion of one's business affairs falls under the category of "*hafazekha asurim*," both the study of Torah, as well as the son's professional education—"*le-lamdo sefer u-le-lamdo umanut*"—are instances of "*hefzei shamayim mutarin.*"

[21] Though the aforementioned *pasuk* in *Kohelet* serves as the source for the father's duty towards his son, it is not necessarily addressed to the father per se, but rather to the individual himself. See *Yerushalmi Kidushin* 1:7 which clearly articulates this idea implicit here in the Bavli.

[22] The Talmud notes that the fundamental difference between the two is that there is no concept of '*lishmah*' in professional training, since if the person already has a profession there is no *mitzvah* to acquire another. Torah study however, is limitless and constantly presents a new *mitzvah* to be done. It is worthy to note that the difference between the halakhic status of acquiring a profession, as opposed to the work itself, is apparent in the *sugya*. The Torah's tale of the woodcutter's accidental killing of an innocent bystander is the classic example of the inadvertent killing ensuing from a *devar ha-reshut*, whereas in a case when this very same carpenter was disciplining his disciple (*shuliya di-nagrah*) and inadvertently caused his death it is classified as a *devar mitzvah*.

[23] More often than not, an academic degree is perceived as a part of one's professional educa - tion. If one's pursuit of wisdom is in and of itself a religious act, its definition as a *mitzvah* is more straightforward. See R. Yosef Kapach in *Techumin* Vol. 2.

patur min ha-mitzvah and thus legitimately enable one to defer the *mitzvah* of *peru u-revu*.

Marriage and Parenthood

As mentioned before, another possible factor in a couple's decision may be their desire to be free to devote themselves fully towards solidifying the emotional foundations of their relationship. Aware of the challenges they may meet up with in the future, they may be interested in setting aside a period of time in which they will be able to focus on each other—nourishing and building that which is yet a young relationship. They may fear, or even be convinced, that assuming the weighty responsibilities and pressures of parenthood prematurely will have a negative effect on the future of their relationship. In order to properly evaluate this concern, we must first clarify the nature of the relationship between marriage and childbearing.

There is surely a functional connection between marriage and procreation since one must marry in order to be in a position to fulfill the *mitzvah* of *peru u-revu*. It appears clear, though, that this functional connection stems from a deeper conceptual bond. That is, the *mitzvah* of *peru u-revu* is directed at the married individual as opposed to the unmarried one.[24] The Torah's intention then, is that childrearing be viewed as the natural outcome of a healthy marriage.

The Netziv (Rabbi Naftali Tzvi Yehuda Berlin 1817-1893) finds proof for this contention in the fact that one's practical obligation vis-a-vis the *mitzvah* of *peru u-revu* is defined as the strict adherence to the marital pattern proscribed by the biblical commandment of *onah*.[25]

The *mitzvah* of *onah*, however, is unique; since its purpose is to regulate and maintain the couple's conjugal rhythm, there is no universal definition or standard that is applicable to all. Instead, the practical demands of *onah* vary in accordance with the demands of the husband's vocation and his relative level of energy.[26] If we find that *peru u-revu* adopts these same unique criteria, this must mean that this *mitzvah* is perceived to be a natural outcome of a healthy marital relationship—not an independent halakhic demand placed upon the couple's relationship.[27]

This same fundamental understanding underlies a rabbinic statement regarding marital sexual ethics known by the category of *"benei tesha midot"*

---

[24] See Rabbi Joseph B. Soloveitchik, *Family Redeemed: Essays on Family Relationships*, ed. David Shatz & Joel Wolowelsky (New York, Toras HaRav Foundation, 2000), 31-72. [See the article by Rabbi Binyamin Lau cited in this edition who discusses this idea. –Editor's Note]

[25] Rabbi Naftali Tzvi Yehuda Berlin, *Ha-Emek She'elah* 165; *Meishiv Davar* 4:11.

[26] *Shulhan Arukh, Even Ha-Ezer* 76:1-2. See also *Igerot Moshe, Even Ha-Ezer* 3:28, who compares *mitzvat onah* to the husband's other obligations of providing his wife with food and clothing, where it is clear that the husband's obligation is relative to his capabilities.

[27] See *Otzar ha-Poskim, Even Ha-Ezer* 76, who brings the opinion of *Derekh Pikudekha* and others who distinguish between these two *mitzvot*.

(*Nedarim* 20b). The Rabbis delineated moral boundaries of sexual contact by listing nine paradigmatic situations in which a couple must refrain from sexual contact.[28] The central theme stressed throughout, is that the marital act must not be allowed to assume the character of an impersonal—and therefore animalistic—release of primal drives. In the ideal situation, the marital act serves as a physical expression and embodiment of the couple's deep emotional and spiritual attachment. The strict halakhic demand however, does not deal with the ideal as such, but rather with the more modest requirement that the physical act be accompanied by a certain minimal emotional and personal component as well.[29]

The fundamental understanding that *peru u-revu* can be fulfilled only from within the framework of a healthy marital relationship can clearly be seen by the fact that this ethic remains in full force even when strict adherence to it will force a delay in its fulfillment.[30] If, as we have demonstrated, *peru u-revu* pre-supposes a healthy marital relationship, then any measure necessary to strengthen and to insure the health and viability of that relationship must then take precedence over the immediate fulfillment of the *mitzvah*. If childrearing is to ensue from a framework of a healthy marital relationship and does not take precedence over it, then it likewise stands to reason that a couple must be advised *not* to have children in the event that such a move would contribute to the weakening (and possible detriment) of their relationship.

A situation then, in which having a child would definitively serve to *weaken* the marital bond between two individuals would then be in utter opposition to the Torah's view of their ideal union as expressed in the *pasuk*: "And he shall cling to his wife and they shall be one flesh." (Gen. 2:24). Procreation here ("and they shall be one flesh") is assumed to flow naturally from the healthy loving marital relationship ("And he shall cling to his wife").

Is the *Mitzvah* of *Peru u-Revu* Completed with the Birth of a Child?

In describing the couple's motives for delaying childbirth, we also mentioned the possibility that they may feel they are emotionally unprepared for parenthood. A powerful self-image of youth and immaturity may lead newlyweds to believe that they are not yet capable of doing justice to the immense responsibilities involved in raising and educating a child. Though they fully intend to assume the responsibilities of parenthood in the future, they hope to do so upon reaching a more mature and established stage in their life.

This basic, almost intuitive understanding closely resembles that which was discussed earlier. If the desire to follow the dictates of *derekh eretz* (cultured practice) demands that one not marry until he is capable of providing a physical home for his family, the same must also be true *a fortiori* in regard to the

---

[28] *Shulhan Arukh, Orah Hayim* 240:3; *Even Ha-Ezer* 25:2.

[29] See *Levush, Orah Hayim* 240 and *Darkhei Taharah* pp. 196.

[30] See *Beit Yosef* and *Bah, Orah Hayim* 240.

necessary ability to provide the child with the emotional and spiritual facets of the home as well.

Furthermore, although we generally perceive the *immediate* fulfillment of a *mitzvah* to be desirable, "*zerizut*" (speed or haste) is not always a positive attribute. When the circumstances of a situation are such, that by delaying a *mitzvah* one will allow for a higher level or quality of fulfillment (a "*hidur mitzvah*"), hastiness quickly loses its shine. It would seem then, that a couple's wish to delay having children until they are in a position which will enable them to more fully care for their child's needs presents us with exactly such a case.

But in order to convincingly argue that this case may indeed be regarded as an instance of delaying the performance of a *mitzvah* in order to perform it more fully at a later time, we must demonstrate that the parents' ongoing care for their child's upbringing and education is directly linked to one's duty vis-a-vis the *mitzvah* of *peru u-revu*. Surely we sense that this can hardly be otherwise, yet the halakhic interdependence of the two must be established nonetheless.

'We learn it from the creation of the world...'

Beit Hillel and Beit Shammai disputed as to the halakhic requirements of *peru u-revu*, with Beit Hillel opining that one fulfills this *mitzvah* after fathering both a male and a female child. The Talmud explains that this is derived from the story of creation, as it says: "Male and female He created them." (Gen. 1:27) (Yevamot 61b). On a conceptual level, it is difficult to see how it is possible to derive man's duty from the divine act of creation. How can the creation of the world serve to teach us this lesson?

The idea implicit in Beit Hillel's view is that *peru u-revu* is perceived as the human duty to emulate and re-enact in miniature the divine act of creation. Earlier we saw that the *Zohar* considers the story of creation as modeling the correct order in which to erect one's home. We can now deeply appreciate how that idea stems from the understanding that *peru u-revu* is a human re-enactment of creation. Understanding the *mitzvah* in this way also implies that one is obligated to continue caring for his creation, just as God continuously cares for our world. The parents' objective, then, must be to insure the success of their "little world"[31] that they have created, doing their utmost to raise

---

[31] Compare with the definition put forth by Rambam, *Mishneh Torah, Hilkhot Ishut* 15:16. We have explained that Beit Hillel viewed *peru u-revu* as a re-enactmant of creation. It would appear from the gemara however, that the measure of one's continued responsibility towards this 'creation' is a matter of dispute. There is an Amoraic dispute (*Yevamot* 62a) as to the basic intention and nature of the *mitzvah:* Is one commanded to bring two souls into this world?— the perspective being that the soul's descent into this world is an end unto itself, or is the commandment to procreate part of Man's general mission to both insure and to further the settling and conquering of God's creation? The gemara explains that the practical difference between these two opinions is found in the tragic case where a father buries his child. Though a soul may have been lowered from the heavens, if that child did not have children of its own

healthy, upright, and God-fearing children.

This understanding acts as a basis for the requirement the Rabbis added to the Torah's definition of the *mitzvah*. The Rabbis determined that even after fulfilling the Torah's requirement of fathering one child of each gender one should continue to have additional children. R. Yehoshua explains that this is intended to raise the probability of succeeding in the ultimate goal of raising healthy, God fearing children, since any single attempt cannot be relied upon to yield the anticipated results.[32] The Rabbis thus expanded the Torah's initial requirement out of concern for the child's future health and spiritual development.

Rabbi Yosef Karo makes explicit reference to this as part of the broader rationale for the commandment and writes that while fulfilling the marital act, one's intention should be: "to fulfill the commandment of his Creator to have sons who are engaged in the [study of] Torah and who are fufilling the commandments of the people of Israel."[33] One may conclude that the overriding rationale of this *mitzvah* entails much more than the physical/biological creation of a child—it encompasses the desire to raise healthy, upright, and God-fearing children.[34]

This claim, that caring for the future character of one's offspring can constitute a *hidur mitzvah* of *peru u-revu*, has already been put forth by the Maharam Schick (Rabbi Moshe Schick 1807-1879).[35] In the general context of the halakhic discussion of whether or not a *hidur mitzvah* takes precedence over the importance of *"zerizin makdimin le-mitzvot,"* the Maharam Schick turns to the example of our forefathers and poses a question: How are we to understand the fact that Avraham—who appears throughout rabbinic literature as the "father" of all *"zerizim"*—did not take any steps to marry off his son Yitzhak immediately upon his coming of age, waiting instead until he reached the relatively advanced age of forty?

The Maharam Schick suggests that Avraham Avinu's behavior can best be understood as proof of the primacy of the perfect (although belated) performance of a *mitzvah* over its immediate execution. He explains that the post-

---

then the father has not yet fulfilled the latter definition of the *mitzvah*. Even though the father succeeded in performing the act of creation, the purpose and goal was not met.

[32] This is derived from the verse: "In the morning sow your seed, and in the evening do not let your hand be idle, for you cannot know which will be successful—this one or that one—or whether both are equally good." (Ecc. 11:6) See Rashi, *Yevamot* 62b, s.v. *ay zeh yekhshar.*

[33] *Shulhan Arukh, Orah Hayim* 240.

[34] A number of sources indicate that when it is clear that one's children will not be raised and educated according to Torah ideals there is no value in having children. God's response to Hizkiyahu in *Berakhot* (10a) does not refute Hizkiyahu's assumption, but is rather viewed as his inability to know God's machinations through history. See Gen. *Rabah* 44:9, where it explains that Avraham Avinu's heartfelt desire to bear children is wholly dependent on their future acceptance of the Torah.

[35] See *She'eilot U-Teshuvot Maharam Schick, Even Ha-Eezer* 1.

ponement was based on the understanding that if Yitzhak were to first perfect his own character, raising himself to a higher spiritual plane, it would in turn have a beneficial effect on the nature and behavior of his future offspring. As our forefathers' deepest wish was that their children continue on in their path, they willfully postponed the *mitzvah*, waiting for the most opportune time in order to fulfill it in the most perfect manner possible.

With this perspective of the Maharam Schick, we can now support our original claim. The couple's decision to wait until they can better execute their charge of parenthood indeed becomes an instance of delaying the performance of a *mitzvah* in order to fulfill it at a later time in a more perfect manner.

Conclusion

Various groups within the larger Orthodox community often deny legitimacy to any valid, alternative halakhic approaches that differ from their own. Many assume naively that any behavioral nonconformity between the different Orthodox streams results from a pervasively lax attitude towards various religious practices rather than from a legitimate, halakhic source and difference of opinion. Since these attacks often go unanswered, are left unchallenged, or disregarded, the popular impression created in the minds of members of both communities is that these alternate perspectives cannot truly be defended.

Based on the sources however, I believe that the common practice of many young Orthodox couples to postpone having children for any of the considerations mentioned above can be fully validated from a Torah perspective and certainly supported from a halakhic standpoint as well. One may indeed choose to differ with a couple's general outlook on life or with their prioritizing of values. However, one should respect the fact that they are attempting to live according to their own religious and moral convictions in a manner that can (and should) be sanctioned halakhically.[36]

---

[36] For two additional recent discussions on the topic see See R. Yuval Sherlow's "Delaying the First Birth by Young Couples," *Tzohar* 27, 83-89; as well as R. Michael Broyde "Birth Control and Jewish Law—A Pastoral Letter," at : http://www.yith.org/newsletter/newsletter.01.5766.pdf. R. Broyde's halakhic position resembles that which we have presented: "Generally speaking, it is my view that there is nothing wrong with delaying fulfilling the obligation to have children (by not marrying, abstaining from sexual relations, or from using a permissible method of birth control) so long as one does not do so in a manner which defeats the fundamental obligation itself to have children."

Rabbi Barry Gelman serves as Rabbi of
United Orthodox Synagogues of Houston.
He is Director of Rabbinic Placement at Ye-
shivat Chovevei Torah Rabbinical School.

MIPNEI TAKANAT HA-SHAVIM – מפני תקנת השבים
OUTREACH CONSIDERATIONS IN PESAK HALAKHAH[1]
Rabbi Barry Gelman

Recently, I met with a couple who were slowly but surely adopting an observant lifestyle. During the course of our conversation this couple mentioned
that they had a set of china dishes that were a family heirloom. The dishes
were given to them by a family member who did not keep kosher and were
most probably used with either *treif* food or interchangeably for both dairy and
meat. They then told me that they were under the impression that the dishes
could not be "koshered." They told me as well that the dishes had important
sentimental value to them, and that they were saddened by the notion of not
being able to use them.

After seeing how difficult this decision was for them, I shared with them the
view of Rabbi Moshe Feinstein who allowed *kashering* china in circumstances
very similar to theirs and told them that I thought that they, too, could *kasher*
their dishes.[2] At that moment, the wife turned to her husband and said with
a gleam in her eye, "See, I told you we could do it." She went on to explain
that they had been bombarded with so many strict interpretations of Orthodox
Judaism that her husband began to doubt whether or not they could pull off
a total assimilation into Orthodoxy.

In hindsight, I could have tried to convince the couple that their attachment
to the dishes should not serve as a barrier for further religious growth and
counsel them how to best integrate themselves into orthodoxy—just without
the dishes!—but instead, I simply removed the barrier. Removing barriers to
religious growth can be a very effective tool towards increasing religious observance, and we see that this method has, in fact, been used by great *poskim*.

In the response in which Rabbi Feinstein records his permissive ruling about
china, he invokes the idea of "*takanat ha-shavim*," regulations or enactments
made in order to help those who wish to repent (literally: return). Rabbi Feinstein understood that the use of permissive rulings in cases such as this would
make the road to observance easier to navigate for those who wish to embrace
an Orthodox style of religious observance.

One primary source for the concept of *takanat ha-shavim* is a mishnah in

---

[1] I am grateful to David Wolkenfeld for his assistance in bringing this article to publication.
[2] Responsa, *Igerot Moshe, Yoreh De'ah* 2: #46

Gitin (5:5):

> R. Johanan b. Gudgada testified: '… and on the beam which
> was stolen and which he [who stole it and already used it and]
> built it into a palace, restitution for [the beam] may be made in
> money, *so as not to put obstacles in the way of penitents…*' [3]

To grasp the import of the mishnah, one must understand that the primary
obligation regarding a stolen object is to return the item to its original owner.
Only if the object no longer exists is repayment an acceptable option. In this
case, the large beam, though it still exists, has already been built into a building, yet the Rabbis allow the thief to repay the value of the beam instead of
returning the beam itself, which would require the destruction of the building in order to retrieve it. Understanding that the thief would not go to the
trouble of destroying the building in order to return the beam, an allowance
was made to make restitution and repentance feasible.

There is another pitfall inherent when not taking this approach and that is
the lost opportunity to help make a halakhic and permissible style of living
accessible to as many Jews as possible. When discussing leniencies and stringencies, we should not focus on the spectrum of less stringent or more stringent,
but rather on the strategic use of leniency to *encourage greater observance.*
Put differently, when rendering halakhic decisions, rabbis should not focus on
whether or not a decision is in line with the most stringent approach or is in
accord with as many opinions as possible, but rather on the long term affects
the particular decision will have on an individual's level of observance.

The case of our mishnah and its application by Rabbi Feinstein are examples
of the use of halakhic leniencies to make the road easier for *ba'alei teshuvah.*
Other *poskim* throughout the generations have also used leniencies in order to
limit sin in situations that are not ideal. Maimonides, for example, regarding
a case involving an improper union between a Jewish man and his non-Jewish
maid, used the notion of *takanat ha-shavim* in such a fashion and openly
stated that even though he was contradicting an explicit Talmudic ruling by
allowing her to convert and be married, ruled accordingly because of *takanat
ha-shavim*—in order to facilitate repentance.[4]

---

[3] Also quoted in *Eduyot* 7:9. Actual translation reads "on account of the 'decree of the pen -
tents'." See Rashi, *Gitin* 55a, s.v. *takanat ha-shavim.* Also Rambam, *Peirush Ha-Mishnayot
Gitin*, ad loc (emphasis added).

[4] Maimonides, Responsa *"Pe'er Ha-Dor"*, 132. The case involved a Jewish man who had rel -
tions with a non-Jewish woman he had hired to be his maid. Maimonides states that Jewish law
requires that the woman be immediately expelled, yet Maimonides realized that the situation
was not ideal and that if the woman cannot be expelled she should be converted so that the
couple can marry in accordance with Jewish law. Maimonides based his opinion on the *mishnaic* ruling that such a couple, though forbidden to marry, if they did so, need not separate.
Maimonides also invoked the halakhic nuance of *"Et La'asot La-Hashem."* [For a detailed and
descriptive analysis of this case and the use of the halakhic idiom *"Et La'asot La-Hashem"* see

Basing himself on this ruling by Maimonides, in a responsum addressed to Rabbi Raphael Chaim Sabban, Chief Rabbi of Istanbul, Rabbi Benzion Uziel ruled in favor of conversion performed for the sake of marriage.[5] While conversion for the sake of marriage is generally frowned upon, Rabbi Uziel argued that when the non-Jewish partner in an intermarriage wishes to convert, rabbis *should perform* such conversions. Doing so, he claims, frees the couple from the sin of intermarriage and saves the couple and their children from being astranged from Judaism entirely.

Rabbi Uziel also notes that, by approaching the rabbi for conversion, the couple has expressed a desire to be part of the Jewish people. He urges rabbis to allow such conversions in order to make Jewish living accessible to these couples. He also addresses and rejects the conceptual notion of *"hal'iteihu la-rasha va-yimot"*—literally "let the wicked stuff themselves with it until they die"—that teaches that sinners should be left to sin and suffer the consequences.[6] Instead, Rabbi Uziel prefers the following Talmudic teaching (*Shabbat* 31b):

> Rav Ulla expounded: "Why is it written, 'Be not much wicked'? Must one not be much wicked, yet he may be a little wicked? Rather, if one has eaten garlic and his breath smells, should he [continue to] eat more garlic, so that his breath should [continue to] smell?"

From this passage, Rabbi Uziel deduces that it is a commandment to prevent people from sinning.[7] It is this approach, one of using halakha to bring people closer to observance, that Rabbi Uziel applies to the question of conversion for the sake of marriage.[8]

These rulings by Maimonides, Rabbi Uziel, and Rabbi Feinstein share a willingness to use rabbinic creativity and precedent to make entrance into the halakhic way of life easier. Using *takanat ha-shavim* in matters pertaining to

---

Zecharya Goldman's article "Emergency Halakha in the Rabbinic Tradition" in this volume. –Editor's Note]

[5] Responsa *Mishpetei Uzi'el*, Vol. 2, *Yoreh De'ah* 48.

[6] *Bava Kama* 69a. The gemara there discusses the procedures for adequately marking one's field during the year of *shemitah* to allow passersby to know which fields, orchards, and vineyards are permissible to eat from, without concern for either the biblical prohibition of *orlah* or *kerem rev'ay*, for in the seventh year of the Septennate cycle, the land is rendered ownerless and all may partake of its yield. Regarding the rest of the years in the *shemitah* cycle however, the gemara, in explanation of Rabbi Shimon ben Gamliel, states that there is no rabbinic requirement to mark one's field appropriately to warn of any inherent prohibitions when taking fruit because to do so would be stealing and counsels to, "let the wicked stuff themselves with it till they die." For a full treatment of *"Hal'iteihu la-rasha va-yimot"* see *Techumin*, Vol. 9, 156 – 170, and Encyclopedia Talmudit, Volume 9, columns 444-448.

[7] Responsa *Mishpetei Uziy'el*, Vol. 2, *Yoreh De'ah* 48.

[8] For a more detailed discussion on the topic of conversion for the sake of marriage, see Rabbi Mark D. Angel's recent publication on this subject, *Choosing to Be Jewish: the Orthodox Road to Conversion*, (Hoboken, NJ: Ktav, 2005).

personal status represents a bold willingness to use halakha to pry open the doors of Jewish living to assist people in their attempts to enter.

Takanat Ha-Shavim Concerns Regarding *Taharat Ha-Mishpahah*

Takanat ha-shavim has also been used to make the burden of ritual observance easier for individuals who find certain aspects of an orthodox, halakhic way of life unbearable. In his collection of responsa entitled *Reshut Ha-Yahid,* Rabbi Yuval Sherlow, Rosh Yeshiva of Yeshivat Hesder Petah Tikvah, addresses the issue of applying leniencies regarding the laws of *Taharat Ha-Mishpahah*— the laws concerning *nidah,* or menstrual impurity—for newly observant women. The question posed to Rabbi Sherlow came in the context of a general concern on the part of newly observant women that the full compliment of the laws of *Taharat Ha-Mishpahah* may be too much to bear. Rabbi Sherlow permitted a woman who was beginning to observe the laws of *Taharat Ha-Mishpahah* to only observe the biblical laws of *nidah*— without the added rabbinic stringencies—so long as she was on a "path" towards full observance of the laws of menstrual purity.[9] He issued his permissive ruling recognizing that it may be the very stringencies that are imposed on newly observant women that cause them not to observe more important *halakhot.*

Rabbi Sherlow further addressed the issue of women who were uncomfortable with the mikvah attendant doing a full body check before immersion.[10] The question stated that women refrained from immersion in the mikvah due to what they perceived as a breach of privacy on the part of the mikvah attendant. The questioner (rightly) states that since immersion is only disqualified by the presence of a foreign substance that covers most of a woman's body, or by a small amount of foreign substance about which the woman cares, there is no real reason for the mikvah attendant to do a full body check for such substances.

Rabbi Sherlow quotes Rabbi Yaakov Ariel, Chief Rabbi of Ramat Gan, who allows the attendant to only view the woman while immersing in the mikvah, to make sure that all of her hair has gone below the surface, and states that he was willing, for the sake of making it more comfortable for women to use the mikvah, to do away with the full body check that is prevalent in most mikvahs. In this case, the attendant would only enter the mikvah chamber once the woman has already descended into the water. Once again we see a *posek* who is willing to recognize that issuing lenient rulings can lead to further observance.

Though Rabbi Sherlow, as we have seen, was willing to allow minimal participation on the part of the mikvah attendant in order to make mikvah use more pleasant for women uncomfortable with an inspection by the mikvah attendant, there are still women who feel uncomfortable with the presence of

---

9 Responsa, *Reshut Ha-Yahid,* pp. 209-210

10 *Ibid.* pp. 211-213

anyone witnessing immersion. In his *Shulhan Arukh,* Rabbi Yosef Karo rules that if there is no mikvah attendant available, the woman immersing should bundle her hair in a loose-fitting net in order to make sure that all of her hair goes beneath the surface of the water.[11] In the spirit of the lenient rulings of Rabbis Sherlow and Ariel, perhaps this position could also be offered as an option to women hesitant to go to the mikvah with an attendant.

But perhaps even more can be done to raise the comfort level of women in order that they be more inclined to use the mikvah. Rabbi Yosef Karo elsewhere quotes a number of authorities who allow a woman's husband to serve as her own mikvah attendant.[12] In his responsum *Nodah Be-Yehuda,* Rabbi Ezekiel Landau also allows a woman's husband to serve as her own mikvah attendant when there is no one else around to do so.[13] He dispenses with the concern that the couple might have forbidden sexual relations before the woman immerses by arguing that the couple will not violate halakha in this case since within a very short period of time they will be permitted to one another.[14] I have personally counseled a woman, who found the idea of her husband acting as the mikvah attendant very appealing to her, to do so, which then helped her move toward greater mikvah use.

Though neither of these ideas serve as the *best* option to make sure that all of a woman's hair goes under the water during immersion, they certainly are better than the alternative, which is, for many women, not using the mikvah at all. It is reasonable to suggest that if a woman is able to get comfortable using the mikvah in general, then she may also be able to overcome the specific hesitancy or discomfort of using the mikvah attendant. Even if this is not the case, nevertheless, if the woman continues to use the mikvah her entire life using one of the two alternative methods outlined above, it would still be a great accomplishment.

Of course, when it comes to the administration of lenient rulings there is always the fear of the "slippery slope"—that perhaps lenient rulings in these and other areas will lead people to seek out ways to cut corners and not conform with Halakha in general. Rabbi Uziel deals with this concern in his ruling regarding conversion for the sake of marriage, positing that perhaps people will believe, based on his permissive ruling, that intermarriage is permissible. Rabbi Uziel declares that such a concern is baseless, for after all:

> Who does not know [of] the prohibition against intermarriage? Precisely because people will see that we [the rabbis] only perform these weddings after a proper conversion, they will understand the prohibition against intermarriage.[15]

---

[11] Karo, *Shulhan Arukh, Yoreh De'ah* 198:40

[12] *Beit Yosef, Yoreh De'ah* 198:40, s.v. *katvu ha-kol bo*

[13] Responsa, *Noda Be-Yehudah Mahadurah Tanina, Yoreh De'ah* 122

[14] *Ibid.*

[15] Responsa *Mishpetei Uzi'el,* Vol. 2, *Yoreh De'ah* 48.

Furthermore, Rabbi Uziel asserts, rabbis have no right to add stringencies in matters where clear halakhic permission exists.[16]

As we have seen in the mishnah dealing with *takanat ha-shavim* and the writings of Rabbi Feinstein and Rabbi Sherlow, the application of halakhic leniencies is the very tool used by rabbis to increase observance. This is especially so when dealing with individuals who have expressed an interest in coming closer to a traditional lifestyle. Regarding penitents, then, it seems that our great rabbis did not necessarily share the fear of the slippery slope.

Notwithstanding the well documented use of leniency as a tool to build greater observance, there will still be rabbis who, based on their own understanding of Halakha, will refrain from offering lenient rulings. Yet, although a rabbi may not alter his understanding of Halakha and rule in a fashion that he thinks is incorrect, he does have the right to refrain from issuing a ruling and may even direct the questioner to a rabbi who he knows will rule differently or more leniently.[17]

As noted by Rabbi Abraham Isaac Kook:

> If rabbis were to permit what was permitted in accordance with Halakha, then people would likewise accept that which the rabbis prohibit as really prohibited by the Torah. On the other hand, when it is revealed that rabbis are ruling stringently on matters that may be deemed permissible, without concern for the hardship that such rulings may cause an individual, a great desecration of God's Name (*hilul Hashem*) will result. [18]

Rabbi Kook realized that permissive rulings, when appropriate, increase the public's trust in rabbinic leadership, and with increased trust will come increased levels of observance from a trusting public. Conversely, needless, stringent rulings can lead to distrust, less observance, and a breakdown in rabbinic authority. While Rabbi Kook issued these warnings regarding Passover stringencies, his words can easily and appropriately be applied to other areas of Halakha as well.

To sum up, rabbis should not be afraid of lenient rulings. When used properly, permissive precedent recorded in Halakha can be a very effective tool in demonstrating that living in accordance with halakha is possible. Such a realization can empower an individual or family and bolster them to even further levels of observance of Jewish law.

Rabbis should use Jewish law to make living in accordance with Halakha more accessible. Sometimes there is a general fear to use lenient opinions found

---

16 *Ibid.*

17 See *Hulin* 99b and Rabbi J. David Bleich, "*Sidur hupah le-kohen,*" *Techumin*, Vol. 9, pg. 45.

18 *Mishpat Kohen*, Responsum #76; Responsum *Orah Mishpat, Orah Hayim* 112.

in classical halakhic works, but rabbis can and *should* use such rulings as a tool to encourage those on the path to observance to take on more *mitzvot*. There is great value in demonstrating to the newly observant, via the use of lenient rulings, that they too can live a halakhic lifestyle. Once people are shown that halakhic living need not be comprised of the most difficult rulings, further steps towards observance may follow. While we are familiar with the contemporary tendency to use Halakha in ways that makes living in accordance with Jewish law seem unbearable, the trend can, and should, be reversed. I have seen the benefits of such an approach with my own eyes, and the results never cease to amaze me.

Zecharya Tzvi Goldman was a student at
Yeshivat Chovevei Torah Rabbinical School
in 2006-2007.

EMERGENCY HALAKHA
IN THE RABBINIC TRADITION
Zecharyah Tzvi Goldman

" עת לעשות לה' הפרו תורתך."
"It is a time to act for God; they have made void your Torah."
(Psalms 119:126)

Introduction

The Torah and its Sages provide us with a system of law and custom to live by. At times, difficult circumstances make living by certain Torah norms untenable. There are a variety of halakhic principles available to the Rabbis as how to address such situations.[1] Herein, we will explore how the verse *"Et la'asot la-Hashem, heferu toratekha,"* ("It is a time to act for God, they have made void your Torah") in Psalms 119:126 has been used by various rabbis throughout the ages to create distinctively lenient halakhic rulings which have guided individuals, local Jewish communities, and Jewish society as a whole through those difficult times. While the focus of this exploration will be how this verse in Psalms has been used in emergencies to permit that which is forbidden, it should be pointed out from the outset that this verse has the capacity to forbid that which is permitted as well.[2]

The first part of this verse *"Et la'asot"* in Psalms—"It is a time to act for God"—declares a rabbinic perception of a state of emergency, whereas the second half of the verse—"they have made void your Torah"—is a mandate for

---

[1] For example, "a threat to life overrides the Shabbat," (*Shabbat* 132a and *Yoma* 82a), and "a threat to life overrides the whole Torah except the three [cardinal] sins," (*Tashbetz* 4, *Tur* 2:7, *Hatam Sofer, Yoreh De'ah* 2:245 and *Mishpetei Uziy'el, Yoreh De'ah* 2:48, and *Helkat Ya'akov Yoreh De'ah* 207.) Also, "a compelled person is exempt" (*Bava Kama* 25b).

[2] For a twentieth-century example of this usage, see *Seridei Eish* 2:95, where he forbids any *mohel* (ritual circumciser) from circumcising a gentile child born to a Jewish man and non-Jewish woman where no conversion of the minor is involved. This was seen on his part, as well as his predecessor Rabbi Ezriel Hildesheimer, as a fence against assimilation and intermarriage, though he acknowledged that there were lenient rulings in this regard. Another earlier historical example is found in the *She'elot u-Teshuvot Maharil* 199, who forbids teaching women Torah, even Torah that is for their practical use—even if it be considered a *mitzvah*—lest they be led astray by the cunning that Torah develops in a person. See also, *Divrei Yatziv, Orah Hayim* 240, where the custom of not learning Torah on *Erev Tisha B'Av* and X-mas night is explained using this principle.

92

the rabbinic authorities to respond with the capacity to override the law, i.e., to "void" the Torah on a temporary basis, whether it be to forbid the permitted or permit the forbidden.[3]

Biblical Precedent

The paradigm for the application of the "*Et la'asot*" mechanism is the biblical story of Elijah the Prophet on Mt. Carmel.[4] Elijah is faced with a situation where the majority of the Jewish people found themselves with a dual faith commitment to both the God of Israel and the false god Ba'al. Elijah challenges the prophets of Ba'al to a sacrificial duel. Whoever's sacrifice is accepted by heaven (evidenced by being devoured by a heavenly fire), his God is the true God. There is one difficulty with Elijah's challenge: it is a severe biblical

---

[3] The verse, "It is a time to act for God, they have made void your Torah" is quoted in the mishnah in *Berakhot* 9:5 and again in *Berakhot* 63a and is divided into two sections: "It is a time to act for God" and "they have made void your Torah." It can then be read from both front-to-back and back-to-front with alternating interpretations. The way of reading the verse that permits the forbidden is rooted in the interpretation of Rabbi Natan found in the mishnah and is later cited in its corresponding talmudic passage. However, Psalms 119:126 has been interpreted in a number of alternative ways to that of Rabbi Natan. The gemara in *Berakhot* 63a, prior to citing the interpretation of Rabbi Natan, states the front-to-back reading of our verse: "'It is a time to act for God' [to punish sinners] For what reason? Because, 'they have made void your Torah.'" Rava then offers Rabbi Natan's back-to-front interpretation which reads, "they have voided your Torah—it is a time to act for God." Rashi explains, "They have voided your Torah—those that do your will like Elijah on Mt. Carmel, that offered sacrifice on a private altar at a time that private altars were prohibited, because it was a time to make a fence and boundary in Israel for the name of the Holy One Blessed Be He." (s.v. *mi-seifa le-reisha*). Another example of an alternative reading of our verse is where the gemara teaches, "If you see a generation where the Torah is not dear, gather [the Torah] in, as it says, 'It is a time to act for God, they have made void your Torah,'" (*Berakhot* 63a). Here, the Talmud is saying that in this instance, one may nullify the Torah by abstaining from transmitting it to others which ordinarily is the obligation of a sage. (See Rambam, *Mishneh Torah, Hilkhot Talmud Torah* 1:2) Rambam, in his commentary on *Berakhot* 9:5, also has a startling interpretation of this verse when read in its front-to-back reading, as it is found in scripture: "when the time comes to collect from them and to take vengeance, causes will occur for people to void the Torah so that the punishment comes to them with justice and this matter is long and distant very, very deep...." Rambam is saying that when "It is a time to act for God" to punish sinners (in this specific case those that do not respect ancient enactments) God brings it about that these individuals "have made void your Torah" in other ways and, as a result, their punishment is fully just and forthcoming. Finally, *Melekhet Shelomoh* in his mishnaic commentary on *Berakhot* 9:5 cites *Yerushalmi Berakhot* 9:5 which states: "He who limits his Torah study to fixed times has voided the covenant. What is the reason? 'They have voided your Torah it is a time to act for God.' " The Yerushalmi Talmud states that by limiting one's Torah study to "It is a 'time' to act for God," one is, as a result of this limitation, "voiding the Torah". (See *Penei Mosheh*, ad. loc. and *Mishneh Torah, Hilkhot Talmud Torah* 1 for an understanding of one's proper fulfillment of the obligation to study Torah.)

[4] 1 Kings, 18

prohibition to slaughter or offer a sacrifice outside of the sanctuary court,[5] and the person who violates this commandment is subject to *karet* (severance),[6] a most harsh consequence.[7] Elijah's sacrifice is nonetheless accepted, the prophets of Ba'al are slain, and the Jewish people who witness the sacrificial duel proclaim, "God is the Lord! God is the Lord!" (1 Kings 18:39) The action of Elijah the Prophet is in no way condemned.[8] Instead, it finds itself enshrined as a precedent in the Talmud[9] for rabbinic-era methods of emergency halakha and is termed a *hora'at sha'ah*—a temporary ruling. Rambam (Rabbi Moses ben Maimon 1138-1204) formulates the halakha as follows:

> And so if a recognized prophet says to us to transgress one of the commandments in the Torah, or many commandments of the Torah, whether of minor or severe status on a temporary basis it is a commandment to listen to him...[10]

Rambam goes on to explain, however, that this does not apply to the prohibitions regarding idolatry even on a temporary basis and uses the story of Elijah as the paradigm of a temporary ruling.[11]

Apparent circumvention of normative biblical commandments is not infrequent in *Tanakh*. Based on varying readings of the early and later rabbinic authorities, one can find nearly thirty examples within *Tanakh* where such a mechanism was utilized.[12] From a rabbinic perspective, the biblical message is clear: though the commandments are norms to live by, a prophet or prophetess has the power to break any of them in time of great need, save those pertaining to idolatry. In other words, *there is a precedent in* Tanakh *to be flexible in our adherence to the commandments* on a temporary basis when deemed necessary by someone of prophetic authority.

The Authority of the Sanhedrin and Rabbinic Court

Although it is prohibited for humans of flesh and blood, when not pro-

---

[5] Rambam, *Sefer Ha-Mitzvot, Lo Ta'aseh* 89,90.

[6] See *Keritut* 1:1.

[7] Severance in Hebrew is *karet*. In *Mo'ed Katan* 28a it is understood as premature death and there is a dispute whether it is defined as age 50 or 60.

[8] The prophet's actions have been interpreted by *Midrash Tanhuma* as being self-initiated, while *Yerushalmi Ta'anit* sees them as being of the command of God. See *Etz Yosef* on *Yevamot* 90b.

[9] See *Yevamot* 90b, and Meiri, *Beit Ha-Behirah*; *Hidushei Rashba*; *Hidushei Ritva*; and *H - dushei Ramban* ad loc. One thing these Rishonim all agree on is that Elijah the prophet is a precedent for a *beit din*, on a temporary basis, to permit a Torah prohibition.

[10] *Mishneh Torah, Hilkhot Yesodei Torah* 9:3

[11] *Ibid.* See *Kesef Mishneh* ad loc.

[12] See 8th Volume of *Encyclopedia Talmudit*, s.v. *hora'at sha'ah*. Biblical personalities unde - stood by the tradition to have utilized this mechanism include Mosheh, Yehoshuah, Devorah, Gideon, Manoah, Shimshon, King David, King Shelomoh, Elishah, and Ezra. See also *Kol Sifrei Maharitz Hayot, Sefer Torat Ha-Nevi'im*, Chapter 5.

phetically directed, to contravene the divine will as expressed in the Torah's commandments, on occasion God might communicate to His vessels and communicators of the divine word[13] a need to act contrary to His normally declared will. In the post-biblical period, the radical power to temporarily circumvent biblical commandments is not limited to a prophet or prophetess. The Rambam speaks directly of the Sanhedrin bearing this authority to permit the forbidden:

> And so, if they saw a need on a temporary basis to nullify a positive commandment or to transgress a negative commandment in order to return the many to the faith or to save many Jews from stumbling in other matters, they do as the hour requires. Just like the doctor amputates the hand or the foot of this person in order that the whole person lives, so, too, the rabbinic court rules on occasion to transgress a few commandments according to the time, in order that they all are established similar to what the original sages have said: "Desecrate for him one Sabbath so that he will keep many Sabbaths."[14]

Ra'avad (Rabbi Avraham ben David 1120-1198) speaks similarly about a court's ability to permit the forbidden without transgressing the prohibition[15] of detracting from the Torah:

> And if they [the court] take away from [the observance of the commandments] by necessity of the hour like the example of Elijah on Mt. Carmel, this too is a matter of Torah, 'It is a time to act for God they have made void your Torah.'[16]

The Rif (Rabbi Isaac ben Jacob Alfasi 1013-1103) explains how the power of a prophet to permit the forbidden has been transferred to a sage. He utilizes the principle, "a sage is preferable to a prophet"[17] and explains that, "everything that a prophet does with his prophecy, the sage does with his wisdom."[18] Indeed the Talmud never questions how a properly constituted Sanhedrin has such power, and furthermore provides instances when they exercised such power.[19]

---

13 See *Tosafot, Yevamot* 90b, s.v. *ve-ligmar mineih.*

14 *Mishneh Torah, Hilkhot Mamrim* 2:4. See also Radbaz's comment in note 4.

15 *Mishneh Torah, Sefer Ha-Mitzvot, Lo Ta'aseh* 314

16 *Hasagot Ha-Ra'avad, Hilkhot Mamrim* 2:9 and *Kesef Mishneh*, note 9

17 *Bava Batra* 12a

18 See Rif's commentary in *Ein Ya'akov* on *Yevamot* 90b

19 In *Yevamot* 90b, we are given some examples of this such as a *Beit Din* executing a man during the times of the Greeks for riding on a horse on the Sabbath which is only rabbinically prohibited (see *Beitzah* 36b), or for lashing a man who had sex with his wife under a tree which, while immodest, is not a biblical prohibition and lashes are not mandated. Lastly, there is the example of Shimon ben Shetah hanging 80 women on one day for their involvement in idolatrous witchcraft (*Sanhedrin* 45b). This extended past the bounds of normal law on several grounds: 1)

In addition, according to the authoritative opinions of Rabbi Yosef Karo (1488-1575) and the Rema (Rabbi Moshe Issereles 1525-1572), this power can still be exercised, and furthermore, the rabbinic courts and Jewish leadership can exercise this power in each and every era, including, in theory, our own.[20]

Mishnaic and Talmudic Precedent

The Babylonian Talmud records three crisis situations where *"Et la'asot"* is invoked to allow for an expression of emergency halakha, thus overriding normative prohibitions. The first of these three situations concerns taking the name of God in vain. The last mishnah in tractate *Berakhot* (9:5) records:

> They [the Sages] instituted that a person inquires as to the well being of his friend with the name of God, as it says (Ruth 2:4): "And, behold, Boaz came from Bethlehem and he said to the harvesters, 'God is with you.' And they said to him, 'God bless you...'" and it says: "It is a time to act for God, they have made void your Torah." Rabbi Natan says, "They have voided your Torah [because] it is a time to act for God."

The Ritva (Rabbi Yom Tov ben Avraham Ashvili 1250-1320) explains that the sages instituted this emergency halakha

> ...because of the concern that the name of God not be forgotten and the name of idols would [then] be fluent in their discourse. Thus, we permit them to make mention of the name of God in vain.[21]

women are not hanged, 2) there seems to have been less then normative judicial requirements, and 3) they were all hanged on one day. (Rashi, ad loc., s.v. *ein danin*, Rambam's commentary on *Sanhedrin* 6:4, s.v. *be-yom ehad*, and *Mishneh Torah, Hilkhot Sanhedrin* 24:4).

20 In *Shulhan Arukh, Hoshen Mishpat* 2:1, Rav Yosef Karo states that a *beit din*—even of today's status—is able to exercise extra-judicial authority. The *Shulhan Arukh* reads, "Every *beit din*— even those that are not ordained in Israel—if they see that the nation is enmeshed in sins (and it is an emergency), they judge, whether it is capital cases or monetary cases, of any kind of legal punishment, and even if there is not complete testimony. And if the person is immune [from their power], they beat him by means of the gentiles. All their actions should be for the sake of Heaven, and this [power] refers specifically to the rabbinic leaders of the generation or the leaders of the city that the public has relied on them." The Rema adds, "They have the ability to remove his possessions from him as they see fit, to mend the breaches of the generation." He continues on to say, "so we are accustomed in every place that the leaders of a city in their city are like the Sanhedrin: they lash and punish and their abrogation of private property is valid according to the custom, even though there are those that disagree [with regards to the extent of this power and drastically seek to limit it]..." See continuation of Rema and *Me'irat Einayim*, note 11. This passage seems to indicate that, in theory, some extra-judicial power is still retained with regards to this more conservative approach of going beyond the norms of the Torah. We will see as we examine the earlier and later authorities how they exercised their power as leaders of the generation in regards to the liberal capacity of this power.

21 *Hidushei ha-Ritva, Berakhot* 63a. Another example worth mentioning is the decree of the

The Meiri (Rabbi Menahem ben Shlomo Meiri 1249-1315) explains this innovation in a different light:

> They [the Sages] instituted that a person inquire as to the well being of his friend with the name of God in order that they know that peace and the rest of the blessings reach one from his [divine] glory.... And even though there is an opening to say not to mention the name of God in vain and by way of commoners. However, it is written: "It is a time to act for God, they have made void your Torah," and it is preferable to us to mention God's name more than it is fitting then not to mention it at all, in order that we make it regular in the speech of people.[22]

It should be understood that while for the Rambam the taking of God's name in vain in such a manner is prohibited biblically,[23] most early authorities, including the Ritva and Meiri, hold it is merely a rabbinic prohibition.[24]

While each of these early authorities sees this Talmudic precedent as an example where "*Et la'asot*" is invoked to override an existing prohibition, Rashi (Rabbi Shlomo Yitzhaki 1040-1105) has an alternative reading of this particular precedent. In the words of Rashi,

> there are times where we nullify the words of Torah in order to act for God. So this [person] who intends to inquire as to the well being of his friend this is the will of God as it says, "Seek peace and pursue it" it is permitted to annul the Torah to do something that *appears* forbidden.[25]

In Rashi's interpretation, the Torah value of "seek peace and pursue it" (Ps. 24:15) serves as the primary justification for this unconventional use of the divine name, whereas "it is a time to act for God" ("*Et la'asot*") is what allows for doing an action that on the surface *appears* forbidden.[26] Thus, according to Rashi, the power of "*Et la'asot*" is used more modestly in this particular instance.

Hashmonaim that God's name should be written in legal documents in response to the attempts of the Greeks to remove faith in God from the Jewish people. The Hashmonaim made this decree despite the inevitable reality that these documents would be discarded and God's name would not be respected in the garbage (*Rosh Hashanah* 18b and *Megillat Ta'anit*, 7 Tishrei). The justification for this was likely, "It is a time to act for God." See *Meshiv Davar* 2:80, where this is presumed.

22 Meiri, *Beit ha-Behirah*, Berakhot 63a

23 *Mishneh Torah, Hilkhot Berakhot* 1:15.

24 *Tosafot, Rosh Hashanah* 33a, s.v. *ha*; *Sefer Ha-Hinukh* 430; *Rivash* 384; *Terumat Hadeshen* 37 in the name of the Geonim.

25 *Berakhot* 54a, s.v. *ve-omer*.

26 See Professor Rabbi Eliezer Berkovits, *Not in Heaven: The Nature and Function of Halakha* (NY: Ktav, 1983), 66.

The second of the three crisis situations regards the wearing of the priestly garments of the *kohen gadol* (high priest) outside of the Temple. The Talmud records a story of how an anti-Jewish group wanted to enlist the support of Alexander of Macedonia to destroy the second Temple. Shimon the Righteous went to meet Alexander with other prominent Jewish leaders and he apparently dressed himself in the priestly garments of the *kohen gadol* in honor of Alexander. However, these sacred garments may not be worn outside the Temple grounds. The meeting was successful, though, due to a recurring vision that Alexander had previously had of Shimon the Righteous greeting him in these same garments before he went out to do battle. Because of this astonishing encounter he reversed his earlier decision which had been influenced by the anti-Jewish group, and the Temple was saved. The Jews then proceeded to punish their enemies and declared the day a *yom tov* (holiday). The Talmud seeks to understand how it was that Shimon the Righteous was permitted to wear priestly garments outside of the Temple grounds; it offers two different resolutions: "If you prefer, say [he wore clothing that] was [merely] fit to be used as priestly garments. Or if you prefer, say, 'it is a time to act for God they have made void your Torah.'"[27]

Meiri explains that based on the quoted verse from Psalms we understand this as an emergency halakha.[28] According to this reading, one can violate the prohibition of wearing priestly garments outside the temple in order to save the temple—an *"Et la'asot."*

The third and final crisis situation concerns the writing down of the oral tradition. The Talmud teaches that, "one is not permitted to say words of the written tradition by heart, and one is not permitted to commit the words of the oral tradition to writing."[29] Yet we find that the sages committed the oral tradition to writing! And, in one instance, the Talmud[30] questions how it was that Rabbi Yohanan and Reish Lakish were reading from a book of *agadah*, a part of the oral tradition. The Talmud offers as its answer, "'it is a time to act for God they have made void your Torah'—it is better that one letter from the Torah be uprooted then the Torah be forgotten."[31]

---

[27] *Yoma* 69a; *Tamid* 27b

[28] Meiri, *Beit Ha-Behirah*, *Yoma* 69a.

[29] *Gitin* 60a; *Temurah* 14b. This teaching also finds expression in the midrash. (See *Shemot Rabah* Vilna Edition Parashah 47:1,3 and *Yalkut Shimoni, Parshat Ki Tisa* 247-404.

[30] *Ibid.*

[31] This is the answer found in *Temurah* 14b. In *Gitin* 60a, Psalms 119:126 is quoted without the latter statement. The words "one letter from" is a correction of *Shitah Mekubetzet*. See also Rabbeinu Gershom ad loc. In *Gitin* 60a the case of a "Sefer Aftarata" is brought as well. Examine there and see the Rif's ruling in chapter 5 of *Gitin*, page 28, where he rules against the Talmud that one can write passages short of a complete book of a Torah scroll instead of the whole Torah scroll for the education of a child. See also Rabbeinu Nissim and *Shiltei Giborim* ad loc. In the latter, he interprets this leniency of the Rif as possibly due to socio-economic reasons.

Rashi explains the reasoning behind this emergency halakha with the following words: "When one acts for the sake of [God's] holy name, it is fitting to void the Torah...."[32] Meiri uses the same language:

> ...similarly with the words of the *agadah*, for these are words of the oral tradition and nevertheless, they relied on [this verse] to write them, since their hearts have become small and the Torah forgotten; and whenever a time comes that it requires the making of an ordinance for the sake of Heaven, we forgive the honor of the Torah on a temporary basis, as it is said, "It is a time to act for God; they have made void your Torah." [33]

Other early authorities explain this passage in the same manner.[34]

Having explored how "*Et la'asot*" has been used as a basis to explain the actions of prophets, the authority of courts, and the decisions of sages, we will now explore how it has been used by earlier and later religious authorities throughout the generations.

Rulings of the Early Authorities

There are two distinct features that the above biblical and Talmudic precedents share in common. The first is that their application of "*Et la'asot*" relates to the collective Jewish people. Whether one is contravening the law to prevent faith in God from being diluted, preventing God's name or power from being entirely forgotten, saving the Temple from destruction, or seeking to preserve the oral law from oblivion, these are all matters that relate to *Klal Yisrael* (the entire nation of Israel)—not to an individual Jew or even an individual Jewish community. The second feature these precedents share in common is that the invoking of "*Et la'asot*" stands on its own, without recourse to other halakhic principles to support the decision in question. Indeed we shall see that the further away from the era of the Talmud one looks, "*Et la'asot*" becomes less independent as an halakhic mechanism.

In light of his understanding of the Talmudic uses of "*Et la'asot*", Ridvaz (Rabbi David Ibn Zimra 1479-1573) does not see it as having application to individuals. In his own words, "certainly we do not say "*Et la'asot*" except in a matter that applies to all."[35] This restrictive view, however, is not shared by Tosafot, Rambam, and several other earlier authorities, who each apply this verse to circumstances concerning individuals.

---

[32] *Temurah* 14b, s.v. *et la'asot la-Hashem*.

[33] *Beit Ha-Behirah, Gitin* 60a.

[34] See *Hidushei ha-Ran, Gitin* 60a; *Nimukei Yosef, Gitin* 60a; and *Hidushei Ha-Ritva, Gitin* 60a.

[35] Ridvaz, *Orah Hayim—Yoreh De'ah* 8:10 here he critiques *Tosafot, Bava Kama* 3b, s.v. *ke-de-me-targem* where *Tosafot* understands the blind Rav Yosef's ability to read Targum by heart as being a invocation of, "It is a time to act for God."

Tosafot (*Bava Kama* 3b, s.v. *ke-de-metargem*), in seeking to understand how the blind *amora* Rav Yosef recited the Aramaic translation of the prophets by heart despite the halakhic ban on doing so,[36] explains "there is no greater "*Et la'asot*" than this." For Tosafot, Rav Yosef's blindness was a personal emergency, for if he could not study the written Torah by heart he would not be able to study it at all. This personal emergency, it seems, allowed for the invoking of "*Et la'asot.*"

Rambam, in a famed and precedent-setting responsum,[37] addressed a situation where a Jewish man bought a non-Jewish maidservant[38] and took her into his house.[39] This aroused the displeasure of his stepmother and her three daughters who claimed that, "he was isolating himself with her and doing what was fitting in his eyes." Based on the complaint of the family, a local judge questioned the maidservant—who claimed to be Jewish—and the judge allowed the girl to return to the man's home. The question posed to Rambam by the local court, skeptical of her claim to Jewishness, was whether or not they were obligated to remove the girl from his house or whether they could allow the situation to stand as it was. The Rambam ruled that they must make every effort to remove her or have him free her from her servitude and marry her. Removing her, while perhaps less effective, posed no halakhic difficulty; forcing him to free her and then marry her, on the other hand, did present a difficulty as it contradicted an explicit *mishnah*: "one who is suspected [of having sexual relations] in regards to a maidservant and frees her, he should not marry her." (*Yevamot* 2:8) The proscription of marriage in such an instance is seen in the mishnah as the halakhic ideal[40] in order to prevent the confirmation of the original suspicions,[41] but for the Rambam, this ideal was set aside because of a decree to make it easier for sinners to repent (*takanat ha-shavim*[42]) and to lessen the sin.[43] Additionally, the Rambam writes that "we rely on that which the sages have said, 'It is a time to act for God they have made void your Torah.'"

---

[36] *Gitin* 60a

[37] This responsa has been quoted by many of the Modern era responsa that address interma - riages where the couple was intimately involved with one another prior to their conversion. See *Otzar Ha-Poskim, Even Ha-Ezer* 11:5 Ot 60; *Ahiezer* 3:21; *Seridei Esh* 3:50; *Tuv Tam Ve-Dat* (Mehadura Kama) 230.

[38] See responsa *Pe'er Ha-dor*, Siman 132 for all the details and differing renditions of the situation.

[39] *Pe'er Ha-Dor*, Siman 132

[40] The end of the mishnah clearly says that if he did marry her he is not forced to divorce her.

[41] Rashi, ad loc., s.v. *lo yisa'enah.*

[42] See article by R. Barry Gelman on *takanat ha-shavim* and outreach considerations in this volume – Editor's Note

[43] Rambam's language is, "It is better that that he eats from the gravy and not the [forbidden] fat itself." Cf. *Kidushin* 21b and *Pesahim* 79a.

Rabbi Yehudah HaHasid (1150-1217), when discussing a situation where non-Jewish enemies or bandits pose a danger to Jewish women, offered this counsel:

> "It is a time to act for God they have made void your Torah." Although the Torah says, "a man's vessel should not be on a woman and a man should not wear a garment of a woman," if enemies have besieged a city or if one is traveling and they will see that they are women, [and] they will rape them, they should go in the garb of men, even with a sword, so that they think that they are men. And if there are only ten [Jewish] men and there are several [Jewish] women, they should wear swords in order that they presume them to be men and not harm them."[44]

Rabbi Yehudah HaHasid uses "*Et la'asot*" to address a situational risk particular to one community and does not rule for the entire nation.

In another early ruling, the Rosh (Rabbi Asher ben Yehiel 1250-1327) addresses the question of whether or not a community may read from a Torah scroll written on parchment which was not processed with the intention of making a Torah scroll (and was thus not prepared in accordance with halakha[45]) if no other Torah scroll is available. He rules that the community may read from it, and relies on the lenient, minority view of a Gaon who saw the proper preparation of the parchment as the ideal fulfillment of the *mitzvah* but not completely necessary. In the words of the Rosh,

> If you have in your place a proper Torah scroll, guard it, and if not, do not remove the reading of the Torah scroll because of it, for the scripture says, "It is a time to act for God they have made void your Torah."[46]

---

[44] *Sefer Hasidim* 200. this is also brought down in *Terumat Ha-Deshen* 1:196. For a conservtive use of this verse, see *Sefer Hasidim* 955, where it is used to direct someone not to travel to a distant place to learn Torah if it will endanger his life or potentially lead to his kidnapping, forced conversion, or being robbed.

[45] For an understanding of the halakha to which this responsum relates, see *Mishneh Torah, Hilkhot Tefillin* 1:11 and *Hilkhot Sefer Torah* 10:1. According to the plain understanding of Rambam in *Mishneh Torah*, such a Torah scroll should not be used for public Torah reading and it does not have the sanctity of a proper Torah scroll.

[46] See Rosh, *Sefer Ha-Itim* in *Hilkhot Ketanot, Hilkhot Sefer Torah* at the end of *Mesekhet Menahot*. In the fifteenth century, Rabbi Israel Isserlin cited this ruling of Rosh as a precedent to permit the tying of the sections of the Torah parchments together with silk when there is no choice, although he acknowledges this is invalid by normal halakhic standards (*Terumat Hadeshen* 1:51). *Mishneh Torah, Hilkhot Sefer Torah* 10:1 lists 20 disqualifying features of a Torah scroll—the very last disqualifying feature is tying the separate parchments of a Torah scroll together with anything other then animal sinews.

Rabbi Aaron ben R. Jacob Hakohen (author of *Sefer Kolbo*, thirteenth and fourteenth centuries), basing himself on the ruling of the Geonim of Nadborna, permits communities that do not have a Torah scroll to use *humashim*[47] for their public readings.[48] The Geonim of Nadborna, had not only permitted the normal Torah blessings to be made over their *humash* reading, but also permitted the calling of the normal number of people for *aliyot* on Shabbat or weekdays. Their ruling overrode the normative prohibition of using a *humash* for a public Torah reading, which was not considered respectful toward the community. (*Gitin* 60a)

In their responsum, the Geonim of Nadborna questioned the halakhic validity of their own Torah scrolls, presuming it unlikely that they lacked *any* disqualifying features. They thus viewed the status of their Torah scrolls, which they had previously read from and made blessings over, as similar to that of a *humash*. Furthermore, they found the situation of lacking a Torah analogous to the Talmudic precedent of the "Book of *Haftorot*," when the reading of consolidated selections of the prophets from a condensed scroll was permitted, despite an earlier prohibition to do so.[49] The Sages in that case invoked "*Et la'asot*" because most communities could not afford to have the entire corpus of prophetic works written for them. Similarly, the Geonim of Nadborna ruled that since the community in question could not afford or otherwise obtain a Torah scroll, public readings from *humashim* should likewise be permitted.[50]

The Maharil (Rabbi Jacob ben Moses Moellin, Germany, 1360-1427) similarly uses "*Et la'asot*" in addressing a question of concern to a particular community. He was asked whether or not a non-skilled Torah reader may read softly from a Torah scroll while the *hazan* reads aloud for the community from a *humash*.[51] He invoked the reasoning of "*Et la'asot*," and deemed it permissible.[52]

---

[47] *Humashim* of their time were made by a scribe on parchment, yet did not qualify as a Torah scroll for a variety of halakhic reasons (see *Mishneh Torah, Hilkhot Sefer Torah* 10:1), but should not be confused with our *humashim* which are printed on paper. *Humashim* of the Talmudic or medieval era were generally an entire book (i.e. *Bereshit, Shemot, Vayikra,* etc. of the Torah written in a scroll), but not all five books like a proper Torah scroll.

[48] *Sefer Kolbo* 20. This ruling of the Geonim of Nadborna is also found in *She'eilot u-Teshuvot Ba'alei ha-Tosafot* #16.

[49] *Gitin* 60a. Rabah and Rav Yosef prohibited writing a selection from a book of the Prophets, but rather required that an entire book of an individual Prophet be written and that the portion of the *Haftorah* be read from it.

[50] The Geonim of Nadborna offered another support for their ruling that although we do not roll a Torah scroll in the presence of the community since this is considered disrespectful, we do so, nevertheless, when there is only one Torah scroll, *Yoma* 70a, *Sofrim* 11

[51] See note 292 as to the definition of a *humash* in their time.

[52] *She'eilot u-Teshuvot Maharil ha-Hadashot* 23.

Rulings of Later Authorities

One of the most significant uses of *"Et la'asot"* by a later authority is found in the *Kesef Mishneh*, Rabbi Yosef Karo's commentary to Rambam's *Mishneh Torah*. In the laws of Torah study, Rambam chastises those who support themselves through charity in order to immerse themselves in Torah study rather than working.[53] In his commentary on this piece, Rabbi Yosef Karo uncharacteristically[54] goes to great lengths to contradict nearly every source the Rambam cites, developing an entire halakhic argument against the Rambam's view. He ends his commentary on this matter with the following statement in support of Torah scholars taking a salary for their religious functions and learning:

> And we have seen that all the sages of Israel before the time of our teacher [Rambam] and after his time are accustomed to take a salary from the community. And even should [the scholars] concede that the law is like [Rambam] in his commentary on the *mishnah*, it is possible that all the sages of the generation have agreed [to go against it] because of, "it is a time to act for God; they have made void your Torah." For if the livelihood of the students and the teachers were not available, they would not be able to exert themselves in Torah as is fitting and the Torah would be forgotten, God forbid. And with it being available, they are able to immerse themselves in it and the Torah will be made great and glorified.[55]

Rabbi Yosef Karo argues that, if for no other reason, communities can justify their paying scholars to study and teach because of *"Et la'asot,"* that is, it is an essential need of the community and a reason to override a previously held halakhic position. This view is accepted as authoritative in later rabbinic rulings.[56]

During the eighteenth and nineteenth centuries, the mechanism of *"Et la'asot"* is used in a variety of circumstances. Rabbi Akiva Eger (1761-1837) questioned how people involved in the burial of the dead can take a salary for such a *mitzvah*.[57] Rabbi Shlomo Kluger (1785-1869) further asked how those who watch the dead before burial can take a salary. Rabbi Kluger offered as one explanation, "It is possible that from the power of 'it is a time to act for God'

---

[53] *Mishneh Torah, Hilkhot Talmud Torah* 3:10. This language is brought down in Tur, *Yoreh De'ah* 246 and Rema *Yoreh De'ah* 246:21. It also corresponds with Rambam's lengthy commentary on *Avot* 4:5 that is well worth examining.

[54] See Introduction to the *Kesef Mishneh*.

[55] See *Kesef Mishnah* on *Hilkhot Talmud Torah* 3:10

[56] *Shakh, Yoreh De'ah* 246:20. See also *Igerot Mosheh, Yoreh De'ah* 2:117 where Rav Moshe goes so far as to say that someone who thinks he will be pious and concern himself with Rambam's view and be stringent and work for a living is following the advice of the evil inclination and will forget what little Torah he has learned. See as well *Avkat Rohel* 20 and *Tashbetz* 1:147.

[57] Quoted in *Ha-Elef Lekha Shelomoh, Orah Hayim* 263.

they permitted it, as there is no one found to do [this job] for free…"[58]

Rabbi Naftali Tzvi Yehudah Berlin (1817-1893) ruled that it is permitted and, in fact, a *mitzvah* to destroy the original templates that were used to print holy books that were being disrespected post-production.[59] In justifying the printing of these holy books which, *ipso facto*, involves the creation of these templates which were inevitably mistreated by their publishing houses, he invoked "*Et la'asot*"—as no way to print books exists without such templates.[60]

Rulings of the Nineteenth and Twentieth Century Poskim

The Rosh Yeshiva of the Berlin Rabbinical Seminary, Rabbi Dovid Tzvi Hoffman (1843-1921)[61] addressed a question as to whether boys who attended public schools on Shabbat,[62] and as a result missed the regular Shabbat services, could read the Torah portion of the week—including the calling of seven men and the reading of the *haftorah* with blessings—prior to the afternoon *minhah* service on a regular basis. This practice was instituted by Rabbi Ezriel Hildesheimer (1820-1899), the founder and first Rosh Yeshiva of the Berlin Rabbinical Seminary. Rabbi Hoffman felt there was support to read the Torah in such a manner on an occasional basis where no other alternative existed.[63] However, he did not see it as truly within the law to do so on a regular basis. He invoked "*Et la'asot*" as his reason to support the practice.

In a 1971 responsum regarding a yeshiva day school in Scranton, Pennsylvania, Rabbi Moshe Feinstein (1895-1986) felt it appropriate to ignore his usual requirement of single-sex education for students over the age of ten. In this instance, the school would have been forced to either send the girls to a

---

58 *Ibid.*

59 *Meishiv Davar* 2:80.

60 The normative halakha is found in Rambam, *Hilkhot Yesodei ha-Torah* 6:8, where he ruled, "All holy writings and their commentaries and explanations—it is forbidden to burn them or destroy them by hand…." Rabbi Berlin found it permissible to destroy these templates because they were not intended nor sanctified to be used for study, but rather from the outset, these templates were made to be destroyed.

61 *Melamed Le-ho'il, Orah Hayim*, 1:14.

62 Rabbi Hoffman ruled that it is permitted for children to attend public school on Shabbat provided they do not write (*Melamed Le-ho'il, Orah Hayim* 1:58). He likewise permitted children under the age of Bar and Bat *Mitzvah* to carry their books without an *eruv*. (He even stated that a religious family that could afford a tutor and could make up the material that the child missed in school on Shabbat should nevertheless send their child to school to strengthen those children who may not be up to the challenge of maintaining observance in such a situation.) Rabbi Ezriel Hildesheimer also allowed himself to look the other way when these students exercised on Shabbat at school, lest they be mocked by the school staff and called lunatics, possibly jeopardizing their ability to get away with not having to write. (See *Sheylot U-teshuvot Rebbe Ezriel, Orah Hayim* 48) This situation, though not ideal, nevertheless proved to be quite illustrative as to how flexible and communally conscious Rabbis Hoffman and Hildesheimer were willing to be.

63 *Orah Hayim* 135:2 *Rema* and *Mishnah Berurah* note 5 and *Biy'ur Halakhah* ad loc.

public school or divide the classes and risk closing the school due to cost and parental displeasure with the small classes.[64] Due to these factors, he invoked "*Et la'asot*" and permitted co-educational classrooms for fifth through eighth graders.

Rabbi Menashe Klein (1925-) is known to have invoked "*Et la'asot*" to justify voting in democratic elections.[65] He based this decision on both the Talmudic principle of choosing the lesser of two evils (*Sotah* 48a) (in this case, the political candidates) and with a general appreciation of the United States as a kind country to Jews. But Rabbi Klein expresses great reticence and conservatism about the dangers of assimilation into a host society, in general counseling radical isolation, and only allows democratic participation through voting because of "*Et la'asot*." In his view, choosing elected officials is not for the individual to do, rather it is for a sage to decide according to the needs of the hour and to be done solely for the sake of heaven.[66]

Rabbi Eliezer Yehudah Waldenberg (1917-2006) permitted men to recite Psalms or learn Torah in public areas or while riding public transportation when there are women dressed immodestly.[67] Supporting his decision, he quoted Rabbi Avraham Yeshaya Karelitz (1878-1953) who permitted giving rebuke to the public—which could include reciting Torah teachings of the Sages—when women who are obligated to cover their hair are present yet have their hair uncovered.[68] Rabbi Karelitz invoked "*Et la'asot*" as part of his lenient ruling, in addition to the view of *Tosafot Rabbeinu Yitzhak* that if one is not paying attention to an immodestly dressed person, it is permitted.[69]

Rabbi Yehiel Ya'akov Weinberg (1885-1966), the Rosh Yeshiva of the Berlin Rabbinical seminary prior to World War II, addressed the validity of the practices of the Yeshurun religious youth organization in post-World War II France. Part of Yeshurun's outreach program involved boys and girls jointly participating in activities together, as well as singing holy songs together at Shabbat meals.[70] Rabbi Weinberg began his response recognizing that these

---

64 *Igerot Mosheh, Yoreh De'ah* 4:28.

65 *Mishneh Halakhot* 12:374. This responsum was written to Dr. Marc Shapiro, author and YCT lecturer.

66 See *Mishneh Halakhot* 12:290 and the conclusion of this essay for other instances where he maintains that applying "*Et la'asot*" should be restricted to the sages.

67 *Tzitz Eliezer* 15:11. Immodesty is defined here by Rabbi Waldenberg as the uncovered hair of women who should have their hair covered, or as a revealed "portion" (*tefah*) of a woman's body that women normally cover.

68 *Hazon Ish, Orah Hayim*, 16:11.

69 Rabbi Karelitz also quotes the *Mordekhai* (Mordekhai ben Hillel c. 1250-1298), who stated that, "Therefore, it is forbidden to say matters of holiness while hearing a women sing and, in our sins, we dwell among the Gentiles and, 'It is a time to act for God, they have made void your Torah,' therefore, we are not careful in learning [Torah] when hearing Aramean women sing...." *Mordekhai* 80, *Berakhot* 8. (Quoted in the name of Rabbi Eliezer of Mintz.)

70 *Seridei Eish, Orah Hayim* #8 (ed. Mossad Harav Kook, Vol. II). For another example of

activities could easily be construed as normatively prohibited.[71] Yet he then went on to develop a sophisticated halakhic argument (including the invoking of *"Et la'asot"*) to permit these activities. He reasoned that since it was acceptable not to insist on a *mehitzah* at a mixed activity of neutral nature (like a wedding or a lecture that did not have mixed seating), the issue here concerned a stringency more than an actual law.[72] Similarly in this case, since the boys and girls sat on separate benches while in the same room, this practice was sufficiently acceptable.

In regards to mixed singing however, he cites the precedent set by a Sefardic rabbi who permitted this practice since there was no issue of "forbidden thoughts" in this context.[73] It should be noted that he also saw the future of French Jewry in grave danger and empirically recognized the effectiveness of Yeshurun's outreach activities. Throughout his responsum he invoked *"Et la'asot"* and viewed the implementation of his own halakhic arguments as in a state of emergency.

There is a noticeable conservative feature of language that emerges amongst the nineteenth and twentieth-century religious authorities who invoke *"Et la'asot,"* in contrast to their predecessors. Some of these later religious authorities make statements that intend to put limits on how and by whom this concept should be employed. Earlier authorities seem much less self conscious when relying on *"Et la'asot"* and—when they sparingly decide to—do so without specifying any qualifications. The need to issue warnings and publicize boundaries regarding valid, halakhic use of this verse was not limited to ultra-traditionalist authorities, but also included those who were considered to be lenient and modern. While it may come as no surprise to find these warnings

---

Rabbi Weinberg's use of *"Et la'asot,"* see *Seridei Esh, Helek Rishon, Kuntrus Rishon, "Shehitat Ofot be-Hatikhat Kol ha-Mafreket"* (ed. Mossad Harav Kook). When the Nazis prohibitted the ritual slaughter of kosher animals unless the head of the animal was completely severed in the process, he permitted this practice for fowl.

[71] Mixed groups because of *kalut rosh*, see *Sukah* 51b-52a and *Shulhan Arukh, Orah Hayim* 529:4; and mixed singing because of *kol ishah* issues, *Berakhot* 24a, Rambam, *Hilkhot Isurei Biah* 21:2, *Shulhan Arukh, Even Ha'ezer* 21:1, *Kuntrus Be'er Mayim Hayim* O t 3.

[72] It should be pointed out that Rabbi Weinberg, upon his arrival in Germany from Poland, discovered devoutly observant Orthodox families (haredim) where men and women sang together on Shabbat. He was perplexed since according to his understanding this seemed to be a blatant disregard for halakha. (See *Shulhan Arukh, Orah Hayim* 75:3 and *Magen Avraham*, ad loc.) Upon searching for an explanation, he was informed that Rabbi Shimshon Raphael Hirsch and Rabbi Ezriel Hildisheimer permitted this practice based on the Talmudic principle, "Two voices are not distinct." (*Megilah* 21b) Rabbi Weinberg was not very satisfied with this basis for the ruling and proceeded to develop his own line of halakhic reasoning.

[73] *Sdei Hemed, Ma'arekhet Kol.* Rabbi Weinberg finds support for this ruling in the teachings of Hida when explaining how Devorah the Prophetess sang in public. "At the time of the manifestation of the Divine presence, it is permitted for a woman to sing and there is no concern for forbidden thoughts." He feels this can be applied to the singing of holy songs on Shabbat.

in the responsa of Rabbi Moses Sofer[74] and Rabbi Menashe Klein,[75] we can also find mention of it in the responsa of Rabbi Yechiel Yaakov Weinberg,[76] a more modern posek and Talmudic scholar.[77] Though in some of these cases these latter religious authorities were concerned with the abrogation of Halakha initiated by the enlightenment or Reform forces that either started to take place or was already in full force at the time,[78] in other cases, their concern was for what havoc this verse could wreak in the wrong, even Orthodox rabbinic hands.

In the Zohar and Hasidism

The verse of *"Et la'asot"* has been interpreted throughout the Hasidic tradition in a spiritual and cosmological manner.[79] The focus here, however, will be the quite radical interpretation of this verse by Rabbi Mordechai Yosef Leiner of Izbica, the nineteenth-century Polish hasidic master, and author of the work *Mei Ha-Shiloah*.[80] Commenting on a mishnah in *Berakhot* (9:5), the *Mei Ha-Shiloah* teaches:

> With regards to certain things in the Holy Torah, when it is clear to a person that now is *the time for the Lord to work*, as Elijah did on Mt. Carmel, then it is necessary to overturn the general principles of the Holy Torah and act only in accord with the understanding [*binah*] that God infuses to man. Rabbi Nathan says that when the understanding is not present, the person is required to conduct himself in accordance with the manifested rules of the Torah without transgressing the bounds of the Halakha. Rabbi Nathan further says, when a person's heart strives after the will of God and he removes from himself all

---

[74] See *Hatam Sofer, Yoreh De'ah* 2:214 where he employs this verse as a basis to find merit in a *mikvah*'s method of water transfer.

[75] *Mishneh Halakhot* 12:374 regarding voting in elections. See also *Mishneh Halakhot,* 12:290, where he states, "But not anyone who wants shall come and utilize the Name, for God forbid we will be left with, 'They have made void your Torah' and this is not in the hand of every person. Rather, all with measurement and weighing and with halakha…"

[76] *Seridei Esh, Orah Hayim,* 2:8

[77] See chapters 4 and 7 in Dr. Marc Shapiro's work, *Between the Yeshiva World and Modern Orthodoxy: The Life and Works of Rabbi Jehiel Jacob Weinberg 1884-1966* (London, England: The Littman Library of Jewish Civilization, 1999).

[78] See Introduction to *Torat Nevi'im* in *Kol Sifrei Maharitz Hayot,* where he explicitly articulates this concern and wrote an entire book to demonstrate that no actions that the prophets or sages did are intended to give the message that "The Torah is relative to the time and place and can be voided at any time."

[79] See *Biy'urei Hasidut le-Nach* by Yishai Chasidah on Psalms 119:126 for interpretations of *Sefat Emet* and *Da'at Mosheh.*

[80] For a more in depth understanding of the Izbica rebbe's background and approach see Dr. Morris M. Faierstein, *All is in the Hands of Heaven: The Teachings of Rabbi Mordecai Joseph Leiner of Izbica.*

personal attachments, God summons him to do an act which
seems to him to transgress the principles of the Torah, heaven
forbid. It is concerning this case that Rabbi Nathan said that
a person whose heart strives after the Lord and has removed
from himself all personal gain can be certain that it will not be
counted as a sin, heaven forbid. He can be certain that *it was
a time for the Lord to work*.[81]

The *Mei Ha-Shiloah* does mention elsewhere that this teaching is not intended for casual application and is intended for a "holy man."[82] Nevertheless,
within this late Polish hasidic tradition, "*Et la'asot*" has been taken out of the
hands of established halakhic authorities and has become a living and intuitive
antinomian teaching in the hands of a *tzadik* or advanced Hasid according to
his individual, spiritual path. The *Mei Ha-Shiloah*'s teaching stands in radical
polarity with the teaching of the Rabbi David ibn Zimra who, as stated above,
does not see "*Et la'asot*" as having relevance for an individual.[83] It has been
noted that the *Mei Ha-Shiloah* in its original publication did not appear with
any approbation and is reputed to have been published by a gentile publisher
and was also consequently subject to burning.[84] Given the Sabbatean cloud
that has hung over Hasidism, the spirit of the enlightenment that was soon to
envelope the Jewish people, and the inherent dangers of a person willing to
take advantage of its radical teachings, it should come as no surprise that the
Mei Ha-Shiloah was not well received even by the *hasidim* themselves.[85]

Conclusion

The halakhic archeology found in this essay points to "*Et la'asot*" having
undergone a type of *decline of the generations*.[86] This is particularly apparent

---

[81] I have declined to offer my own translation of such a radical teaching and have preferred to
rely on the translation of Dr. Morris M. Faierstein in his work, *All is in the Hands of Heaven:
The Teachings of Rabbi Mordecai Joseph Leiner of Izbica* (Hoboken: KTAV, 1989), 38. Italics
are mine.

[82] *Mei Ha-Shiloah*, Volume I, *Parshat Kedoshim* s.v. *ish imo ve-aviv*.

[83] Rabbi David Ibn Zimra (*Ridbaz*), *Orah Hayim, Yoreh De'ah*, 8:10.

[84] See Faierstein, *All is in the Hands of Heaven: The Teachings of Rabbi Mordecai Joseph Leiner
of Izbica* (Hoboken: KTAV, 1989), 7-8.

[85] Many attribute the current widespread popularity of the *Mei Ha-Shiloah* to Rabbi Shlomo
Carlebach z'l who popularized its teachings over a span of more than 30 years. For an example
of authors who see Rabbi Carlebach as personally responsible for this resurgence in the teachings of the Izbica, see the dedication to Eliahu Klein, *Meetings with Remarkable Souls: Legends
of the Baal Shem Tov* (Northvale, NJ: Jason Aronson, 1995).

[86] The rabbinic expression "the decline of the generations" suggests that just as the passing
of time and generations has taken us further and further away from the original revelation at
Sinai, so too our understanding of Torah and human nature, as well as our personal stature
(and even rabbinic authority) has decreased with time. This view however, is not universally
accepted. See Menachem Kellner, *Maimonides on the Decline of the Generations and the Nature*

when one contrasts the way the verse was used to support the actions of the Prophets and Talmudic-era sages and how it came to be utilized in the responsa literature of later religious authorities and *poskim*. In general, the further in time an authority was from the biblical era when he employed this verse, the more he applied it to prohibitions of gradually lesser weight, with additional halakhic principles as support or available as alternatives, a more self-conscious usage.

A second understanding that is borne out through an overwhelming preponderance of halakhic precedent and opinion is that "*Et la'asot*" is to be employed highly judiciously by recognized religious authorities. Even the nineteenth-century Hasidic master Rabbi Mordechai Yosef Leiner of Izbica, who takes this verse out of the hands of the established halakhic authorities, restricts the implementation of this teaching to an elite cadre of rebbes and *hasidim*, and, even according to his view, is considered to be at best marginal.

Above all, "*Et la'asot*" clearly demonstrates a certain flexibility of the halakhic tradition to enable adjustment to situations of crisis and change. In every generation there have been sages who have shown themselves capable of transcending a mindset that would lead to enforcing the law to its own detriment and, in the words of the sages, create a "stringency that leads to a leniency."[87] With a broader understanding of how "*Et la'asot*" has been employed throughout the different eras of our rabbinic tradition, we are left to wonder how—and if—future Orthodox *poskim* will employ this verse in the halakhic emergencies that confront us in the twenty-first century.

---

of Rabbinic Authority (Albany, NY: State University of New York Press, 1996).
[87] See *Pesahim* 48b, *Yevamot* 30b, *Bava Kama* 11a, *Nidah* 24b.

Rabbi Hayyim Angel is the Rabbi of the
Spanish and Portuguese Synagogue in New
York City, and an instructor of Bible at Ye-
shiva University.

Seeking Prophecy in Historical Narratives: Manasseh and Josiah in Kings and Chronicles[1]
Rabbi Hayyim Angel

I. Introduction

The prophetic authors of biblical historical narratives, such as those in Kings, included material selectively. They were relating prophetic messages using history as their primary vehicle of expression.

Chronicles provides a divinely inspired alternative presentation of the historical information related in Kings. Almost half of Chronicles has parallels in earlier biblical books. The rest of the material was likely drawn from other written sources and oral traditions extant at that time.[2] It is a retelling of history, which stands independently as a theologically significant narrative. A close comparison of the parallel accounts in Kings and Chronicles will enable us to refine our understanding of each book, especially when we focus on which events each book includes, and how each presented history in accordance with its own religious outlook. In this study, we will explore this relationship, specifically with regard to Kings Manasseh (697-642 B.C.E.) and his grandson Josiah (640-609 B.C.E.).

---

[1] This essay is based on a lecture given at the fourth annual *Yemei Iyun* in *Tanakh* of Yeshivat Chovevei Torah (June 2006) and is a sequel to my article, "Seeking Prophecy in Historical Narratives: Ahaz and Hezekiah in Kings and Chronicles," *Milin Havivin* 2 (2006), 171-184. In addition to the classical commentators on Kings and Chronicles, I have drawn from: Moshe Eisemann, *I & II Chronicles: A New Translation with a Commentary Anthologized from Talmudic, Midrashic, and Rabbinic Sources* (Brooklyn, NY: Mesorah Publications, 1987); Sara Japhet, *The Ideology of the Book of Chronicles and its Place in Biblical Thought* (Hebrew) (Jerusalem: Mosad Bialik, 1977); Sara Japhet, *Old Testament Library: I & II Chronicles* (Louisville, KY: Westminster/John Knox Press, 1993); Yehudah Kiel, *Da'at Mikra: I & II Kings* (Hebrew) (Jerusalem: Mosad ha-Rav Kook, 1989); Yehudah Kiel, *Da'at Mikra: I & II Chronicles* (Hebrew) (Jerusalem: Mosad ha-Rav Kook, 1986); Bustenay Oded (ed.), *Encyclopedia Olam ha-Tanakh: I & II Kings* (Hebrew) (Tel-Aviv: Dodzon-Iti, 1994); Bustenay Oded (ed.), *Encyclopedia Olam ha-Tanakh: I & II Chronicles* (Hebrew) (Tel-Aviv: Dodzon-Iti, 1995).

[2] Isaac Kalimi, *The Reshaping of Ancient Israelite History in Chronicles* (Winona Lake, IN: Eisenbrauns, 2005), 1. See further discussions in Abarbanel, introduction to Early Prophets, 8; introduction to Kings, 428; Kiel, *Da'at Mikra: I Chronicles*, 51-55.

II. Manasseh in Kings

Manasseh was involved with more forms of idolatry and categories of sinfulness than all the Northern and Southern kings *combined*.[3] The elaborate description of Manasseh's iniquities justifies the decree for the destruction of the Temple and the Babylonian exile:

> Therefore the Lord spoke through His servants the prophets: "Because King Manasseh of Judah has done these abhorrent things—he has outdone in wickedness all that the Amorites did before his time—and because he led Judah to sin with his fetishes, assuredly, thus said the Lord, the God of Israel: I am going to bring such a disaster on Jerusalem and Judah that both ears of everyone who hears about it will tingle. I will apply to Jerusalem the measuring line of Samaria and the weights of the House of Ahab; I will wipe Jerusalem clean as one wipes a dish and turns it upside down. And I will cast off the remnant of My own people and deliver them into the hands of their enemies. They shall be plunder and prey to all their enemies because they have done what is displeasing to Me and have been vexing Me from the day that their fathers came out of Egypt to this day." (II Kings 21:10-15)[4]

This decree becomes a refrain in Kings (II Kings 22:15-20; 23:25-27; 24:1-4), highlighting that Manasseh ultimately caused the destruction.

Despite his unrivaled idolatry and murder, Manasseh appears to have died of natural causes, having reigned for fifty-five years—longer than anyone else in Israel's history. It appears that only later generations suffered for his sins, while he and his generation lived in relative peace.

III. Josiah in Kings

Kings underscores Josiah's unique stature by noting that he had been prophetically predicted centuries before his birth, during the reign of Jeroboam son of Nebat:

> "O altar, altar! Thus said the Lord: A son shall be born to the House of David, Josiah by name; and he shall slaughter upon you the priests of the shrines who bring offerings upon you. And human bones shall be burned upon you." (I Kings 13:2)

Kings further stresses that Josiah eradicated the idolatry of its three main

---

[3] See the detailed charts in Klaas A.D. Smelik, *Converting the Past: Studies in Ancient Israelite and Moabite Historiography* (Leiden: Brill, 1992), 141, 149.

[4] Translations of biblical passages are, with small adjustments, from the *Tanakh: A New Translation of the Holy Scriptures, According to the Traditional Hebrew Text* (Philadelphia & Jerusalem: Jewish Publication Society, 1985).

promoters in the period, i.e., Solomon, Jeroboam, and Manasseh:

> The king also defiled the shrines facing Jerusalem, to the south of the Mount of the Destroyer, which King Solomon of Israel had built for Ashtoreth... As for the altar in Bethel [and] the shrine made by Jeroboam son of Nebat who caused Israel to sin—that altar, too, and the shrine as well, he tore down... (II Kings 23:13-15)

Unfortunately, Huldah the prophetess had informed Josiah of the sealed decree prior to his reformation (II Kings 22:15-20), and the narrative concludes that Josiah's superior efforts could not reverse the metaphysical damage of his grandfather Manasseh:

> However, the Lord did not turn away from His awesome wrath which had blazed up against Judah because of all the things Manasseh did to vex Him. The Lord said, "I will also banish Judah from My presence as I banished Israel; and I will reject the city of Jerusalem which I chose and the House where I said My name would abide." (II Kings 23:26-27)

Despite his unrivaled reformation, Josiah met with a violent death at the hands of Egyptian archers (II Kings 23:29-30). In fact, his arrow-induced demise is paralleled by that of the notorious king Ahab (I Kings 22:34-35).[5]

Some Midrashim attempt to justify Josiah's premature death by blaming his generation. Though the king eliminated public shrines, many idolaters went underground, re-emerging after Josiah's death (*Ta'anit* 22b; *Lam. Rabah* 1:53). This midrashic explanation receives textual support from the nation's rapid regression to idolatry after Josiah, and from Jeremiah's complaint of insincere repentance, dated to Josiah's reign:

> The Lord said to me in the days of King Josiah: Have you seen what Rebel Israel did, going to every high mountain and under every leafy tree, and whoring there? [...] And after all that, her sister, Faithless Judah, did not return to Me wholeheartedly, but insincerely—declares the Lord. (Jer. 3:6, 10)

Alternatively, Josiah's death might present an unsolvable theological quandary. One Midrash plays off verses in Ecclesiastes lamenting the reality that everyone dies:

> For the same fate is in store for all: for the righteous, and for the wicked; for the good and pure, and for the impure; for him who sacrifices, and for him who does not; for him who is pleas-

---

[5] See further analysis of this connection in Rafi Yaakovi, "Ahab and Josiah: Matter and Spirit" (Hebrew), *Megadim* 5 (1988), 69-78; Sara Japhet, *Old Testament Library: I & II Chronicles*, 1042-1043.

ing, and for him who is displeasing; and for him who swears, and for him who shuns oaths. That is the sad thing about all that goes on under the sun: that the same fate is in store for all. (Ecc. 9:2-3)

> "For him who sacrifices," applies to Josiah [...] and "for him that does not sacrifice," applies to Ahab. [...] The former [Josiah] died by arrows and the latter [Ahab] died by arrows. (*Lev. Rabah* 20:1)[6]

Similarly, R. Yosef Ibn Caspi expresses disdain toward those who would question why Manasseh died peacefully, whereas Josiah was killed:

> There are fools who ask: "How could [Manasseh] die peacefully as did Hezekiah his father, and more than Josiah?" Who knows if this is [how he died]...? And let us grant that he indeed died peacefully—who understands God's thoughts and judgments?[7]

The narratives following Josiah's death fulfill the predestined decree, predicated on God's "visiting the guilt of the parents upon the children, upon the third and upon the fourth generations" (see Exod. 20:5; Deut. 5:9). Zedekiah, the king at the time of the destruction of the Temple, was the third generation from Manasseh. Jehoiakhin, who was exiled along with the Judean nobility, was the fourth.

IV. Chronicles
A. *Manasseh*

While Chronicles' description of Manasseh begins similar to that of Kings, it then relates that Manasseh paid for his sins and was exiled to Babylonia. Shockingly, Manasseh became the greatest penitent in Chronicles:

> In his distress, he entreated the Lord his God and humbled himself greatly before the God of his fathers. He prayed to Him, and He granted his prayer, heard his plea, and returned him to Jerusalem to his kingdom. Then Manasseh knew that the Lord alone was God. (II Chron. 33:12-13)

Manasseh returned to Judea, where he promptly cleared away much of his idolatry. This repentance is particularly impressive in Chronicles, where five kings moved from a distinct period of righteousness to a distinct period of wickedness: Rehoboam, Asa, Joash, Amaziah, and Uzziah. Manasseh is the *only* king in Chronicles whose religious life took an upward turn.

---

6 Translations of passages from the Talmud and *Midrash Rabah* (with minor modifications) taken from Soncino.
7 Ibn Caspi, II Kings 21:18.

B. *Josiah*

While the Chronicles account of Josiah is largely parallel to that of Kings, Chronicles reports that Josiah initiated the reformation years before Hilkiah found the Torah scroll. It is noteworthy that Josiah's death receives considerably more attention in Chronicles:

> After all this furbishing of the Temple by Josiah, King Nekho of Egypt came up to fight at Kharkemish on the Euphrates, and Josiah went out against him. [Nekho] sent messengers to him, saying, "What have I to do with you, king of Judah? I do not march against you this day but against the kingdom that wars with me, and it is God's will that I hurry. Refrain, then, from interfering with God who is with me, that He not destroy you." But Josiah would not let him alone; instead, he donned [his armor] to fight him, heedless of Nekho's words from the mouth of God; and he came to fight in the plain of Megiddo. Archers shot King Josiah... (II Chron. 35:20-23)

In Kings, Josiah's death was cast in purely political terms, i.e., he opposed the Egyptian army so they shot him. In Chronicles, however, Josiah sinned by shirking the word of God through Nekho.[8]

While Kings repeatedly attributes the destruction of the Temple and the Babylonian exile to Manasseh's sins, Chronicles points its finger at Zedekiah and his generation:

> Zedekiah... did what was displeasing to the Lord his God; he did not humble himself before the prophet Jeremiah [...]. He also rebelled against Nebuchadnezzar, who made him take an oath by God; he stiffened his neck and hardened his heart so as not to turn to the Lord God of Israel. All the officers of the priests and the people committed many trespasses, following all the abominable practices of the nations. They polluted the House of the Lord, which He had consecrated in Jerusalem [...]. They mocked the messengers of God and disdained His words and taunted His prophets until the wrath of the Lord against His people grew beyond remedy. He therefore brought the king of the Chaldeans upon them [...]. (II Chron. 36:11-17)

---

[8] The rabbis and later commentators debate whether Nekho spoke in the name of his gods or in the name of God, since "*elohim*" is ambiguous. *Tosefta Ta'anit* 2:10 believes that "*elohim*" here is secular, i.e., he spoke in the name of his pagan deities. Cf. *Ta'anit* 22b: "What is meant by 'God who is with me?' Rav Judah said Rav said: 'Idols.' Josiah said [to himself], 'Since he [Pharaoh-Nekho] puts his trust in his idols, I will prevail over him.'" *Soferim* 4:23, followed by Radak and Yehudah Kiel (*Da'at Mikra*), on the other hand, maintains that "*Elokim*" here is sacred, i.e., Nekho spoke in the name of God. Regardless, Chronicles holds Josiah accountable for this misdeed.

V. Addressing the Discrepancies

Faced with conflicts between Kings and Chronicles, some interpreters attempt to resolve each problem locally. While many explanations have been offered, Abarbanel's responses underscore the difficulties inherent in local reconciliations.

Addressing the irreversible intergenerational decree in Kings, Abarbanel cannot believe that God would refuse to rescind His decree if Josiah's generation repented.[9] Consequently, he asserts that many of Josiah's contemporaries remained closet idolaters.[10] Thus, despite the refrain in Kings that the decree was irreversible, Abarbanel insists that a more genuinely righteous generation in Josiah's time, in fact, would have abrogated the decree.[11] Similarly, Abarbanel refuses to read II Kings 24:3-4 as evidence of a decree. Rather, he interprets these verses to mean that Jehoiakim and his generation continued to sin as did Manasseh:

> All this befell Judah at the command of the Lord, who banished [them] from His presence because of all the sins that Manasseh had committed, and also because of the blood of the innocent that he shed. For he filled Jerusalem with the blood of the innocent, and the Lord would not forgive.[12]

It appears that Abarbanel's valiant efforts to eliminate the sealed decree stray from the simple meaning of the verses in Kings.[13]

Even more extraordinary is Abarbanel's explanation of the opposing accounts of Manasseh's repentance.[14] Abarbanel adopted Rambam's theological distinction between *Nevi'im* and *Ketuvim*:[15] people who had attained full visionary prophecy wrote the books included in *Nevi'im*, whereas the authors of the psalms, wisdom, and historical narratives canonized in *Ketuvim* wrote while in a conscious state; God guided those authors' writing with "divine inspiration."[16]

---

[9] Abarbanel, II Kings 23:26, 29.

[10] Cf. *Ta'anit* 22b; *Lam. Rabah* 1:53; Jer. 3:6-10 discussed above.

[11] Cf. Ralbag, II Kings 23:22; Kiel, *Da'at Mikra: II Kings*, 401-402.

[12] Abarbanel, II Kings 24:3-4.

[13] Alternatively, Kiel quotes *Keli Yakar* (in *Da'at Mikra: II Kings*, p. 773 n. 31b): since M - nasseh could not undo the murders he committed, Kings omitted his repentance. Chronicles, on the other hand, tells the story as it happened, i.e., at least he repented of his idolatry (Malbim also; cf. Ralbag, II Kings 23:4, 25). This reconciliation is difficult as well, since idolatry certainly is emphasized in Manasseh's reign, and continues to be mentioned in later references to the decree.

[14] Abarbanel, commentary on II Kings 23:29.

[15] Rambam's view is not universally accepted in Jewish thought. For discussion and sources, see Sid Z. Leiman, *The Canonization of Hebrew Scripture: The Talmudic and Midrashic Evidence*, 2nd ed. (New Haven: The Connecticut Academy of Arts and Sciences, 1991), 56-72, and especially, 167-170, nn. 287, 293, 294.

[16] Maimonides, *Guide to the Perplexed* II:45.

Consequently, Abarbanel suggests that Kings was composed through prophecy, by Jeremiah (*Bava Batra* 15a). This heightened insight enabled Jeremiah to see through Manasseh's self-serving motivations for repenting, so he omitted that repentance from Kings. Chronicles, however, was composed by Ezra (*Bava Batra* 15a) through divine inspiration—a lesser level of revelation. Consequently, Ezra failed to recognize the shortcomings of Manasseh's motivations, so he recorded his repentance. This, though, is a surprising claim. Even *the reader* of Chronicles can see that Manasseh's repentance came under duress. It is difficult to imagine that Ezra missed this point.

It appears that the perspectives of Kings and Chronicles cannot be "reconciled." In *Sanhedrin*, *Hazal* debate Manasseh's status in the World to Come:

> Three kings and four commoners have no portion in the World to Come: the three kings are Jeroboam, Ahab, and Manasseh. Rabbi Yehudah said: "Manasseh has a portion therein, for it is written, 'and he prayed.'" They [the Sages] answered him: "They restored him to his kingdom, but not to [his portion in] the World to Come." (*Sanhedrin* 10:2)

This tannaitic argument revolves around which text is primary. The anonymous first opinion relies on Kings' harsh treatment of Manasseh, whereas R. Yehudah turns to Chronicles' presentation of Manasseh's repentance.

> Rabbi Yohanan said: "He who asserts that Manasseh has no portion in the world to come weakens the hands of penitent sinners." (*Sanhedrin* 103a)[17]

Rabbi Yohanan offers a religious-educational point to support Rabbi Yehudah, but not an objective argument to resolve the tension between Kings and Chronicles, since that resolution does not exist. The first opinion in the mishnah would respond to Rabbi Yohanan that, like it or not, Kings unambiguously teaches that there are some sins that generate irreversible decrees. Thus, *Hazal* remain deadlocked in disagreement as a result of the divergent perspectives of Kings and Chronicles.[18]

VI. Why the Accounts are Different

Rather than reconciling individual contradictions, a more thoroughgoing approach attempts to ascertain the underlying religious principles of each book. The Talmud states that prophetic books were included in the canon because

---

17 Cf. *Sifrei Deuteronomy* 348, which casts Moses' final blessing to Israel as including a prayer that God should forgive even Manasseh.

18 The Jerusalem Talmud poignantly relocates this debate to the heavenly court: "The minister-ing angels were shutting the windows [of heaven] so that Manasseh's prayer should not reach God. They said to God: 'Master of the universe! One who worshipped idols and who placed a statue in the Temple—will You accept his repentance?' He said to them: 'if I do not accept his repentance I will be locking the doors before every penitent'" (J.T. *Sanhedrin* 10:2, 28c).

of their enduring religious value:

> Only the prophecy which contained a lesson for future genera-
> tions was written down, and that which did not contain such
> a lesson was not written. (*Megilah* 14a)

At the same time, however, Rashi distinguishes between the Torah and
Nakh:

> *Torat Moshe* is called "Torah" because it was given for all gen-
> erations. The prophets are called only "*kabalah*," since they
> received each prophecy through divine inspiration for the needs
> of their time and generation.[19]

Thus, the Torah's primary audience is all Jews of all times, and it is eternally
relevant. While also containing eternal messages, however, prophetic books
simultaneously address the generations in which they were composed as their
primary audience.

Traditionally, Kings was composed in the era of the destruction of the
Temple, by Jeremiah. Chronicles was composed at the beginning of the Second
Temple period, by Ezra (*Bava Batra* 15a). One of the main purposes of Kings
is to vindicate God for the destruction—it was Israel's fault, rather than God's
abandonment or injustice. Chronicles, on the other hand, wanted to inspire faith
and hope in the Returnees to Zion.[20] Rather than viewing Kings and Chronicles
primarily as histories, they are prophecies that employ historical narratives to
teach eternal messages about God and His relationship with Israel.

A. Reward and Punishment in Kings and Chronicles

Like many other biblical books, Kings leaves many events—good and bad—
unexplained theologically. In contrast, Chronicles links virtually everything
political and personal to direct reward and punishment. If, for example, a sin is
mentioned in Kings, Chronicles almost always supplies a relevant punishment
to its narrative. If an act of righteousness is mentioned in Kings, Chronicles
supplies a reward. If suffering is mentioned in Kings, Chronicles supplies a sin.
If a good event occurs in Kings, Chronicles supplies an act of righteousness.
Thus, Chronicles presents a far more systematic and transparent theological
framework than Kings.[21]

Kings teaches that the political and religious actions of one generation—both
good and bad—can affect later generations. In contrast, Chronicles adopts the
view of Ezekiel 18 and almost completely eliminates intergenerational merit

---

[19] Rashi, *Hulin* 137a, s.v. *Torat Moshe*.

[20] Cf. Abarbanel's introductions to Samuel and Kings.

[21] See Japhet, *The Ideology of the Book of Chronicles*, 147-148. For an important modification
of this absolute position, see Ehud Ben Zvi, *History, Literature and Theology in the Book of
Chronicles* (London: Equinox, 2006), 21-24, 161-163.

and retribution from its historical narrative. Chronicles contends "the person who sins, only he shall die" (Ezek. 18:4).[22]

Within the theological framework of Kings, then, Manasseh could be singularly wicked, yet suffer no repercussions during his lifetime. Josiah could be singularly righteous, yet die a violent death. Manasseh's sins could cause destruction several generations later. In contrast, Chronicles reports punishment within Manasseh's lifetime, i.e., he was exiled to Babylonia. The moment he repented, he returned to Israel and went on to reign longer than anyone else. Similarly, Josiah was killed because he ignored the word of God. The destruction of the Temple and Babylonian exile are blamed on the sins of Zedekiah's generation, not that of Manasseh.

Chronicles' recasting of history neither disputes nor replaces the Kings account. Instead, each book selects and presents its historical material in accordance with the underlying theological lessons it wishes to convey.

B. A Longer View of History

In Isaiah 7, the prophet pleaded with Ahaz not to appeal to Assyria for military assistance. Ahaz, however, refused to listen. Isaiah subsequently prophesied that Judea would indeed achieve a short term victory against Aram and Samaria, but then Judea would suffer devastation. Thus, Ahaz sowed the seeds for the downfall of both the Northern and Southern Kingdoms by inviting the Assyrians to the region.

The destruction of the Temple and the Babylonian exile form the climax to the Book of Kings. That decree was sealed during the reign of Manasseh, and fulfilled in Zedekiah's time. Therefore, Kings casts Manasseh as the worst king, whereas Ahaz is presented as much less wicked.

By the time of the writing of Chronicles, however, much of the damage from Babylonia was undone, i.e., the Babylonian exiles had permission to return to Israel and the Second Temple was standing. In contrast, the effects of the Assyrian invasions remained, i.e., the Northern tribes still were lost. Since the Assyrian damage ultimately proved more permanent than the Babylonian damage, Chronicles casts Ahaz as the worst king. It could afford to cast Manasseh as a penitent.

C. Purposes of Kings

Kings opens with instability in the monarchy. David was frail, Adoniyah attempted to usurp the throne, and Solomon was forced to eliminate threats before finally securing his throne (I Kings 1-2). Solomon then achieved an ideal state because of his faithfulness to God and His commandments (I Kings 3-10).

---

[22] See further discussion in Japhet, *The Ideology of the Book of Chronicles*, 138-154; Kiel, *Da'at Mikra: I Kings*, 124-127. See also Gershon Brin, *Studies in the Book of Ezekiel* (Hebrew), (Tel-Aviv University: The United Kibbutz Press, 1975), 80-105; Mordekhai Tropper, "The Ethical Principles of Ezekiel the Prophet" (Hebrew), *Shematin* 114 (1994), 33-38.

That came to an abrupt collapse when he promoted idolatry (I Kings 11). His empire began to unravel during his lifetime, and God visited the decree for the division of the monarchy onto his son Rehoboam.

This pattern continues throughout Kings. The three great disasters, i.e., the splitting of the kingdom, the exile of Northern kingdom, and the destruction of the Temple, all came as a result of idolatry. All three punishments were intergenerational decrees. Several Northern dynasties likewise followed this pattern of idolatry leading to intergenerational punishment.

Many at the time of the destruction were complaining: "Our fathers sinned and are no more; and we must bear their guilt" (Lam. 5:7; cf. Jer. 31:29; Ezek. 18:2). Kings addresses their concern by agreeing that they were in fact suffering primarily for the sins of their ancestors. Rather than being unfair, this was part of a broader pattern in God's judgment—many disasters of Israel's history may be explained this way. The generation of the destruction did not have to be the worst generation to experience the nation's worst disaster.

D. The First Nine Biblical Books

Aside from its internal consistency, Kings forms the completion of the first nine biblical books, which flow as a coherent narrative unit. The world began with instability (*tohu va-bohu*); people were placed in the Garden of Eden conditional on their faithfulness to God's command; sin undermined the fabric of creation by leading to exile from Eden, and ultimately the Flood. In Kings, the monarchy also started with instability; through faithfulness to God, Solomon built a stable empire and a Temple that symbolizes the Garden of Eden;[23] and sin undermined the stability leading to destruction and exile.

Additionally, Israel was dispossessed four generations after Manasseh's sins, just as their Canaanite predecessors were dispossessed after four generations of sin: "And they shall return here in the fourth generation, for the iniquity of the Amorites is not yet complete" (Gen. 15:16). Finally, Kings concludes with the surviving Jews returning either to Babylonia—the homeland of Abraham; or to Egypt (II Kings 25:26), thus effecting a complete reversal of the earliest biblical narratives. Anticipating these disasters, Jeremiah poignantly laments the reversal of creation to its primeval state of desolation:

> I look at the earth, it is unformed and void (*tohu va-bohu*); at
> the skies, and their light is gone. I look at the mountains, they

---

[23] See, e.g., *Num. Rabah* 12:6: "Rabbi Simeon bar Yohai said, '[...] From the beginning of the world's creation the Divine Presence had dwelt in this lower world; as it says, "And they heard the voice of the Lord God walking in the garden, [...]" (Gen. 3:8), but once the Divine Presence departed at the time when Adam sinned, it did not descend again until the Tabernacle had been erected.'" Also *Pirkei de-Rabbi Eliezer* 20: "'He drove the man out,' (Gen. 3:24)—He was driven from the Garden of Eden, and settled on Mount Moriah, for the entrance to the Garden of Eden opens onto Mount Moriah."

are quaking; and all the hills are rocking. I look: no man is left, and all the birds of the sky have fled. I look: the farm land is desert, and all its towns are in ruin—because of the Lord, because of His blazing anger. (Jer. 4:23-26)

The four-verse appendage of Yehoyakhin's release from prison (II Kings 25:27-30) seems intrusive to the stark conclusion to Kings, providing only a marginal degree of comfort.

E. Purposes of Chronicles

"Adam, Seth, Enosh; Kenan, Mahalalel, Yared; Enokh, Methuselah, Lamekh; Noah, Shem, Ham, and Yapheth" (I Chron. 1:1-4). By opening from the beginnings of humanity, Chronicles casts itself as a "new version" of the first nine biblical books, culminating with the building of the Second Temple. The Returnees to Zion were led by Zerubabel, a Davidic descendant; and Joshua, the High Priest from the Zadokite line.

The nine chapters of genealogies connect the Returnees to the beginnings of humanity, and also to a much-idealized Golden Age represented by David and Solomon. David, Zadok, and the Levitical choir families have their pedigrees traced back to Adam. I Chronicles 9 parallels the roster of returnees in Nehemiah 11, stressing that all of human history from Adam until the Second Temple period is linked. Sara Japhet extends this idea to the overall purpose of Chronicles:

> By reformulating Israel's history in its formative period, the Chronicler gives new significance to the two components of Israelite life: the past is explained so that its institutions and religious principles become relevant to the present, and the ways of the present are legitimized anew by being connected to the prime source of authority—the formative period in the people's past. Thus, Chronicles [...] strengthens the bond between past and present and proclaims the continuity of Israel's faith and history.[24]

Chronicles characterizes the reigns of David and Solomon as stable from their outset. Chronicles omits references to rebellions, divisions, or the major sins of these individuals; its narrative demonstrates the ongoing stability of Israel.

Chronicles downplays intergenerational punishment (and merit), and presents an almost transparent correlation of reward and punishment. In contrast, Kings left many issues unexplained theologically such as Manasseh's long life and Josiah's violent death. Thus, Chronicles teaches that the people are unburdened by their bleak past. Additionally, even regular people—not just prophets—can witness God's hand in history.

---

[24] Japhet, *Old Testament Library: I & II Chronicles*, 49.

Manasseh is not explicitly blamed for the destruction in Chronicles (though Huldah alludes to the decree in II Chron. 34:23-28). Chronicles focuses on individual responsibility, so it can include Manasseh's repentance. Kings, which depends on Manasseh's unprecedented sinfulness and intergenerational punishment to justify the destruction, could not include any sign of his repentance.

Furthermore, Yehudah Kiel notes that Chronicles wanted to explain why Manasseh merited longest reign. His favorable acts *must* be included.[25] Perhaps Chronicles teaches that "in the place where penitents stand even the wholly righteous cannot stand" (*Berakhot* 34b), insofar as Manasseh reigned longer than any other king. At any rate, Chronicles teaches that *anyone* can repent, and God never shuts the door to penitents.

Moreover, the destruction of the Temple is cast in Chronicles as one disaster among many caused by sins, but it is not the overwhelming climactic event it is in Kings. Sara Japhet observes that this is the *only* post-Rehoboam narrative in Chronicles that is shorter than its counterpart in Kings.[26] Chronicles' conclusion with Cyrus' permission (II Chron. 36:22-23) fits naturally with the flow of the narrative, and paves the way for the opening chapters in Ezra. Thus, the destruction of the Temple was tragic, but only a temporary setback for a permanent nation.

On a broader level:

Manasseh's sin → exile to Babylonia → repentance → return to Israel

can symbolize Israel. This parallel is made even stronger from the fact that the Assyrians exiled Manasseh to *Babylonia*, instead of their capital, Nineveh! Thus, Manasseh serves as a microcosm for the Returnees: despite committing horrible sins warranting the destruction of the Temple, God heard his prayers, accepted his repentance, and returned him to Israel from a Babylonian exile. So too, the Jewish people had endured the destruction of the Temple and exile to Babylonia for their sins; but God accepted their prayers and repentance and returned them to Israel.

When Chronicles was written, it must have stunned the Jews who already knew the bleak Kings narrative, and who still felt rejected by God. Thus, it functions as a prophecy more than as an objective history, teaching that God's relationship with Israel is stable and eternal.[27] Additionally, Chronicles enables us to sharpen our understanding of the underlying themes of Kings, since we now can appreciate the elements Kings chose to omit or present differently, in order to present its own prophetic messages.

---

[25] Kiel, *Da'at Mikra: I Chronicles*, 41.

[26] See Japhet, *The Ideology of the Book of Chronicles*, 309-314.

[27] See Kiel, *Da'at Mikra: I Chronicles*, 7-9.

Dr. Michelle Friedman is an Assistant Professor of Psychiatry at Mount Sinai Medical
Center in New York City and the Chair
of Yeshivat Chovevei Torah Rabbinical
School's Department of Pastoral Counseling.

A CASE OF UNUSUAL HOSPITALITY:
SAMUEL, SAUL, AND THE WITCH OF EIN DOR[1]
Michelle Friedman, M.D.

Towards the end of I Samuel (28:1-25), the tragic descent of King Saul is
interrupted by the mysterious and touching story of his visit to the witch of
Ein Dor. The narrative prompts an exploration into the role of hospitality
earlier in *Tanakh* and invites the reader to compare the meal described in I
Samuel 28 with other great biblical meals of welcome. Yet why does the text
cast a female witch as the heroine of the story? Furthermore, how might the
reader interpret the story of Saul's visit to the hospitable witch of Ein Dor in
the larger context of *Tanakh*?

To briefly review, the story begins after the death of the prophet Samuel,
a time of spiraling crisis for King Saul. Saul's earlier failure to eradicate all of
Amalek as commanded resulted in complete estrangement from his mentor,
Samuel. Contemporaneous with formal mourning of Samuel's death, Saul ban-
ishes all mediums and witches in his domain but then, in the face of imminent
battle with the Philistines, becomes frantic with terror. Failing to get any sign
of contact with God, Saul disguises himself and journeys to Ein Dor to consult
the reluctant witch. Saul's encounter with the spirit of his dead mentor unfolds
into a worsening nightmare. Samuel's first words rebuke the distraught Saul
for disturbing the dead prophet's rest. Samuel goes on to foretell a series of
devastating events: the forthcoming battle will be disastrous, and Saul, together
with his sons, will die. Hearing this news in his already depleted state, Saul
loses all hope and falls to the floor:

> At once Saul flung himself prone on the ground, terrified by
> Samuel's words. Besides, there was no strength in him, for he
> had not eaten anything all day and all night. (I Sam. 28:20)[2]

---

[1] My special thanks to my Hebrew teacher, Alexander Templeman z'l, who introduced me to
the witch of Ein Dor in the poetry of Saul Tchnernichowsky, and to Rabbi David Silber of
Drisha Institute, who guided my more recent explorations of this topic and suggested many
of the ideas in this paper.

[2] All biblical translations are from *Tanakh: A New Translation of the Holy Scriptures According
to the Traditional Hebrew Text* (Philadelphia & Jerusalem: The Jewish Publication Society,

Suddenly, the action shifts to a detailed description of tender, yet firm, hospitality extended by the witch:

> The woman went up to Saul and, seeing how greatly disturbed he was, she said to him, "Your handmaid listened to you; I took my life in my hands and heeded the request you made of me. So now you listen to me: Let me set before you a bit of food. Eat, and then you will have the strength to go on your way." He refused, saying, "I will not." But when his courtiers as well as the woman urged him, he listened to them; he got up from the ground and sat on the bed. (I Sam. 28:21-23)

Taking charge of the situation, she prepares an elaborate menu of dressed calf and freshly baked bread and commands the unwilling king to eat:

> The woman had a stall-fed calf in the house; she hastily slaughtered it, and took flour and kneaded it, and baked some unleavened cakes. She set this before Saul and his courtiers, and they ate. Then they rose and left the same night. (I Sam. 28:24-25)

Saul obeys, regains some strength, and exits. Though he will die the next day, he will fall with dignity, a king in battle.

Stories of hospitality occur frequently in *Tanakh* and, like other repeated motifs, invite interpretation. At a most basic level, providing nourishment is the starting point for welcoming strangers and creating relationship. True hospitality implies acceptance of otherness and affirms the core value of shared humanity. The openhearted host serves before asking questions. This is demonstrated in what is perhaps the most famous of biblical meals of welcome in which Abraham, despite the pain of his recent circumcision, together with his wife Sarah, hurries to prepare a meal of bread and calf meat for the three visitors at Mamreh:

> Looking up, he saw three men standing near him. As soon as he saw them, he ran from the entrance of the tent to greet them and, bowing to the ground, he said, "My lords, if it please you, do not go on past your servant. Let a little water be brought; bathe your feet and recline under the tree. And let me fetch a morsel of bread that you may refresh yourselves; then go on – seeing that you have come your servant's way." They replied, "Do as you have said." Abraham hastened into the tent of Sarah, and said, "Quick, three *se'ahs* of choice flour! Knead and make cakes!" Then Abraham ran to the herd, took a calf, tender and choice, and gave it to a servant-boy, who hastened to prepare

---

1985).

> it. He took curds and milk and the calf that had been prepared
> and set these before them; and he waited on them under the
> tree as they ate. (Gen. 18:2-8)

Abraham's spontaneous hospitality finds a skewed echo in Genesis 19:3 where his nephew Lot prepares a feast for the two angels visiting Sodom. Lot's generosity goes awry when he tries to placate the depraved mob outside his door clamoring for the guests. By offering them his daughters, Lot makes his children into commodities and perverts hospitality. Judges 19 reprises the story of Lot where in the incident of the concubine thrown to the rabble at Gibeah—once again, misplaced hospitality leads to vicious brutality.

In contrast, the striking similarity of specific foods and the string of action verbs used in the narratives of Mamreh and Ein-Dor suggest that the witch's ministrations follow in the admirable tradition of Abraham's unambivalent generosity. The situation at Ein-Dor is desperate. Saul, at the nadir of his life, desperately needs guidance and tenderness. He is utterly lost without Samuel, the stern prophet who plucked young Saul from the simple life of a shepherd, made him Israel's first king, and then abandoned him.

Samuel's background and his development as a prophet inform the kind of mentorship he provides to Saul as king. Samuel comes by his harsh and unforgiving nature honestly. His mother Hanah, in fulfillment of her vow, left him with the high priest Eli when little Samuel is newly weaned. She visits him but yearly, bringing her son a coat at pilgrimage time, and then returns home to care for her other five children.

Samuel's first call to prophecy comes in boyhood when he hears God saying his name twice. The classic divine double call followed by young Samuel's response *"Hineni"*—"here I am"—alerts the reader that an event of monumental importance in *Tanakh* is taking place. At this moment, when God calls to Samuel, the institution of the prophet is established. As God recedes from direct communication with humankind, the prophets serve the emerging nation as religious and moral compass, advising, rebuking, and inspiring the people and their kings.

Prophecy exacts a terrible toll on Samuel. At the beginning, and then again at the end of his lonely life with Saul, Samuel has to tell a man whom he loves that he and his sons will perish.

> The Lord said to Samuel: "I am going to do in Israel such a
> thing that both ears of anyone who hears about it will tingle.
> In that day I will fulfill against Eli all that I spoke concerning
> his house, from beginning to end. And I declare to him that
> I sentence his house to endless punishment for the iniquity he
> knew about – how his sons committed sacrilege at will – and
> he did not rebuke them." (I Sam. 3:11-13)

"Further, the Lord will deliver the Israelites who are with you
[Saul] into the hands of the Philistines. Tomorrow your sons
and you will be with me; and the Lord will deliver the Israelite
forces into the hands of the Philistines." (I Sam. 28:19)

Samuel's first prophetic assignment comes at excruciating cost. He must tell
his surrogate father Eli that the high priest will be destroyed together with
his sinful sons. Aside from his bearing the pain of Eli's delinquent children,
Samuel also must face the impact of his own two sons' corrupt lives, which
prompts the people's demand for a new form of leadership—the Israelite nation
wants a king (I Sam. 8:1-5). Samuel reluctantly searches out and anoints Saul
and comes to care for him so deeply that, when the time comes, God has to
shake the prophet out of mourning over his failed monarch Saul in order that
Samuel install a new king in his stead (I Sam. 16:1). Samuel dutifully obeys.
He selects David, anoints him, and then effectively exits the text. Without
Samuel's direction, however, Saul unravels completely—and so we find him
collapsed on the floor at Ein Dor.

Whether the reader believes that the apparition conjured at Ein Dor was truly
the spirit of the dead prophet or rather a deception perpetrated by a masterful
illusionist, Saul is devastated by the encounter. Enter the witch. Up to this
point in the story, she has been in the background, serving to procure Samuel
for the distraught Saul. She now moves into center stage as a principal actor.
Her character takes on a whole new dimension—counterbalancing Samuel's
scathing rejection with a diametrically opposite manner—of compassionate
hospitality. This arresting juxtaposition of the nameless witch with the great
prophet Samuel dominates the scene.

But why a witch? Why does a woman sorceress who should be in exile along
with her banished peers appear in King Saul's darkest hour to offer him food
and comfort? Perhaps only a character entirely different from Samuel could
take on the challenge of contradicting the prophet's stern dictate. The witch of
Ein Dor, as a woman and as a practitioner of the dark arts, meets ample criteria
that establish her outsider status *vis-á-vis* the power base of early Israel. First,
as a woman, she assumes a familiar role as facilitator. Women in *Tanakh* typically serve as conduits for insight and understanding and are often portrayed
as having an ability to perceive important meanings in private surroundings
and then translate their wisdom into the action sphere. Sarah, for example, sets
the banishment of Hagar into motion; Rebeccah determines which blessings
will go to each of her twin sons; and so on.

The second striking feature of the hostess of Ein Dor's identity that sets her
beyond the normative pale is her profession. Witches are the most marginalized
of women. Throughout classical literature, witches are single females. No man
neutralizes her power or controls her, but at the same time, she has no chil-

dren.[3] Witches typically live on the outskirts of the community and are feared by regular citizens. The witch of Ein Dor is sufficiently disconnected from the people and traditions of Israel that she can call Samuel's final methods into question. Her straightforward speech and unhesitant food preparation challenge the prophet's rejection of Saul. She not only feeds the defeated king bread and meat, she absorbs his fear and extends hope. Her mission is to bolster Saul's failing spirit and to help him complete his kingly trajectory.

The books of I and II Samuel introduce prophecy and monarchy. From Genesis onward, biblical narrative develops literary cycles of creation, destruction and revision. The creation of the world is followed by the flood after which the pattern repeats in the re-creation of the world by the inhabitants of Noah's ark. The patriarchs go back and forth between Israel and Egypt, each journey adding experience and wisdom to the individual and collective community that will become Israel. *Tanakh* traces the spiraling religious and moral development of humankind as well. Stories of conflict and resolution between parents and children and between siblings illustrate the progressive evolution of a family, tribe, and nation.[4] At the same time, God's presence becomes more hidden. As God retreats from direct communication with mankind, prophecy arises to guide the fledgling people.

Samuel and Saul are the first prophet–king dyad. Their partnership produces greatness but also tragic misery; it is a template for a relationship that requires further development. When Saul spares the Amelekite king Agag, along with the best spoils, he demonstrates a misplaced notion of compassion. When Saul compounds his sin of disobedience by shirking responsibility for his action, he further confirms that he is inadequate to be king. Samuel, on the other hand, in refusing Saul's effort at repentance, displays a different failure of compassion. The prophet lacks tolerance for human imperfection. Rather than support the vulnerable king whom he created, Samuel abandons Saul, his protégé.

The witch of Ein Dor, however, has no investment in Saul. Outsider that she is, the witch models a critical value: compassion. Saul, after all, was God's chosen king. He should not end his life crawling out of a witch's hut or dying on the floor. Recall that Saul descends from the tribe of Benjamin whose mother, Rachel, also possesses a passionate and sometimes desperate nature that leans over the normative edge. In her frantic attempts to bear children, she makes a deal to borrow her sister's presumably fertility-enhancing mandrakes and then later ignites Jacob's wrath by charging him with the double responsibility of her infertility and her mortality, "Give me children or else I will die" (Gen. 30:1). Finally, while preparing to leave her father's house, Rachel steals Laban's

---

[3] Shaul Stampfer, "How Jewish Society Adapted to Change in Male/Female Relationships by 19th/ Early 20th Century Eastern Europe" (paper presented at Orthodox Forum, New York, 2005).

[4] Devora Steinmetz, *From Father to Son: Kinship, Conflict, and Continuity in Genesis* (Louisville: Westminster/John Knox Press, 1991).

idols, the *teraphim*. She dies giving birth to Saul's ancestor, Benjamin, and is buried *ba-derekh*, on the road, to Efrat: "Thus Rachel died. She was buried on the road to Ephrath—now Bethlehem" (Gen. 35:19).

The witch of Ein Dor feeds and comforts Saul in his worst hour, giving him the strength to go on his way, *"ba-derekh"* (I Sam. 28:22). In using this word, the witch recognizes the mythological connection between Saul and his ancestress, Rachel. Neither for Rachel nor Saul is death the end of their legacy. Both characters evoke poignant feelings despite, or even because of, their flawed humanity. Rachel stirs deep love as an eternal protective mother of Israel, and her descendant, Saul, retains nobility as the first king of Israel.

In making a meal and consoling Saul with her own hands, the witch also reminds the reader of Hanah's tender act of bringing a home-made coat to her little son Samuel when she made her annual pilgrimage to the high priest. The unusual hospitality demonstrated by the witch of Ein Dor teaches us that in a most desperate hour, compassion has a special place. The spark of hope kindled by simple, direct kindness can revive the spirits of nobles and commoners alike, and thus allow for the dignity befitting God's creation.

Rafi Farber is a student at Yeshivat Chovevei
Torah Rabbinical School. He received his
BA in Philosophy from Brandeis Univer-
sity.

RAMBAM: LIBERTARIAN OR DETERMINIST?
Rafi Farber

I. Rambam the Libertarian

To study a philosopher who appears to contradict himself requires a fine-
toothed comb. The Rambam (Rabbi Moshe ben Maimon 1138-1204)[1] seems
inconsistent numerous times, on many significant issues, between his *Guide
of the Perplexed* and his earlier works the *Mishneh Torah* and the *Peirush Ha-
Mishnayot*. Two general approaches may be taken toward explaining the apparent differences in outlook. One approach suggests that he simply changed his
mind. Alternatively, the Rambam may have been well aware of the contradictions, yet left it to the reader to separate philosophical deception from his real
opinions—essentially, to distinguish truth from decoy.

Depending on the method used to resolve these inconsistencies, the process
of separating the Rambam's decoys from his truths may yield a variety of results.
On one hand, the decoy may be scrapped entirely, labeled as nothing but a
distraction for the simple-minded, intended to be ignored by the scholarly who
are wise enough to identify it as simply a smokescreen. On the other hand, it
may be a passage linguistically and contextually structured in such a way so as
to make the reader think that it is saying what in fact it is not. In such a case,
the decoy need not be scrapped, but simply reread and reinterpreted.

This essay will attempt to address the Rambam's true opinion concerning
freedom of human will. While certain passages in his earlier works suggest he is
a full libertarian, ascribing free will to every conceivable human action, others
in the *Guide* suggest that he is a full-blown determinist. To discern what the
Rambam actually thought, I will use the second method suggested—a critical reinterpretation of apparent inconsistencies in relevant texts—rather than
simply scrapping what is believed to be the smokescreen in favor of a so-called
esoteric opinion.

It is the seeming clash between statements found in both the *Shemoneh Perakim* (a work contained in the *Peirush Ha-Mishnayot* as an introduction to his
commentary on *Masekhet Avot*) and the *Mishneh Torah* against his philosophical assessments of causality found mainly in parts II and III of the *Guide* that
necessitate this rereading. As a rule of thumb, whenever the Rambam makes
inconsistent statements between his earlier works, which principally include his

---

[1] Also referred to herein as "Maimonides."

Peirush Ha-Mishnayot and the *Mishneh Torah*, and his later work the *Guide*, the latter is usually taken as his true, esoteric opinion. The inconsistencies contained in the Rambam's works regarding free will follow this understanding.

Scholar Lenn E. Goodman demonstrates this uncertainty forthright. In attempting to mesh the libertarian statements of both the *Shemoneh Perakim* and the *Mishneh Torah* with the deterministic statements of the *Guide*, Goodman tries to place the Rambam between libertarianism and determinism by entertaining the notion that he is a soft determinist, another term for a compatibilist. He writes that the Rambam "is a voluntarist within the context of his determinism. Is he a soft determinist?"[2] Whereas a hard determinist denies any possibility of freedom by saying that causality is the only deciding factor, a soft determinist concedes that causality alone is responsible for human action, however moral responsibility still exists. The compatibilist tries to argue this seemingly paradoxical position by distinguishing between external and internal persuasive force. If a man[3] is forced, by factors external to himself, to do a certain thing, he is not free and therefore not morally responsible for its ensuing consequences. However, if he is forced by his internal nature as a causal being, he is, what can be called, "free," and therefore morally responsible, even though his internal causal nature determines his actions anyway.

Ultimately, though, Goodman rejects any possible soft determinism inherent in the Rambam's philosophy in that the libertarianesque statements and his categorization of them as foundational to Torah and the commandments found in both the *Shemoneh Perakim* and the *Mishneh Torah* preclude any possible rejection of the human ability to freely choose, despite what may be implied otherwise in the *Guide*. Goodman, then, seems to avoid the problems that the *Guide* introduces for the Rambam as a libertarian, preferring to passively label them as something far too cryptic to deal with and almost "other worldly."

It is my contention that the *Guide* need not be passed up, and that a careful rereading of the Rambam's statements in both the *Mishneh Torah* and the *Shemoneh Perakim* will clear away much of the confusion surrounding the subject of free will as dealt with in the *Guide*. Further, this rereading will absolve any need to temper the tone of the statements found in those two works in light of others found in the *Guide*. But even if the inconsistencies can be resolved through a rereading, the question remains as to why the Rambam would shroud his language in confusion concerning such a pivotal topic as free will. Generally, it can be assumed that he is trying to hide something from the simpleton. Which aspect of free will is considered dangerous to the average mind, however, is a subject for further study and will be addressed later.

The earliest and one of the strongest statements the Rambam makes about

---

[2] Lenn Evan Goodman, "Determinism and Freedom in Spinoza, Maimonides, and Aristotle: a Retrospective Study," in *Responsibility, Character and the Emotions*, ed. Ferdinand Schoemam (New York: Cambridge University Press, 1987), 145.

[3] Following the Rambam's formulation, the masculine is used throughout.

free will can be found in the eighth chapter of the *Shemoneh Perakim*, which is an introduction to his commentary on *Masekhet Avot*. *Avot*, unlike other *masekhtot* in the Mishnah, does not deal with halakha in terms of the permitted versus the forbidden. Rather, it deals with human character traits, behavioral patterns, and moral qualities that a person should have, and is written in the form of anecdotes, sayings, and aphorisms said by *Tanaim*. Written during the Rambam's youth in his early twenties, the *Shemoneh Perakim* serves the purpose of explaining to the reader why *Avot* is relevant to one's life in the first place. The Rambam, who largely dealt with commenting on the permitted and forbidden in Jewish law as delineated in the *Mishnah*, felt it appropriate to begin his commentary on *Avot* with a treatise on human nature and the composition of human character, being that *Avot* is a morality and character guide as opposed to a law code. As he says in the introduction to the *Shemoneh Perakim*:

> I found it fitting to [compose an] introduction before I begin
> explaining each law individually with [a few] helpful chapters
> that will introduce to the reader the context [of *Avot*], and will
> also set for him the foundational axioms to what will be said
> explicitly later.[4]

Among the pivotal issues dealt with by the *Shemoneh Perakim* is the freedom of human will, seen by the Rambam as a necessary precursor to a study on human character, for such a study would be futile if one were not convinced of his very ability to improve himself morally. The ability for self-improvement is one of the axiomatic principles that the Rambam wishes to elucidate here as a precursor to a study of the actual *mishnayot*.

There are many passages relevant to free will in particular, which are located mostly in the final chapter. The most compelling and comprehensive is this:

> But the doubtless truth is that all the actions of man are subject
> to his own power. If he wants to, he does [something] and if
> he wants to he doesn't [do that something] without force or
> coercion upon him in this matter. (*Shemoneh Perakim* Ch. 8)

A very similar passage can be seen in the *Mishneh Torah*, in *Hilkhot Teshuvah* [Laws of Repentance], where the Rambam talks explicitly about human will. He uses the phrase "deed among deeds," saying that a man is not forced to do "any deed" at all.[5]

Reading just these passages, one may be persuaded to believe that the Rambam holds that every activity in which a man may engage is subject to his own free will. Such a view would make the Rambam a full libertarian, and would imply that absolutely everything one may do in his life is subject to his choice, and his choice alone. However, to assess the Rambam as a full libertarian leads

---

4 This, as well as any other uncited translations to English in this article are my own.

5 Rambam, *Mishneh Torah, Hilkhot Teshuvah* 5:4

to a contradiction by implication with his moral philosophy as elucidated in the *Guide* and presented in the *Mishneh Torah*.

In the *Mishneh Torah*, *Hilkhot Teshuvah* 1:1, in explaining the verse "man has become like one of us to know good and evil" (Gen. 3:22), the Rambam says,

> This species—man—is unique in the world, and there is no other species similar to him in this regard, namely, that he himself under [the power of] his own knowledge and thoughts, knows the good and the evil, and does whatever he desires.

This passage can be seen as a categorical denial of any similarity between animal and man in any essential quality, man being unique in the world in this respect. It follows then that this is also a denial of any possibility of free will in the animal. To assume that the Rambam is a full-blown libertarian in that he holds that every situation a man may find himself in is subject to his free will would conflict with this statement in the *Hilkhot Teshuvah*, for reasons that will soon be explained.

Scholar Marvin Fox in his interpretation of *Guide* I:1-2 explains as follows:

> An animal is what it is at birth and becomes what it becomes by virtue of the natural realization of the potential present in it. Its line of development is predetermined, and it is either aided or obstructed by outside forces impinging upon the animal but over which it has no control. The young horse does not have the option of deciding that it wants to become the most perfect horse possible, and then striving toward that goal.[6]

According to the Rambam, then, animals do not have free will, nor do they have any possibility to achieve it. This deficiency is a natural consequence of the fact that the animal has no intellect.[7] As the Rambam writes in the *Guide*, "That which was meant in the scriptural dictum, 'let us make man in our image' (Gen. 1:26), was the specific form, which is intellectual apprehension, not the shape and configuration. Nothing else was made in the image of God, and therefore nothing else can experience intellectual apprehension."[8]

Animals, then, lacking an intellect, are forever stuck in the realm of physicality, and are forced to operate solely within that realm for their entire lives. It is

---

[6] Marvin Fox, *Interpreting Maimonides* (Chicago: The University of Chicago Press, 1990), 183.

[7] This is not to say that the intellect, or intellectual apprehension, is equivalent to free will. Rather, possession of an intellect is a necessary—though not sufficient—condition for the attainment of free will.

[8] Rambam, *The Guide of the Perplexed*, Trans. by Shlomo Pines, (The University of Chicago Press: Chicago, 1963) I:1. Refers to man's knowledge of good and evil, insofar as it detracts from the knowledge of God.

because of this that they have no ability to perfect themselves, and hence they have no free will, nor would they have any use for it. In logical form consequent here, the reasoning can be formulated as follows: Insofar as a being is operating solely within the realm of physicality, that being has no free will.

Man, though, has two realms within which to operate, the physical and the intellectual, but this does not mean that he must function in both of them always. There are inevitably situations in the life of man that do not require any intellectual processing. For example, assuming both are permitted by the Torah, one may choose what to drink when thirsty, Coke or Pepsi. If he likes Coke, he'll take the Coke. If he likes Pepsi, he'll take the Pepsi. There seems to be no room for the intellect to factor into the decision here, so it might as well not exist in this situation, and the outcome would be the same. Whatever he likes most, he'll drink, whether he be a man or an animal. Objections can be made by attempting to find differences between the products, say, whether one was processed ethically versus whether the other was processed in a sweatshop in the third world and wedge the intellect within that variable, but manipulating the variables does not change the fact that there are conceivably existing scenarios in which the intellect cannot possibly play any role. Thus in those instances in which the intellect by its nature can simply play no role, man is equivalent to animal.

The Rambam states this explicitly in his introduction to the *Peirush Ha-Mishnayot*:

> That man, before he studies, is nothing more than an animal, since man is not separate from the rest of the animal kingdom except regarding *higayon* [intellect], that he lives as a *higayon* being, my intention with regard to the word *higayon* being conceptual understanding.

Now if, outside of "enlightened understanding"[9] man is nothing more than an animal, then it follows that in those instances, man has no free will. If this is not so, then the Rambam is being inconsistent. He cannot at the same time deny any free will in animals and be a full libertarian. If man is using his free will in all circumstances but at the same time can be nothing more than an animal, then by implication, animals have free will. Yet this is what the Rambam categorically denies.[10]

Though there seems to be no instance in the Rambam's works where he explicitly states that humans can be strictly involved in the mundane and *not* be

---

9 *Peirush Ha-Mishnayot*, Introduction. Later in that passage the Rambam cites the example of knowledge of the unity of God being the highest level of such "enlightened understanding."

10 The lack of free will in an animal would mean that its actions are determined, but "determined," is not to say that God has any direct role in forcing an animal to do whatever it does, for as the Rambam says in numerous places throughout the *Guide*, animals have no divine providence. Rather, they are determined by their own natures.

subject to free will, a gathering of evidence implies this. First, there is evidence in the *Shemoneh Perakim* that would suggest that the libertarian statements have a more relatively limited scope. In Chapter Eight of *Shemoneh Perakim*, the Rambam writes:

> [With regard to] all of the actions of man that are subject to his power [to do], it is concerning these that, without a doubt, are to be found [the phenomena of] obedience and rebelliousness, since we have already explained in the second chapter that the commandments and warnings of the Torah only concern those [actions] concerning which man has free choice to do or not to do. It is [with regard to] this part of the soul in which the fear of heaven is not in the hands of heaven, but rather is left up to the free choice of man as we have explained.

What the Rambam is saying here is that that which the Torah applies to concerns only that to which man has, or is regarded as having, a choice. What he has a choice about is whether or not he fears heaven. He continues on with this theme, explaining the rabbinic statement, "everything is in the hands of heaven save the fear of heaven." The word "everything," according to the Rambam, only applies to that which man has absolutely no control over, such as whether he will be short or tall, whether rain will fall or not, etc. Granted, these are not even under the control of man, whereas the so-called mundane decisions purported to be non-applicable to free will are. In other words, if "everything" does not include the so-called mundane decisions, then the exception to that "everything" has nothing to do with those decisions either. Now, if we were to reapply the Tanaitic statement with the Rambam's interpretation in mind, we get the following:

That which cannot be controlled by man is controlled by heaven, yet the fear of heaven, which by all accounts should be in the control of heaven, is not controlled by heaven; it is controlled by man.

The fear of heaven, thus, is controlled by man—under the free will of man to choose. By implication, then, mundane matters are not.[11]

What is important here is what the Rambam excludes in his interpretation of the Tanaitic statement. He does not say anything about (assuming the permitted and the forbidden do not play a role) choosing what food to eat, what game to play, or what clothes to wear. Apparently those "choices" are completely irrelevant to the saying, because they are of no concern to human perfection, and therefore are ignored under the subject of choice. The only thing applicable under the realm of choice is the specific realms of good and evil—fearing or not fearing heaven—concerning which the Rambam quotes

---

11 This does not mean that the mundane is controlled directly by God, meaning that God is not forcing me to choose Coke over Pepsi. Rather, insofar as these mundane choices are inconsequential, they are determined by the Aristotelian imperative to pursue happiness.

a verse from Lamentations: "From the mouth of [He who sits] on high, good and evil are not sent out" (3:38).

More direct evidence that the mundane is not included in the subject of free will comes from the *Guide* III:51, where the Rambam deals with the case of a prophet engaged in mundane matters. Divine providence, he says, only applies to the prophet insofar as he is contemplating God. The prophet is still considered a perfect man, though he is not using his intellect to think about God at the moment.[12] Instead, he is thinking about business decisions, which he may have to do at times. Since the Rambam's opinion is that divine providence watches over a man in proportion to his intellect, if divine providence is not extended over a prophet, he must not be using his intellect.[13] If he is not using his intellect, he is, by implication, equivalent to an animal at that moment, where divine providence does not and cannot extend. And just as animals have no free will, neither does this prophet at the moment he is deciding upon a business matter.

Also important to keep in mind is that the Rambam never explicitly says that free will *does* apply to mundane situations. Objections can be raised that the superior man always applies himself and turns mundane choices into intellectual (meaning, spiritual) ones. That may be true, but it excludes the average man who doesn't always spiritualize his decisions. Free will is not reserved for the superior alone.

One might still retort that the Rambam does make recommendations in *Hilkhot De'ot* [Laws of Character] in his *Mishneh Torah*, concerning what foods to eat and when, as well as what clothes to wear and when (such as in the clothes of the high priest). However, when he does make such recommendations and expound on such laws, he is transporting the mundane and nonintellectual realms of food and clothing into the realms of good and evil by introducing health issues and elucidating Torah laws. It is good to stay healthy and evil to harm one's body unnecessarily. Therefore, certain foods are recommended at certain times. Yet, take away the variable of health, and the intellect vanishes once again. The same is true with clothing in situations where halakha plays no role. The point at stake here is that wherever free will resides, it must involve the intellect in some fashion, which limits its scope of applicability, and prevents the Rambam from being a full libertarian.

There are phrases the Rambam uses in the *Shemoneh Perakim* and the *Mishneh Torah*, however, that make it seem as if the functional realm of free will includes more than just good versus evil. For example, just a few lines before his explanation of the Tanaitic statement concerning the fear of heaven in Chapter Eight, the Rambam uses the phrase "all activities of man," saying that man has power to freely choose all of these activities. There are two ways to explain this: either the sentences immediately following the phrase "all activities of man"

---

12 *Guide* III:51.
13 *Guide* III:51 and III:17.

are speaking of a slightly different subject, or "all activities of man" actually only applies to the good versus the evil. For a number of reasons, the former, I believe, is a better answer.

The first reason is a passage in Section Three of the *Guide*, where in a rejection of determinism, the Rambam equates animal with man. Animals, he says, are not controlled by external forces any more than humans are, and he affirms that animals move by virtue of their wills alone:

> It is a fundamental principle of the Law of Moses our Master, peace be on him, and of all those who follow it, that man has an absolute ability to act; I mean to say that in virtue of his nature, his choice, and his will, he may do everything within the capacity of man to do, and this without their being created for his benefit in any way any newly produced thing. Similarly, all the species of animals move in virtue of their own will and He has willed it so; I mean to say that it comes from His eternal volition in the eternity a parte ante that all animals should move in virtue of their will and that man should have the ability to do whatever he wills or chooses among the things concerning which he has the ability to act. (*Guide* III:17)

This statement which, at first, seems to affirm a free will in animals thereby contradicting the previously quoted passages, really serves to mark a crucial distinction between the will itself, and free will as a particular type of will. This passage further can be used as a template with which to interpret the statements of Chapter Eight in *Shemoneh Perakim* and *Hilkhot Teshuvah* in the *Mishneh Torah,* and can help remove the contradictory implications in those passages as well. Animals, according to the Rambam, indeed have control over their own wills, as it is God's wish that they do. However, the fact that they can do what they want—what they *will*—does not mean that their will is at all *free*. It seems that when speaking of will alone, the Rambam is speaking to the effect of denying total external causality over one's actions. Specifically, there is nothing external, God or proximate physical cause, that forces any animal to do any action. This, though, does not imply anything about internal realities within the animal. Their wills may be able to function on their own, but they are not free.

Libertarian passages concerning will as found in the *Shemoneh Perakim* and *Mishneh Torah,* are statements defining the nature of the physical world at large (or God, insofar as God created the physical world). In these cases, they are saying that nothing about the physical world forces either animal or human to do anything in particular. The passage in *Guide* III:17 is not a statement about the nature of will, meaning whether it is a free type of will or not. Rather it is simply a statement about the physical world, a statement that seeks to lay the groundwork for the possibility of a free will by affirming the very existence of volition by virtue of the physical world that predicates its existence. Since the physical world does not impinge on its existence, it does, indeed, exist.

One other crucial factor concerning all of these statements is that the term "*behirah*" ["choice"] is rarely used. It is used, in fact, in the passage previously quoted from *Shemoneh Perakim* concerning "all activities of man."[14] The Rambam there says that free will only applies to that which "*behirah*" applies, which, as he had explained earlier,[15] is that which man has sway over. He seemingly even further restricts it to that which is not in the hands of heaven—namely the fear of heaven. This kind of evidence supports the contention that when the Rambam makes these types of statements about will, saying that animals have it as well, he is not describing human nature as containing within it a certain *type* of will (in this case a free will); rather, he is explaining to the reader the nature of the physical world as not precluding the possibility of will or volition in the first place. In other words: these statements do not concern free will as a metaphysical reality, but merely provide the initial basis for it in affirming the possibility and existence of the will itself.

The division between volition as an existent phenomenon and free will as a certain type of volition can be seen in other passages in the *Guide*, and in some cases quite explicitly:

> For inasmuch as the deity is, as has been established, He who arouses a particular volition in the irrational animal and who has necessitated this particular free choice in the rational animal and who has made the natural things pursue their course, chance being but an excess of what is natural, as has been made clear, and its largest part partakes of nature, free choice, and volition—it follows necessarily from all this that it may be said with what proceeds necessarily from these causes that God has commanded that something should be done in such and such a way or that He has said: Let this be thus. (*Guide* II:48)

Although this passage is difficult to understand, the distinction between free will and volition in general is clear. But a more difficult problem is introduced here: the Rambam seems to be affirming determinism! The Rambam as libertarian now seems a far-off possibility indeed! Why would a libertarian make such a deterministic statement as "necessitate this particular free choice"? It is undoubtedly passages such as these which drove scholars like Goodman to at least consider branding the Rambam a closet determinist. Indeed, Shlomo Pines and Alexander Altmann even interpreted this passage as a betrayal of the Rambam's esoteric opinion as a determinist.[16] Moshe Sokol has also advocated

---

14 *Shemoneh Perakim*, Ch. 8.

15 *Ibid.*, Ch. 2.

16 Altmann, "The Religion of the Thinkers: Free Will and Predestination in Saadia, Bahya and Maimonides," *Religion in a Religious Age*, ed. S.D. Goitein (Cambridge, MA: Association for

this position,[17] despite the fact that he writes in the same article that:

> [I]t should not be particularly surprising if Maimonides adopts an esoteric view closer to religious orthodoxy in his more popular works and an esoteric view in the *Guide*. On the other hand, in a recent article, Shlomo Pines himself warns against such facile generalizing.[18]

This passage in *Guide* II:48 is the axis around which much of the confusion concerning the Rambam's actual position on the subject of free choice revolves and we will return to it later. For now, I will present two possible ways to understand this passage without necessitating the labeling of the Rambam as a determinist. First, the medieval commentator on the *Guide*, Shem Tov ben Joseph ibn Shem Tov (fifteenth century) attempted to answer this question by saying that the Rambam's intent in saying that God causes a particular free choice in the rational animal means that God, as the ultimate cause of everything, brings into being the proximate cause that brings a man into a certain situation in which he can, then, actually exercise his free choice. Insofar as God is only the general, ultimate cause of free choice, He does not determine it or force a particular free choice on the rational animal. He uses a parable to explain his meaning more clearly in this regard:

> A fitting analogy for this: A certain king levies a tax that he commands be taken from the men of the city. Afterwards, the tax collector comes to collect the tax, and generated from this are fights and quarrels in the city, as well as many activities involving money and trade. It is said [regarding these activities] that the king caused all of them as he was the ultimate reason for them. When you understand this analogy, you will understand everything that the Rabbi said in this chapter and how he related all of these activities to God, may he be blessed.[19]

God, explains Shem Tov, like a king creating the effects of a tax collection by intially ordering it, only causes a free choice in the rational animal insofar as he is the ultimate cause of free choice in the first place. The Rambam is not advocating determinism here according to Shem Tov. Rather, he is merely identifying God as the ultimate cause of everything in the physical world, including the reality of free choice itself.

The obvious objection to Shem Tov's assessment is that the Rambam actu-

---

Jewish Studies, 1974), 25-51.

[17] Sokol, "The Rambam on Freedom of the Will and Moral Responsibility," *Harvard Theological Review* 91, no.1 (January 1998), 25.

[18] *Ibid.*

[19] Shem Tov ben Yosef ibn Shem Tov. Commentary to *The Guide of the Perplexed* of Moshe ben Maimon, (Traditional edition, trans. to Hebrew by Shmuel ibn Tibon).

ally uses the word "particular" in his construction, saying that God "causes the *particular* free choice in the rational animal."[20] Shem Tov cannot simply ignore the words of the sentence and say that the Rambam is labeling God as the ultimate general cause when the words themselves say that God is necessitating a particular free choice in the rational animal. The answer to this question is in the parable. Much as the king who levies the tax starts a process that causes particular things to happen, so too, does God. What is meant by the phrase "necessitates a particular free choice" is not that God causes someone to choose one particular thing over another; rather, that as a general cause, certain things stem from God's initiation.

Jerome Gellman similarly interprets *Guide* II:48 by reversing the causal reasoning of the passage in question. He says that the passage asserts not that God is the cause of a human being's choice but that what follows from that choice is ascribable to God, since what happens as a consequence of the choice follows natural law.[21]

Returning to our earlier point, these passages in the *Guide* have been used in order to facilitate a certain reading of the phrase "all the activities of man" in the *Shemoneh Perakim*, namely that the Rambam is not saying that everything a man does is subject to free will. Rather, insofar as the physical world does not preclude will, man has free will regarding whether or not to fear heaven. This meaning can be extracted from the text in *Shemoneh Perakim* itself, if read carefully:

> But the doubtless truth is that all the activities of man are given over to his power. If he wants to do [an action] he does it, and if he wants to, he doesn't do it, without force or coercion upon him in this matter. Therefore, the obligatory commandments were made, and [God] said, "See, I have given before you today the [path to] life and the good, the [path to] death and the evil, and you shall choose life" (Deut. 30:15), and He gave us the power to choose regarding these [paths]. (*Shemoneh Perakim* 8:1)

In the opening lines of this passage, the Rambam begins with a denial. Namely, that there is no external force compelling man to do anything he does not want to do. This is the general statement that, because it is a denial of external force, affirms the existence of the will in general. There are four things to note about the lines beginning with the word "therefore" that support the restricted reading, as opposed to the full libertarian one ascribing free will to all human action.

---

20 *Guide*, II:48 (emphasis added).
21 Jerome I. (Yehudah) Gellman, "Freedom and Determinism in Maimonides' Philosophy," *Moses Maimonides and His Time*, ed. Eric L. Ornsby (Washington, DC: Catholic University Press of America, 1989), 139-150.

First, the verse he quotes from Deuteronomy as the source for free will itself restricts the realm of choice to two options—good and evil. This is much narrower than the aforementioned "all activities of man." Second, is the phrase "and He gave." If, as the Rambam had just previously mentioned, all the actions of man are already up to him without any external force compelling him, there would be no reason for the Torah, or God, to give man freedom of choice, or "*behirah*," because it would already be an established fact concerning human nature in its own right. All the Torah would have to do is remind man of its existence rather than give something that is already given. If the first two lines are affirming the existence of *behirah* itself, then the words "and He gave" have no place in this passage. A more appropriate word in that case would be "and he mentioned" that free choice exists regarding these paths.

Third is the phrase "regarding these." These words confirm the restrictions placed on the realm of *behirah* by specifying that it is indeed in this specific area of good and evil mentioned in the verse that *behirah* indeed applies. In other words, it is only "regarding these" that freedom of choice was "given" to man by the Torah, or God. Fourth is the word "therefore." With that word as the transition between the denial of external compelling forces guiding man and the actual nature of freedom of choice given by God, the restricted reading advocated here becomes clear: the very nature of the physical world created by God, says the Rambam, necessitates that there be nothing inherently compelling man to commit any action whatsoever, whether that action be under the realm of *behirah* or not. It is because of this reality—"therefore"—that God was able to give his people freedom of choice, for if man's actions were forced, then there would be no possibility of it. This freedom of choice given to man, though, is restricted to the realm of good and evil. It is only "regarding these" that man has true freedom. There still remains a question, however, of why God had to "give" this freedom to man, or whether it was natural in the first place as a result of man's nature. This question, as well as the question of how this freedom is able to function given human nature, will be taken up in the next section.

II. Rambam the Determinist

The main conclusions reached at this point are: 1) that passages in the Rambam's writings that refer to such things as "all activites of man" (including sections of the *Shemoneh Perakim*, as well as phrases in chapter five of *Hilkhot Teshuvah* in the *Mishneh Torah*) serve only to affirm the existence of volition as a general phenomenon and applicable to every voluntary deed, and 2) that the Rambam cannot possibly be advocating unrestricted free will in every situation for man, since this would affirm the existence of free will in animals as well. What remains to be seen is if the Rambam can advocate any type of free will in man without getting himself stuck in other philosophical conundrums.

One of the main objectives of the Rambam's *Guide of the Perplexed* is to resolve, or at least explore, difficulties between Greek philosophy—and in particular Aristotelian philosophy—and the Torah. The Rambam can rightfully be considered an Aristotelian, but he certainly did not agree with Aristotle on every issue. In fact, his disagreements with Aristotle can be found explicitly in the *Guide*. Most notable among them are disagreements over the possibility of divine creation of the universe and over the nature of divine providence. It is unclear whether the Rambam himself held that God actually created the universe from nothing or whether that is only one conceivable possibility. What is certain though, is that the Rambam does not hold, as Aristotle does, that divine creation is a metaphysical impossibility. Their differences of opinion concerning the realm and role of divine providence are equally as sharp, if not more so.

Aristotle's opinion regarding providence, as summed up by the Rambam, is that "God [...] takes care of the spheres and of what is in them and that for this reason their individuals remain permanently as they are" (*Guide* III:17). God's nature as the unmoved mover necessitates this result. The Rambam's opinion, on the other hand, is that:

> [I]n this lowly world—I mean that which is beneath the sphere of the moon—divine providence watches only over the individuals belonging to the human species and that in this species alone all the circumstances of the individuals and the good and evil that befall them are consequent upon the deserts [...].
> (*Guide* III:17)

Though Aristotle would deny the above sentiment, regarding everything else besides humanity the Rambam says he agrees with Aristotle in the realm of providence.

Since the Rambam is an Aristotelian, and since his disagreements with Aristotle are brought up in the *Guide*, it can be assumed that where he does not mention a disagreement there is none. On that note, there is a principle brought down in Book 1 Chapter 7 of the *Nichomachean Ethics* where Aristotle writes, "Happiness, then, is something final and self-sufficient, and is the end of action." In Book 10 Chapter 6, he continues on this theme:

> Evidently happiness must be placed among those [activities] desirable in themselves, not among those desirable for the sake of something else; for happiness does not lack anything but is self-sufficient. Now those activities are desirable in themselves from which nothing is sought beyond the activity. And of this nature virtuous actions are thought to be; for to do noble and good deeds is a thing desirable for its own sake.

What this means is that happiness, because it is always necessarily sought for its own sake, is inescapable. When one decides whether or not to do something, he is really doing it or abstaining from it in order to secure his own happiness. Succinctly, every decision made in the span of a human life can be considered to be selfish. A person may go shopping because he is running low on milk; which he wants his children to drink; because he wants their bones to be strong; because he wants them to be healthy; because he has an emotional investment in their well-being; which, if secured, will make him happy as a father. Let us consider two examples more apt to the discussion at hand:

1) A man may rob someone knowing that it is a sin, because he has estimated that the disadvantages inherent in defying the will of God and breaking the law pale in comparison to his suffering at the hands of abject poverty, and therefore doing this right now will make him happier than abstaining. Put simply: a man sins for whatever reason, ultimately because he wishes to secure his own happiness.

2) A man may abstain from committing adultery with a married woman because even though his desire is great, and even though he will attain some degree of happiness from the act, he estimates that the pleasure gained from the sin will not be worth the consequences of transgressing God's will (or his wife's), and in the end he will come out in the negative in terms of his own happiness.

No matter how many links there are in the chain, in the Aristotelian conception, the end always ultimately comes down to happiness and nothing else. This principle, if understood correctly, can be applied to any situation, including altruism and self-sacrifice. The only reason a man may help out another—even if there is no seeming benefit to himself—is that by doing so he feels happy, and coincidentally derives it from making someone else happy as well. Someone may sacrifice his life for the purpose of sanctifying the name of God because he has determined, ultimately, that allegiance to God will make him happier than any temporary extension of his physical life would.

There is little indication that the Rambam disagrees with this principle. In fact, there are various hints throughout his writings affirming it. For instance, in his introduction to the *Shemoneh Perakim*, he says that one of the reasons why he is writing the composition is that following the prescriptions of *Masekhet Avot* can bring one to "great fulfillment and true happiness." It seems one purpose of *Masekhet Avot*, therefore, is to bring a person to true happiness. Even if one claims that the ultimate purpose is to enable a person to follow the will of God, it is still notable that the Rambam chose to specifically mention "true happiness" to the exclusion of other factors in his treatise focusing specifically on free will.

It is noteworthy as well to mention the opinion of Jehuda Melber on this issue, who considers man's purpose, for the Rambam, as other than happiness alone.[22] Melber asserts that according to the Rambam, "all of man's conduct

---

[22] Jehuda Melber, *The Universality of Maimonides* (Jonathan David Publishers: New York: 1968).

can therefore be summed up in the rabbinic saying: 'Let all thy deeds be done for the sake of God,'" quoting Chapter 5 of the *Shemoneh Perakim* to this effect. Melber continues:

> Maimonides has thus parted widely from the Aristotelian goal for man: the attainment of happiness [...]. While Aristotle sees the highest goal for man in the attainment of happiness, albeit a happiness that is not material or hedonistic, Maimonides sees the highest goal for man in the attainment of the knowledge of God.[23]

With Melber's position in mind, it is possible to say that the Rambam's goal for man wasn't formulated in the exact same way as Aristotle's, but to say that the Rambam "parted widely" from the Aristotelian viewpoint is an overstatement. It is true that Aristotle's formulation is to the effect that man should strive for ultimate happiness, and the Rambam's formulation is that man should strive for knowledge of God, but the two formulations can be said to pick out the very same goal for man. The Rambam would not disagree that happiness is the end goal for man because he would essentially agree that knowledge of God will inevitably lead man to ultimate happiness. Aristotle may disagree with the Rambam's religious specification of his formulation, but the two still agree on the general principle.

There is yet another challenge that can be put forth to the agreement between Aristotle and the Rambam on this issue. If, for the sake of argument, knowledge of God *didn't* lead to the ultimate happiness of man, would the Rambam continue to insist that it is still the ultimate goal for man? If the answer is yes, then one can say they disagree. To resolve this question, let us delve into the Rambam's writings where we find an unexpected source in *Hilkhot Geirushin*:

> With regard to he whom the law prescribes that we [are permitted to] force him to divorce his wife and he doesn't wish to divorce, a Jewish court, regardless of where or when, lashes him until he says, "I am willing [to grant a divorce]." When he writes the bill of divorce, it is valid. So, too, if gentiles beat him and said to him "do what the Jews are telling you," and the Jews pressured him by the hands of the gentiles until he grants the divorce, it is valid. (*Hilkhot Geirushin* 2:20)[24]

Here, the Rambam is saying that, contrary to any other conceivable case where physical force is used to seal a contract, beating a man until he agrees to give a *get*, a divorce contract, does not invalidate the contract. In the next law, he explains exactly why a *get* that is attained through physical force is

---

[23] *Ibid.*, 105-106.
[24] *Halakha* 17 in some editions.

considered valid:

> And why is this bill of divorce not null and void? For behold, he
> is forced, whether by the hand of Jews or gentiles! [The reason
> is] that we don't consider [someone to be] forced except he who
> was pressured and pushed to do something that he was not un-
> der a biblical obligation to do. For example, someone who was
> beaten [into] selling [something] or giving [something away].
> However, he whose evil inclination took hold of him, [persuad-
> ing him to] ignore a commandment or to commit a sin, and he
> was beaten until he did whatever it was he was obligated to do,
> or until he distanced himself from that which was forbidden to
> do, [to force him by beating] is not considered forcing. Rather,
> he forced himself with his perverse opinions. (*Ibid.*, 2:21)

Apparently, even though the man is "forced" in this case to do what he
seemingly doesn't want to do, he is not halakhically considered forced because
he is being forced to conform to Torah law, a situation that does not recognize
the "forced" category. The most crucial passage, though, is found shortly
thereafter:

> Therefore, he who doesn't wish to divorce, since he already
> wants to be considered of the Jewish people, [it can be assumed]
> that he wants to do all of the commandments and to distance
> himself from sin, and it is his inclination that has taken hold
> of him. (*Ibid.*, 2:23)

According to the Rambam, every Jew who accepts his status as a Jew, *by
definition* wants to follow the commandments, and therefore forcing him to
do something he already wants to do does not invalidate any contract he was
forced to sign in the process. His "perverse opinions" forced him to not want
to give the bill of divorce to his wife, and the physical beatings, rather than
forcing the man *qua* man to write the contract, forced the perverse opinions to
let go of the man so he could make the decision he, *qua* man, would want to
make in the first place. If the Rambam can say that every Jew naturally wants
to follow the commandments of the Torah and therefore forcing him to do so
would not invalidate a contract insofar as everyone naturally does what they
want to do, he is admitting that man, by nature, does what he wants, and not
what he doesn't want. If man does what he wants by nature, he is forced by his
nature into making specific decisions, those he wants. Saying that what man
wants guides his decisions is synonymous with saying that happiness guides
his decisions.

What would the Rambam say about the goal of man if knowledge of God
didn't lead to ultimate happiness? It's simple: To not follow what one wants—
what makes one happy—is *by nature impossible*. Insofar as forcing someone to

do what he really wants to do is basis enough to say that no contract can be invalidated by such force, the Rambam is saying that *every* man—by nature— does what he wants. If he didn't, then whether the *get* would be invalidated or not would have to be judged on a case by case basis according to whether the specific man—by his nature—does what he wants to or not. To separate knowledge of God from happiness for the Rambam is impossible. Therefore, the end goal for man is the same for both him and Aristotle.

One final question can still be asked concerning the equation of Aristotle to the Rambam on this issue. Ironically (or fittingly), it comes from Plato. In Plato's Euthyphro dialogue, Socrates challenges Euthyphro to give him the precise form which makes pious things pious. Eventually he comes to the conclusion that what makes pious things pious is the fact that all the gods love it. Socrates then asks the classic question, "Is the pious pious because it is beloved of the gods? Or is it beloved of the gods because it is pious?" As Socrates continues to make logical moves through the dialogue, the conclusion is reached that the latter is true. Piety is beloved of the gods because it is pious, and not the other way around. This being so, the precise form of piety itself has not been found. Rather, only a quality of it has been discovered—that it is beloved of the gods.

The same type of question can be applied here. Using knowledge of the Divine as our substitute for piety, we can formulate it this way: Aristotle clearly believes that knowledge of the Divine is the goal for man because it leads man to ultimate happiness. Does the Rambam reverse this causal structure and say that ultimate happiness is the goal for man because it leads him to the knowledge of the Divine? If so, then the Rambam does to a degree depart from Aristotle.

While this may be true, there are passages in the *Guide* that imply otherwise. The Rambam says that "when a perfect man is stricken in age and is near death, his knowledge [of God] mightily increases, his joy in that knowledge grows greater" (*Guide* III:51). When describing the kiss of death as experienced by Moses, Aaron, and Miriam, he says "these three died in the midst of the pleasure derived from the knowledge of God and their great love for Him" (*Ibid.*). Regardless, even if Aristotle and the Rambam can be split on the Euthyphro line, they would both still agree that happiness, in essence, is inescapable.

If this is so, where does free will reside in the Rambam's conception of humanity? If man already wants to follow the commandments as explained in *Hilkhot Geirushin*, what, if anything, is he choosing when he decides to actually follow through with what he already wants to do?

It has already been deduced that if free will resides anywhere, it must reside somewhere in the intellectual or spiritual part of man. Furthermore, all decisions involving following commandments certainly involve the intellect, as it has already been stated by the Rambam that the choice between good and evil (which, in the context of Deuteronomy means following or not following the commandments) is applicable to the realm of free choice.

But there are two philosophical issues that seem to block free will from functioning even in this situation, and seem to label the Rambam a determinist. First, according to the Rambam (as implied by *Hilkhot Gerushin* 2:22), it seems as if every intellectual decision is already decided upon. Man knows what he wants or what makes him happy, and by nature will do what he wants. Secondly, even if it isn't decided upon, since his perverse opinions can yet take hold of him in these situations, the ultimate deciding factor in these decisions is nevertheless what a man wants, whether he is correct about what he really wants and follows the Torah or makes a mistake and does not. Whether or not a man makes a mistake regarding his happiness, it does not mean he never intended to pursue it. In reality, he was forced to pursue it by his own nature. And if a man must inescapably choose what he wants, even in cases of altruism and self-sacrifice, then there really is no more room left for him to make a free choice. The Rambam, then, seems to be a determinist.

III. The Rambam's True Opinion on Free Will

There are two last, remaining issues that must be resolved. 1) If the Rambam affirms that not only volition, but free will as a specific *type* of volition that is given by God exists, *and* that man necessarily does what he wants, then how does the Rambam have room to fit free will into his conception of humanity? 2) If the Rambam does believe in a restricted free will, why would he shroud such a view in relatively amorphous language? After all, if the entire pillar of Torah and the commandments rests upon its reality, as he says it does in *Hilkhot Teshuvah* 5:5, why not state forthright what its exact nature is, what it applies to, and when it applies?

To tackle the first problem requires a fine reading and detailed analysis of chapter five of the *Hilkhot Teshuvah*. This chapter is where the Rambam makes his most detailed account of his opinion on free will in that work. The chapter begins:

> The ability of every man [to act] is his own. If he wants to incline himself toward the path of good and become a righteous man, he has the ability. And if he wants to incline himself toward the path of evil and be a wicked man, he has the ability. This is what is written in the Torah, "Now man has become like one of us, knowing good and evil," (Gen. 3:22).

First, as this is a treatise on repentance, the subject matter is *a priori* restricted to that which repentance applies to—following or not following the commandments of the Torah. So even before we start reading this chapter, we know that the Rambam here is not particularly concerned with volition itself. This chapter concerns itself almost entirely with the nature of free will as a metaphysical reality given by God to man specifically.

This is evident in the language the Rambam uses throughout the chapter. He qualifies the specified domain of actions almost every time to good versus evil. For instance, in 5:1 he states, "that he is now, regarding his [Man's] thoughts and opinions, essentially a knower of good and evil and a doer of anything he desires. There is nothing to hold him back from doing the good or the evil." Even when he uses the language "anything he desires," he immediately qualifies it back to good and evil.

In 5:3 he refers to "one of the two paths" again in the restrictive tone, and repeats the denial of divine compulsion for good or evil. Even when in 5:5 he uses the language "all that man desires to do among the actions of man," he immediately qualifies it again with the words "whether good or evil."

Returning to 5:1, one might be tempted to read the word "wants" as an affirmation of the Aristotelian principle supported by the Rambam's statements in *Hilkhot Geirushin*. A man will do what he wants, and then the problem of man always doing what he wants without any other option comes into play again. However, if read carefully, the use of the word "wants" actually serves to use that very Aristotelian principle in order to necessitate the existence of free will in man.

There are many important nuances to note in 5:1. The first is the Rambam's use of the word *le-hatot*, meaning, "to incline towards." He chooses this word over something more concrete, such as *le-hahlit*—"to decide." Second is his use of the word "path." He seems to be speaking of leaning toward a general path as opposed to executing a particular good or evil decision. Third are the words "to be a righteous person" which seem superfluous and out of place. Superfluous because the reader already knows that he is talking about being good when he says "to incline himself toward the path of good," and out of place because it is impossible to simply decide to be a righteous person. Being a righteous person seems to be more a culmination of a lifetime of decisions, and not just a split-second choice made by one act of *behirah*. The same can be said about the Rambam's use of the words "to incline toward" with regard to "path of evil" and "to be a wicked person." Everything taken together, though, the Aristotelian conundrum is solved.

If one accepts the dualist conception of humanity that the Rambam maintains, namely, that man consists of a divine soul on one hand and an animal soul on the other, or an intellectual part and a physical part,[25] then there are three possibilities as to what type of decision-making process a man can undergo. The first possibility is that the particular decision needed to be made involves strictly physical factors such as what shirt to wear, what drink to drink, or what food to eat. (Again, this is assuming that no halakhic questions exist and all other factors remain equal.) In that case the Aristotelian principle kicks in and man will, by necessity of his own human nature, pick whichever path he wants. Though there is still no external force compelling him in either direction, the irresistibility of his internal nature (that which seeks happiness) does not allow

---

25 *Guide* I:1-2.

his will to be free in such a case.

The second possibility is that the particular decision needed to be made involves strictly intellectual factors with no interference from the physical drive. In such a theoretical case, for instance, where there is no desire to transgress the commandments of the Torah, in essence a man will naturally choose what he wants, which is to follow the commandments in order to attain "true happiness." The Aristotelian principle applies here as well, and free will is left with no room to operate.

The third possibility, however, is that the intellectual part of man comes into conflict with the physical part of man. In such a case, what a man decides he wants, or what will make him happy, becomes relatively more confusing. There is, though, already an example of such a conflict in the passage from *Hilkhot Geirushin* discussed earlier. In that case, the man in question was in conflict between what he *qua* man really wanted (to fulfill his obligation and give his wife the document of divorce), and what his inclination wanted (which was to keep his wife against her will). In such a case, the Rambam admits that the Aristotelian principle of happiness still applies, except that the man must struggle between which type of happiness he intends to fulfill, the true happiness which would be to obey the will of God by following the commandments, or the happiness of the inclination. In reality, he wants to do both, except that he must choose one over the other. His human nature is irresistible—he must choose what he wants over what he doesn't want. However, deciding what is the *correct thing to want* in a specific situation is a different matter not subject to Aristotle's rule. Perhaps this is why the Rambam uses the word "wants" in the first sentence of *Hilkhot Teshuvah* 5:1. He is admitting that whatever a man chooses, he will choose what he wants regardless. But he must in fact choose the thing he determines is best to want, which, according to the Rambam, is left up entirely to his free will.

It seems, in accordance with the Rambam's language in the *Shemoneh Perakim* that was analyzed earlier on, and from chapter five of *Hilkhot Teshuvah* in the *Mishneh Torah*, that there are two possibilities as to when free will takes full effect. The first possibility is when the physical part of man is in conflict with the intellectual and he must decide whether or not to do a specific good versus a specific evil action. The second possibility is when man must make a general life decision concerning which path to happiness he will take for the remainder of his life. In my opinion, the correct interpretation of the Rambam is that both situations engender free will, though the latter is the primary free will scenario.

As is evident from the language of the *Hilkhot Teshuvah* 5:1, the Rambam is not referring to any one specific decision. His use of the words "to incline toward" and "path" belie the fact that he is referring to something more general and long-lasting. His reference to choosing to be a righteous or a wicked person contributes to this, in that choosing to be either righteous or wicked is not anything concrete, but is rather a long-standing path for the future. And while it is true that man will choose what he wants, he must make a decision regarding which path to happiness he chooses to take. Deuteronomy gives two options: "life and good" on one hand, and "death and evil" on the other. (Deut. 30:15)

At the same time, the Rambam does not deny that free will can operate during any time when man must choose between good and evil. Though the primary case is where one must choose between the paths themselves, whenever the inclination conflicts with the path to true happiness, man must still make a choice. Chapter Two of *Shemoneh Perakim*, for example, speaks of deciding upon doing or transgressing any commandment in particular.

We can now return to Chapter Eight of *Shemoneh Perakim* and see how it fits into the recent interpretation of free will:

> But the doubtless truth is that all the actions of man are given over to his power. If he wants to do [an action] he does it, and if he wants to, he doesn't do it, without force or coercion upon him in this matter. Therefore, the obligatory commandments were made, and [God] said, "See, I have given before you today the [path to] life and the good, the [path to] death and the evil, and you shall choose life," and He has given us the power to choose regarding these [paths].

In accordance with the interpretation just given, the purpose of the word "given" makes more sense. Since the physical world allows for man to will his actions on his own, the Torah is able to command man to choose life and good over death and evil. This free choice, "*behira*," was given to man in this regard alone in that the Torah clearly demarcated two separate paths towards living one's life. Now that those paths are known and set out by God, man has the ability to choose between them. Had they not been clarified by God through the Torah, man may never have discovered what good and evil actually are, and therefore may never have known the path to true happiness, and consequently never have been able to exercise free will at all. Insofar as God, through the Torah, gave man full knowledge of the good and the evil, it is as if he gave us access to free will.

Note that reading these passages of the *Shemoneh Perakim* as well as the *Mishneh Torah* under these interpretations eliminates the contradictions between the former works and the *Guide*. Whereas in the first two works the Rambam uses language that denies any type of determinism, in the *Guide* he affirms determinism of a certain type, in that nature functions on necessary causality, and everything goes back to God. On this topic, Goodman writes:

> [A]ll events are ascribed to God, whether these are events of nature, acts of will, or outcomes of pure chance. All, in fact, are

causal. For nature is governed by causal law, wills are motivated by the ends they choose, and what we denominate as chance is a superfluity of causes; it is, as Aristotle explained, a mere confluence of normally unrelated causal streams.[26]

Under the standard reading of the Rambam, the determinism of the type advocated by the *Guide* comes into direct conflict with his statements in *Shemoneh Perakim* and the *Mishneh Torah* because if one assumes that the earlier statements are completely libertarian, then any type of causal determinism undermines that thesis. However, under the reading advocated here, there is no contradiction. Wills are, as Goodman says, motivated by the ends they choose, but this need not contradict the Rambam's statements in his previous works because will, even though it must choose what it wants over anything else, is still man's, in that he is the one deciding what, indeed, he actually wants.

Whether read from the perspective of *Shemoneh Perakim*, the *Mishneh Torah,* or the *Guide*, free will as the choice between good and evil remains the same. The Rambam chooses to be more open about his views on deterministic causality in the *Guide* because it is a work of philosophy. Likewise, the Rambam uses language expressing the ability of man to exercise his *own* will in *Shemoneh Perakim* because it is primarily a treatise on human nature. Finally, he chooses to reveal the actual nature of free will in full in the *Mishneh Torah*, because *Hilkhot Teshuvah*, the Laws of Repentance, deal primarily with the realm of good versus evil, rather than human nature as a whole.

IV. Why the Rambam Chose to Subvert his Opinion

The Rambam's language on the subject of human freedom and determinism has led to much confusion throughout the centuries. With scholars trying to figure out the popular and the esoteric, the decoys and the truths, the contradictions and the inconsistencies, people begin to lose track of what the Rambam is trying to say to his readers. The question is, why would he try to confuse us? If human freedom is indeed the pillar of Torah and the commandments, how has all this disagreement concerning what the Rambam really believed on the subject cropped up so often? While I believe that the Rambam's true opinion can be teased out of his texts if read closely and correctly, he could have made the whole endeavor easier by explaining to us in clear language what exactly the nature of free will is versus what the nature of volition is, *in general*, and why determinism in the form of causality in the latter does not conflict with free will as a separate reality.

In *Guide* III:28, the Rambam says the following:

[I]n regard to the correct opinions through which the ultimate perfection may be obtained, the Law has communicated only their end and made a call to believe in them in a summary

---

26 Goodman, "Determinism and Freedom in Spinoza, Maimonides, and Aristotle," 115.

way, that is, to believe in the existence of the deity, may He be exalted, his unity, his knowledge, his power, his will, and his eternity. All these points are ultimate ends, which can be made clear in detail and through definitions only after one knows many opinions. In the same way the Law also makes a call to adopt certain beliefs, belief in which is necessary for the sake of political welfare. Such, for instance, is our belief that He, may He be exalted, is violently angry with those who disobey Him and that it is therefore necessary to fear Him and to dread Him and to take care not to disobey.

This passage can be interpreted in a variety of ways. The thrust of it seems to differentiate between what the Rambam terms "true beliefs" versus "necessary beliefs". The true beliefs are those of God's existence, his knowledge, his power, his will, and his eternity. These have no secondary benefit to them other than that they are true in themselves, and must be believed because of their inherent character as truth. The necessary beliefs, though, are put forth by the Torah for secondary purposes of the political, religious, and ethical welfare of the populace. The central question is whether the Rambam held these so-called "necessary" beliefs as true in that they lead to behavioral truths and eventually ultimate truths, or whether he held that the Torah is in fact lying to us by telling us pure falsities with the intent of getting us to act in a certain ethically or religiously desirable way.

In his book on the Rambam's principles of Jewish faith, Professor Marc Shapiro[27] gathers numerous rabbinic opinions that disagree with each of the Rambam's thirteen principles. In the chapter on the Eighth Principle, namely, "that the Torah in our hands is exactly the same as the Torah that Moses presented to the Children of Israel,"[28] Shapiro gathers over twenty-five pages of evidence of rabbinic disagreements with the Rambam on this issue, including the Talmud itself, as well as textual realities of differences in versions of the Torah's text that no one can deny. For Shapiro, it is evident that the Rambam did not himself believe in his own principle, as he writes:

> [I]t is impossible to believe that Maimonides should be taken at his word when he writes that all are obligated to believe that our Torah scrolls are the same as the one given to Moses. Who better than Maimonides knew the problems implicit in such a statement? He was perfectly aware of the textual differences in various scrolls, and it was he who went to such great lengths to establish a correct pentateuchal text[...].[29]

---

[27] Dr. Shapiro authored an article in the Hebrew section of this edition—Editor's Note.
[28] Marc B. Shapiro, *The Limits of Orthodox Theology: Maimonides' Thirteen Principles Reappraised* (Portland, OR: Littman Library of Jewish Civilization, 2004), 91.
[29] *Ibid.*, 115.

Furthermore, citing the Talmudic opinion that the last eight verses of the Torah were written by Joshua, Shapiro writes that:

> For the Rambam to declare a Talmudic opinion heretical appears extremely unlikely, especially when one bears in mind his view on the impossibility of deciding authoritatively between rabbinic opinions in theoretical matters.[30]

To explain how the Rambam could possibly brand as dogma something even he himself didn't believe, he turns to the *Guide* III:28 and the Rambam's own distinction between true and necessary beliefs. Principle Eight, he says, is a necessary—rather than a true—belief, in that, taken literally, it isn't exactly true, though belief in it enables the masses to retain their faith in the authenticity of the Torah. Shapiro writes:

> In his time, Muslims were challenging the Jews, claiming that they had altered the text of the Torah [...] In the face of such an assault, it is not hard to see why Maimonides felt it was important for the masses to believe that their text was the exact equivalent of Moses' text. The masses then (and today) could not be expected to understand the problems relating to the biblical text. Exposing them to some of this knowledge could have undermined their unquestioned faith, especially in the face of Islamic polemics. It was thus necessary for the masses to affirm what, in reality, was not true [...].[31]

Here, Shapiro is taking the Rambam's coinage of "necessary belief" to mean an actual false belief used for advantageous purposes. Though many scholars dispute that this is what the Rambam meant, for it would suggest that parts of the Torah are lies, Shapiro has support in classical Maimonidean commentators like Shem Tov ben Joseph ibn Shem Tov:

> And the Torah further commanded us to subscribe to a few beliefs, belief in which is necessary for the welfare of the state, just as it commanded us to believe that God has flaring anger against the transgressors of his will. This belief *is not true*, for He is not active and he doesn't get angry, as it is said, "I am the Lord, I change not." But the average man needs to believe this belief, [namely] that He is active [in his anger]. And *even though it is a lie*, it is necessary for the continued establishment of the state.[32]

It is obvious that according to Shem Tov, necessary beliefs according to the

---

30 *Ibid.*, 117.

31 *Ibid.*

32 Shem Tov, *Guide* III:28 (emphasis added).

Rambam are purely lies meant to further social and religious equilibrium. If by "necessary beliefs," the Rambam did indeed mean "false beliefs," and stuck one in as one of the thirteen principles of faith of Judaism itself, one could easily expect the Rambam to do something less radical, like convolute his language so as to make it appear that he is saying something that he actually is not. If he can lie about his beliefs in one of his most central and celebrated documents, the "Thirteen Principles of Faith," he can certainly hide his beliefs through difficult language.

In the *Shemoneh Perakim*, the Rambam makes it a primary goal that the reader understand that he has the freedom to act on his own. Without this conviction, he will not take the advice of *Masekhet Avot* seriously, and moreover, he will not take the Torah or any of its commandments seriously. Therefore, he chose to speak in categorical terms: every single thing a man does is given over to his own power; that there is nothing that can prevent him from doing what he wants; and that man has free will. While true that if read carefully, he is really saying something slightly different by qualifying the functional nature of free will to a very restricted field, if he were to say that outright, it would be dangerous for his ends, and for the reader. For example, one cannot tell a five-year-old never to lie except in very special circumstances. While everybody lies at some point or another for a good reason, to try to explain forthright to a child that there are circumstances when it is appropriate, even encouraged to lie, will confuse him and he will inevitably misapply those special circumstances through rationalization to situations that do not match them.

Had the Rambam clearly explained his view as to the relatively restricted functionality of free will in the *Shemoneh Perakim*, a reader may come to think that in any given situation, he might not be under that realm of functionality for whatever reason. He may come to think that since free will is in reality as restricted as it is, he might as well do what he wants. If free will is explained to be a lifestyle choice, he may come to believe that he has already decided, and live his life deterministically. He may, like the five-year-old, misapply his own situation of free will and rationalize to himself that he, in truth, is not responsible for his actions.

The same is true for readers of the *Mishneh Torah*. If the Rambam is to be clear and precise as to his true opinion in *Hilkhot Teshuvah*, the same thing may occur. A reader may assume to himself that either he used his free will in choosing his path already, or that what he is doing at the present moment does not fit those definitions, and will abandon all responsibility for his actions. Better for man to know the ultimate reality—that he *has* free will—and mistakenly think that he uses it at all times (when in fact it is a rarity), than read the statement incorrectly and misapply it to his own situation.

The *Guide*, though, is a different story entirely. It is here that the conflict between the Rambam as a libertarian, occasionalist, and soft determinist engenders itself. Passages such as *Guide* II:48 and the later chapters of Part I where he talks of divine causality and strikes a more deterministic tone have caught many off balance, creating a whirlwind of argument over the Rambam's position on the issue. This is because the affirmation of any type of causality whatsoever was unnecessarily seen as contrary to his libertarian statements in *Shemoneh Perakim* and the *Mishneh Torah*. But this need not be the case. To attempt to view the former works as a decoy, or frame them as the popular opinion, as set against the esoteric, true opinion in the *Guide* is to miss the point. To attempt to redefine and resettle the Rambam onto some kind of pseudo-deterministic ground is equally unnecessary, though this is a popular view in Maimonidean scholarship today. Moshe Sokol writes:

> Maimonides' affirmation of a determinism flowing from his conception of divine causality and will is compatible with the ascription of moral responsibility, perhaps the most important consideration Maimonides advances in favor of human free will. The difference between the *Guide* and Maimonides' popular works is that in his popular works he stresses only his affirmation of free will, largely on the grounds that to deny it would be to deny the possibility of human responsibility. Only to the more elite audience of the *Guide* does he hint at his real view in [*Guide*] *II:48*, that human choice is determined.[33]

This, in my view, is simplistic and wrong. Considering that free will is held by the Rambam to be "the pillar of the Torah and the commandments," this simply cannot be possible. The truth is that in the *Guide,* the Rambam could afford to reveal his true opinions on causality *of the will alone*, given the book's intended audience and philosophical structure.[34] But those opinions do not conflict at all with his statements in *Shemoneh Perakim* and the *Mishneh Torah.* They merely say in clearer language what was only implied in the former works: that causality of whatever nature does not interfere with man's actions being his own, because volition itself is caused by the necessary human pursuit of happiness anyway. Despite this causality, man will choose what he wants. This, in fact, *is* causality. It just isn't spelled out that way. Whatever layers of causality are above are only relevant to the philosophical speculation of the *Guide*, and make no difference in reality.

The Rambam, in consideration of the above, is a complete libertarian in terms of free will as a functional system. Man will choose what path he wants

---

[33] Sokol, "The Rambam on Freedom of the Will and Moral Responsibility," *Harvard Theolog - cal Review* 91, no.1 (January 1998).

[34] The determined nature of the will does not entail determination by God. The will is dete - mined, rather, simply by the internal nature of man and animal as seekers of happiness. Man has the added ability to seek a qualitatively different kind of happiness, and thus has free will in the fullest sense regarding which happiness to pursue. Yet, when operating solely under physicality, his will becomes determined once again by that very nature.

to take, what happiness he wants to pursue, and what he really wants in life. In terms of volition in general, he may be labeled a determinist. But insofar as they are two separate subjects (though highly related), differing positions on volition versus free will need not be combined or seen as conflicting with each other. There are no contradictions, only seeming ones, so as not to confuse the populace about their nature as free choosers. Just as he did regarding his eighth principle of faith, so too the Rambam did here—not by lying to us however, just by selecting his language very carefully.

The answer to the question, "is the Rambam a libertarian or a determinist?" depends on what issue you are currently dealing with. Regarding volition in general the Rambam is a hard determinist, regardless of whether the causality is seen as stemming from God or from nature. If the issue is free will however, then the Rambam is a libertarian, and, well, the choice is up to you.

Drew Kaplan is a rabbinical student at Ye-
shivat Chovevei Torah Rabbinical School.
He earned his BA in Jewish Studies from
Indiana University.

BIRKAT HA-MAPIL:
THE RABBINIC PRE-SLEEP BLESSING[1]
Drew Kaplan

Sleeping is a regular occurrence for every human being. Sleep is not a sudden occurrence, though; it is an occurrence for which one prepares. It is during this *approach* to sleep that a person experiences an intersection between the waking world of consciousness and the world of unconsciousness, of sleep. With this daily liminal experience, a need was seen by the Rabbis to impart to it religious meaning.[2] The Rabbis sought to frame the process of lying down to go to sleep by constructing a meaningful liturgy.

A society's particular attitude toward sleep is reflected in the types of activi-ties that occur surrounding sleep. For instance:

> Going to sleep means going through a number of culturally defined motions, such as dressing in a certain way, modifying light and sound conditions, assuming one of a limited number of postures, closing one's eyes even in darkness… These mo-tions, together with the perceptions of the actual state of sleep, and motions associated with awakening, constitute the role of the sleeper.[3]

The Rabbis' representation of the behaviors surrounding sleep then, reveals much about their conception of sleep in general, as well as a great deal about how they saw their daily lives.

The focus in this article will be on the liturgical behavior of the sleeper (or attempted sleeper). Investigating liturgy prescribed to be said while on one's bed can help us understand rabbinic thought regarding sleep,[4] and how they

---

[1] I would like to thank Michael Katzman and Benji Shiller of the *Milin Havivin* editorial staff, as well Rabbi Josh Yuter, for all of their comments, notes, and suggestions on this paper. All statements, including any errors herein, remain my own.

[2] See, especially, the words of Maimonides introducing the chapter in which this blessing is found: "When the Sages instituted the words of these prayers, they also instituted other prayers, and these are they…" (*Mishneh Torah, Hilkhot Tefilah* 7:1). After this introduction follows a number of blessings, beginning with our blessing of *Ha-Mapil*.

[3] Vilhelm Aubert and Harrison White, "Sleep: A Sociological Interpretation I," *Acta Sociologica* 4, no. 2 (1959), 48.

[4] For other work on rabbinic thought on sleep, see Joshua Schwartz, "Material Culture and

sought to guide the thought of the one attempting sleep. As the "rabbinic appreciation of the religious significance of the physical world comes through in their theology of blessings,"[5] we shall see the nature of the rabbinically-constructed role of "sleeper," as found in the relevant blessings.[6]

Birkat Ha-Mapil: Talmudic Source

The text of the *Ha-Mapil* blessing appears in the context of a *beraita*[7] which discusses three blessings for three other situations: prior to letting blood, going to the bathhouse, and going to the bathroom (*Berakhot* 60a-b).[8] Similar to the act of going to sleep, all three of these situations are frequent, and in all three, danger could befall those involved.[9] Furthermore, these places of potential danger are also places where one undergoes amelioration of their physical condition.[10] At the stage between being outside of these places and being in them, a blessing is a particularly useful psychological tool. It is helpful for one to frame these situations within a religious context, beseeching God to assist in this undertaking.[11] The pre-sleep text as found in the Romm edition of the

Rabbinic Literature in the Land of Israel in Late Antiquity: Beds, Bedclothes, and Sleeping Habits," in ed. Lee I. Levine, *Continuity and Renewal: Jews and Judaism in Byzantine-Christian Palestine* (Jerusalem: Dinur Center for the Study of History, Yad Ben-Zvi and Jewish Theological Seminary of America, 2004): 197 209 (Hebrew), as well as my previous article, "Rabbinic Sleep Ethics: Jewish Sleep Conduct in Late Antiquity," *Milin Havivin* 2 (2006): 83-93.

5 Reuven Kimelman, "The Rabbinic Theology of the Physical: Blessings, Body and Soul, Resurrection, and Covenant and Election," in *The Late Roman-Rabbinic Period*, vol. 4, *The Cambridge History of Judaism*, ed. Steven T. Katz (Cambridge, UK & New York: Cambridge University Press, 2006), 947.

6 It seems logical that the Rabbis would have instituted such a blessing, regardless of precedent, as the pre-sleep time seems to call for a religious context. However, the etiology of this blessing is unclear. Professor Lawrence Schiffman has suggested that, originally, one would say the [full] *Shema* upon one's bed accompanied with its evening blessings, including *Hashkiveinu*; when these were moved to the evening service to be said in in the synagogue, a rabbinically-required recitation of the *Shema* accompanied by this new *Ha-Mapil* blessing took their stead (Professor Lawrence Schiffman, "The Other Talmud: The Jerusalem Talmud, Its History and Text," *Edah Lehrhaus* #3, JCC of Manhattan, New York City, 14 June 2007). Nevertheless, I am not altogether convinced of this particular possibility. Perhaps *Ha-Mapil* is a stand-alone blessing that was created on its own and not simply as a replacement for another blessing.

7 The blessing appears in only one place within the entire Talmud (including both the Babylonian and Palestinian Talmuds). The *beraita* is punctuated by Amoraic and Stamaitic statements; whether or not *Ha-Mapil* is a part of the *beraita* will be discussed later.

8 For more information, see Julius Preuss, *Biblical and Talmudic Medicine*, trans. & ed. Fred Rosner (New York & London: Sanhedrin Press, 1978), 248-257, 533-537 & 541-544, and 546-551, respectively.

9 See, for instance, *Berakhot* 62a for dangers of going to the privy (including damaging spirits).

10 For instance, "The bath was not only considered to be an amenity, but most importantly a means for the maintenance of health" (Preuss, *Biblical and Talmudic Medicine*, 543).

11 It is worthy to note that this text is a collection of blessings, whereas this is not speaking

Talmud reads as follows:

> One who enters onto his[12] bed to sleep says from *"Shema Yisra'el"* until[13] *"Ve-hayah im shamo'a."*

> And he says, "Blessed is the one who causes sleep to descend upon my eyes and slumber upon my eyelids and gives light to the pupil of the eye.

> "May it be willful from before You, O Lord, my God, that You will lay me down peacefully; give me my lot in your Torah; accustom me to come to *mitzvah*; do not accustom me to come to transgression; bring me neither to iniquity, to sin, to temptation, nor to humiliation; may the good inclination rule over me; may the evil inclination not rule over me; save me from unfortunate accidents and illnesses; may neither bad dreams nor bad thoughts confuse me; may my bed be complete before You; light my eyes lest I sleep the sleep of death.

> Blessed are You, Lord, who illuminates for the entire world in all of his entire glory."[14]

First, the Talmud considers the spatiotemporal setting, that is, one's entrance into bed.[15] The Talmud's setting is not immediately before one falls asleep, nor

---

about the total procedure for entering these places. See, for instance, *Tosefta Berakhot* 2:2 and *Shabbat* 10a in addition to *Ta'anit* 20a for what to do procedurally upon entrance into a bath house.

[12] Although the reader should be referred to my comment ("Rabbinic Sleep Ethics," 84, n.4) on the default usage of the masculine gender, that is not to say that women were necessarily either excluded nor included in this prescription (it may, however, hinge upon the saying of the "Shema").

[13] Although most texts use the language of "until," Rabeinu Hananel, the early eleventh-century Talmudic commentator, has the version to say "and," thus it would be the first two paragraphs, rather than simply the first paragraph. The reason that this is a possibility is that each of the two paragraphs uses the language of lying down. (Rabbenu Asher, *Berakhot* 9:23).

[14] *Berakhot*, vol. 1, *Talmud Bavli* (Vilna: Romm, 1860), 60b. (Henceforth, Romm edition.)

[15] Why this language of "entering *into*" is used in relation to beds as opposed to "lying down on", "going onto", or anything similar, is on account that "beds were usually high, and were entered by a footstool." Furthermore, canopies were not unusual, which added to the sense of 'entering' into another domain. (S. Safrai, "Home and Family," in *The Jewish People in the First Century: Historical Geography, Political History, Social, Cultural and Religious Life and Institutions*, vol. 2, eds. S. Safrai and M. Stern (Amsterdam: Van Gorcum, 1976), 736.) See, for instance, *Sukah* 10b for canopied beds. For a sense of space beneath beds in the Talmudic era, see, for instance *Berakhot* 62a (and its parallel in *Hagigah* 5b) where Rav Kahana hid under Rav's bed, as well as *Bava Batra* 58a, where Rabbi Binah answers to Rabbi Yohanan that a bed of an *am ha-aretz* seems like a packed storehouse.

is it when one is already in their bed, but rather when they are making their way into bed. Moreover, it is not when they enter into their bed for any purpose (such as eating or reading, for instance) that they follow this ritual, but rather, it is for sleeping, *per se*.[16] By saying this upon entrance into one's bed—by beseeching God to help one get to sleep,[17] as well as to mark their entry into this space, separating themselves off from their concerns of the day—the intended effect may be soporific.[18] As to the potential danger of the situation, like the other three situations mentioned in the *beraita*, the reason for the blessing here is for the Rabbis to show that we "are grateful that He bestows sleep upon us, because sleep rejuvenates us and allows us to function, but we are also scared of the physical and spiritual dangers that we may encounter while we sleep."[19]

It is no surprise that the first component of the Talmud's bedtime prescription is not the blessing of *Ha-Mapil*, but saying the first paragraph(s) of the *Shema*. The recitation of *Shema*, consisting of three separate sections of scriptural verses,[20] dates back to antiquity.[21] Outside of the above text from *Berakhot*, however, discussion of the *Ha-Mapil* blessing is absent from the Talmud's discussions regarding the reading of the *Shema* on one's bed.[22] Since our text in *Berakhot* is the only mention of reciting *Ha-Mapil* along with the

---

[16] One vague aspect of this line is the timing: is it simply once a day, when one goes to sleep at night? Or is it any time one goes to sleep? What about napping—should one say it then? What about sleeping (or napping, for that matter) in a place aside from one's bed (perhaps on a chair or on the ground)—or is it only when sleeping in a bed? The only other usage of the term "one who enters to sleep" is found in a *beraita* where "one who enters to sleep in the day…" or "one who enters to sleep in the night…" (*Sukah* 26b). It may be that the unqualified term in our text leaves open the possibility that one going into one's bed to sleep *at anytime* says the blessing. One further issue of the action is whether this line excludes or includes "bed usage" (a rabbinic euphemism for sex)—an issue we shall see later in this paper.

[17] For a survey of insomnia in the Bible and the Talmud, see Sonia Ancoli-Israel, "'Sleep Is Not Tangible' or What the Hebrew Tradition Has to Say About Sleep," *Psychosomatic Medicine* 63, no. 5 (2001), 781-783.

[18] Cf. Franz's words on this matter: "[p]sychologically, sleep is a condition of disinterest for the presented situation or, in other words, it is a condition of total distraction" (Shepherd Ivory Franz, review of "La Fonction du Sommeil", *Riviste di Scienza* 2 no. 3 [1907] by E. Claparède, *The Journal of Philosophy, Psychology and Scientific Methods* 5, no. 6 (1908), 163). The function, then, of this blessing would be to help set apart this person's concerns from the day and help them focus on their present situation of trying to fall asleep for the night.

[19] Naomi Gerszberg, "*Ha-Mapil*," *Kol Mevaseret* 2 (2002), 85-86.

[20] Deuteronomy 6:4-9, 11:13-21, and Numbers 15:37-41. However, in the selected *Berakhot* text, only the first and second sections are mentioned, which is logical, since they both contain the line of "reciting them… when you lie down and when you get up" (Deut. 6:7, 11:19).

[21] For instance, see I. Elbogen, "Studies in the Jewish Liturgy," *The Jewish Quarterly Review* 19 OS, no. 2 (January 1907), 229-233. Cf. Ismar Elbogen, *Jewish Liturgy: A Comprehensive History*, trans. Raymond P. Scheindlin (Philadelphia, New York & Jerusalem: The Jewish Publication Society & The Jewish Theological Seminary), 22-23.

[22] *Berakhot* 4b-5a, *Berakhot* 13b, *Yerushalmi Berakhot* 1:1, and *Yerushalmi Berakhot* 2:1 are all amoraic discussions.

Shema, it seems that *Ha-Mapil* was at least not a great matter of concern to the Amoraim. This point is especially salient in the *Talmud Yerushalmi*, where *Ha-Mapil* is not mentioned at all.

In our *Berakhot* text, it is unclear if the *Ha-Mapil* blessing is part of the *beraita* discussed earlier or if it is an addendum to the text of the *beraita*. If the *Ha-Mapil* blessing is indeed within the *beraita*, its source would seem Tannaitic, and either the Amoraim are not as concerned about its recitation as they are the saying of the *Shema*, or the need to say the *Shema* on one's bed is amplified by the Amoraim for other reasons.[23] But if the *Ha-Mapil* blessing is not within the *beraita* but has been appended to the *beraita*, its origin may be later, possibly even post-Amoraic, and we can thus understand why it was neither discussed, nor was it a desideratum among the Amoraim. Alternatively, the blessing may be of Tannaitic or Amoraic origin and was just not recorded until later.

Structure of *Birkat Ha-Mapil*

The overall structure of this blessing is a tripartite composition, consisting of an opening line of blessing, a middle section of requests, and a concluding line of blessing. It thus may be considered a full rabbinic blessing, fulfilling the rabbinic requirements to open and conclude a blessing (*Berakhot* 46a-b, *Pesahim* 104b).[24] The language employed is in the first-person singular, as opposed to a common plural language, which makes sense, since this person is undergoing this event on his or her own and is "concerned with personal, physical, and mental wellbeing."[25]

Among the multiple Talmudic manuscripts and medieval commentaries, we find numerous versions of the wording of this composite blessing.[26] While the opening and concluding lines of the blessing remain more or less consistent throughout the various texts, the middle sets of requests differ widely. A number of possibilities account for these different versions. There may have

---

[23] This amplification is either that the need is emphasized in a prescriptive manner by Rabbi Yehoshua, son of Levi (*Berakhot* 4b), or that he meant to mandate saying either all three, or just the first two, in addition to the first paragraph mentioned in our text.

[24] Cf. Ruth Langer, *To Worship God Properly: Tensions Between Liturgical Custom and Halakha in Judaism* (Cincinnati, OH: HUC Press, 1998), 24-27 for the structure of rabbinic blessings.

[25] Rabbi Dr. Elie Munk, *The World of Prayer: Commentary and Translation of the Daily Prayers*, vol. 1, *Daily Prayers*, trans. Henry Biberfeld (Jerusalem & New York: Feldheim, 1963), 224.

[26] Rabbi Raphael Rabbinovicz, *Variae Lectiones in Mischnam et in Talmud Babylonicum*, vol.1, *Tractate Berachoth et totus ordo Seraïm* (in Hebrew) (Munich: H. Roesl, 1867; Jerusalem: Ohr Hahakhmah, 2002), 345, n. 7. Not only are there various versions, but even different recensions within a given author's work – in this case, Maimonides' *Mishneh Torah* on this text has a few different ones (Nachum L. Rabinovitch, *Sefer Ahavah*, vol. 1, bk. 2, *Mishneh Torah According to Bodleian MS. Huntington 80 with a Comprehensive Commentary* (in Hebrew) [Jerusalem: Ma'aliyot, 1984], 266.).

been initially a shorter version upon which people added lines, or a longer form which became shortened.[27] Alternatively, it may have been a medium-length blessing with various strophes being added and/or deleted. Therefore, the most valuable method by which to look at this blessing is to inspect each of the three main sections separately.[28]

First Section: Opening Blessing

Although there are over a dozen different texts sampled here, each has the same beginning of "Blessed is the One who causes bonds of sleep to fall…"[29] with variations thenceforth:

(1)…upon eyes.[30]

(2)…on Man and gives light to the pupil of the eye.[31]

(3)…upon me and the One who gives light to the pupil of the eye.[32]

(4)…on my eyes and the One who guards me like the pupil of the eye.[33]

(5)…on my eyes and sets slumber upon my eyelids.[34]

(6)…upon my eyes and slumber upon my eyelids.[35]

(7)…upon my eyes and gives light to the pupil of the eye.[36]

(8)…upon my eyes and slumber upon my eyelids and gives light to the pupil of the eye.[37]

(9)…upon my eyes and sets sleep of slumber and the One who gives light

---

[27] Shlomo Naeh, "*Hergel Mitzvah,*" *Tarbitz* 65, no. 2 (January-March 1996), 232.

[28] While one could alternatively study the blessing by looking at each of the versions on their own and then comparing them, the structure, nevertheless, remains the same amongst them.

[29] All translations are mine.

[30] Rav Netronai Gaon, Teshuvot Rav Netronai Gaon OH 9 (*Teshuvot Rav Netronai bar H - lai Ge'on*, vol. 1, ed. Yerahmiel Brody (Jerusalem & Cleveland: Ofeq Institute, 1994), 113). (Henceforth, Netronai.)

[31] Menahem ben Rabbi Shlomoh, *Beit ha-Behirah,* vol. 1, *Masekhet Berakhot,* ed. Shmuel Dyc - man (Jerusalem: Yad haRav Herzog, 1965), 212. (Henceforth, Meiri.)

[32] Rabbi Isaac ben Jacob Alfasi, *Hilkhot Rav Alfasi,* vol. 1, ed. Rabbi Nissan Sacks (Jerusalem: Mossad Harav Kook, 1969), 50. (Henceforth, Rif.)

[33] MSS Oxford 366, Paris 671. (Henceforth, Oxford (for both).)

[34] *Sefer Mitzvot Katan, Mitzvah* 151. (Henceforth, SeMaK.)

[35] Rosh, *Berakhot* 9:23. (Henceforth, Rosh)

[36] Rambam, *Mishneh Torah, Hilkhot Tefilah* 7:1 according to *Mishneh Torah,* vol. 1, *Book of Ahavah,* vol. 2 (in Hebrew) (Jerusalem & Bnei Brak: Hotzaat Shabse Frankel, 2007), 74. (Henceforth, Rambam-Frankel.)

[37] Found in both the Soncino (Soncino, Italy: Joshua Solomon Soncino, 1483) and Romm printed editions of the Talmud (and, for that matter, the Bomberg version (Venice, Italy: Dan - iel Bomberg, 1520), p. 62b, which is identical in this matter to that of the Soncino version). So, too, Rambam, *Mishneh Torah, Hilkhot Tefilah* 7:1 according to *Sefer Mishneh Torah al-pi Kitvei Yad Teimanim,* vol. 2, *Sefer Ahavah,* ed. Yosef Kapah (Jerusalem: Mekhon Mishnat haRambam, 1983), 174. (Henceforth, Rambam-Kapah.) It is noteworthy here to mention Kapah's words in a note on this passage (my translation): "and in the printed [editions], they added and emended as they liked" (Kapah, *Sefer Mishneh Torah,* 174, n. 1).

to the pupil of the eye.[38]

(10)...upon my eyes and sets sleep of slumber upon my eyelids, and light-giver to the pupil of the eye.[39]

(11)...upon my eyes and the One who gives light to the pupil of the eye, and the One who sets sleep of slumber.[40]

(12)...upon my eyes and sets sleep of slumber upon my eyelids and rest upon the pupil of the eye.[41]

(13)...upon my eyes and sets sleep of slumber upon my eyelids and rest upon the pupil of the eye and guards me like the pupil of the eye.[42]

(14)... upon my eyes and the One who sets sleep of slumber to descend and the One who lights up the pupil of the eye.[43]

A common aspect running through each of these versions is thanking God for being the One to cause sleep to fall upon the person. This is perfectly reasonable considering that this is the liminal moment that the person is moving from becoming tired in the waking realm, to accepting upon themselves their hypnagogic state and entering into sleep. The common language of "causes bonds of sleep to fall" utilizes the language of 1 Kings 20:31,[44] which imagines that ropes are binding up the sleeper. Indeed, the language used throughout the blessing repeatedly borrows from biblical verses.

The phrasings of both "sleep" and, separately, "slumber" were adapted from Psalms 132:4 and/or Proverbs 6:4. The two terms are separate forms of sleeping,[45] with the second ("slumber") used as an intensification.[46] Thus, the phrase "sleep of slumber" is likely a mistake. Furthermore, it is interesting that this phrase is used as the object of "placing"[47]—hinting perhaps that this

---

[38] Rambam, *Mishneh Torah, Hilkhot Tefilah* 7:1 according to *Mishneh Torah*, vol.1, *Sefer Ahavah*, bk. 2 (Jerusalem: Segula, 2003), 38-39. (Henceforth, Rambam-Segula.)

[39] Simhah ben Shmuel of Vitri, *Mahzor Vitri*, vol. 1, ed. Rabbi Aryeh Goldschmidt (Jerusalem: Mekhon Otzar Haposkim, 2004), 163. (Henceforth, MzVitri.) It is noted there that one MS has "returner" instead of "lightgiver."

[40] *Sefer Hilkhot Gedolot*, siman 1, ch. 9 (*Sefer Hilkhot Gedolot* (Jerusalem: Mekhon 'Or Ha - izrah, 1992), 89). (Henceforth, Hil. Ged.)

[41] Rabbi Avraham ben Rabbi Yitzhak, *Sefer ha-Eshkol*, ed. Hanoch Albeck (Jerusalem: Mekitzei Nirdamim, 1938), 94. (Henceforth, Eshkol.)

[42] Rav Amram Gaon in *Seder Rav Amram Ga'on*, vol. 1 (Warsaw: Ch. Kelter'a I Spolki, 1865; Jerusalem: Kiryaah Ne'emenah, 1965), 19. (Henceforth, Amram.)

[43] Rambam, *Mishneh Torah, Hilkhot Tefilah* 7:1 according to *Mishneh Torah: Mahadura Menuk - det Im Perush Le-Am*, vol.3, *Sefer Ahavah*, ed. Rav Shmuel Tanhum Rubenstein (Jerusalem: Mossad haRav Kook, 1958). (Henceforth, Rambam-Kook.)

[44] Rabinovitch, *Sefer Ahavah*, 266. Rabinovitch goes on to suggest that this understanding is reflected in the morning blessings with the saying of "the One who releases the bound" – that those bonds of sleep which had held back the sleeper are now removed.

[45] See Rabbi Meir Leibush's commentary on the Proverbs verse.

[46] Michael V. Fox, *Proverbs 1-9: A New Translation with Introduction and Commentary*, Anchor Bible 18A (New York & London: Doubleday, 2000), 213. See also 214, n. 163 there.

[47] Rabinovitch suggests that this language is based off of Job 40:25 (Rabinovitch, *Sefer Ah -*

word was not originally part of the blessing.

In a number of versions, the blessing borrows from Psalms 17:8, which says "guard me like the apple of your eye"[48]—describing the pupil, lying in the midst of the iris. Those versions that have adopted the language of "guard me" request protection, especially at this vulnerable moment. Those versions which speak about lighting up the pupil of the eye rather than guarding it use such a phrase to balance the sleep that is about to descend upon the person's eyes, with hopes of their post-sleep experience. Either way, this ocular focus seems to be due to the eye being the main sensing interface with one's waking world. Thus, there is a movement from wakefulness to sleeping, then from sleeping to wakefulness—all brought on by God.

The first two versions of the opening blessing listed above offer an impersonal blessing of God, matching the concluding blessing. Although the third version offers a personal placement of the bonds of sleep upon the person, the last nine versions, also more personal, have the bonds of sleep being placed specifically on the eyes.[49] Additionally, the first and sixth versions have only one action verb, whereas the remainder use multiple action verbs.

Middle Section: Personal Requests

The middle section of the *Ha-Mapil* blessing, which includes a series of requests, also varies greatly among the manuscripts and commentaries' versions. While many of the elements remain the same, even some of the common phrases are found in some versions and not in others. Most versions start off with the introductory language of "May it be Your will, Lord, my God,"[50] remaining with the personal, first-person theme of this blessing, and then all move to requests, starting off with "that…." What follows in each of them is a string of verbal strophes connected by the word "and." In the chart that follows, I have omitted the connecting "and" and have provided ordinal numeration for each of the verbal strophes as they appear in each version:

---

vah, 266).

[48] Translations of Scripture in this paper are from *Tanakh: A New Translation of the Holy Scriptures According to the Traditional Hebrew Text* (Philadelphia & Jerusalem: The Jewish Publication Society, 1985).

[49] The logic behind suggesting that the bonds of sleep are upon the person would be that one is bound up, as it were, as their physical mobility is limited.

[50] *Sefer Mitzvot Katan* has added onto this "and the God of my fathers," while *Mahzor Vitri* has a pluralized form of that. Additionally, while the Talmudic manuscripts have no mention of God, it is clear that this is meant to be inserted when pronouncing this blessing.

[51] "Stand me up from my bed to life and to peace."

[52] "Stand me up from it to life and to peace."

[53] "Stand me up from my bed to life and to peace."

[54] "Stand me up from my bed to life and to peace."

[55] "Stand me up to peace and to a good life."

[56] "Do not bring me to iniquity, to sin, to temptation, nor to humiliation"

	Romm	Oxford	Soncino	Rif	Rambam	Hil.Ged.	Netronai	Amram	Rosh	MzVitri	Eshkol	SeMaK	Meiri
That You will lay me down peacefully	1		1				1	1	1	1		1	6
Stand me up peacefully		6		7[51]	4[52]	3[53]	2	2	2[54]	2		2	7[55]
Give me my lot in Your Torah	2	1	2	1			3	3		3		3	1
Accustom me to come to *mitzvah*	3	2	3	2				4		4			2
Do not accustom me to come to sin	4	3	4	3				5		5			3
Do not bring me to sin, to temptation, nor to humiliation	5[56]	4	5			1[57]		6		6			
May the good inclination rule over me	6	5		4				7			1		4
May the evil inclination not rule over me	7		6	5				8		8[58]	2		5
Save me from unfortunate accidents and illnesses	8		7		1[59]			9			3[60]	4[61]	
May neither bad dreams nor bad thoughts confuse me	9		8		2	2		10	3	9	4		
May my bed be complete before You	10		9	6	3			11	4	10	5	5	
Light my eyes lest I sleep the sleep of death	11		10	8	5			12	5	11	6	6	8
Guard me from coming into blood									7				

Looking at all of these different versions of the text can certainly obfuscate interpreting the blessing.[62] For instance, while the smallest version is three

57 "Do not bring me to temptation nor to humiliation."

58 "…and from evil thought."

59 The Bodleian MS (as does Rambam-Kook) has "Save me from evil inclination and from unfortunate accident" (see Rabinovitch, *Mishneh Torah*, 266).

60 "Save me from mishap, from bad dreams, and from bad thoughts."

61 "Save me from the evil inclination, from mishap, and from bad dreams and [bad] thoughts."

62 Whether the mixing and matching came about through active recensions—whether via written or oral means—or whether there came about scribal and oral transmission changes. Curiously, the blessing with which *Ha-Mapil* shares the most similarity is that of *ha-Ma'avir*

lines long, the longest version includes twelve lines. Additionally, there is no clear chronology to range of length, as demonstrated by both the smallest and largest being Geonic. In any event, we shall now proceed to identify the major themes in this portion of the blessing.

The first line, "that You will lay me down peacefully," appears in a little over half of the represented examples and almost always is the first line in this section (Meiri's version has it toward the end). It expresses one's hope to be able to sleep. The language of "lying down" seems to once again draw from biblical language.

The next line of "stand me up peacefully" occurs either as the second line, last line, or penultimate line in the listing in this section. This line along with the previous one works well as a mirror to those versions of the first blessing wherein both sleeping and waking are mentioned. This seems to be why it is found either directly juxtaposed to the first line or at the opposite end of the section.[63]

The next line of "give me my lot in Your Torah" is mentioned in one of the first few lines of this section, sometimes the first, indicating that this is one of the more significant requests here. In fact, when one goes to sleep, they do relinquish their attempts to study more Torah. Therefore, at this time they recognize that sleeping and studying Torah are two mutually exclusive activities, and that regardless of their current pursuit of seeking sleep, they still hope to have a portion in God's Torah.[64]

The next two requests of "accustom me to come to *mitzvah* and do not accustom me to come to sin" are always found in tandem. Although it may seem strange that one would request these active actions as one is going to sleep, they may have a bed-related intention. As Shlomo Naeh has pointed out, these terms relate to euphemistic language for sexual intercourse.[65] The request then is for the sexual activity in which one may engage to be proper. Interestingly, whereas the discourse to this point has been centered on sleep, this line shifts the focus to bedtime activity in general, or in a non-sexual understanding of "accustom me to come to *mitzvah*" the focus has shifted beyond the bed entirely.

The following four lines of "bring me neither to sin, to temptation, nor to humiliation," "may the good inclination rule over me," "may the evil inclination not rule over me," and "save me from unfortunate accidents and illnesses" seem

---

Sheinah, the last of a series of daily *berakhot* which are recited later in the morning order of blessings. This is peculiar since one would expect the blessing immediately following sleep, that of *Elokai Neshamah* found directly after *Ha-Mapil* in the Talmud, to be most like the one to directly precede it, in order to provide blessing "bookends" for sleep. This is not the case and instead, it is recited later [on the same page in the Talmud].

63 It is unclear why the corresponding language of "rising" as found in the *Shema* paragraphs of Deuteronomy 6:7 and 11:19 is not used here, as it would seem to be particularly appropriate.

64 Cf. Rabbi Yechezkel Landau, *Sefer Zion Le-Nefesh Hayah,* vol. 1, rev. ed. (Jerusalem: Vagshal, 1995 (orig. Prague: 1791)), 218, s.v. *she-tashkiveini le-shalom ve-ten helki be-Torahtekha.*

65 Naeh, "*Hergel Mitzvah,*" 234.

similar to the two preceding lines in that they seem waking-activity oriented. They may also be related to the bed in terms of sex.[66] This is certainly true for the phrase "guard me from coming into blood" that appears uniquely in *Mahzor Vitri*, seemingly referring to blood of either *nidah* or *zivah* that may occur during sexual intercourse.

The early fourteenth-century scholar Rabbi Ya'akov ben Asher suggests that these non-sleep-related requests were added by the ninth-century sage Rav Amram Gaon.[67] If so, it could have been done for one of three reasons. 1) Because this blessing is said prior to entering one's bed, the locus of sexual activity, and, as there is no other liturgical outlet for making these requests, this moment becomes optimal. 2) These requests are actually intended to relate to general waking hours and are said now as a means of preparation for the day ahead. 3) A mixture between the previous two: some requests may have been meant for bedtime and others for the next day.

The next line of "may neither bad dreams nor bad thoughts confuse me" is borrowed from the end of Daniel 5:10, which includes the following: "Let your thoughts not alarm you [...]." This line requests of God not to allow the sleeper to be perturbed with nightmares.

The request "may my bed be complete before You" seems, at first, to be speaking of the physical bed. Thus, one is praying for the bed to remain sturdy throughout the night and for the sleeper to remain sleeping, rather than disturbed by a collapsing bed. However, the language of "before You" seems to indicate a further meaning. It may be that the completeness refers to that which comes from the bed—the progeny conceived there.[68] Thus, it is likely speaking about sexual activity while on the bed.[69]

---

66 See *Kidushin* 81b for Rabbi Hiyah, son of Ashi's daily request of "May the Merciful One save me from the evil inclination," beseeching God to help him to have a disinterest in sexual activity.

67 *Tur, Orah Hayim* 239. Although, whether Rav Amram added them from his own thought or had a different version is unclear. (Naeh, "*Hergel Mitzvah*," 232.)

68 Rashi, *Berakhot* 60b, s.v. *u-te-hei mitati sheleimah lefanekha*.

69 While at first glance, the phrase "my bed" has no special connotation – including the biblical *hapax legomenon* of Psalms 6:7 – the Rabbis construe this phrase with sexual meaning. While the phrase "usage of my bed" in tannaitic texts (*Ta'anit* 1:6, *Ketuvot* 5:6, *Eduyot* 4:10, *Nega'im* 14:2, *Tosefta Ta'anit* 1:5, 2:4, *Tosefta Yoma* 4:1, *Tosefta Ketuvot* 5:6, *Tosefta Nega'im* 8:6, *Tosefta Nedarim* 7:1, *Tosefta Zavim* 1:9, and *Nedarim* 81b) is of a sexual nature, the phrase "my bed" by itself is not (see *Ta'anit* 21a, *Megilah* 28a, and *Berakhot* 5a). Of particular interest in this shift of meaning is Abba Binyamin's statement: "For two things, I pained myself all of my days: On my prayer: that it should be before my bed; and on my bed: that it should be placed between the north and the south" (*Berakhot* 5b). At face value, Abba Binyamin seems to be talking about both the physical or temporal juxtaposition of his prayer and his bed in the first case, and how he wanted to position his bed in the latter case. On the latter element of Abba Binyamin's statement, the *stam* of the gemara connects the geographical positioning of the bed to a statement by either Rabbi Hama, son of Rabbi Hanina, or Rabbi Yitzhak, that one who positions his bed this way will merit male children (*Berakhot* 5b), thus reading Abba

The final line of "light my eyes lest I sleep the sleep of death" is taken from the last half of Psalm 13:4. Not only was a connection between sleep and death made in the Bible,[70] but a *beraita* in the Babylonian Talmud explicitly suggests that sleep bares a resemblance to death (*Berakhot* 57b).[71] Moreover, as one is preparing for a loss of consciousness, one hopes that it is temporary.[72] Thus, this line is used as a request that this sleep should be not be a permanent one. Furthermore, the language of lighting up of eyes is similar to some versions of the first and concluding blessings.

There are two main motifs woven into this section of requests. On one hand, we find preparation for sleep leading to arising to a new day. The second motif, however, is one of seeking blessing while engaged in sexual activity. A number of these are requests from the petitioner directly to God, but there are also several indirect requests, with the blesser hoping for his or her desired outcome to occur. In each of these modes, one gives up their authority over themselves and places themselves in the trust of God.[73]

Binyamin's statement with sexual connotation. Two additional amoraic usages of this term further illustrate their understanding of "my bed" as sexual. The first is Rav Yehudah quoting Rav expounding on Psalms 6:7, the biblical verse mentioned earlier, that even at the time of David's pains, he still had sex (*Sanhedrin* 107a). While this understanding is not the simple understanding of the verse, Rav interprets "bed" as being "usage of bed" (Rashi, *Sanhedrin* 107a, s.v. *mitati*). The second amoraic usage is that of Reish Lakish, who also expounds a biblical verse: "And Jacob called his sons and said, 'Come together that I may tell you what is to befall you in days to come'" (Genesis 49:1), an apparent discontinued clause. Reish Lakish seeks to fill this narrative gap by saying that Jacob, after becoming concerned with his loss of prophetic ability, began considering that "[P]erhaps there is an invalidation on my bed, like Abraham, out of whom came Ishmael, and like my father Isaac, out of whom came Esau" (*Pesahim* 56a). Reish Lakish presents Jacob being concerned not about his physical bed, but rather representing the bed as the locus of generating progeny. Indeed the amoraim see more meaning in a bed on which one engages in the sexual act rather than simply a bed for sleeping (Cf. *Shabat* 118b and *Gitin* 56a).

[70] See, for instance, Thomas H. McAlpine, *Sleep, Divine & Human in the Old Testament*, JSOTS 38 (Sheffield, England: Sheffield Academic Press, 1987), 144-149.

[71] The specific language used is that sleep is one-sixtieth of death, along with four other rel-tionships between various items—mostly non-physical.

[72] See the fascinating statement of Johnstone: "structurally the beginning of death is exactly like the beginning of sleep. Each is a loss of waking consciousness. That death is not merely the loss of waking consciousness, but the loss of *all* consciousness does not affect the extrapolation; sleep, too, can be, or at least seem to the erstwhile sleeper, a loss of all consciousness." (Henry W. Johnstone, Jr., "Toward A Phenomenology of Death," *Philosophy and Phenomenological Research* 35, no. 3 [1975], 396-397.)

[73] Cf. "When people sleep, some of the responsibility they have for taking care of their own and society's interests, is transferred to others" (Vilhelm Aubert and Harrison White, "Sleep: A Sociological Interpretation, II," *Acta Sociologica* 4, no. 3 [1959], 14). The theological import of this blessing then, is that the sleeper puts his or her trust in God, beseeching divine protection.

Third Section: Concluding Blessing

The concluding blessing line is the least varied of the three *Ha-Mapil* sections. Not only are there only several different versions, but they also differ little in message:

Blessed is the Light-giver of the world.[74]
Blessed is the One who gives light to the entire world with his glory.[75]
Blessed is the One who gives light to the whole entire world with his glory.[76]
Blessed is the One who gives light to the whole world.[77]
Blessed is the One who gives light to the world with his glory.[78]

The theme of God giving light to the world seems to reflect the notion of giving light to the pupil of the eye included in most versions of the opening blessing line. The usage of this motif in the closing blessing creates a literary envelope—closing on a theme with which the blessing began. But the language of lighting up the world may seem out of place, right before sleeping—one might expect language about good sleep, sweet sleep, or even a renewed spirit or energy upon waking. So why is the blessing formulated in this way?

The blessing speaks of lighting up the world with the person thinking about their waking day ahead—once darkness has fallen over the land, they are in a moment of diminished opportunity, such that the pervading darkness forces a cessation of daily labors, crafts, and other regular activities. But the words of *Ha-Mapil* serve to give them hope, something to which to look forward. The nineteenth-century physician Robert Macnish describes that, upon awakening, "the eyes are painfully affected by the light, but this shortly wears away, and we then feel them stronger than when we went to bed."[79] The motif of the light in *Ha-Mapil* suggests the same kind of powerful first moment upon our return to consciousness.

Some of the versions mention God lighting up "the whole world." What is gained by adding the element of "the whole"? Perhaps this phrase suggests a stronger recognition of the greatness of God, demonstrated further in some versions through the inclusion of "in His glory." This further appendage clarifies the results of God's acts in "the whole entire world"—that his glory is so magisterial that He lights up the world.

---

74 Oxford (& Paris).
75 Soncino, Romm, Rambam-Segula, Hil. Ged, Rosh, and Eshkol.
76 Rif, Rambam-Kook & Amram.
77 Rambam-Kapah & Rambam-Frankel.
78 MzVitri & SeMaK.
79 Robert Macnish, *The Philosophy of Sleep*, 2nd ed. (Glasgow: W.R. M'phun, 1834), 38.

Conclusion

While the Talmudic manuscripts and early medieval commentators[80] (*rishonim*) vary greatly in their representations of the *Ha-Mapil* blessing, certain themes, nevertheless, emerge.[81] Throughout the *Ha-Mapil* blessing, motifs of heading to sleep, hoping to arise from sleep, sexual conduct, and the lighting up of eyes appear. All of these fit within the standard rabbinic rubric of a lengthy blessing, with a full opening blessing line, a middle section continuing the themes and requests, and then concluding with a short, closing blessing line. Although a semblance of sleep to death is suggested, "no anticipation of any metaphysical crisis is implied."[82] That is to say, the text of the blessing does not suggest a concern about contact with spirits or that one's spirit necessarily leaves one's body.

For a Jew approaching their bed to sleep, the Rabbis of the Talmud seek to provide a religious orientation for this pivotal experience. They use liturgical prescriptions, both from Scripture, as well as from their own blessing formulations to do so. While "sleep did not take up much of their attention in their halakhic system, as it was more likely seen as a very normal, quotidian activity,"[83] once the moment arrives and an individual has physically prepared for sleep, the Rabbis provide a frame for this moment that marks the transition from consciousness to unconsciousness. Upon the recital of this blessing, one becomes mentally prepared to move into a different mode of existence.

---

[80] Amongst these, one of the most significant is Maimonides' *Mishneh Torah* among which are found several versions of this text. Rabbi Rapoport suggested that "it is axiomatic to all students of the *Mishneh Torah* that this work was written with extreme meticulousness and precision. An accurate text is therefore all the more critical for the student who seeks to appreciate its proper meaning and decipher the delicate nuances of its phraseology" (Rabbi Chaim Rapoport, "Maimonides, Mishneh Torah, Manuscripts and Indices," *Jewish Action* 65, no. 3 [Spring 2005]: 40). Thus, for Maimonidean scholars, there is yet still room to investigate this blessing in the *Mishneh Torah*.

[81] One problem that arises with private liturgy such as *Birkat Ha-Mapil*, that gives rise to such a divergence in versions, is that it is generally confined to a textual sphere as opposed to public liturgy, where people may more easily be more familiar with a certain way of saying it.

[82] Martin L. Gordon, "*Netilat Yadayim Shel Shaharit*: Ritual of Crisis or Dedication?", *Gesher* 8 (1981), 66, n. 80.

[83] Kaplan, *Rabbinic Sleep Ethics*, 93.

Alexander Kaye is a student at Yeshivat
Chovevei Torah Rabbinical School. He is
also pursuing a doctorate in Jewish History
at Columbia University.

FAITH, HISTORY AND INTERPRETATION: REFORM AND ORTHODOX RESPONSES TO MODERN HERMENEUTICS
Alexander Kaye

The history of Judaism is the history of Jewish interpretation. To understand it, the discipline of hermeneutics—the study of how interpretation happens, the rules by which people read and understand—is a crucial tool. In *People of the Book*, Moshe Halbertal argues that throughout the Middle Ages, Jewish thinkers often held diametrically opposed positions on key subjects. These opinions were nevertheless all considered Jewish because they were grounded in interpretations of Judaism's key texts, especially the Bible. For Jews, Halbertal suggests that the Bible is a "formative text." "A formative text," he states, "is one in which progress in the field is made through the interpretation of the text itself. A text-centred culture that has formative texts proceeds in that mode; its achievements are interpretative."[1] This means that developments within Jewish thought are always made in relation to that text.

A hermeneutical model similar to Halbertal's sheds new light on the struggles between Reform and Orthodox Judaism in nineteenth-century Germany. Historians have typically focused on the theological and social differences between Orthodox and Reform thinkers regarding fundamentals such as the nature of revelation, the significance of ritual observance and the importance of rabbinic legal precedent. A hermeneutical approach however, adds an important dimension because it reveals the common ground *shared* by the Reform and Orthodox camps that is often obscured by the polemical nature of their writings. This applies on a general level. No less than in the middle ages, nineteenth-century developments in Jewish religious thought were couched in new readings of classical texts. But it also applies on a more specific level. As a close analysis of the methodology of scriptural interpretation of key figures in Orthodox and Reform Judaism demonstrates, they share not only the fact that they interpret texts but also, to a large extent, the way that they interpret texts. Although the conclusions drawn from their interpretation are very different, the methods used to reach them are often very similar.

---

[1] Moshe Halbertal, *People of the Book: Canon, Meaning, and Authority* (Cambridge, Mass., 1997), 90 ff. especially 94.

This approach can be used to look behind the rhetoric of the Reform-Orthodox debates. If their polemics were taken at face value, it would seem that whereas Reform interpreters embraced the modern hermeneutics crystallized by Spinoza and lionized by nineteenth-century German historicists, Orthodox interpreters remained true to a pre-modern traditionalist hermeneutics that shunned both the historicization and the critical examination of sacred texts. This perspective can be challenged through an analysis of the interpretative principles of three key Jewish thinkers of nineteenth-century Germany. R. Abraham Geiger, the founder of Reform Judaism, did indeed embody the modern hermeneutical methods of *Wissenschaft des Judentums*, a movement for the scientific (i.e. critical historicist) study of Judaism. But the Orthodox response was ambiguous. R. Samson Rafael Hirsch, one of the most vocal and prolific (not to mention conservative) Orthodox thinkers of the period, fought for decades to resist the conclusions of *Wissenschaft*. He dedicated himself to bolstering the authority of rabbinic law and the importance of tradition. And yet it can be shown that his scriptural interpretation, while it led to conclusions worlds apart from Geiger's, was built on the same basis of a modern Spinozan hermeneutics. Lastly, an investigation of R. David Zvi Hoffmann, a younger contemporary of R. Hirsch, brings to light a subtly different Orthodox response to modern hermeneutics, which may presage the paradigm shift in models of understanding that was brought about in the works of Martin Heidegger and refined by his pupil Hans-Georg Gadamer.

Abraham Geiger (1810-74) has been called the "founding father of Reform Judaism."[2] Born to an Orthodox family, he became a proponent of *Wissenschaft des Judentums*. He received his doctorate from the University of Marburg and held rabbinic positions in a number of communities, most notably Breslau, Frankfurt and Berlin. He used various journals and teaching positions to air his views, including the Berlin *Hochschule fur die Wissenschaft des Judentums*, where he spent his final years. Like the Reform movement in general, Geiger's conception of history operated upon two fundamental assumptions: that Judaism, like any other phenomenon in history, developed; and that despite this development, it has a continuous essence underlying it that with each successive stage in historical development achieves a higher form.[3] This conception allowed a departure from traditionalism whilst simultaneously creating (Geiger would say discovering) the underlying essence of the Jewish spirit as it was relevant to that time.[4]

Geiger's conception of history translated directly into his hermeneutics,

---

2 Michael Meyer, "Abraham Geiger's Historical Judaism," in *New Perspectives on Abraham Geiger: An HUC-JIR Symposium*, ed. Jakob J. Petuchowski` (Cincinnati, OH: HUC-JIR, 1975), 3.

3 Ismar Schorsch, "Ideology and History in the Age of Emancipation," in *From Text to Context: The Turn to History in Modern Judaism* (University Press of New England, 2003), 12.

4 Meyer, "Abraham Geiger's Historical Judaism," 5.

which were a reflection of Spinoza's. Spinoza, a seventeenth-century Dutch Jew, revolutionized the reading of the Bible in a number of ways. He effaced the distinction between sacred and profane texts and applied the same hermeneutical rules to the Bible as he did to any other text. He also distinguished between meaning and truth. It was possible to understand the meaning of a statement in scripture (for example "tablets of stone engraved by the finger of God") without necessarily believing in the truth of that meaning (and instead believing that the Bible was compiled by a number of people over a period of time). Indeed, Spinoza was the first to engage in what would later be called "higher criticism" of the biblical text. Spinoza also lay out his methodology for interpreting the meaning of the text. He maintained that "all knowledge of Scripture must be sought from Scripture alone," taking into account the historical context of the language and concepts within it.[5] In this sense the method of understanding the meaning of scripture was the same method used to understand nature:

> The method of interpreting Scripture is no different from the method of interpreting Nature [...] The method of interpreting Nature consists essentially in composing a detailed study of Nature from which, as being the source of our assured data, we can deduce the definitions of the things of Nature. Now in exactly the same way the task of Scriptural interpretation requires us to make a straightforward study of Scripture, and from this, as the source of our fixed data and principles, to deduce by logical inference the meaning of the authors of Scripture.[6]

Spinoza's methods and assumptions were extremely influential for historians and theologians in Geiger's milieu, who adopted a historicist reading of scripture, believing that the events and texts of the past should be understood on their own terms and any biases of the reader should be ignored. It is not by chance that as Geiger was beginning his critical study of the Bible, similar developments were taking place in Christian circles where Strauss's historical approach to scripture in *The Life of Jesus* (first published in 1835) had a far-reaching effect.

This was the background to Geiger's hermeneutics. Hermeneutics were critical to Geiger because he believed that the "inner development of Judaism [...] [is] the history of the biblical text and the translations."[7] Although earlier in life he thought that a close examination of the biblical text could yield the

---

5 Benedictus de Spinoza, *Tractatus Theologico-Politicus* (Leiden; New York, 1989), 142. For an analysis of this principle in the Tractatus, see Leo Strauss, *Persecution and the Art of Writing*, (Westport, CT: 1973).

6 Spinoza, *Tractatus Theologico-Politicus* (Gebhardt Edition, 1925), 141.

7 Quoted in Ken Koltun-Fromm, *Abraham Geiger's Liberal Judaism: Personal Meaning and Religious Authority* (Bloomington, 2006), 46.

"natural sense of scripture," he later abandoned this belief for a new theory in which the text had no natural sense but rather was produced by political forces in Jewish history.[8] Using variations among early translations as evidence, Geiger proposed that as the Jewish community developed and had to adapt to different historical circumstances, the text of the Bible itself was amended in response to contemporary concerns. The text therefore bares "traces" of earlier versions of itself.[9] Later in history, with the advent of what became the rabbinic age, the text was no longer amended. Instead, creative exegesis, which often conflicted with the plain meaning of the text, was required to make it relevant to the present. These rabbinic interpretations, also called *midrashim*, were presented by the rabbis as the Oral Law, and were considered by Jews to be binding. While admirable in its time as a way of making scripture relevant for contemporary historical circumstances, rabbinic law was now anachronistic and a new Jewish identity had to be formed. So a modern reader attempting to understand the real meaning of the biblical text must approach it with the realization that it has been altered over the generations with "expansions, clarifications, typological and symbolic explanatory schemes."[10] As such, "the eternal word does not belong to a particular time [...]. Each and every time, direction of thought and individuality brings to the Bible its own point of view."[11]

Geiger's hermeneutics are very close to Spinoza's approach to the interpretation of scripture. He shared Spinoza's crucial distinction between meaning and truth, which allowed Geiger to understand the Bible not as a representation of the will of God, or a prescription for religious action in the present, but merely as a reflection of its authors' opinions from a particular point in time. He also adopted a historicist approach to the text, insisting that the biases of generations of interpretation be put aside in favor of a reading in the terms of the text itself. As Michael Meyer has put it, for Geiger, "the history of Judaism must be understood in its own terms, each period in its own context, possessing relative validity as the revelation of the religious consciousness of the community of faith at a practical point in Jewish history."[12]

However, Geiger fell short of this stated intention. As we now know, it is never possible to ignore one's own contexts. And indeed, Geiger's hermeneutics were ideologically motivated. He claimed that his intention was "to prove how every element in the Judaism of his day had come into being historically and hence did not possess binding force."[13] As such, he failed on one level as a

---

[8] For the earlier theory, see especially Geiger's *Das Verhältnis des natürlichen Schriftsinnes zur thalmudischen Schriftdeutung* (1844). For the later theory, see especially his *Urschrift und Übersetzungen der Bibel* (1857). For more on the shift in Geiger's thinking, see *ibid.*

[9] *Ibid.*, 46.

[10] *Ibid.*, 47.

[11] *Ibid.*

[12] Meyer, "Jewish Religious Reform and Wissenschaft des Judentums: The Positions of Zunz, Geiger and Frankel," 28.

[13] Meyer, "Abraham Geiger's Historical Judaism," 5.

historian because he failed "to distinguish adequately between his own historically founded Judaism from the Judaism of history."[14] In one important sense,
then, Geiger differed from Spinoza. Despite his radical historicism, Geiger
always maintained that there was an underlying truth to scripture – if not in its
meaning then in its method. If, as Geiger believed, Judaism continually adapted
to its contemporary historical circumstances, then to remain true to the inner
essence of Judaism, he also believed that Jews in his own time had to abandon
the traditional practices of earlier generations in order to adapt to the political
requirements of the age of emancipation. As Jay Harris notes, for Geiger, "a
proper historical conceptualization of the emergence of Jewish law is required,
so that its essential temporally conditioned nature will be recognized. Once
this is accomplished, Judaism can be put back on the proper path as a religion
with a progressive dynamic, able to respond to the demands of the time."[15]

It was this historicism and its theological ramifications that R. Samson Rafael
Hirsch considered to be ill-founded and dangerous. R. Hirsch (1808-88) was
a life-long spokesman for Orthodox Judaism. He became friendly with Geiger
when they were both young students at the University of Bonn, though the
friendship was marred by their ideological divergences over the next decade.
In 1851, R. Hirsch became the Orthodox rabbi in Frankfurt am Main. His
many publications were characterized by his defense of Orthodoxy against the
growing popularity of Reform Judaism. Like Geiger, R. Hirsch thought that
the correct approach to scriptural hermeneutics was essential. "There is no
evil," he wrote, "no wrongful development in Judaism which does not owe its
origin to the improper or sinful conception of the Torah."[16] This sentiment
was reflective of his struggles with the Reform movement, whose historicist
understanding of scripture undermined the authority of the text as a product
of a single divine revelation. It also threatened the traditional rabbinic interpretation of the text which, according to Orthodox tradition, was consistent
with the Oral Law, which was also divinely revealed.

R. Hirsch's defense of traditional Judaism (he shunned the label "Orthodox"
as he recognized that "it was the modern 'progressive' Jews who first applied
this name to the 'old', 'backward' Jews as a derogatory term") was based on
his articulation of certain hermeneutic principles.[17] He shunned a historicist
reading of scripture and granted traditional interpretations primacy over historical ones, asserting that "there is no evidence or guarantee for the truth
and reality of a historical fact, save our trust in tradition."[18] Reading scripture

---

14 *Ibid.*, 13.

15 Jay Michael Harris, *How Do We Know This?: Midrash and the Fragmentation of Modern
Judaism* (Albany: SUNY Press, 1995), 163.

16 Samson Raphael Hirsch, *The Nineteen Letters on Judaism*, trans. B. Drachman (New York:
Feldheim, 1969), 117.

17 Samson Raphael Hirsch, "Religion Allied to Progress," 229.

18 Quoted in I. Grunfeld's introduction to Samson Raphael Hirsch, *The Pentateuch* (New

as a historically contingent text, dependent for a proper understanding upon contextualization, marred scriptural hermeneutics with what R. Hirsch called a "sickly subjectivism."[19] He sought to reintroduce the distinction between sacred and profane texts that Spinoza and his descendants had erased.[20] Even if historical context may be useful for understanding some texts, scripture is different. In fact, it is unique.

R. Hirsch also refused to recognize Spinoza's distinction between meaning and truth, at least as regards scripture. His journal *Jeschurun* ran many articles which sought to defend traditional Judaism against those who would change it to keep "up to date" or "allied with progress." One of the recurrent arguments against this point of view assumes the authority and truth of scripture itself:

> Is the statement: "And God spoke to Moses saying," with which all the laws of the Jewish Bible commence, true or not true? [...] If this is to be no mere lip-service, no mere rhetorical flourish, then we must keep and carry out this Torah without omission and without carping in all circumstances and at all times.[21]

Of course to a Spinozan, "And God spoke to Moses saying" may well be a mere rhetorical flourish, or at the very least, something that the author of the text believed to be true but has no binding authority on the contemporary reader.

One of R. Hirsch's most pressing projects, which he shared with many of his Orthodox contemporaries, was to defend the unity of the Written and Oral Law against the new criticism of the Reform movement. A principle goal of the historicism of the Jewish Reform movement was to demonstrate that the Oral Law was nothing more than a collection of rabbinic exegeses. Geiger and his colleagues considered these *"verkehrte"* (absurd) interpretations, that flew in the face of the plain meaning of the Written Law (i.e. scripture) so as to produce a corpus of man-made edicts.[22] The tendentious extraction from minute scriptural hints of volumes of laws regarding the observance of the Sabbath, for example, were certainly not a straightforward reading of the text. Whether this exegesis was ingenious or seditious, it was certainly not divine, and, because it was historically contingent, it was also not binding for contemporary Jews.

York, 1971), xxi.

[19] Quoted in Myers, *Resisting History: Historicism and its Discontents in German-Jewish Thought*, 31.

[20] For a discussion of the effect of a universal hermeneutics on the distinction between sacred and profane texts with special reference to Schleiermacher's hermeneutics, see Jeffrey F. Keuss ed., *The Sacred and the Profane: Contemporary Demands on Hermeneutics* (Aldershot, England: Ashgate Publishing, 2003), especially pp. 61-76.

[21] Samson Raphael Hirsch, "Judaism Up To Date," in *Judaism Eternal; Selected Essays from the Writings of Samson Raphael Hirsch*, ed. I Grunfeld (London, 1956), 216. See also R. Hirsch, "Religion Allied to Progress."

[22] Harris, *How Do We Know This?: Midrash and the Fragmentation of Modern Judaism*, 159.

Orthodox thinkers had to defend themselves against this attitude, which stood in direct opposition to the traditional understanding that the Oral Law originated in divine revelation and was therefore authoritative and eternal. Furthermore, the Written and Oral Law, both originating from the same divine source, were absolutely consistent with one another. Indeed, through careful use of the 13 hermeneutical rules of Rabbi Ishmael, themselves divinely revealed, principles of the Oral Law can also be extrapolated from the text of scripture itself. What is more, scripture is silent on many details of divine service—we are told to wear *totafot* between our eyes, and make *tzitzit* for the corners of our garments, but what are these *totafot,* and how are the *tzitzit* to be made? And the Oral Law is required to fill in these lacunae. So, far from being a distorted departure from the true meaning of scripture, the Oral Law was necessary to understand it properly, even as it could also be extrapolated from the text itself.[23] Having said all this, it was clear to traditional Jews that a straightforward reading of scripture would not yield an interpretation consistent with the exegesis of the Oral Law. In an age when traditional interpretations were being challenged, the relationship between the Oral and Written Law had to be explained and defended.

It is not surprising, then, that every major Orthodox commentary on scripture published in nineteenth-century Germany emphasized the unity between the Written and Oral Laws and sought to describe the precise relationship between them. R. Jacob Zvi Mecklenburg's *Ha-Ketav Ve-Ha-Kabalah,* which was first published in 1839 and ran into many editions, maintained that the text of scripture is multivalent and so contains not only the *peshat* or plain meaning but also the *derash* or exegetical interpretations of the Oral Law. And what of the times when the Oral Law seems to actually contradict the *peshat?* The text is intentionally ambiguous to give the reader a chance to demonstrate his faith by submitting to tradition against the rational reading. Scripture therefore serves as a kind of mnemonic for the Oral Law, but a mnemonic with an added dimension. Because the *derash* style of interpretation, which links Oral with Written Law, is itself divinely revealed, it serves not just as an aid-memoire but also sheds light on the specific nature of the law being extrapolated. This explains the energy that the Talmudic rabbis put into preserving the precise mnemonics and squeezing from them every ounce of significance. R. Meir Loeb Malbim's *Ha-Torah Ve-Ha-Mitzvah,* first published in 1844, has a similar project to R. Mecklenburg's commentary, but comes to a different conclusion. The verses quoted by the sages are not merely mnemonic devices. Rather, the Oral Law can be derived from scripture following logical and philological rules. A true reading of scripture will yield the same conclusions as rabbinic *derash.*

---

[23] This is a necessarily brief portrayal of the traditional approach to the relationship between the Oral and Written Law. For recent treatments of the significant variety between traditional models, see Michael S. Berger, *Rabbinic Authority* (New York, 1998), and Moshe Halbertal, *People of the Book: Canon, Meaning, and Authority* (Cambridge, Mass., 1997).

R. Hirsch, too, tried to defend the traditional understanding of the Written and Oral Laws against historicist criticism. This was a primary goal of his commentary on the Pentateuch, which he published between the years 1867 to 1878. Was his position closer to R. Mecklenburg, who maintained that *derash* is mnemonic, or to Malbim who claimed that the Oral Law can actually be derived from scripture? In fact, R. Hirsch claimed that both were right. The Oral Law was revealed before the Written Law and is not dependent on it; the Written Law was revealed as a summary of the Oral Law: "to be to the Oral Law in the relation of short notes on a full and extensive lecture on any scientific subject."[24] But the notes are only of value if the original lecture can be successfully reconstructed from them. This is the function of Rabbi Ishmael's 13 hermeneutic rules, also divinely revealed, which enable the extrapolation of the Oral Law from scripture through the principles of *derash*. The Written and Oral Laws are thus mutually authenticating. On the one hand, "it is not the Oral Law which has to seek the guarantee of its authenticity in the Written Law; on the contrary, it is the Written Law which has to look for its warrant in the Oral tradition."[25] On the other hand, the fact that the Oral Law can be derived from scripture does give it a greater authority and militates against the claim made by Geiger and others that it was simply a human innovation of the early rabbinic period. It was no doubt to bolster the authority of the Oral Law that R. Hirsch felt the need to explain why, if the Oral Law was revealed before the Written Law, scripture contains no reference to it whatsoever:

> Jewish tradition – a phenomenon unique in its kind – [...] refuses any documentation by the Written Torah which, after all, is only handed down by that oral tradition and presupposes it everywhere. This itself is the most trustworthy sign of its truth [...] The fact is that Holy Writ contains no direct documentary evidence of this truth of the Oral Tradition. And yet, a whole nation has joyfully committed the preservation of its existence during more than 3000 years in the authority of this Oral Tradition.[26]

In fact, R. Hirsch claims, it would be counter-productive for scripture to make reference to the authority of Oral Law, because others could claim that the reference had been forged. Better to omit any mention of it. In this way, R. Hirsch sought to support the divine authority of both Written and Oral Law and to demonstrate the relationship between them.

So far the hermeneutical positions of Geiger and R. Hirsch are predictable. Geiger, an advocate of a historically contingent Judaism that should be updated to reflect the changing times, understood scripture itself as a historically

---

[24] Commentary to *Exodus* 21:2 in Volume 2 of R. Hirsch, *The Pentateuch*, 288.

[25] *Ibid.*, xxii.

[26] *Ibid.*

contingent document that has to be placed in the context of its production, and the Oral Law as a human innovation that is certainly not binding to the modern Jew. R. Hirsch, defender of traditional Jewish law, regarded scripture as an eternal, divine document that can be understood only on the basis of a traditionalist, a-historicist approach through the interpretations of the Oral Law which was *itself* divinely revealed. In reality, however, their hermeneutic positions are not so straightforward. Although R. Hirsch always presents his hermeneutic techniques as a continuation of traditional methods of interpretation, he shares more assumptions with the historicist school than he himself admits. I have already discussed the nuances within Geiger's position: although he is strongly founded on a scientific historicism descended from Spinoza, he does seek justification in the inner nature of scripture as he sees it. R. Hirsch's position is also nuanced. It has more in common with Spinozan methods of interpretation than it first appears.

Much has been written about R. Hirsch's relationship to modern science and philosophy. In fact, R. Hirsch himself embraced modern intellectual life and coined the famous motto *Torah im Derekh Eretz* as an educational and philosophical approach to the relationship between traditional and modern life (although what R. Hirsch intended to be the parameters of this relationship are still hotly debated). It has been well established that R. Hirsch's own religious philosophy was heavily influenced to some degree by Hegel, and more so by Kantian ideas of an autonomous ethics.[27] His commentary on scripture took for granted that at the root of Torah law was an ethical imperative. Like Jewish reformers, albeit in a slightly different way, he believed that Judaism was a religion of enlightened ideals and cultural values. Relatively little work, however, has been done on the debt that R. Hirsch's hermeneutics owed to Spinoza and nineteenth-century historical objectivism. This is no doubt regarding R. Hirsch's own repeated opposition to this method of interpreting scripture in countless books and articles. But despite his own protests against *Wissenschaft*, his interpretative method shared a great deal of common ground with it. As Spinoza, and after him Geiger, insisted on reading scripture on its own terms, within its own historical context, so did R. Hirsch.

Like Spinoza, R. Hirsch insisted that the text should be interpreted *"aus sich selber"* (out of itself).[28] His goal was "to derive the explanation of the text from the words themselves."[29] Like Spinoza, he resisted imposing onto the text categories or explanations not already contained within it. R. Hirsch even criticized Maimonides on these grounds, who "entered into Judaism from without, bringing with him views of whose truth he had convinced himself

---

[27] For an overview of R. Hirsch's religious philosophy, see Noah H. Rosenbloom, *Tradition in an Age of Reform: the Religious Philosophy of Samson Raphael Hirsch* (Philadelphia, 1976).
[28] R. Hirsch, *The Pentateuch*, xxii.
[29] *Ibid.*, vi.

from extraneous sources."[30] No doubt R. Hirsch's motivation for attacking Maimonides in this way was the manner in which the theory in the *Guide for the Perplexed*, that the mitzvot had historically contingent explanations, was used by many reformers as justification for abandoning them. Nonetheless, R. Hirsch saw the value in interpreting scripture in its own terms only. In a passage that bears striking similarity to the section of Spinoza's *Tractatus* quoted above, R. Hirsch advocates interpreting scripture as we interpret nature:

> Two revelations are open before us; that is, nature and the Torah. In nature all phenomena stand before us as indisput-able facts, and we can only endeavor *a posteori* to ascertain the law of each and the connection of all [...] [The same is true of Torah.] Its ordinances must be accepted in their entirety as undeniable phenomena and must be studied in accordance with their connection to each other, and the subject to which they relate. Our conjectures must be tested by their precepts, and our highest certianty here also can only be that everything stands in harmony with our theory.[31]

And how do we go about understanding scripture in its own terms? Here too, R. Hirsch adopts a Spinozan approach. The meaning of the text can only be grasped with a proper understanding of both the historical context of scrip-ture and its language. Like Spinoza, R. Hirsch believed that an appreciation of the real meaning of the original language of scripture is essential. Only then, from the text itself rather than from assumptions foreign to it, can we reach an understanding of the underlying meaning of scripture as a whole:

> The beginning should be made with the Bible, its language should first be understood, and then, out of the spirit of the language, the spirit of the speakers therein should be inferred [...] [The Bible] should be studied as the foundation of a new science [...] the doctrine of God, world, man, Israel and Torah should be drawn from the Bible, and should become an idea, or system of ideas, fully comprehended.[32]

In addition to this linguistic knowledge, R. Hirsch believed that an aware-ness of the context of scripture is also required. It is impossible to understand the Written Law without the appreciation that the Oral Law preceded it. In his comments on the Pentateuch, R. Hirsch had to contend with the fact that its main section dealing with civil law starts not with basic principles, but with the laws of slavery. This anomaly can be explained with an understanding of the context in which the Written Law was revealed and an appreciation that it

---

[30] R. Hirsch, *The Nineteen Letters on Judaism*, 119.
[31] *Ibid.*, 143 fn 6.
[32] *Ibid.*, 127-8.

comes after the revelation of the Oral Law:

> What a mass of laws and principles of jurisprudence must have
> already been said and fixed, considered, laid down and ex-
> plained, before the Book of Law could reach these, or even
> speak of these, which, after all, are only quite exceptional cas-
> es.[33]

Although the context that R. Hirsch assumes and, therefore, the conclusions
he reaches are very different from Spinoza's or Geiger's, and although unlike
them he regarded the eternity and integrity of scripture as fundamental, it is
nonetheless clear that he shares with them some basic assumptions about how
to understand scripture.

In several places, R. Hirsch indicates that his approach is consistent with
the interpretations of Oral Law, that it is possible "to derive the fundamental
meaning of the words [of scripture] from the rich fund of linguistic explanations which we posses in our traditional writing."[34] But although he purports
to support traditional exegesis, he more often uses his own methods, which are
based on a philological approach to the text or rely on symbolic readings that
are largely unprecedented in rabbinical exegesis. His symbolic readings of the
Tabernacle and the sacrifices, for example, are highly innovative. So even as R.
Hirsch criticized *Wissenschaft*, he assimilated its interpretative techniques; he
fought against it based on its own weapons. On occasion, he even tried to be
more scientific than *Wissenschaft* itself, claiming, for example, that *Wissenschaft*
is unscientific because it is no more scientific to assume that the Torah is human than that it is divine.[35] No wonder that R. Hirsch's approach to scripture
has been labeled "unprecedented traditionalism – an oxymoron if ever there
was one."[36]

An interesting counterpoint to R. Hirsch is his younger contemporary, R.
David Zvi Hoffmann (1843-1921). Born in Hungary and trained by R. Moses
Schick, R. Hoffmann received his doctorate from Tübingen and in 1873 joined
the *Berlin Rabbinerseminar* under R. Esriel Hildesheimer and later replaced
him as Dean. R. Hildesheimer's school differed in orientation from R. Hirsch's
Frankfurt Rabbinerseminar in that it more explicitly embraced the techniques
of *Wissenschaft*, even while it remained Orthodox in its theology and practice.[37]
R. Hoffmann, like R. Hirsch, was unwavering in his support of traditional

---

[33] Commentary to *Exodus* 21:2 in: Volume 2 of R. Hirsch, *The Pentateuch*, 287.

[34] *Ibid.*, vi.

[35] See Mordechai Breuer, *"Hokhmat Yisrael: Shalosh Gishot Ortodoksiyot,"* in *Sefer Yovel Likhvod Moreinu Ha-Ga'on Rabbi Yosef Dov Soloveitchik Shlit"a*, ed. Lamm Israeli, Rafael (Jerusalem and New York, 1984), 857.

[36] Harris, *How Do We Know This?: Midrash and the Fragmentation of Modern Judaism*, 227.

[37] For more on the differences between the two schools, see Mordechai Breuer, *Modernity Within Tradition: the Social History of Orthodox Jewry in Imperial Germany* (New York, 1992), and Breuer, *"Hokhmat Yisrael: Shalosh Gishot Ortodoksiyot."*

religious law and resisted the notion of updating religion to keep up with the times. He also maintained, as did R. Hirsch, that "authentic Judaism regards the Oral Law as well as the Written Law [to be] of divine origin."[38] However, he differed from R. Hirsch in a number of important respects. Although he believed that the content of Oral Law was divinely revealed, and that the Oral Law was required for a true understanding of the Written Law, he maintained that the midrashic exegeses by which the rabbis linked the Oral Law to the Written Law, were mnemonic devices invented by men. In this, he had ample precedent in R. Mecklenburg's *Ha-Ketav Ve-Ha-Kabalah*.

R. Hoffmann also differed from R. Hirsch in more extreme ways that are representative of the more general differences between the Berlin and Frankfurt Seminaries. He openly utilized the tools of *Wissenschaft* in a way that R. Hirsch never did, and saw no contradiction between a historical-critical approach to rabbinic texts and his faith. As Mordechai Breuer put it, "for a deeply pious man like David Zvi Hoffmann, critical investigation into authoritative sources was the soul of Torah study, and, altogether, piety was unthinkable without thorough knowledge."[39] Despite his belief that the Oral Law was divinely revealed, when it came to rabbinic texts R. Hoffmann advocated a historical-critical analysis that included an investigation into the chronological layers of the text and believed that criticism of the mishnaic text is "required for the scientific examination of the tradition."[40] His understanding that rabbinic texts need to be approached as documents which changed over time was closer to the approach of his Reform counterparts than to that of R. Hirsch. R. Hoffmann believed, for example, that "it is obvious that very many of the old *mishnayot* have undergone transformations through the diverging explanations of later *Tannaim*. It is, of course, impossible to reconstruct [...] the original *mishnah* with certainty. It can only be guessed."[41] He also recognized that rabbinic lawmakers may have been affected by the non-Jewish cultures that surrounded them, an element of his work that R. Hirsch considered heretical. If for R. Hirsch rabbinic law was eternal and unchanging, for R. Hoffmann it was firmly entrenched in history.

R. Hoffmann's approach to the Written Law was quite different. He differentiated between the Oral Law, which "is for the best part of divine origin as far as its content is concerned, but the form has only been fixed at a relatively later time," and the Written Law, which "is the word of God in content as well as in expression."[42] As such, the historical-critical approach that

---

[38] Jenny Marmorstein, "David Hoffmann: Defender of the Faith," *Tradition* 7-8 (1966), 92.

[39] Breuer, *Modernity Within Tradition: the Social History of Orthodox Jewry in Imperial Germany*, 182-3.

[40] Quoted in David Ellenson, *Between Tradition and Culture: the Dialectics of Modern Jewish Religion and Identity* (Atlanta, Ga., 1994), 37.

[41] *Ibid.*, 11-12.

[42] David Hoffmann, *The First Mishna and the Controversies of the Tannaim: The Highest Court*

R. Hoffmann required for the interpretation of rabbinic texts, he considered inadmissible for the interpretation of scripture. He believed in the divine origin and Mosaic authorship of the entire Pentateuch, the integrity of the received Jewish text of the Bible and the consistency between the Written and Oral Law, which are both divine. Although he seems to accept that the text of Scripture may have become corrupted over the ages, he still advocates against altering it:

> Even if we have to admit that the text has not remained intact in some places, we must on the other hand agree that we lack means of restoring a text which was written in the holy spirit and that any conjecture, no matter how well supported on exegetical and historical critical grounds, does not offer us even the probability that the Prophet, i.e. the author of the sacred text, had originally written it in this form rather than according to the text before us.[43]

Ostensibly, then, although R. Hoffmann differed sharply from R. Hirsch when it came to the interpretation of rabbinic texts, he agreed with him regarding the interpretation of scripture. But in fact, there is an important point of contrast between their approaches to scriptural interpretation too. R. Hirsch did not typically distinguish between his *a priori* assumptions and the principles he attempted to prove objectively "from the text itself." His writings, which seek to demonstrate the unity of Written and Oral Law and the uniqueness of the Torah, never self-consciously address the fact that these were also beliefs that he held because of religious tradition, prior to and independent of a scientific interpretation of the text. He held in common with Geiger this failure to identify personal prejudices that preceded interpretation. Both R. Hirsch and Geiger's work was shaped, at least in part, by ideological motivations, but was presented as a series of objective, positivist arguments, that were intended to appeal to any rational thinker independent of his or her intellectual tradition.

It was precisely in this way that R. Hoffmann's hermeneutical approach differed from R. Hirsch's. R. Hoffmann had the same religious tradition as R. Hirsch, and he also believed that the assumptions of his tradition (such as the unity of the Oral and Written Law) could be demonstrated with critical methods. But unlike R. Hirsch, he explicitly noted his *a priori* assumptions. His commentary to Leviticus begins with an introduction in which he states:

> I willingly agree that, in consequence of the foundation of my belief, I am unable to arrive at the conclusion that the Pentateuch was written by anyone other than Moses; and in order to avoid raising doubts on this score, I have clearly outlined the

---

in the City of the Sanctuary, trans. Paul Forchheimer (New York: 1977), 1.
[43] Marmorstein, "Introduction to Leviticus," 100.

principles in which my commentary is based [...].[44]

He then sets out these principles:

> We believe that the whole Bible is true, holy, and of divine ori-
> gin [...] Authentic Judaism regards the Oral Law as well as the
> Written Law as being of divine origin [...] Just as the Torah as
> a divine revelation must not contradict itself, in the same way
> it must not contradict the Oral Law which is of divine origin
> [...] [We hold] the assumption of the integrity of the Massoretic
> or traditional text.[45]

To be sure, R. Hoffmann does attempt to justify these assumptions, which
form a backdrop for his commentary. For example, while he acknowledges that
his faith requires him to resolve apparent contradictions within or between
the Written and Oral Laws, he also defends this position by appealing to an
ancient hermeneutical principle of assuming consistency throughout a work.[46]
He also dedicated a monograph to exposing certain flaws in the documentary
hypothesis.[47] Likewise, R. Hoffmann's commentary is an attempt to justify
his traditional assumptions using modern historical-critical tools. He himself
admits as much:

> We shall [...] exclude completely every criticism of the text which
> is not rooted in Massoretic soil [...] we shall subordinate our-
> selves entirely to the words of the Bible [...] [and] dispute with
> the so-called higher criticism which sets itself up as a judge over
> the bible [...] We shall always consult [tradition] in explaining
> the words of Scripture. Nevertheless, we shall also consider the
> commentaries which adopt a different point of view and make
> an effort to justify our interpretation in the face of theirs.[48]

But although the fact that R. Hoffmann's scientific analysis, circumscribed
and directed by his traditional assumptions, is reminiscent of R. Hirsch, the
fact that he explicitly accepts and describes his assumptions distinguishes his

---

44 *Ibid.*, 91.

45 *Ibid.*

46 *Ibid.*, 94-5. "[...] even in other realms of law there are frequent differences which have to
be reconciled by means of certain rules of interpretation, and it has not occurred to anybody
to find fault with this. Within the three law-books of the Code of Justinian (Digests, Institutions, Codex) which are certainly to be considered as one large connected work, the general
rule applied to the treatment of contradictory passages is to demonstrate the illusory nature of
the conflict wherever possible, primarily because, in view of the unity of the three-fold work,
harmony is to be considered natural in itself, secondly since Justinian himself promised that if
one were only to look at it *subtili animo*, one would find a concealed basis of unity."

47 David Hoffmann, *Die Wichtigsten Instanzen Gegen die Graf-Wellhausensche Hypothese* (Be -
lin, 1904).

48 Marmorstein, "Introduction to Leviticus," 101.

work in a significant way. It could be said that this move presages the hermeneutics of the later twentieth century that was built on the work of Martin Heidegger and his student Hans-Georg Gadamer. In *Being and Time* (first published 1927, six years after R. Hoffmann's death), Heidegger made a fundamental shift from a Cartesian hermeneutics that described interpretation as an encounter between the interpreting subject and the interpreted object (the text). He asserted instead that interpretation and interpreter are intrinsically bound together and thereby challenged the claim that the interpretation of a text can stand independent from the interpreter and his or her personal prejudices. Gadamer refined this idea by constructing a theory of hermeneutics in which the prejudices of the interpreter, which nineteenth-century historicists did all they could to overcome, were not only inevitable, but also necessary for the act of interpretation, which could only take place by setting up the *a priori* assumptions of the reader against the text itself.[49] This powerful hermeneutical model has been suggested by contemporary Jewish thinkers as a way of interpreting tradition and rabbinic authority today and as a basis for reconciling a religious reading of the text with modern critical sensibilities.[50]

Clearly, R. Hoffmann's hermeneutics are not at all identical with the Heideggerian model. Although he recognizes and states his own prejudices, he nonetheless attempts to demonstrate the truth of his interpretation in objective critical terms. However, his methodology could be seen to bridge the gap between R. Hirsch's traditionalist historicism and a Heideggerian hermeneutics. While R. Hirsch does not recognize his prejudices, and claims that his conclusions are born out of the text itself, and Heidegger insists that an interpretation cannot exist independent of the reader's prejudices, R. Hoffmann falls between these two approaches. He shares R. Hirsch's assertion that whatever his own prejudices, his conclusions can be objectively verified. But his identification of pre-existing beliefs in his introduction, outside of the body of his commentary, is perhaps a move towards the recognition that prejudices precede his interpretation and therefore inevitably inform it.

It could be claimed that this subtle shift in R. Hoffmann's work was rooted in a fear that the refusal, required by traditional faith, to engage in a critical examination of scripture could not be adequately justified on the grounds of a historicist hermeneutics alone. A new hermeneutics, which recognized the inevitable place of tradition in all interpretation and the futility and self-deception of a claim to pure objectivism, would lend itself more readily to a defense of traditional interpretation. It seems unlikely that Hoffman consciously pursued this line of reasoning. But perhaps the difference of his approach from

---

[49] See especially Hans-Georg Gadamer, *Truth and Method*, 2nd rev. ed. (London: Continuum, 2004).

[50] See, for example, Tamar Ross, *Expanding the Palace of Torah: Orthodoxy and Feminism*, 1st ed. (Lebanon, NH, 2004), 168-71. For a similar theory based on the work of Stanley Fish, see Berger, *Rabbinic Authority*, 140-144.

R. Hirsch's, however subtle, marks the beginning of the shift towards a new religious hermeneutics in the twentieth century.

If this is true, the three personalities discussed here map out three different attempts to navigate the impact of historicism on Jewish hermeneutics during the nineteenth century. Geiger, eager to justify the *Wissenschaft* program of "updating" Judaism, embraced historicism and its criticism of traditional interpretation. R. Hirsch, while claiming that the proponents of *Wissenschaft* would destroy Judaism, that they "laboured with vicious energy to undermine that which they pretend to represent," nonetheless saw fit to defend his traditionalism on the very same hermeneutical grounds.[51] R. Hoffmann was more extreme than R. Hirsch in his use of modern critical methods, but he was also more sensitive to the drawbacks of using them to defend a traditional approach. Ironically, it was the Orthodox thinker more accepting of modern hermeneutics who more forthrightly stated his traditionalist assumptions before attempting to justify them critically. In doing so, he pointed towards an entirely new hermeneutics formulated in Germany in the years following his death.

A hermeneutical approach to the Reform-Orthodox debates of nineteenth-century Germany provides important insights on the way we construct modern Jewish identity. It reinforces the thesis that an opinion is "Jewish" when it is presented as an interpretation of central Jewish texts. Given that the specifics of any interpretation are always contestable, this broad definition is one possible way of distinguishing between those positions that fall within the realm of Judaism, (whether or not one agrees with them,) and those that fall without. Furthermore, hermeneutics provides alternative grounds for comparison between Jewish religious groups, beyond a comparison of theological positions or ritual practice. If some groups are considered to be close to each other in religious practice, they may be very far from each other in the way they understand that practice. Alternatively, and perhaps more importantly, denominations that are far from each other with regard to theology or ritual may share an interpretative methodology. Without minimizing the differences between denominational positions, a hermeneutical analysis may demonstrate similarities in the way these positions are developed. If *what* Jews think is not necessarily the same, *the way* they think it might be. What would be the effect of such an approach on the practical reality of Jewish inter-denominational relationships?

---

[51] Hirsch, *The Nineteen Letters on Judaism*, 137.

David Wolkenfeld, a student at Yeshivat
Chovevei Torah Rabbinical School, has a
B.A. in History from Harvard College and
is completing an M.A. in Jewish History
at the Bernard Revel Graduate School of
Yeshiva University.

Pacifism, the Jewish Mission, and Religious Anti-Zionism: Rabbi Aaron Samuel Tamares in Context[1]
David Wolkenfeld

Introduction

During the Russian-Ottoman War (1877-1878), Aaron Samuel, a young Jewish boy in the Lithuanian *shtetl* of Maltsh, witnessed his neighbors receive news of their son's death. Many decades later, Rabbi Aaron Samuel Tamares (1869-1931), a writer, philosopher, and community rabbi for the Lithuanian village of Milejczyce,[2] described his memory of that day in his autobiography:

> During the Russian-Turkish War the terrible news came to [R. Tamares]'s gentile neighbor that his son had fallen in the war. The mother of the soldier cried out bitterly and the little Jewish boy cried along with her. From that time onward, the boy was obsessed by thoughts regarding the terror of war.[3]

This experience infused in R. Tamares a deep hatred of warfare and violence that would lead him to espouse a fierce pacifism that shaped his reactions to social movements, such as revolutionary socialism, and informed his imagination as a *darshan*. R. Tamares's pacifism was also connected to an idealistic vision of Jewish destiny. Pacifism, to R. Tamares, was not just a spiritual ideal, but an inherent part of the mission and purpose of the Jewish people.

R. Tamares's support for Jewish spiritual renewal and skepticism towards the separatist orientation of the Eastern European rabbinate, together led R. Tamares to support Zionism. However, he was quickly disillusioned with the

---

[1] This article was originally written for a course on Zionism taught by Professor David Fishman at the Bernard Revel Graduate School of Yeshiva University.

[2] R. Tamares inherited the rabbinic post in Milejczyce from his father and held it until his death. In addition to the interests discussed here, R. Tamares is known for his unique fulminating against the fossilization of halakha.

[3] Aaron Samuel Tamares, "Biography of *Ahad ha-Rabbanim ha-Margishim*," in *Pacifism and Torah* (Hebrew), ed. Ehud Luz (Jerusalem: Dinur Center, 1992), 3. All translations of R. Tamares are my own. R. Tamares's autobiography is written in third person.

movement and became a vocal opponent of Zionism. To R. Tamares, the
Zionist focus on developing Jewish nationalism and the creation of a territorial nation-state based on the model of contemporary European nationalism
amounted to a betrayal of the vital Jewish mission in world history: to be a
non-political, and even "anti-political," nation. R. Tamares recanted the essays he had written supporting Zionism, forbade them from being reprinted,
and penned new essays and books explaining his pacifist vision of Judaism and
ideological opposition to Zionism.

Of course, R. Tamares was not the only East-European rabbi to write essays or books characterizing Zionism as a betrayal of essential elements of the
Jewish faith. However, whereas some Hasidic rabbis, R. Shalom Dov Baer of
Lubavitch among them, attacked Zionism as a betrayal of the Jewish dream of
redemption, R. Tamares argued that Zionism was a betrayal, not of the vision
of a perfect and miraculous redemption, rather of the spiritual mission, pacifist
message, and necessarily non-political methods of Judaism.

The outbreak of World War I confirmed R. Tamares's negative assessment of
European civilization. He witnessed the carnage brought by nationalism and
political activism. He saw the noble ideals of democracy and socialism tainted
by a quest for power. His belief that only a pure, non-political Judaism could
offer humanity hope for a different future was reinforced. In the first decades of
the twentieth century, R. Tamares looked with scorn on a discredited European
civilization, with alarm at Jewish attempts, through Zionism and assimilation,
to mirror what he perceieved to be the worst attributes of that civilization, and
continued adamantly to advance a message of Jewish pacifism.

R. Tamares's idiosyncratic vision of pacifist Orthodoxy is more than just a
"road not taken" in Jewish intellectual history. For those who have thrown
in their lot with Zionism and the State of Israel today, his writings are worth
revisiting. Post-Zionist Jews and others searching for a new purpose to Jewish
national life and a peaceful existence in the modern Middle East may find value
in both R. Tamares's vision of the Jewish nation as well as his pacifist ideals.

Pacifism and Anti-Nationalism

As his early encounter with his gentile neighbors demonstrates, R. Aaron
Samuel Tamares recoiled in horror in reaction to warfare and violence. As the
young Aaron Samuel cried together with his neighbors, he wondered to himself
how those same neighbors could decorate their home with a patriotic picture
of a Russian army engaging the enemy:

> The boy would stand there for hours unable to break his gaze
> from the picture. He was dumbfounded by people. How could
> they find it in their hearts to commit the acts of violence de-
> picted in the picture [...]? And together with those questions he
> was perplexed by this mother, stricken by fate, how could she

tolerate the presence of this picture in her home? And what was it that compelled her to look, without any break, at that same cursed vision, that had caused agony to so many mothers?[4]

At the age of nineteen, Aaron Samuel Tamares went to learn at the *mussar*-movement affiliated *Kolel Perushim*. While studying there, he attracted a circle of like-minded *batlanim* [idlers], so called for their lack of interest in discussing rabbinic placements and careers. When not immersed in study, they would gather to hear the young R. Tamares expound upon the "evil oppression that exists" in the world.[5] The worst form of oppression, young Tameres would exclaim, was war: "taking people from their homes, against their will, and setting them in front of the firing cannons [...] this is the pinnacle of dread against which a special struggle must be initiated."[6]

Warfare, for R. Tamares, was the worst form of injustice, not only in degree, but in quality as well.[7] The recognition of justifiable violence, such as exists when violence is yielded by a state, allows violent urges to corrupt the intellect with lies. Justified violence was therefore qualitatively more harmful and pernicious than violence with no claimed justification. In a *derashah* for Passover, which will be discussed in greater detail below, R. Aaron Samuel Tamares expounded upon the types of wickedness that can be found among people:

> The evil that is intellectual, the evil that is lying, the evil that is political—that is to say, evil that brings alongside itself an excuse, is the greatest source of destruction in the world. It is the source of all of the disasters and destruction since the time when humanity began, in a small way, to perfect its intellectual capabilities, such as they are. For from that time, private murder, the natural murder of an individual falling upon another, has decreased. But, in place of that decrease, the lying form of murder has increased. And what is that lie? The formation of nations, which are "clubs" organized together for the sake of pursuing and afflicting other nations weaker than they are.[8]

Here, R. Tamares links the artificial groupings of people into nations, and the ensuing national sentiments coupled with "intellectual violence," corrupt minds that justify murder.

---

[4] *Ibid.*

[5] *Ibid.*, 4.

[6] *Ibid.*, 15.

[7] Aaron Samuel Tamares, "Freedom," in *Pacifism and Torah* (Hebrew), ed. Ehud Luz (Jerusalem: Dinur Center

1992), 125.

[8] *Ibid.*, 130.

Aversion to Violent Revolution and Marxism

R. Tamares's commitment to nonviolence led him to reject the violent tactics of revolutionaries. Although he recognized the same oppression and injustice as the most ardent bomb-throwing anarchist, he could not countenance the use of terror, even in the most noble of goals. While still in the *Kolel Perushim*, R. Tamares told the other *batlanim* that their hatred of oppression and injustice must not lead them to violence:

> When he told them of the need to struggle against oppression, his intention was not terror, i.e. placing a bomb under the carriage of some minister. First of all, because such behavior was against the spirit of the *gemara*, second, because that very act is itself an act of war. The proper way to struggle against oppression is to educate the masses and to give them the ability to distinguish between good and evil.[1]

R. Tamares's pacifism pulled him towards and also away from socialism. Initially, the socialist disdain for war earned R. Tamares's strong support.[2] However, when the various European socialist parties supported their governments during the First World War, R. Tamares's pacifism lead him to turn against them:

> He [R. Tamares] was silenced when he found out that the socialists from all the different lands, and the Russian socialists included, who only a moment before the war had agitated each one against his own government, once those same governments declared war and invited the socialists to participate in the fight, the socialists were instantly appeased and began to shout patriotic cheers. Each one handed authority to his own government to play with them in the comedy of "national liberation."[3]

But even deeper than a political disillusionment with the socialist parties over their support for the various war efforts of their own nations, R. Tamares, already before the First World War, had found the entire Marxist way of thinking unsatisfying. "Marxism was a food that was too dry, he desired a socialism of the heart, not a socialism of numbers."[4] R. Tamares was greatly moved by socialist literature that aimed at arousing sympathy for the struggling workers and contempt for wealthy capitalists. But he could not bring himself to endorse a political program that sought to replace one ruling class for another. A "socialism of numbers," he felt, would only replace one type of oppression with another. Marxist materialism would guarantee that a rising

---

[1] Tamares, "Biography," 4.

[2] *Ibid.*, 15.

[3] *Ibid.*, 16.

[4] *Ibid.*, 15.

proletariat would seek to gain only material benefits for itself, and never seek to reform the human heart.[5]

Even still, R. Tamares was sensitized to the oppression and injustice that socialists were struggling against. Yet because R. Tamares considered violence to be the worst form of injustice and oppression, he could not support any movement that would attempt to use those tools in the service of even the highest ends. Ultimately, R. Tamares believed that the most pressing problems facing humanity were not political problems, nor did they have political solutions; rather, R. Tameres believed they were spiritual problems, and he felt that oppression, injustice, and violence, could only be confronted through spiritual resistance and spiritual renewal, first on an individual level, and then on a broader scale.[6]

Passover and Spiritual Resistance

R. Tamares's *derashah* [sermon] for *Shabbat ha-Gadol* in 1906 is a particularly eloquent explication of his vision of spiritual renewal, opposition to oppression, and commitment to pacifist methods. The *derashah*, given the title *"Herut,"* is collected in a volume called *Musar ha-Torah ve-ha-Yahadut*, published in Vilna in 1921. This collection of *derashot* that R. Tamares gave on *Shabbat Shuvah*, *Shabbat ha-Gadol*, and other occasions, demonstrates the facility with which he utilized the *derashah* genre to develop his thinking in a creative fashion and to organize his challenging thoughts around simple and familiar homiletic units. Additionally, the *derashah* format allowed him to inject his lofty idealistic vision of Jewish pacifism into the annual celebrations and religious observances of his community.

"Herut" begins with praises of freedom: Passover is a holiday devoted to that value, and it is indeed a worthy ideal to not only yearn for, but to actively strive to achieve. In *"Herut,"* R. Tamares presents the experience of the Seder night and the memory of the Exodus from Egypt as two cornerstones of a distinctly Jewish strategy for achieving freedom that is different from the freedom as sought after and practiced by Western revolutionaries:

> We can see a little bit of difference between the methods of "taking one's freedom" of the European political parties, and our way of achieving freedom. They took freedom, for example, during the French Revolution, by "barricades" or by throwing bombs upon some despot or another. And we try to achieve freedom by making a seder, eating *matzah*, singing *hallel*...that is to say, by means of repeating well on our lips the memory of the freedom of the Exodus, the Godly flame will be fanned within our souls and we will remember His kindness and His

---

[5] *Ibid.*

[6] *Ibid.*, 10.

actions.[7]

Not surprisingly, R. Tamares found the Jewish method of achieving freedom superior to the political struggles of non-Jews:

> Their strategy of making those revolutions, to respond with evil to the evil of the wicked, can possibly succeed, but it is also possible that they will make matters worse. And in any case, they are nothing more than a temporary cure that is effective for only a short period of time. Just as we have seen take place in all of the lands where freedom was won through a violent revolution, again a short time later, the affliction of despotism returns to the body politic as before. The true cure against despotism, burning out the evil to its roots, is to be found precisely in the Jewish "revolution" of making a Seder if only Israel understand well the idea that is contained in the Seder [...] and the true meaning of *zeman heruteinu*.[8]

R. Tamares then sets out to explain the specific understanding of freedom and slavery that Passover is designed to impart. First, he articulates the philosophical distinctions between two types of wickedness:

> There are two types of evil actions that occur among human beings. That is to say, they emerge from one of two distinct sources. There is evil that comes from physical and bodily sources, and there is wickedness that comes from the intellectual side [...] The bodily destruction falls under the framework of "good and bad" and the intellectual component is under the framework of "truth and falsehood."[9]

Physical and material evil is the cause of "simple, natural murder,"[10] as well as other acts motivated by anger alone. Theft and other actions that are motivated by greed, envy, or lust are likewise the outcomes of this physical wickedness. Intellectual evil on the other hand, causes murderous actions that are "accompanied by justifications and excuses."[11] There is a lie or falsehood at the root of intellectual evil since an unjust act gets disguised as a justifiable one. According to R. Aaron Samuel Tameres, this justified wickedness is the greatest evil, both because it is caused by the corruption of man's higher mental faculties, and because it is responsible for large scale massacres and oppression, even as civilization has slowly stamped out simple physical wickedness and "natural

---

[7] Tamares, "Freedom," 127.
[8] *Ibid.*, 128.
[9] *Ibid.*
[10] *Ibid.*, 129.
[11] *Ibid.*

murder."[12]

R. Tamares next explains that the enslavement of one people by another is a manifestation of the second, more pernicious, form of wickedness. Only a corrupt intellect justifies the malicious rule of one person over another.[13] The spiritual message, therefore, of the Exodus is that God's opposition to falsehood, and in particular the intellectual corruption that can justify slavery, is so severe that he intervened in history to rescue the Israelites and make clear that opposition. Furthermore, Egyptian slavery and Exodus was a necessary precursor to revelation to ensure that the Torah itself would not become a tool in the arsenal of the wicked. We are meant to learn from the Torah's laws an elevated ethical sensitivity, not use them to attack other Jews for their minor transgressions.[14]

Thus far, R. Tamares has provided a richer understanding of Passover as a holiday of freedom, but he has not yet explained how freedom can be achieved in the absence of divine intervention and why pacifist methods are the superior method of achieving freedom. To answer those questions, R. Tamares explains that the superiority of pacifist methods is the result of the intellectual nature of the Egyptian slavery, and other large-scale oppressions. The slave can only be kept in bondage if he himself acknowledges the legitimacy of the arrangement.[15] The path to freedom, and the ability to maintain that freedom, depends upon internalizing the message of the Exodus, namely, that God defends the weak, represents truth, and is opposed to the falsehood and intellectual corruption that is expressed in oppression.[16] If the victim of oppression denies the legitimacy of that oppression, and asserts that God, too, is opposed to oppression, then the victim is already better off; the slave is already partially free. This is the purpose of the rituals of Passover. They remind us what God's values are, and that freedom from oppression is our birthright as people.

In contrast to utilizing peaceful Passover rituals, R. Tameres believed that the use of violence to achieve freedom or justice is doomed to failure for two reasons. First, R. Tamares was concerned that an individual who used violent means in self-defense, would ultimatey come to use those same means aggressively.[17] Second, he believed that any use of violence would in the long-run only strengthen the rule of force and weaken the forces of justice:

> A whole nation, just as an individual, must arrange its way of life on the foundation of the aphorism mentioned by Tosafot (*Bava Kama* 23), "one must be more concerned about harming others than in being harmed by others." Indeed, for when a

---

[12] *Ibid.*, 130.
[13] *Ibid.*, 131.
[14] *Ibid.*
[15] *Ibid.*, 136.
[16] *Ibid.*, 133.
[17] *Ibid.*, 137.

person strives to guard his own fists from causing harm to others he causes, through this, the reign of the God of truth and justice over the world, and he gives strength to the kingdom of righteousness. This strengthening of righteousness will in turn guard him against being harmed by others. This is not the case if he prioritizes his own self-defense and keeps his fists ready to defend against the attacks of others. Behold, by this very way of thinking he weakens the power of justice and arouses the characteristics of wickedness.

As the text of the Passover Haggadah states, "And I shall pass [through Egypt] on this night—I and not an emissary." The Holy Blessed One could have given Israel the ability to exact revenge on the Egyptians themselves. However the Holy Blessed One did not want to show them how to use their own fists. Even though at that moment it would be to protect themselves from the wicked, it would end up causing the spread of the use of the fist throughout the world, and the defenders would eventually become pursuers [...]

We can now explain the *beraita* that discusses the verse, "and you shall not leave, not any one, from the door of his home until the morning." Rav Yosef taught, "once permission was given to the destroyer, he will not differentiate between wicked and righteous." At first glance, this *beraita* is a deep contradiction to the statement in the Haggadah of "I and not an emissary." How can the *beraita* say, "once permission was given to the destroyer!" But according to our ways the two statements match. For the *beraita* is coming to explain why the Holy Blessed One sought to exact vengeance Himself and did not allow the Israelites even to look. The answer is that God acted in this way so as not to arouse the destroyer that is within the Israelites themselves. For once permission is given, he will not distinguish between wicked and righteous and the defender will in the end become a pursuer.[18]

These passages recognize that violence in self-defense can be just, yet R. Tamares argued that resorting to violence was always self-defeating when confronting wickedness of the intellectual variety. This type of wickedness emerges out of a distorted mind. Such a mind wrongly believes that the strong are allowed to abuse those weaker than they. By responding to this unjustified violence with yet more violence, the victim is agreeing with his oppressor that

---

[18] *Ibid.*

force should be the prime determinant in human relations. In R. Tamares's wording, he "strengthens the power of the fist." R. Tamares does not discuss the use of violence in personal self-defense. Since such "natural and physical" wickedness is not accompanied by a corrupted intellect, on the contrary it is accompanied by a guilty conscience,[19] there is no risk that responding violently in individual self-defense will strengthen a false belief about force.

The pacifist orientation of "*Herut*" is focused on the use of nonviolence in the quest for freedom. Although the message is universally applicable, "*Herut*" addresses the Jewish people and their own quest for freedom. Yet, in R. Tamares's other writings, pacifism is given a more important place: the very purpose of Jewish existence is to spread a pacifist morality throughout the world.

The Pacifist Mission of the Jewish People

R. Tamares wrote of a universal mission of the Jewish people. The basic idea is this: Jews exist as a people to spread the moral precepts of the Torah, including a pacifist aversion to bloodshed, to the rest of humanity. Since an aversion to bloodshed is part and parcel of the moral message of the Torah, the Jewish mission to humanity must be accomplished without the use of force. The suffering of the Jews in exile and attempts to alleviate that suffering, must therefore by evaluated in light of the Jews' purpose for existing as a people.

In "*Te'udat Yisrael: Kivush ha-Tevel u-Kivush ha-Yetzer*," another *derashah* published in the collection *Musar ha-Torah ve-ha-Yahadut*, R. Tamares develops a dialectical conception of progress. Material and spiritual progress follow one from the other and lift humanity from barbarism to moral civilization. Progress, in both of its aspects, is the selection of the good from the bad. Material progress is the refinement of what is useful from what is not useful. Spiritual progress is the refinement of good moral character from bad moral character. "Enlightenment" is R. Tamares's term for the effort to increase good over bad in the physical realm; "Torah" is the term for God's method to increase the good over the bad in the spiritual realm.[20]

R. Tamares argued that both aspects of progress were valuable and necessary. Indeed, "*derekh eretz kadmah la-Torah*," that is, it is first necessary for civilization to establish a beachhead through material progress.[21] However, technological civilization alone without concomitant moral development will result in great evil. The Pharaoh who enslaved the Jewish people, in R. Tamares's conception, was attempting physical technological development without moral development.[22] The form of enlightenment that yields mastery over nature is the common destiny of humanity. Israel, however, was entrusted with the Torah to

---

[19] *Ibid.*, 129.
[20] Aaron Samuel Tamares, "The Destiny of Israel: Conquest of the Earth or Conquest of the Heart," in The Morality of the Torah and Judaism (Hebrew) (Vilna: 1912), 80.
[21] *Ibid.*, 79.
[22] *Ibid.*, 84.

promote morality among all people.²³ In a 1913 essay *"Le-She'eilat ha-Yahadut,"* R. Tamares reiterated this point, "Judaism, throughout its long existence, has but one destiny—to uplift the spirit of humanity in the image of the people of Israel, chosen by the Higher Intelligence to receive its Word."²⁴

Once R. Tamares has claimed that the "Higher Intelligence" has imparted a moral model for all humankind upon the People of Israel, R. Tamares must flesh-out the salient content of that moral message. The pinnacle of Judaism's moral message is an aversion to bloodshed, and the "extreme revulsion of the Jew towards murder and bloodshed," was for R. Tamares, a source of confidence in the moral success of Judaism:

> For what is there that is more precious and more holy to a living person than the blood that flows in his heart? Therefore, there can be no test more exacting, to make known the moral perfection of a person, than his attitude towards the blood of his fellow. "For the soul is in the blood," the Torah says with the intention of increasing the value of the soul of one who has blood. But this verse will not lie if we interpret it also as reflecting on the soul of the other side. That is to say, the way in which a person treats the blood of his fellow is the prime test of the character of his soul.²⁵

We have already seen how R. Tamares, writing in his autobiography, reflected upon his childhood commiseration with his gentile neighbors over the loss of their son during the Russian-Ottoman War. That event did not merely sear into the consciousness of the future rabbi the grim reality of war. For R. Tamares, the co-mingled tears of the stricken parents and the Jewish boy symbolized the role of the Jewish people:

> That action from long ago, the little Jewish boy crying alongside a gentile woman over the death of her son, a sacrifice of war, served [years later] as a symbol for the Jewish mission in the midst of the other nations, to arouse among all peoples the appropriate feeling of hatred for warfare. For it is only the free and refined Jewish spirit, that is composed of a combination of Torah and *galut* [exile], that is capable of feeling with exceeding poignancy the disgrace that it is to drag a human-being to be a "bull in the arena," the horror that is bloodshed.²⁶

For R. Tamares, all people could come to appreciate the horror and injustice

---

23 *Ibid.*, 90.

24 Aaron Samuel Tamares, "On the Jewish Question," in Pacifism and Torah (Hebrew) ed. Ehud Luz (Jerusalem: Dinur Center 1992), 149.

25 *Ibid.*, 152.

26 Tamares, "Biography," 16.

of war. For many, such as the young Tamares's gentile neighbors, that realization only came when a son died in battle, and even then not completely. Nationalism clouded the vision of most people. The Jews, however, their moral consciousness refined by the experiences of the *galut*, were capable of a keen moral awareness and therefore had a crucial role to play in history.

A Reevaluation of *Galut*

As we have seen, R. Tamares believed that *galut* was responsible for purifying the moral sensitivity and moral judgment of the Jewish people. Several of his writings discuss *galut* and evaluate its hardships in light of the spiritual gains that can accrue to a nationless people. The arch evils afflicting the world, nationalism, warfare, and violent revolutionary struggle, were all evils that exilic existence had spared the Jews. The viability of the Jews' educational mission to humanity, and therefore the betterment of all humanity, was dependent upon the continued exilic existence of the Jews.

Furthermore, the powerlessness of exilic existence and the frequent victimization of the Jews in *galut* reinforced the moral teachings of the Torah. A victim of injustice understands the importance of justice; a victim of violence appreciates the horror of violence:

> This destiny [of the renewal of the world through moral transformation] cannot be undertaken by any new political party or sect as effectively as that ancient people, whose yearning for freedom and justice are its ancient heritage from days gone by, that is to say the Nation of Israel in *galut*.[27]

> The long education of the Jew on the knees of the noble spirit of the Torah, on the one hand, and the low spirit of the burden of exile, on the other, removed from our midst all base egoism which is the filth of the primordial serpent.[28]

As an individual too, R. Tamares grappled with the question of *galut*. He weathered his entire career serving as a rabbi in a small community, rejecting offers for a teaching position in Odessa.[29] Reflecting upon this self-imposed exile, R. Tamares concluded that a positive impact upon the world could be effected even in relative isolation and obscurity:

> He [R. Tamares] involved himself, principally, in improving his own spiritual status [...] However, his inward concentration and focus did not mean that he despaired of repairing the world and considered that task to be lost from the outset. On the contrary, he believed that the redemption of the world, its

---

[27] Tamares, "Jewish Question," 155.

[28] *Ibid.*, 154.

[29] Tamares, "Biography," 12.

renewal, and its improvement were sure to come. However, he was convinced that the renewal of the world would not come by means of shrewd politics nor through artificial organizations of society, rather only through sharpening the moral-esthetic sense—sharpening the ability to distinguish between good and evil. And, since according to this "war plan," an individual went to battle first and foremost with his own self, it followed that there was no need for a freedom fighter to be in a central urban area, among the multitudes who can be organized into demonstrations in the street. Rather, it is possible to sit in a small village, and even in the forest, and be involved with liberating the world.[30]

If an individual could liberate the world sitting in a small village or in the midst of a forest, a nation could also play a role in world history, even without a territory under its control. On the contrary, R. Tamares argued, exile could be advantageous for the truly crucial task of moral refinement:

Contemporary youths, members of the new movements, do not understand at all that Israel has a special destiny in the world [...] Because of this, they present the *galut* as a simple and secular phenomenon that does not contain within itself any advantage [...] Recently, they have decided amongst themselves "*beli neder*" to remove the *galut* with all the means at their disposal, whether to find some new land or to change the organization of the lands where they already reside. But all of their struggles are for naught.[31]

Exile, and accompanying antisemitism, are not, God forbid, some sort of incitement or pogrom from the Holy Blessed One when we fall behind in offering up to him "taxes" in the form of *mitzvot*. Rather, exile is a necessary result of our destiny and our role.[32]

The exile scattered the Jews among the nations of the world and gave Jews the potential to serve as a pacifist and non-nationalist element within their host countries—freed by their statelessness from the morally corrupting effects of nationalism—bearing witness to the true outrage and horror of violence. Jewish patriotism during the First World War was therefore particularly upsetting to R. Tamares. Instead of serving as a moral example, offering sympathy to all victims of the war and condemnation to all combatants, Jewish communi-

---

[30] *Ibid.*, 13.

[31] Aaron Samuel Tamares, "The Destiny of the Prophets," in *The Morality of the Torah and Judaism* (Hebrew) (Vilna: 1912), 132.

[32] *Ibid.*, 133.

ties offered blind support for their homelands and an opportunity for moral excellence was lost.[33]

Zionism: From Early Support to Intense Rejection

Given his positive evaluation of exilic Jewish existence, it is not surprising that R. Tamares was an opponent of the Zionist attempt to end the exile. Considering his disdainful attitude towards political activism, it is also not surprising that R. Tamares doubted that any meaningful gains could result from Zionist activities. Moreover, given R. Tamares's wholly spiritual and pacifist conception that he feels makes up the true Jewish identity, it is not so surprising that the Zionist dream of normalizing the Jewish condition—including a return to national life—was seen by R. Tamares as a betrayal of the Jewish mission.

What is somewhat surprising, however, is that R. Tamares was present in 1900 at the Fourth Zionist Congress in London—not as a protester or observer, but as a delegate![34] R. Aaron Samuel Tamares's presence at the Fourth Zionist Congress was the culmination of a decade of vocal support for Zionism that began in his days as a yeshiva student and included offering the talents of his caustic pen in service of the new movement. The London Congress marked the pinnacle of R. Tamares's involvement with Zionism. As the character of the Zionist movement, its goals, and its means became clear to R. Tamares, and as his own thinking matured, R. Tamares retreated from his earlier support, recanted his pro-Zionist essays, and emerged as a passionate voice of religious anti-Zionism.

R. Tamares first identified as a Zionist during the years that he was a student at the yeshiva of Vollozhon, beginning in 1890. R. Tamares was a member of *Netzah Yisrael*, a student Zionist organization allied with *Hovevei Tziyon*.[35] This identification continued after Herzl's first Zionist Congress in 1897. R. Tamares was particularly attracted by Ahad Ha-Am's call to create a spiritual center for the Jewish people. R. Tamares understood Zionism to be an idealistic movement that would spark positive spiritual renewal among the Jews.[36] In "*Shilumim le-Riv Tziyon*," published in *Ha-Melitz* in 1899, R. Tamares predicted that Zionism and Jewish independence would enhance the spiritual heritage of the Jewish tradition.[37]

Years later though, writing in his autobiography, R. Tamares described, with some sarcasm, his early attraction to Zionism:

> Sometime later, starting in 1897, the Zionist Movement appeared: Herzl, the Congresses, the speech of Max Nordau from

---

[33] Tamares, "Biography," 17.

[34] Ehud Luz, introduction to *Pacifism and Torah* (Hebrew), by Aaron Samuel Tamares (Jerusalem: Dinur Center 1992), x.

[35] *Ibid.*, viii.

[36] *Ibid.*, ix.

[37] *Ibid.*,

the podium at the Congress, rebuking the nations and their governments for pursuing the Jews, his demand to the nations that they repair this injustice by handing *Eretz Yisrael* to the Jews (why an injustice which they had committed should be fixed with what is in the hands of others—i.e. the Turks—nobody had yet thought to ask that question). The rabbi [R. Tamares] supported this movement with all of his might and soul on account of his thinking that Zionism was a movement of freedom and justice, fighting against evil and oppression. He was dragged into this error by the above mentioned speech by Nordau; this rabbi was still lacking, (asking his forgiveness for saying so), the correct discernment to evaluate that type of "justice" which is found on the lips of those who fight—not for the redemption of man, but for territory [...] At that time no person had yet occasion to witness freedom fighters, of noble spirit, after they have achieved their goals, afflict and choke others with the same pain that had been done to them, all in the name of freedom.[38]

R. Tamares had been particularly drawn to the cultural Zionism of Ahad Ha'am.[39] Although the cultural activities that the cultural Zionists advocated were a direct challenge to European Orthodoxy, which was quite happy to see the regnant European Jewish culture continue unabated, the cultural Zionist emphasis on a broader Jewish revival, that would encompass culture in all its forms, appealed to religious Jews whose conception of Judaism was more spiritual and idealistic than national or territorial. "The best of Orthodoxy," in R. Tamares's words, were drawn to Zionism by the cultural Zionist appropriation of the most "lofty verses of the Bible," and the "brightest statements of *Hazal*." Writing in his autobiography, R. Tamares responded to the appeal of cultural Zionism with a brief sarcastic remark, "How noble the spirit, how wonderful the Judaism, that depends upon ownership of a 'private yard.'"[40] R. Tamares looked askance at a form of Judaism that primarily depended upon a piece of territory. He came to view the cultural Zionist linkage of Jewish renewal with Zionist political goals as a negation of the possibility for any spiritual potential of cultural Zionism.

Putting aside R. Tamares's sarcastic remarks in his autobiography, written many years after his disillusionment with Zionism, the proximate causes of that disillusionment came precisely during the time that R. Tamares was most connected to the Zionist movement and its formal leadership. As a known rabbinic supporter of Zionism, following the publication of his 1899 article in

---

38 Tamares, "Biography," 6.
39 *Ibid.*, 6.
40 *Ibid.*

Ha-Melitz, R. Tamares participated in a regional meeting in Vilna of the Zionist movement. R. Tamares was distressed by the assimilated youth who dominated the meeting, leaving the rabbis present to sit and watch in silence:

> The rabbis sat before them with guarded breath, as if afraid, God forbid, to disturb the great intelligences there, speakers of Russian, who used lofty words, completely new to the rabbis— such as "agitation," "propaganda," and "party discipline." Not one word of "Jewish" was spoken from the mouths of those youths during the entire gathering, and certainly there was no remembrance of the "lofty and great Jewish ideal." For two days these children sat and prattled above the heads of the rabbis—some of whom's hair had already fallen from their beards—in Russian, a language that most of the rabbis could not even understand.

He [R. Tamares] left that gathering with a great cooling of his prior fervor. About one month later, in the summer of 5660 (1900), *"Ahad ha-Rabanim ha-Margishim"* [R. Tamares] was chosen by the Zionists of Brisk to attend the Fourth Zionist Congress, that was to take place in London, and he traveled there. All of those same flaws of emptiness, bureaucracy, and formality that were revealed at the meeting in Vilna, returned in greater force at the London Congress, and were the entirety of the Congress, except for the addition of a verbal announcement, which was met with applause deafening to the ears, when it was heard by the delegates who had gathered from all parts of the world: Dr. Herzl had been invited to eat lunch with the Turkish sultan!

> The fantasies he had previously held regarding raising the Jewish spirit and struggling against oppression, that he had first thought to find within Zionism, melted away completely. Immediately, while still in London, he sent word to the Kovno Zionists forbidding them to print his [pro-Zionist] article in a booklet. He returned home with his spirit broken by disappointment.[41]

The practical and political orientation of official Zionism, together with its fixation on what to R. Tamares were trivialities—such as Herzl's meetings with world leaders—lead R. Tamares to realize that the attraction he had felt towards Zionism was due to elements of the movement that were marginalized within the circles that counted. R. Tamares could not entertain an allegiance to an idealistic Zionism, devoted to confronting oppression and raising the Jewish spirit high, after sitting through regional Zionist meetings and international Zionist congresses where nobody with any influence within the movement was remotely interested in R. Tamares's concerns. It was not the irreligiosity per-se

---

[41] *Ibid.*, 7-8.

of the youths in Vilna, or the delegates in London, that was off-putting to R. Tamares. Indeed, the *haredi* intolerance for religious lapses among Zionists had originally pushed R. Tamares into the arms of Zionism.[42] What R. Tamares found so offensive was the lack of Jewish spirit among the Zionist leadership, as R. Tamares defined it, a failing that was deeper than a simple binary of allegiance to, or non–observance of, the rituals of Judaism. R. Tamares saw an assimilationist spirit of the worst kind leading the Zionists in Vilna to conduct their meeting in sophisticated Russian. No Jew devoted to a true spiritual revival of Judaism could be seduced by the superficial nationalism of the Congress and visions of Herzl dining with princes and sultans.

As his own thought matured, R. Tamares's opposition to Zionism became far more categorical and absolute. It became more than a rejection of a particular movement with particular flaws. As R. Tamares's pacifist philosophy developed, and with it his positive evaluation of exilic Jewish existence, the very goals and material methods of Zionism became anathema to him. In his later, mature writings, Zionism became nothing less than a betrayal of a prime element of the Jewish mission in history: to impart ethical living and pacifist values to humanity while in exile.

The earliest manifestations of religious anti-Zionism were motivated by opposition to the irreligious lifestyle of many Zionists, the secular orientation of Zionist leaders from Leon Pinkser to Theodor Herzl, and the implicit challenge of Jewish nationalism to the traditional rabbinic leadership of Jewish communal life. Even Zionist sympathizers and supporters such as R. Naftali Zvi Yehudah Berlin came into conflict with the leadership of *Hovevei Tziyon* over the emerging irreligious character of the early *Hovevei Tziyon* settlement of Gadera and the Zionist movement's response to the *shemitah* of 1887. The denunciations of rabbis less favorably disposed to Zionism, such as Rabbi Hayim Soloveitchik of Brisk, were even more strident.[43] A common denominator between the equivocal support of Zionism by R. Berlin and the harsh denunciation of R. Soloveitchik was their characterization of the elements of Zionism that they each condemned as rebellious departures from proper and appropriate Jewish lifestyle.

Hasidic opposition to Zionism however, had been more intrinsic. As Aviezer Ravitzky observes in his *Messianism, Zionism, and Jewish Religious Radicalism*, Hasidic anti-Zionism, specifically of the Munkacz and Satmar schools of thought, has always viewed Zionism and the State of Israel through an entirely theological lens, rather than through a pragmatic analysis of the movement and the state. They have claimed that Zionism is an inherently demonic force and deterministically doomed to failure, irrespective of the level of religious observance of the Zionists or the religious character or policies of the State of

---

42 *Ibid.*, 9.

43 Aviezer Ravitzky, *Messianism, Zionism, and Jewish Religious Radicalism*, trans. Michael Swirsky and Jonathan chipman (Chicago: University of Chicago Press, 1996 (orig. Tel Aviv: Am Oved, 1993)), 13.

Israel.[44]

Ravitzky highlights how Zionism was attacked by Hasidic thinkers, specifically as a betrayal of the true redemption. Rabbi Shalom Dov Baer Schneersohn of Lubavitch, writing in 1899, attacked Zionist activities for undermining the perfect redemption of the future. The long awaited redemption of Israel, R. Schneersohn wrote, would be complete and entirely miraculous, beyond any event in Israel's history:

> The redemption that took place through Moses and Aaron was also not a full one, for the Jewish people were once again enslaved; and even less so was the redemption at the hands of Hananiah, Mishael, and Azariah [...] In the present exile we must expect redemption and salvation only at the hands of the Holy One, Blessed be He, Himself, not by flesh and blood, and thus will our redemption be complete.[45]

By characterizing the biblical redemption of Israel's history as incomplete in comparison to the future redemption, R. Schneersohn denied Zionists the ability to use those events as historic precedents or inspirations for their own planned liberations. "Let my people go," may have been a Zionist slogan, linking modern political liberation with the Exodus, but R. Schneersohn could respond that the authentic liberation and redemption of the future would transcend even the paradigm of the Egyptian Exodus.

The Bialer Rebbe, Rabbi Yitzhak Yaakov Rabinowitz, also attacked Zionism in his book, *Divrei Binah* (1913), for betraying the authentic faith in a miraculous Redemption:

> Zionism represents the struggle of the Evil Urge and its assistants, who wish to bring us down, heaven forbid, by false and harmful opinions, claiming that, if Israel will not perform some concrete action to settle in the Holy Land and to actually work the land, then they will be unable to leave this bitter exile [...] In fact, Israel have no greater foe and enemy, who wish to deprive them of their pure faith, that our salvation and redemption transcends the way of nature and human intelligence.[46]

In this passage, any attempt to improve the Jewish condition is a dangerous force eroding the sustaining faith in a perfect, complete, and entirely divine redemption.

Ravitzky portrays R. Schneersohn as the originator of religious anti-Zionism

---

[44] *Ibid.*, 137.

[45] S.Z. Landau and Joseph Rabinowitz, *Or la-Yesharim* (Warsaw: 1900), 58. Quoted and translated in Ravitzky, 17.

[46] Yitzhak Yaakov Rabinowitz, *Divrei Binah* (Lublin, 1913), 27a. Quoted and translated in Ravitzky, 18.

based in large part on his messianic argument. Only R. Schneersohn had developed this line of thinking among the contributors to the anti-Zionist booklet *Or la-Yesharim*, published in 1900. The other contributors focused their attacks on the irreligiosity of many Zionists.[47] By 1903, however, *Da'at ha-Rabanim*, a second booklet of anti-Zionist essays, contained numerous essays based upon the messianic argument first developed by R. Schneersohn.[48]

This growing trend within religious anti-Zionism, that would reach its apotheosis in the anti-Zionism of Munkacz and Satmar, shares certain aspects with the anti-Zionism of R. Tamares's mature thought, but also departs from it in significant ways. Both varieties of religious anti-Zionism have surpassed a simplistic reaction against Zionist irreligiosity, but rather are responding to the essential nature of Zionism. A broadly tolerant outlook, such as what lead R. Naftali Zvi Yehudah Berlin to support Zionism despite his misgivings, would not have provided an answer to the religious anti-Zionism of either Rabbis Schneersohn or Tamares. Indeed, R. Tamares displayed great tolerance towards less observant Jews in his writings, yet he was a staunch opponent of Zionism. Observance of Jewish ritual would not have mollified R. Tamares, because for R. Tamares, the Zionist movement was intrinsically a movement that betrayed an essential (if not *the* essential) component of Judaism.

If R. Tamares shared the broader religious anti-Zionist perception of Zionism as an inherent betrayal of an essential characteristic of Judaism, he differed in his analysis of the nature of that betrayal. It was not a betrayal of the faith in redemption, per se, but rather a betrayal of an essential Jewish attribute of pacifism and anti-nationalism. As we saw above, R. Tamares rejected the assertion of both Zionists and Hasidic anti-Zionists that exile was entirely a punishment for Jewish sin. Exile, for R. Tamares, was intrinsic to the Jewish spiritual mission. It was the spiritual mission of Judaism iself that was threatened by Zionism. Jews were faced with a choice between becoming a nation operating on the political plane or remaining faithful to a religious tradition that demanded pacifism and rejection of the political.

Ironically, R. Tamares's understanding of the idealistic nature of Jewish peoplehood was mirrored by one of the strongest proponents of religious Zionism: Rabbi Abraham Isaac HaCohen Kook. Writing in the aftermath of "the war to end all wars," R. Kook discussed the timing of the return to Jewish national life:

> We left the political arena under duress but also with a certain inner willingness, until that happy time when a polity could be governed without wickedness or barbarism. The delay has been necessary. We have been disgusted with the terrible iniquities of ruling during the evil age. Now the time has come, is very

---

[47] Ravitzky, 19.

[48] *Ibid.*

near, when the world will be refined and we shall be able to prepare ourselves [...] It is not for Jacob to engage in government as long as it entails bloodshed, as long as it requires a knack for wickedness.[49]

As Ravitzky explains, based upon the messianic orientation of R. Kook's Zionism, R. Kook implicitly accepted the *haredi* critique of pre-messianic Jewish statehood. It seems from the above quote that R. Kook also implicitly accepted R. Tamares's critique of Jewish warfare and political activity. R. Kook's messianic Zionism was dependent upon a messianic framework through which R. Kook understood both Zionist colonization and the broader post-World War I international scene. R. Tamares saw the First World War as the nail in the coffin of European civilization and final proof of the horrors of war. Any remaining sympathy he felt towards Zionism was lost when the Zionist movement involved itself in the Allied war effort. In his words, "during the global bacchanalia, Zionism was revealed to be a twin sister to all the monsters of the world."[50] R. Kook was taken by the lofty rhetoric surrounding the war and believed that it was indeed the final war of an old global political paradigm and the dawn of a newer, "refined" world.

The First World War marked the dying of an old civilization and the end of a global political paradigm as both R. Tamares and R. Kook understood it. However, the Second World War and the Holocaust, which occurred only a few years after the deaths of R. Tamares in 1931, and R. Kook in 1935, might very well have shaken the attitudes of each towards Judaism and Zionism. R. Kook's messianism and belief in historical progress would have been challenged by humanity's sinking to new depths of brutality and violence and a State of Israel gaining and maintaining its independence through warfare in an as-of-yet-unredeemed world. Perhaps R. Tamares as well, so perceptive in his awareness of the costs of power, would have recognized in the destruction of the Holocaust, the costs of powerlessness.

---

[49] Abraham Isaac Kook, *Orot* (Jerusalem: 1963), 14. Quoted and translated in Ravitzky 120.
[50] Tamares, "Biography," 19.

העורכים המאוחרים.

כעת, לאור מסקנה זו, כאשר אנו באים לבדוק את ההבדלים התרבותיים והלכתיים בין א״י לבבל, המצויים במסורותיהם של הנחותי. יהיה קשה לאפיין הבדלים אלו לתקופת האמוראים בני הדור השלישי והרביעי, יתכן שהם משקפים תקופה מאוחרת יותר. אפשר שההבדלים אלה אינם משקפים הבדלים הסטוריים בין המרכזים כלל, אלא משקפים את תוצאת עיונם ולימודם התיאורתי של העורכים.

אתא רב דימי אלא את הלשון 'יתיב רב דימי'. לדוגמא (שבת קמה ע"א): 'יתיב רב דימי וקאמר
לה להא שמעתא. אמר ליה אביי לרב דימי: אתון משמיה דרב מתניתון ולא קשיא לכו, אנן משמיה
דשמואל מתנינן לה—וקשיא...'.[38] וכן (פסחים מד ע"א):'יתיב רב דימי וקאמר לה להא שמעתא.
אמר ליה אביי לרב דימי... והתנן: המקפה של תרומה...'.[39] הבחנת לשון זו מלמדת שעורכי
התלמוד מודעים לחשיבותו של המונח 'כי אתא רב דימי', ואינם רוצים שאביי יערער על המונח
הזה. לכן הם אינם מביאים את המונח כאשר אביי דוחה את דברי רב דימי.

גם במקרים בהם אביי דוחה את 'כי אתא רב דימי' (וכפי שציינתי, מעט מאוד), יהיה בנוסף
לדחיית זו, 'כי אתא רבין'—שמעה א"י סותרת. התלמוד לא מסתפק בדברי אביי לדחות את שמעת
א"י, אלא דוחה את שמעת רב דימי בשמועה א"י נגדית מא"י. כגון (שבת עב ע"ב):

כי אתא רב דימי אמר למאן דאמר אשם ודאי בעי ידיעה בתחילה... אמר ליה
אביי: הרי חטאת, דבעינן ידיעה בתחלה ופליגי רבי יוחנן ורבי שמעון בן לקיש!
אישתיק. אמר ליה: דלמא במעשה דלאחר הפרשה קאמרת, וכדרב המנונא?—
אמר ליה: אין. כי אתא רבין אמר: הכל מודים בשפחה חרופה...[40]

ולא בכדי אביי הוא זה שדוחה את עמדתו של רב דימי, חשיבותו של אביי רבה מכוון שנטל
חלק חשוב בעריכת התלמוד הבבלי. ועל כך כבר עמדו חוקרים רבים וכבר כינה אותו רי"ן אפשטיין
"מראשי הבונים של התלמוד הבבלי".[41] אביי, כעורך אחד השלבים הראשונים בעריכת הבבלי, אינו
מסכים לקבל את מסורתו של רב דימי, מא"י, כלא ניתנת לערעור. ההפך, הוא חולק עליה ואינו
מסכים לכל מסורת ארצי ישראלית. אך העורכים המאוחרים שכבר מצאו את הלשון 'כי אתא רב
דימי' אינם מוכנים לקבל את ערעור דברי רב דימי על ידי אביי, ולכן משתמשים ברבין, בלשון
'כי אתא רבין'.

לסיכום, בעבודה זו השתדלתי לעקוב אחרי הלשון 'כי אתא רב פלוני'. להפתעתי גליתי שלשון
זו חשובה לעורכי התלמוד. כמות המסורות העלה בי את החשד, שלפנינו מונח של עורכי התלמוד,
שכבר בשלב קדום(הדורות המאוחרים של האמוראים?) של עריכת התלמוד הצמידתהו לדברי
רב דימי. מכוון שמצאם של המסורות שהנחותי מביאים הוא מא"י. העורכים ערכו את הסוגיא,
כך שהמונח ישמש לנעילת הדיון ההלכתי, או התחלת דיון בבסיס הלכתי מוצק מא"י. עורכים
מאוחרים היו שמודעים לערכו של המונח, אך המונח גרם להם קושי, מכוון שאינו הסתדר עם
מגמתם בסוגיא התמודדו עם הקושי הנ"ל בשתי צורות, שהעיקרית שבהם היא דחיית המסורת
של רב דימי בנחותי אחר, רבין. רבין המופיע בתלמוד עם מינוח דומה, 'כי אתא רבין'. מינוח זה
נוצר ,וכן גם המסורות של רבין, שהשתעתקו כלשונם כפי שמובאים ע"י רב דימי[בעיקר השמות]
אך בשינוי ההלכה, כתוצאה מהתמודדות עם המינוח 'כי אתא רב דימי, ז"א שזו פיקציה של

[38] תגובה באותה לשון(העברה) ישנה בערובין כא ע"א–ע"ב: 'יתיב רב דימי וקאמר לה להא שמעתא. אמר ליה אביי
לרב דימי: מאי טעמא... אמר ליה: קרקפנא, חזיתיה לרישיך בי עמודי כי אמרה רבי יוחנן, להא שמעתא. איתמר
נמי, כי אתא רבין אמר רבי יוחנן...'.
[39] וראה עוד: נזיר לו ע"א; זבחים ע ע"א; חולין צט ע"ב; בכורות יא ע"א; בכורות כב ע"ב; תרומה ד ע"ב.
[40] עוד לדוגמא: שבת עו ע"א; ב"ק מג ע"א.
[41] רי"ן אפשטיין, מבוא לנוסח המשנה, עמ' 369. ועיין עוד הנ"ל, מבואות לספרת האמוראים עמ 12; ד. רוזנטל
"פרקא דאביי", תרביץ מז(1977), עמ' 98 הערה 6 ושם מסכם את הדיון בענין זה. ולאאחרונה י. זוסמן, "וישוב
לירושלמי נזיקין", מחקרי תלמוד א', 103 הערה 194.

רב דימי, אמר רבי יצחק בר אבודימי, משום רבינו אמרו: עובד כוכבים ועבד
הבא על בת ישראל—הולד ממזר. רבי יהושע בן לוי אומר: הולד מקולקל.
למאן? אילימא לקהל, הא אמר רבי יהושע: הולד כשר! אלא לכהונה, דכולהו
אמוראי דמכשרי, מודו שהולד פגום לכהונה מק"ו מאלמנה... אמר ליה אביי:
מאי חזית דסמכת אדרב דימי? סמוך אדרבין! דכי אתא רבין אמר: רבי נתן
ורבי יהודה הנשיא מורים בה להיתירא...

בדוגמא זו אביי מתייחס לדברי ר' יוסף ומביא את מסורותו של רבין. אם כך אנו מוצאים
שאביי מכיר את שתי המסורות, של רבין ושל רב דימי. אך כלעיל, איני טוען שבכל מקום שרבין
מופיע עם רב דימי, לפנינו מעשי העורכים. אלא שהשאלה שצריכה להשאל היא—האם הלשון
'כי אתא רב פלוני' שמשה את אביי ורב יוסף? ותשובתי היא לא. זה הוא מעשה עורכים. יתכן
שהמסורת המובאת בשמם אכן נכונה היסטורית. אך ההצעה כי אתא אי מאוחרת. ואכן מצאנו
פעמים ספורות מאוד שרב דימי יופיע ללא הפתיחה 'כי אתא רב דימי', למרות שהוא ראוי להיות
שם.[35] כלומר, גם אם נטען שרב יוסף ואביי מביאים לידי התנגשות את מסורת רב דימי ורבין, אופן
הצגת הדברים מלמד אותנו על ייחסם של העורכים ללשון 'כי אתא רב דימי'.

כעת נעבור לדרך השניה שבה דוחה התלמוד את דבריו של רב דימי. והיא הבאת אי הסכמה
מצד האמורא אביי, רבו ומורו של רב דימי.[36] כגון, יבמות עח ע"א:

כי אתא רב דימי אמר רבי יוחנן: מצרי שני שנשא מצרית ראשונה—בנה שני
הוי אלמא בתר אימיה שדינן ליה. אמר ליה אביי אלא הא דאמר ר' יוחנן
הפריש חטאת מעוברת וילדה רצה מתכפר בה, רצה מתכפר בולדה... אישתיק.
א"ל: דלמא שאני התם, דכתיב... א"ל: קרקפנא! חזיתיה לרישך ביני עמודי כי
אמר רבי יוחנן להא שמעתא.

רב דימי הבקי בשמועותיו, ואומר על מה של שמע, לא שמעתי (פסחים לד ע"ב). מקבל ביקורת
נוקבת על שמעל בתפקידו בשעת לימודו אצל רבי יוחנן, ולכן אין מתקבלת שמעתו להלכה.[37]
אציין שהמקרים בהם אביי סותר את 'כי אתא רב דימי' מעטים מאוד. בבדיקתי מצאתי שישנה
דרך אחרת, בה התלמוד מציג את דחיית רב דימי ע"י אביי. במקומות אלו אין התלמוד יציין 'כי

[35] ראה לדוגמא ברכות מד ע"א:
א"ל אביי לרב דימי מאי ניהו ברכה אחת מעין שלוש? א"ל אפירי דעץ על העץ ועל פרי העץ ועל
תנובת השדה ועל ארץ חמדה טובה ורחבה שהנחלת לאבותינו לאכול מפריה ולשבוע מטובה רחם ה' אלהינו על
ישראל עמך ועל ירושלים עירך...
אביי בן הדור הרביעי לחכמי בבל אינו יודע מהי 'ברכה מעין שלוש'(!), להם ישנה ברכה אחת לאחר סיום האכילה.
ורק כאשר בא רב דימי לבבל, מפרש לו מהי ברכה זו. עד דור רביעי ברכה זו אינה מוכרת בבבל, אך בא"י (ובמקורות
א"י, כתוספתא והירושלמי) היא מוכרת. לכן במשנה בבל נוסח המשנה הוא "וחכמים אומרים ברכה אחת"(כך בכ"י
היד של הבבלי; וכן במשנת בבל בכ"י פריז 329–328; וכך בתוספתא ע"י וינה. ראה תוספתא זרעים, מהדורת
ליברמן פ"ד ה"ו, עמ' 19. וראה תוספתא כפשוטה, עמ' 61), ולא "וחכמים אומרים ברכה מעין שלוש" כבמשניות
נוסח א"י. בדוגמא בניגוד לדוגמאות האחרות דברי רב דימי לא מופיעים עם הפתיחה 'כי אתא רב דימי', למרות
שברור שמסורת זו היא מא"י.
[36] עיין מבוא לתלמודים, עמ' 360.
[37] דוגמאות נוספות: עירובין י ע"ב; שבת סג ע"ב; פסחים מד ע"א.

דאנא ורבי יהושע בן לוי לא פליג'ן אהדדי, מאי בתחלה דקאמר רבי יהושע
בן לוי? תחלת חופה, ומאי סוף? סוף ביאה, וכי קאמינא אנא בין בזו ובין בזו
מחלוקת—תחלת חופה וסוף חופה דהיא תחילת ביאה. כי אתא רבין, אמר רבי
שמעון בן פזי אמר רבי יהושע בן לוי משום בר קפרא: מחלוקת—לבסוף, אבל
בתחלה—דברי הכל מוחלת; ורבי יוחנן אמר: בין בזו ובין בזו מחלוקת.

בסוגיא זו רב דימי מוסר את שמועת אמוראי א"י, אך בעקבות ערעורו של ר' אבהו התלמוד
מביא את מסורתו של רבין. גם בדוגמא זו אנו רואים שרק בעיקבות אי קבלת דעתו של רב דימי,
מופיע 'כי אתא רבין' עם מסורת שונה, בשמם של אותם חכמים, מוסרי המסורת, המצויים
במסורתו של רב דימי.

דוגמא ג (ברכות כב ע"א):

רב נחמן תקן חצבא בת תשעה קבין. כי אתא רב דימי אמר, רבי עקיבא ורבי
יהודה גלוסטרא אמרו: לא שנו אלא לחולה לאונסו, אבל לחולה המרגיל ארבעים
סאה. אמר רב יוסף: אתבר חצביה דרב נחמן. כי אתא רבין אמר: באושא הוה
עובדא בקילעא דרב אושעיא, אתו ושאלו לרב אסי, אמר להו: לא שנו אלא
לחולה המרגיל, אבל לחולה לאונסו פטור מכלום. אמר רב יוסף: אצטמיד חצביה
דרב נחמן... אמר רבא: הלכתא, בריא המרגיל וחולה המרגיל—ארבעים סאה,
ובריא לאונסו—תשעה קבין, אבל לחולה לאונסו—פטור מכלום.

התלמוד אינו מוכן לקבל את פסיקתו של רב דימי שחולה לאונסו צריך תשעה קבין. התלמוד
מתמודד עם מסורת זו, עד שבסוף הסוגיא, התלמוד מביא את פסיקתו של רבא. המיוחד במקרה
הנ"ל הוא שהתלמוד משלב את דברי רב דימי ואת המסורת הסותרת של אבין בסיפור על מקרה
שארע לרב נחמן, ותגובתו של רב יוסף למאורע זה. איני יודע אם לפנינו מאורע היסטורי, ואכן
כך התרחשו הדברים, או אין זה אלא מעשי עורכי התלמוד. אך בכל מקרה ישנה סתירה בין
המסורות.

איני רוצה לטעון שכל המקרים שהתלמוד מצמיד את רבין לרב דימי הם מעשי עורך מאוחר.
פעמים חכמים בני זמנו של רב דימי מכירים את שתי המסורות ומתיחסים אלהם. למרות שבמקרים
אלה קשה להכריע האם לפנינו מעשה עורך מאוחר או לפנינו מסורת אוטנטית של אמורא המתיחס
לדברי רב דימי ורבין , לדעתי אפשר לראות עקבות לעריכה מאוחרת.

לדוגמא (יבמות מה ע"א):

דכי אתא רב דימי, אמר רבי יצחק בר אבודימי, משום רבינו אמרו: עובד כוכבים
ועבד הבא על בת ישראל—הולד ממזר... ר' יוחנן ור' אלעזר ור' חנינא דאמרי:
עובד כוכבים ועבד הבא על בת ישראל—הולד ממזר. אמר רב יוסף: רבותא
למחשב גברי? הא רב ושמואל בבבל, ורבי יהושע בן לוי ובר קפרא בארץ
ישראל, ואמרי לה חלופי בר קפרא ועיילי זקני דרום, דאמרי: עובד כוכבים
ועבד הבא על בת ישראל—הולד כשר! אלא אמר רב יוסף: רבי היא דכי אתא

והשניה, דעתו של רב דימי נדחת או ע"י ראש ישיבת פומבדיתא ,מעסיקו של רב דימי, אביי. רבין[33] ה"נחותי" בין דורו של רב דימי (דור שלישי רביעי לאמוראי בבל), מופיע בתלמוד כמוסר את מסורותיה של אי, 'כי אתא רבין...'. לרוב הוא יופיע אחר דבריו של רב דימי, 'כי אתא רב דימי כי אתא רבין'. לרוב הופעתו לאחר רב דימי משמשת לשתי מטרות. האחת, לסתור את דבריו של רב דימי (והיא העקרית). והשניה היא לחזק את מסורתו של רב דימי (כאשר יש ערעור או ספק בדברי רב דימי[34]). נתון זה מעורר בי ספק שיתכן שכל תכליתו של 'כי אתא רבין' והצמדתו לרב דימי מציג שלב עריכה של עורכים מאוחרים, שמטרתם היא לערער את מסורותיו של רב דימי. הביא מספר דוגמאות לכך.

דוגמא א (סנהדרין עד ע"א):

א"ר ישמעאל מנין שאם אמרו לו לאדם עבוד ע"ז ואל תהרג, מנין שיעבוד ואל יהרג? ת"ל "וחי בהם" ולא שימות בהם. יכול אפילו בפרהסיא? ת"ל ולא תחללו את שם קדשי ונקדשתי...

כי אתא רב דימי א"ר יוחנן לא שנו אלא שלא בשעת גזרת המלכות אבל בשעת גזירת המלכות אפילו מצוה קלה יהרג ואל יעבור. כי אתא רבין א"ר יוחנן אפילו שלא בשעת גזירת מלכות לא אמרו אלא בצינעא אבל בפרהסיא אפילו מצוה קלה יהרג ואל יעבור.

דבריו של רב דימי משמו של ר' יוחנן, אינם מתיישבים עם דבריו של ר' ישמעאל שהובאו לפני כן בסוגיא. לדבריו של רב דימי בשעה שאין גזירת מלכות יעבור ולא יהרג .ולא פרש בפרהסיא או בצנעא, משמע בכל מקרה אל יהרג. ולכן בעקבות כך הובאו דבריו של רבין בשמו של ר' יוחנן לאמר שאין המסורת הארצי ישראלית שהובאה משמו של ר' יוחנן סותרת את הברייתא, אלא בפרהסיא יהרג ועל יעבור, כפסק של ר' ישמעאל. כרב דימי, רבין מוסר את ההלכה משמו של ר' יוחנן. התלמוד המביא להתנגשות את שתי המסורות(כמעט תמיד בהתנגשות בין רבין לרב דימי שמות החכמים זהים אך המסורת שונה), בוחר לפסוק כמסורת שהובאה ע"י רבין. מבדיקתי את המופעים בהם רב דימי ורבין מביאים מסורת שונה מא"י, לא מצאתי אף לא פעם אחת שהתלמוד מקבל את רב דימי. בכל מקום שהם מופעים יחד התלמוד מסיים את הסוגיא בדבריו של רבין. ולא בכדי, דבר זה מלמדנו על עריכתו של התלמוד וגיבוש המסורות המצויים ביד העורכים.

דוגמא ב (כתובות נז ע"א):

כי אתא רב דימי, אמר רבי שמעון בן פזי אמר רבי יהושע בן לוי משום בר קפרא: מחלוקת—בתחלה, אבל בסוף—לדברי הכל אינה מוחלת; ורבי יוחנן אמר: בין בזו ובין בזו מחלוקת. אמר רבי אבהו: לדידי מיפרשא לי מיניה דרבי יוחנן,

---

[33] עיין מבוא לתלמודים, עמ' 353–352; באכר, הנ"ל, עמ' 515–510.

[34] יבמות נה ע"ב: אמר שמואל—אמר רבה בר בר חנה אמר רבי יוחנן: העראה—זו נשיקה, משל, לאדם שמניח אצבעו על פיו, אי אפשר שלא ידחוק הבשר. כי אתא רבה בר בר חנה אמר רבי יוחנן: גמר ביאה בשפחה חרופה—זו הכנסת עטרה. מתיב רב ששת: שכבת זרע—אינו חייב אלא על ביאת המירוק; מאי לאו מירוק גיד? לא, מירוק עטרה. כי אתא רב דימי א"ר יוחנן: העראה—זו הכנסת עטרה. אמרו ליה: והא רבה בר בר חנה לא אמר הכי! אמר להו: או איהו שקראי, או אנא שקרי. כי אתא רבין א"ר יוחנן: העראה—זו הכנסת עטרה.

בדוגמא זו ישנו ספק לתלמוד, 'כמה רובו'. עורכי הסוגיא מביאים את מסורת א"י שהובאה לבבל בידי רב דימי. התלמוד מציג שרב פפא, דור מאוחר יותר, מקבל מסורת זו. ובכך מסיים העורך את הסוגיא.

דוגמא נוספת:

> איבעיא להו: מהו להפסיק ליהא שמו הגדול מבורך? *כי אתא רב דימי אמר, רבי יהודה ורבי שמעון תלמידי דרבי יוחנן אמרי: לכל אין מפסיקין, חוץ מן יהא שמו הגדול מבורך, שאפילו עוסק במעשה מרכבה פוסק. ולית הלכתא כותיה.*[31]

עפ"י דוגמא זו נראה שטענתי לעיל, שהמונח 'כי אתא רב דימי', הינו מונח של עורכי הסוגיא, לסיום הלכה, אינו נכון. מכוון שהתלמוד פוסק, בסופה של הסוגיא 'ולית הלכתא כותיה', בניגוד למסורת א"י המובאת ע"י רב דימי. אכן כך אנו מוצאים גם בכתבי היד של התלמוד. אך י.ש. שפיגל, בדיסרטציה, הוספות מאוחרות (סבוראיות) בתלמוד הבבלי, עמ' 195, טוען שביטויי סתמי זה המופיע בסוף סוגיא, הנו מאוחר. בעמ' 196-197 הוא דן בדוגמא שלנו וכך כתב: הנציב בפרושו "העמק שאלה" לשאילתא א' אות כה סבור ע"פ דברי בעל ה"ג [ד"ו דף ב סע"ד, ד"ב עמ' 42, ד"י עמ' 55] כי "ולית הלכתה כותיה" לא היה לפני בה"ג והשאילתות. אבל ר"ש הורוויץ חולק עליו בזאת, עמ"ש בהערתו למחזור ויטרי דף 21 הערה כו, וכשישיטתו סבור גם רל"ג ב"גנזי שכטר", ח"ב עמ' 100 אות יג". עכ"ל. מדיון בלשון 'ולית הלכתא כותיה', בחיבורו של שפיגל, נראה לי שלשונו זו היא הוספה מאוחרת. העורך הנ"ל אינו מכיר בערכו של הביטוי 'כי אתא רב דימי', ולכן פוסק בניגוד למסורת זו.

לסיכום, בסוגיות שהבאתי לעיל נסיתי להראות את חשיבותם של המסורות מא"י שהובאו ע"י רב דימי. התלמוד מוסר מסור הלכות של רב דימי מרבותיו בארץ ישראל: (בעיקר32)(ר' יוחנן, ר"ל, ר' אלעזר ,ר' חנינא, ואחרים. עורכי התלמוד עורכים את הסוגיא כאשר מטרתם הוא ש'כי אתי רב דימי' ישובץ בסוף הסוגיא. לביטוי זה ישנו ערך ספרותי חשוב בעיניהם. ביטוי זה בעיני העורכים הנו מעצב ופוסק הסוגיא.

כעת אעבור לתופעה אחרת, שמחזקת בעיני את ההנחה שמאמריו של רב דימי משקפים עריכה ספרותית מכוונת ע"י עורכי התלמוד. בעיון בסוגיות 'כי אתא רב דימי' למדתי שהתלמוד בוחר בדרך מיוחדת ויחודית להתמודד עם המסורת של 'כי אתי רב דימי', כאשר אינו מוכן לקבלן. הרבה פעמים מגמת הסוגיא היא בניגוד ל'כי אתא רב דימי', לכן העורכים ינסו בדרכים יחודיות להתמודד עם קושי זה. לדעתי דבר זה מלמד על שלבים קדומים ומאוחרים בעריכת הסוגיא. כאשר בשלבי העריכה הקדומים 'כי אתא רב דימי', שימש כפסק הלכה וחתימת סוגיא. אך בשלבי עריכה מאוחרים, שפסקם אינו מתישב עם המסורת של רב דימי, היה קשה לעורכים להתעלם מהדומיננטיות של המסורות לכן מצאו דרך עוקפת להתגבר על קושי זה.

ישנם שתי צורות דחיה, בהם התלמוד משתמש להדוף את 'כי אתא רב דימי'. האחת, דעתו של רב דימי נדחת ע"י רבין, הנחתוי בין דורו של רב דימי (בן זוגו של רב דימי באגרתו של רש"ג). שגם הוא מכונה נחותי בתלמוד (השני, אחרי רב דימי, מבחינת התפוצה של הביטוי 'כי אתא רב פלוני').

התלמוד מביא את פרושיהם של רב, שמואל, ר' יוחנן ורבנן. אך התלמוד אינו מקבל את
פרושיהם, אלא את פרושו של רב דימי. חשוב לי להדגיש שנית , שלא רק שהתלמוד מביא את
פרושו של רב דימי בסוף, כפרוש החותם את הסוגיא. אלא התלמוד מביא את דברי רב דימי
בפתוס: 'כי אתא רב דימי'—רק בעקבות כך אנו מקבלים את פרושו. המונח הספרותי והעריכה
משפיעים על חתימת הסוגיא.

כעת אעבור לפסקי הלכה הנמסרים ע"י רב דימי אחרי הבאת המונח 'כי אתא רב דימי'. אדון
במספר דוגמאות בהם רב דימי מוסר בבבל הלכה ארצי ישראלית. גם כאן ברצוני להראות את ערכם
הדומיננטי של מסורות אלו אצל עורכי התלמוד. לעורכי התלמוד ישנה חשיבות יתרה שהמסורות
הארצי ישראליות בידיד רב דימי, 'כי אתי רב דימי', יהיו פסק ההלכה, סופה של הסוגיא,כלעיל.
מסורותיו של רב דימי מא"י אינם חשובים רק בגלל ידיעת הלשון או הראליה של א"י, אלא בגלל
היותם מא"י. אני מוצא, שעורכי הסוגיא סדרו את הסוגיא כך שרב דימי יסיים ויחתום את הסוגיא
בפסק הלכתי שהובא מא"י. לעורך התלמוד בואו של רב דימי מא"י ולפסקי הלכה שאותם מביא,
הוא בעל חשיבות רבה. ולכן מסיים את הסוגיא בצורה דרמתית-ספרותית 'כי אתא רב דימי'. כעת
אביא מספר דוגמאות לכך:[27]

...רבי אלעזר בן עזריה אומר מרחיצין את הקטן ביום השלישי שחל להיות
בשבת אי אמרת בשלמא תנא קמא מזלפין קאמר היינו דקאמר ליה ר"א בן
עזריה מרחיצין, אלא אי אמרת תנא קמא מרחיצין ביום הראשון קאמר ומזלפין
ביום השלישי האי ר"א בן עזריה אומר אף מרחיצין מיבעי ליה? *כי
אתא רב דימי אמר רבי אלעזר אמר רבי הלכה כר"א בן עזריה.*[28]

איני רוצה לדון בפרטי הסוגיא, ובדיון בין תנא קמא לר"א בן עזריה. לענייננו העורך מביא את
מסורת ארץ ישראל במחלוקת זו. אין העורך דן בערכה של המסורת זו ונאמנותה. מבחינתו מספיק
שהיא הובאה ע"י רב דימי, 'כי אתי רב דימי'—שתקבל הערכה רבה.
דוגמא נוספת:

...תנו רבנן נשבר העצם ויצא לחוץ אם עור אם בשר חופין את רובו מותר אם
לאו אסור. וכמה רובו. כי אתא רב דימי אמר ר' יוחנן רוב עוביו ואמרי לה [29]רוב
היקפו. אמר רב פפא הלכך בעינן רוב עוביו ובעינן רוב הקיפו.[30]

---

[27] סוגיות מעין אלו נמצאות במקומות רבים בתלמוד ואציין לאחדים מהם: יומא יב ע"ב; סוכה י ע"א; יבמות נט ע"א;
בבא בתרא קסט ע"ב; סנה' סט ע"א; ע"ז לח ע"ב.

[28] שבת קלד ע"ב.

[29] 'אמרי ליה' מובאת בארמית כאשר לשונו של רב דימי היא בעברית (ראה ש"י פרידמן, פרק האישה רבה, עמ'
310). ולא ברור האם ה'אמרי לה' היא לשונו של רב דימי או לשונו של סתם התלמוד. אם אכן זהו לשון 'סתם תלמוד',
אזי רב פפא מכיר סתמא זו. קשה לי להכריע בשאלה זו. אך בבדיקתי העלתית, שבתלמוד ישנם שני סוגי 'ואמרי לה':
1) מסורות שונות של שמות החכמים מוסרי ההלכה. 2) מסורות שונות בעניין הלכתי כלשהו.

בעוד הסוג הראשון הוא סתמי, ולא ברור לי זמנו. הסוג השני כנראה מוקדם, והאמוראים מכירים אותו. לכן ישנה
אפשרות סבירה שבדוגמא הנ"ל רב דימי הוא זה שאמר את 'ואמרי לה'. ועיין ד. הלבני, "מחקרים ומסורות", פסחים,
עמ' שפ"ג הערה 6; וכן מה שכתב מ.ש הכהן פלדבלום, "פרופ' אברהם וייס –הערכת דרכו בחקר התלמוד וסיכום
מסקנותיו", מתוך: ספר היובל לאברהם וייס, עמ' כג-כה.

[30] חולין עו ע"ב .

רב דימי לאביי מסתימת הסוגיא, למרות שסביר להניח שעורכי התלמוד עדיין לא יודעים את פרושו של 'נקלס'-'קורטי', כאביי.

לעורכי הסוגיא חשוב המונח 'כי אתא רב דימי'. הסיום במונח זה בסוגיא זו וסוגיות רבות אחרות[23] מלמד שלפנינו עריכה מכוונת של התלמוד. כל תכליתו של המונח הוא להראות שהמסורת הארצי ישראלית היא בעלת משקל רב בעיני העורכים, ולכן הם מסיימים בו את בסוגיא. מטרת הסיום במונח זה היא לאמר שכך הוא פסקו של התלמוד. אם כן לפנינו ישנה עריכה ספרותית של התלמוד.

דוגמא נוספת:

...וחרס הדריני—מאי חרס הדר' אמ' רב יהודה[24] אמ' שמואל חרס של אדרינוס קיסר. דכי אתא רב דימי אמ' קרקע בתולה היתה שלא היתה עבודה מעולם ונטעה, ורמי לה חמרא בגולפי חיורי ושביק ליה עד דמייצו לחמרייהו ותברי להו לחספי ודרו להו בהדייהו וכל היכא דמטו תרו להו במיא ושתו...[25]

הן בדור הראשון לחכמי בבל (שמואל) והן בדור השני (רב יהודה—עפ"י הגיליון) פרשו מילה זו בצורה אסוציאטיבית ולא עפ"י משמעותה המלולית-ריאלית משום אי ידיעתם את הראליה הארצי ישראלית. ורק כאשר בא רב דימי מא"י מפרש מילה זו.[26] סיום הסוגיא בדברי רב דימי מראה שהעורך קיבל את פרושו הסופי של מילות המשנה. ויותר מכך, הסוגיא הבאה דנה בצורה סתמית ב'חרס הדרייני'. והדיון מניח כמובן מאליו שזהו פרוש המילה ולא מתייחס כלל לפרוש שהובא ע"י אמוראי בבל(שמואל ורב יהודה) למילה זו. בכך מראה העורך שקיבל את פירושו של רב דימי כפרוש הלגיטימי במשנה.

הדוגמא השלישית היא פרוש פסוק בידי רב דימי (ברכות לא ע"א):

ונתתה לאמתך זרע אנשים, מאי זרע אנשים? אמר רב: גברא בגוברין; ושמואל אמר: זרע שמושח שני אנשים, ומאן אינון—שאול ודוד; ורבי יוחנן אמר: זרע ששקול כשני אנשים, ומאן אינון—משה ואהרן, שנאמר: משה ואהרן בכהניו ושמואל בקוראי שמו; ורבנן אמרי: זרע אנשים—זרע שמובלע בין אנשים. כי אתא רב דימי, אמר: לא ארוך ולא גוץ, ולא קטן ולא אלם, ולא צחור ולא גיחור, ולא חכם ולא טפש.

---

[23] דוגמאות מעין אלא מצויים בעשרות מקומות בתלמוד, לדוגמא: ברכות ו ע"א; שבת עו ע"א; עירובין ג ע"א; עירובין נד ע"ב; תעניות י ע"ב; מגילה יח ע"א; מו"ק י ע"א; נדרים נה ע"ב; כתובות קה ע"ב; נדרים מ ע"א; סוטה כא ע"א; גיטין נט ע"א; ב"מ קה ע"א; ב"ב עד ע"א; סנהדרין ז ע"ב; סנהדרין לט ע"ב; סנהדרין מד ע"ב; סנה' סח ע"ב; סנה' ע ע"א; סנה' ק ע"א; סנה' קח ע"א; שבועות כ ע"ב; ע"ז ב ע"ב; ע"ז יט ע"א; ע"ז לב ע"א; כריתות כה ע"ב.

[24] אמ' רב יהודה—נוסף בגליון כתב היד.

[25] ע"ז לב ע"א. עמ' 56 כתב היד אברמסון.

[26] עיין בערוך השלם, ח"ג, עמ' 189,ערך "הדריינא", ופרוש מילה זו היא הרכבה של שני מילים יווניות ύδωρ שמשמעו מים ו οίνο שמשמעו יין.

מדגישים הן התלמוד הבבלי והן התלמוד הירושלמי את היותו 'נחותי', שמשמעותו מקצוע, תפקיד, ולא תואר. יותר מכך, נראה לי שרב דימי מועסק ע"י ישיבת פומבדיתא, ע"י ראש הישיבה אביי. רב דימי מופיע בתדירות גבוהה עם ראש הישיבה אביי,18 שנושא ונותן איתו בהלכות ובמסורות ארץ ישראל (בכ25%–20% מהמקרים בהם התלמוד מדגיש "כי אתא רב דימי" המסורת שהוא מוסר היא לפני אביי), וכן עם חכמים אחרים הקשורים לישיבה זו. ואכמ"ל.

כעת אדון בחלק מן הסוגיות בהם רב דימי מוסר את מסורות א"י בבואו לבבל. סוגיות בהם התלמוד מדגיש 'כי אתי רב דימי'. מטרתי בדיון זה היא להראות את יחסם וערכם של מסורות אלו בעיני עורכי תלמוד. בחלק בראשון אעסוק במסורותיו של רב דימי בפרושי פסוק או מילה, ובחלק השני מסורות העוסקות בשמועות הלכתיות.

פעמים אמוראי א"י או עורכי התלמוד מתקשים בהבנת פרושה של מילה בעברית/יוונית או פסוק מן המקרא. אי ידיעה זו נובעת מאי הכרת הלשון העברית והריאליה הארצי ישראלית. אחד מתפקידי רב דימי הוא לפרש לחכמי בבל את הריאליה והלשון של א"י. ואכן רב דימי עושה זאת בהרבה מן המקרים. פעמים רבות מופיע בתלמוד שאמורא או 'סתמא דתלמוד' פתרו את הקושי. אך פתרונם הוא לא כפי המובן הלשוני-ראלי של הפסוק או המילה, אלא פרוש אסוציאטיבי. הפתרון המספק את התלמוד מופיע בבואו של רב דימי מא"י, שבעקבותיו חכמי בבל מבינים את המשמעות ה'נכונה' של המילה או הפסוק, ע"פ הלשון והריאליה של א"י. התלמוד רואה בדברי רב דימי את 'המילה האחרונה' של הסוגיא, ובעקבות פתרונו מסיים את הדיון. והביא לכך מספר דוגמאות :

...מאי דקל טב פירות דקל טב חצב קשבי נקלס *כי אתא רב דימי* אמ' קורטי. אמ' ליה אביי לרב דימי תנן נקלס ולא ידעינן, אמרת לן קורטי ולא ידעינן מאי אהנית לן אמ' ליה אהנאי19 לכו דכי אזליתו להתם אמריתו להו נקלס ולא ידעי אמריתו להו קורטי וידעי20

את דברי ר' מאיר במשנה: "אף דקל טב חצב ונקליבס"(במשנת בבל21 גרסו עפי כ"י הספרדי נקלס22) לא הבינו חכמי בבל והתקשו בפרושה, במיוחד בפרושה של המילה "נקלס". את תמיהתם בפרוש המשנה הביע רב חיסדא: 'א"ל רב חסדא לאבימי, גמירי דעבודת כוכבים דאברהם אבינו ארבע מאות פירקי הויין, ואנן חמשה תנן ולא ידעינן מאי קאמרינן'. התלמוד ממשיך ומספר שרק כאשר רב דימי הגיע לבבל פרש פרוש מילה זו. ואף אחר שמפרש מילה זו, כקורטי, אין אביי יודע פרושה, וזאת מכוון שאין הוא מכיר את הלשון והריאליה בא"י(וכנראה שגם רב דימי מתקשה בהסבר העצם הנ"ל). החשוב לעניינינו, שבפרושו של

<hr/>

18 ראה פסחים לד ע"ב :'יתיב רב דימי וקאמר לה להא שמעתא. אמר ליה אביי הקדישן בכלי קאמר אבל בפה לא עבוד רבנן מעלה, או דילמא בפה נמי עבוד רבנן מעלה? אמר ליה: זו לא שמעתי, כיוצא בה שמעתי. וכן ראה שבת קמה ע"א; ערובין י ע"ב; ערובין כב ע"א; פסחים מד ע"א.

19 "אהנאי" –בכתב היד זוהי תוספת הגהה אחר מחיקה.

20 ע"ז יד ע"ב. השתמשתי בכ"י הספרדי מהדורת ש. אברמסון, עמ' 24.

21 השתמשתי בהגדרתיו של ד. רוזנטל. "משנה עבודה זרה", מהדורה מדעית, חלק המבוא עמ' 187-179.

22 עיין ד. רוזנטל, שם, עמ 14. בנוסחה של מילה זו ישנו הבדל בין הנוסח הבבלי לנוסח הארצי ישראלי. ועיין בפרוש מילה זו אצל רוזנטל מבוא עמ' 165-164, 233-232. ובמיוחד עמ' 250-247. וראה הנ"ל, מסורות א"י ודרכן לבבל, קתדרה 92(תמוז תשנ"ט), עמ' 12 הערה 28.

ברצוני בעבודה זו להתמקד באחד מן הנחותי—רב דימי.[10] בירידתו של רב דימי לבבל הוא מביא אתו את תורתה של ארץ ישראל: מסורותיה ההלכתיות,[11] פרשנות לשונית,[12] ריאליה,[13] מאורעות שהתרחשו בא"י,[14] מאמרי חכמה,[15] ועוד. במאמר זה אדון בצד הספרותי של התלמוד הבבלי, ואבדוק כיצד התלמוד(העורכים) מתייחס למסורות הארצי ישראליות המובאת ע"י רב דמי ה"נחותי"? מה משקלם ומה ערכם בעיני עורכי התלמוד? מה בין היסטוריה לפיקציה במסורות אלה? בסוף המאמר יהיה באפשרותנו למצוא את היחס הערכי-חשיבתי של מסורות אלה בעיני עורכי התלמוד הבבלי.

במאמר זה בדקתי את כל מובאותיו של רב דימי בתלמוד הבבלי ובתלמוד הירושלמי.[16] ומתוך מאות הסוגיות אשר עיינתי בהם, והסקתי את מסקנותי, בחרתי במספר סוגיות שבהם ארצה לדון ולהדגים את ממצאי הדיון.

רב דימי, החכם הבבלי,[17] מופיע כ–200 פעמים בתלמוד הבבלי. בדרך כלל כאשר הוא מופיע בתלמוד, מביא התלמוד את שמו עם הקידומת 'כי אתי'('כי אתי רב דימי'), וכך ב–139 מופעים (בערך 70% מכלל הזכרת שמו בתלמוד). מכך ניתן להסיק שבואו של רב דימי לבבל הנו מאורע חשוב ומשמעותי לעורכי הבבלי, המדגיש פורמולה זו כמעט כל פעם שמזכיר את רב דימי. הבחנה זו מתחדדת ומתחזקת לאור כך שהפורמולה "כי אתא רב פלוני" מופיעה ב–177 מקומות בתלמוד, וכפי שציינתי מתוכם 137 ה'פלוני' הוא רב דימי(77%). לפיכך, ניתן להסיק כי המונח 'כי אתא רב דימי' הוא מינוח ספרותי שהוצמד למאמרי רב דימי ע"י עורכי התלמוד.

ראוי לציין שבתלמוד הירושלמי מופיע רב דימי[אבדימי, אבדומה, אבודמא, אבודמי] עם הכינוי "נחותא", "אבודמא נחותא". התלמוד הירושלמי מצמיד את הכינוי 'נחותא'(או 'נחותה'), המופיע שבעה פעמים, רק לשני חכמים עולא ואבודמא. כאשר עולא פעם אחת[כלאים לב עג], והשאר אבודמא [ערובין יט ע"ב; ב"ב יג ע"ד; סוכה נט ע"ד(= רה"ש נו ע"ד); שקלים נא ע"א; חגיגה עו ע"ג; קדושין ס ע"ד]. תוצאות מעניינות אלו מלמדות שהן התלמוד הבבלי והן התלמוד הירושלמי רואים ברב דימי יורד. אך הוא אינו סתם 'יורד' אלא ישנה חשיבות מיוחדת לכך שהנו נחותי.

כפי שציינתי לעיל, נראה לי שה'נחותי' הינו מוסד, קבוצת אנשים שזה תפקידם. שאחד החשובים שבהם, אם לא החשוב ביותר, הוא רב דימי. רב דימי הוא בן בבל, ההולך ובא, מבבל לא"י וחוזר לבבל, ומביא את מסורותיהם של חכמים ושל ישיבות א"י. מכמות המסורות שמובאות בתלמוד ע"י רב דימי, כפי שהצגתי לעיל, נראה שאין רב דימי איש עסקים או מטייל שדרך אגב מביא את מסורותיה של ארץ ישראל לבבל, אלא מטרת נסיעותיו היא הבאת מסורות א"י לבבל. לפיכך

---

[10] ח.אלבק, הנ"ל, עמ' 358-360.

[11] דוגמא: ברכות כא ע"ב; שבת ח ע"ב.

[12] ברכות ו ע"ב; ברכות לא ע"ב.

[13] שבת קח ע"ב.

[14] שבת יג ע"ב; שבת נ ע"א; שבת עד ע"א.

[15] שבת קנב ע"א.

[16] בעבודה זו נעזרתי בשו"ת בר-אילן, וכן ב'תוכנת ליברמן'—כתבי היד של התלמוד(לא התיחסתי לשינוים שאינן מעניינו, אלא רק לשינוים שהם בעלי משמעות לדיון).

[17] לדעתו של אלבק, מבוא לתלמודים, עמ' 358-361, ה'נחותא' –הוא מי שעלה מבבל לארץ ישראל וחזר לבבל ותורת ארץ ישראל בידו ושוב עלה לארץ ישראל וחזר לבבל [וזאת על פי הסוגיא בכתובות קיא ע"א. שם מסופר על עולא שהיה רגיל לעלות לארץ ישראל ולחזור. ונקרא בירושלמי 'עולא נחותא'(כלאים לב ע"ג)]; באכר בספרו Tradenten Und Tradition p. 506-510. , אינו מזכיר(נזהר?) היכן נולד או היכן התחנך רב דמי , אלא רק קובע שרב דימי ירד מבבל לא"י.

בקטע השלישי אין רש"ג מזכיר את המילה 'סליק', כבקטעים הקודמים. ובכלל, רש"ג מציג את
שלושת הקטעים אלה בצורה מיוחדת, כך שהתוצאה היא שישינה הדרגתיות ביחס לא"י. בקטע
הראשון, המציג את הדור השני לאמוראי בבל, רש"ג מזכיר 'רבנן דהתם דסליקו מן הכא'.[5] כלומר,
ישנם חכמים ארצי ישראלים שבאים לכאן ללמוד תורה, אך ישנם גם חכמים בבלים שהולכים
לארץ ישראל ללמוד תורה (רב אמי ורב אצל ר' יוחנן). בקטע השני, הדור השלישי, חכמים
אמנם 'סליקין ונחתין', אך רש"ג מזכיר רק את עזיבתם של חכמי ארץ ישראל לבבל, כגון ר' יצחק
נפחא, ר' זירא וכו', אך אינו מזכיר חכמים דסליקין מהכא להתם. אך בקטע השלישי, כפי שציינתי,
ישנה נהירה לבבל, ישנה תנועה חד צדדית מא"י לבבל. רש"ג לא תולה את הבריחה כתוצאה
ישירה של שעת השמד, אלא תוצאה של התמעטות התורה.

בהצגת ההשתלשלות באופן זה (הדרגתיות) רש"ג מראה את התרת קשרי הכניעה של המרכז
הבבלי מא"י, והתפתחותו כמרכז תורה. אם בדור השני ישנם עוד חכמים בבלים שהולכים לא"י
ללמוד תורה אצל גדול הדור, בדור הרביעי ישנה כניעה מוחלטת לחכמי בבל בעקבות התמעטות
התורה.

לאור הצגה מגמתית זו, לדעתי, לא ניתן למצוא ולחפש את ההיסטוריה של הנחותי באגרת.
דעת של רש"ג שהנחותי הנם בעיקר תלמידי חכמים הבאים לבבל ללמוד תורה (מלבד רב אמי
ורב אסי הבאים לא"י ללמוד תורה), היא כתוצאה ממניעיו להאדיר את ישיבת בבל. ולכן אין
לקבל את המסורת על רב דימי שהוא 'נחותי' שחזר לבבל באופן סופי, אחרי התמעטות התורה.
וכפי שציינתי כל הצגת הקטע היא מגמתית במטרה להציג את התמעטות התורה בא"י, והגדלת
קרנה של בבל. לדעתי, רש"ג בחר את רב דימי עם נחותי נוסף, ראבון, שהנו בן בבל,[6] מכוון ששני
חכמים אלה הם החכמים שאותם מכנה התלמוד בצורה דומיננטית 'נחותי'.[7]

מלשונו של רש"ג נראה שהנחותי הם חכמים בודדים שעולים ויורדים (בעיקר יורדים)[8] ומביאים
אתם את מסורת א"י. מהתרשמותי במהלך עבודה זו, נראה לי שהנחותי בתלמוד הבבלי הם לא
אנשים בודדים שהולכים מבבל לא"י ויורדים חזרה, ומביאים אתם מידע על הנעשה בא"י. אלא זהו
"מוסד", קבוצה של חכמים מסוימים שזה היה תפקידם. וכדברי י.א הלוי 'שכל ענינים של ה'נחותי'
היה ללכת מבבל לארץ ישראל ומארץ ישראל לבבל להביא את כל דברי המתיבתות מזה לזה,
דברי חכמי ארץ ישראל לבבל, ודברי חכמי בבל לארץ ישראל'.[9] ואשוב לכך בהמשך.

י.א הלוי; י.זוסמן במחקרי תלמוד א, עמ' 132 הערה 187; וכן הנ"ל, עמ' 103הערה 194.

5 המסורת לגבי רב אסי שהנו בן בבל מוזכרת בתלמודים, ראה ח. אלבק, מבוא לתלמודים עמ' 228-229. אך
המסורת לגבי מוצאו הבבלי של רב אמי אינה ברורה, אלבק(הנ"ל עמ' 227-228) אינה מזכירה כלל. אך ראה
א.הימן, תולדות תנאים ואמוראים, עמ' 225-219,המצדד במסורת זו.

6 ראה אלבק, הנ"ל, עמ' 352-353.

7 לגבי הנחותי האחרים, לא מצאנו שכולם ירדו/ באו בקרו בבבל. המסורת לגבי ר' שמואל בר נחמן שירד לבבל אינה
ברורה כלל. אפשר לאסוף פיסות מידע בתלמוד ולהסיק מסקנה זו, כדוגמת א. הימן, הנ"ל, עמ' 1143. אלבק מתעלם
מהקשרים הבבלי של ר' שמואל בר נחמן ואינו מזכירו כלל (וכן אינו מתייחס למסורת הנ"ל ברש"ג). וכן לגבי ר' יצחק,
ישנה מסורת בודדת במו"ק כד ע"ב שירד לבבל(ראה הימן, עמ' 801-802). לגבי ר' חנינא פאפי, בן א"י, לא מצאתי
כלל מסורת שביקר בבבל. כנראה שרש"ג מסתמך על מסורות קדומות, שלא הגיעו לידינו.

8 על העלייה לא"י בתקופה זו ראה L. Schwartz, Tension between Palestinian scholars and Babyl-
nian Olim in Amoraic Palestine, *Journal for the study of Judaism in the Persian Hellenistic and
Roman period,*11(1981), p 78-94 ; וכן י. גפני, העלאת מתים לקבורה בארץ—קיום לראשיתו של המנהג
והתפתחותו, קתדרה, 4(תשל"ז) עמ' 113-120.

9 י.א הלוי, הנזכר לעיל.

יהורם ביטון לימד תלמוד באוניברסיטה העברית
בירושלים. הוא כיהן כמרצה אורח בישיבת חובבי תורה
בשנת תשס"ז.

'כי אתא רב דימי'—בין היסטוריה לעריכה
יהורם ביטון

ה"נחותי", [1] היורדים ממערבא לבבל, [2] מופיעים רבות בספרות התלמודית. חכמים אלו מביאים
איתם בבואם לבבל מסורות מישיבות ארץ ישראל ומהנעשה בה. המסורות הם בעניינים שונים,
כגון—הלכה, אגדה, לשון וידיעות הארץ. רב שרירא גאון באיגרתו מציין את ה"נחותי", ומביאם
בסקירתו את דורות האמוראים:

I) ובתר דאריהון רב נחמן ורב יהודה ורב הונא ורב חסדא ורב ששת ורבנן אחריני דהוה
סליקו ונחתין, כגון עולא ורבי חייא בר אבא ור' שמואל בר נחמני ורבנן דהתם דסליקו מן הכא
ר' אמי ור' אסי.

II) ובתר הכין רבה ורב יוסף בבבל ורבנן דהוו סליקו ונחתין כגון ר' אבא דהוה יתר הנך
דראשונים ור' יצחק נפחא ור' זירא ור' ירמיה ור' אבהו ור' חנינא פאפי.

III) ובתר הכין אביי ורבא. ונפיש שמאדא בארץ ישראל ואתמעטא הוראה תמן טובא *ונחית
מאן דהוה התם [מן]* בבלאי כגון ראבון כגון רב דימי וכולהון נחותי דינחיתו להכא[3]

בקטע זה רש"ג סוקר את ההיסטוריה של הנחותי בתקופת האמוראים. לפי תיאורו בדור השני
והשלישי לאמוראי בבל חכמים 'סלקין ונחתין'—הגבול בין בבל לא"י פתוח. חכמים באים וחוזרים
מבבל לא"י, והקשרים בין המרכזים אדוק. אך בדור הרביעי, התנועה היא חד צדדית מא"י לבבל,
חכמי בבל חוזרים לביתם כתוצאה מהשמד.[4]

---

[1] ראה: M. Sokoloff, *A Dictionary of Jewish Palestinian Aramaic*, p.346 ערך 'נחות'; וכן מלונו לארמית
בבלית *The Dictionary of Jewish Babylonian Aramaic*, p.740 ערך 'נחותי'.

[2] לעניני הנחותי עיין: ש. קליין, "הנחותי ורבה בר בר חנה על עניני ארץ ישראל, ציון ה-ו (תרצ"ג) עמ' א-יא; י.א
הלוי, דורות הראשונים, כרך ב, עמ' 467 – 473; ע.צ מלמד, פרקי מבוא לספרות התלמוד, עמ' 599 (בשם פרופ'
מהרי"ן אפשטין); ח. אלבק, מבוא לתלמודים, עמ' 303-302; מ. בר, ראשות הגולה בבבל בימי המשנה והתלמוד,
עמודים 8, 80 וכן שם הערה 147-145, 83; *Encyclopaedia Judaica*, כרך יב, עמ' 943-942; ע. שטיינזאלץ,
"הקשרים בין בבל לארץ ישראל", מתוך: תלפיות יב, עמ' 301 (מאמר זה מצריך ביקורת מתודולוגית, דיונו של
שטיינזאלץ הוא בא הופעתם של אמוראי בבל מהדור הרביעי והלאה בתלמוד הירושלמי והסיבות לכך. אך את
האפשרות הפשוטה שסוף עריכת הירושלמי נעשתה בתקופה זו, דור רביעי לאמוראי בבל, הוא דוחה בלי שום טענה
ואינו מקבלה. בנוסף, אין שטיינזאלץ עושה הפרדה בין המקורות. לדעתו, הבבלי הכיר את התלמוד הירושלמי, הוא
אינו מוכן לקבל שהתלמוד הבבלי אינו מכיר את מסורת התלמוד הירושלמי [ועל כך עיין י.זוסמן "ושוב לירושלמי
נזיקין" מחקרי תלמוד א,עמ' 104 הערה 192, וכן עמ' 128 הערה 52]. לדעתו, כל חכם ארצי ישראלי מחויב
לדעת את כל המסורות הארצי ישראליות כאשר ירד לבבל. ואם התלמוד הבבלי לא מביא דעה ארצי ישראלית,
אשר מופיעה בתלמוד ירושלמי בשמו של חכם אשר ביקר בבבל, המסקנה היא שזו התעלמות מכוונת של התלמוד
הבבלי מחכמי א"י ומתורת א"י);W.Bacher; "Tradition Und Tradenten" p 506 – 523 (רב
דימי) שם עד עמ' 510.

[3] איגרת רש"ג, עמ' 61, עפ"י הנוסח הצרפתי.

[4] על השמד עיין דורות הראשונים, ח"ב, עמ' 399-366; א. ה וייס, דור דור ודורשיו, עמ' 100-97; ג. אלון, תולדות
היהודים בארץ ישראל בתקופת המשנה והתלמוד, ח"ב, עמ' 257-252; אבי-יונה, בימי רומא וביזאנטיון, עמ' 177-
136; צ. גרץ, דברי ימי ישראל, עמ' 405-394 [ובעיקר עמ' 399, הערה 2 (הערתו של רבינוביץ)]; וכן בקורתו של

היא מסייעת ביד הרוצה לספור בבין השמשות בערב שבת.שיקול זה של צעירי
המתפללים הוא בעל משקל רב עבורנו, שהרי מעת ייסודה של הקהילה ביכרנו את הדגש על
פרחי קהילתנו בתקווה לשלבם ולהעצימם בכל הקשור למתרחש בבית הכנסת וקירבה למסורת
ישראל.

מסקנות בקצירת ה"אומר"

א. לכתחילה אין לספור את העומר לפני צאת הכוכבים.

ב. אם בבין השמשות מישהו שואל "כמה ימי הספירה הלילה?", יש להשיב "אתמול
היה כך וכך" שהרי אם ינקוט במספר ייתכן שכבר יצא חובת אותו הלילה, ואינו
יכול לברך שוב באותו הלילה.

ג. במידה וקיים צורך יש מקום לפי מנהג אשכנז לספור את העומר בבין השמשות.
לפי מנהג עדות המזרח, אין לנהוג כן.

ד. טוב לקטן השוכב לישון לפני צאת הכוכבים לספור את העומר בבין השמשות.

ה. בקהילתנו, המבוססת על אדני מנהג אשכנז ואשר מעניקה משקל רב להתחשבות
בצעירי המתפללים, ניתן לספור את העומר בבין השמשות במיוחד בשבתות
ובחגים.

ו. היה ומישהו ספר בבין השמשות, ראוי לחזור ולספור ללא ברכה לאחר צאת
הכוכבים. מומלץ לעשות סימן כדי שלא ישכח לספור שוב.

ז. מי שספר בבין השמשות ולא חזר לספור לאחר צאת הכוכבים, רשאי להמשיך
לספור את העומר בברכה.

ח. ראוי להבהיר כי כל האמור לעיל אינו תקף לעניינים אחרים, לרבות: זמן התפילה
בליל שבועות, תפילת ערבית מוקדמת, קריאת שמע בזמנה, הפסק טהרה, וכו'.
כמו כן, אין באמור לעיל קביעה לגבי ספירת העומר לפני בין השמשות.

אף שהיא לא מקובלת על כל חכמינו, מציבה תריס בפני השכחה.[32]

2. צעירי המתפללים

אנו, כהורים, חפצים לחנך את ילדינו במצוות ה', ובכללן מצוות ספירת העומר.[33] יש וילדינו הצעירים שוכבים לישון לפני צאת הכוכבים, וראוי להסתמך על האפשרות של ספירה בבין השמשות כדי לאפשר להם לספור בברכה מידי ערב.[34]

מכתבי הראשונים הגיע לידינו תיאור מדהים על המנהג במגנצא המעיד על הרצון למסד את ספירת העומר של ילדים ולשלבה בחיי הקהילה:[35]

> והיה מנהג במגנצא ששמש העיר היה מקבץ אליו בבית הכנסת כל הנערים אחר
> סיום התפלה, והיה מברך עמהם בקול רם—ברוך אתה ה' א-להינו מלך העולם
> אשר קדשנו במצוותיו וציונו על ספירת העומר שהיום יום אחד. והולך ומונה
> כן כל מנחה עד סוף השבוע, אמר—שהיום שבעה ימים שהם שבוע אחד; י"ד
> ימים שהן שני שבועות; כ"א שהן שלשה שבועות; כ"ח שהן ארבעה שבועות;
> ל"ה שהן חמשה שבועות; מ"ב שהן ששה שבועות; מ"ט שהן שבעה שבועות,
> ולמחרתו הוא ערב שבועות. וכל בעלי בתים חוזרין ומספרין אחר הסעודה
> בבתים. ובכל פעם אחר שספרו אומרים יהי רצון מלפניך ה' א-להינו וא-להי
> אבותינו שיבנה בית המקדש במהרה בימינו ותן חלקנו בתורתך.

אמנם יש גמישות בהלכות ספירת העומר לקטנים, אך ההתחשבות בצעירי המתפללים משפיעה לא רק על ספירתם, אלא אף על הספירה שלנו בשבתות ובחגים. האפשרות ההלכתית להקל עבור הקטן, יכולה להשפיע על המתרחש בבית הכנסת, שהרי איחור התפילה גורע מהזמן היקר והמיוחד הניתן לשבת בסעודת החג ובסעודת שבת עם ילדינו. ממבט זה, כל המאחר את התפילה מרוויח ספירת העומר לאחר צאת הכוכבים אך מנכה מהזמן שניתן לשבת בחיק המשפחה בהארה של קדושת החג וקדושת השבת.

כפי שראינו, המנהג אשר רווח בקהילות אשכנז היה להקדים את הספירה לפני צאת הכוכבים. העדויות על ספירה בבין השמשות מסייעות לנו ומאפשרות תמיכת יתדותינו במנהגי ישראל. יתירה מזו, ראינו כי היו קהילות אשר נהגו להקדים את הספירה דווקא בשבתות, ועובדה זו אף

---

[32] ר' עובדיה יוסף, פוסק כי יש לספור לאחר צאת הכוכבים, ומוסיף: "ומכל מקום ציבור שסיימו תפילת ערבית מיד אחר השקיעה, שהוא עדיין זמן 'בין השמשות', ספק יום ספק לילה, ואינם ממתינים עד צאת הכוכבים, וקיים חשש שחלק מן הציבור יבוא לידי שכחה ויפסידו מצות הספירה, יכולים לספור בברכה" (ילקוט יוסף, לעיל הערה 64, סעיף יד). מכל מקום, הוא דוחה את האפשרות של ספירת העומר לפני בין השמשות, ואכמ"ל. עיינו: ר' עובדיה יוסף, שו"ת יביע אומר, חלק ו, סימן לא; הנ"ל, שו"ת יחוה דעת, חלק א, סימן כג.

[33] ילקוט יוסף, לעיל הערה 64, סעיף ט: "מצוה לחנך את הקטנים לספור את העומר בכל יום, ויש לחנכם לספור עם ברכה כדת, ואפילו אם שכחו לספור יום אחד, יכולים להמשיך לספור בברכה, משום חינוך." ניתן להסיק כי יש על הקטן לספור מהדיונים בכתבי האחרונים על השאלה האם קטן שהגדיל באמצע העומר רשאי להמשיך לספור בברכה לאחר שגדל, ואכמ"ל.

[34] ר' גבריאל ציננער, נטעי גבריאל, הלכות פסח, חלק שלישי, פרק כה, אות י: "יש להקל לקטן לספור בבין השמשות, ובפרט שבימות הקיץ זמן צה"כ מאוחר".
האפשרות להקל עבור קטן מצויה בהלכה במקרים אחרים, עיינו לדוגמא: ר' אברהם אבלי גומבינר, מגן אברהם, אורח חיים, סימן רסט, סק"א שכאשר יש דעות להקל ראוי להקל ואמץ קולות אלו עבור קטן.

[35] ר' יעקב מולין, ספר מהרי"ל—מנהגים, הלכות ספירת העומר, אות טו.

גם מספרי הלכה מארצות אשכנז עולה כי נהגו לספור בבין השמשות. כך מעיד המהרש״ל[26] כי "בספק חשיכה רגילין לספור", למרות שבכל הנראה הוא עצמו לא נהג כך.[27] כך גם מעיד הב״ח: "אבל מנהג העולם עכשיו לברך בספק חשכה".[28] וכן ר׳ שניאור זלמן מליאדי: "ומ״מ המנהג ההמון עכשיו ... לספור בביה״ש".[29]

היו מחכמי אשכנז אשר נהגו לספור לפני צאת הכוכבים בערב שבת בלבד כאשר הכניסו את השבת מבעוד יום, וזאת כדי להכניס את השבת מוקדם מפאת המצווה של תוספת שבת.[30] אמנם היו חכמים אשר קראו תגר על מנהג זה.[31]

ככל הנראה, מנהגים אלו נוצרו בגלל המציאות בקהילות אלו—אם מפני השעה המאוחרת של צאת הכוכבים ואם מפני הנוהג של חברי הקהילה להתפלל ערבית לפני צאת הכוכבים ולאחר מכן לחזור לביתם. תהא הסיבה אשר תהא, רואים אנו כיצד המנהג בקהילות אלו לספור בבין השמשות הכריע את ההלכה הפסוקה אשר דגלה בספירה רק לאחר צאת הכוכבים. אם כן, לעיתים המציאות הכתיבה, ואולי ממשיכה להכתיב, את ספירת העומר בבין השמשות.

כיצד ראוי לנו לנהוג?

בקהילתנו, ישנם שיקולים הנוטים בעד הספירה בבין השמשות בנסיבות מסוימות. מבחינה ראשונית מנהגי הקהילה הקהילה מבוססים על מנהג אשכנז, ובשל כך קיימת אפשרות לנהוג כפי שנהגו בקהילות אשכנזיות אחרות ולספור לפני צאת הכוכבים. אמנם "מנהג ההמון" לכשעצמו אינו נימוק מכריע לסטות מן ההלכה הפסוקה. אולם, דומני כי יש גם שיקולים מהותיים המעוגנים בערכי מסורת ישראל והמדברים בעד הספירה בבין השמשות, והם שניים:

1. "ואין שכחה לפני כסא כבודך"

לא פעם קורה כי כאשר מסיימים את התפילה לפני צאת הכוכבים, מכריזים בבית הכנסת כי על כל אחד ואחד לספור בביתו. אולם, השכחה מצויה בין אנשים בשר ודם, ואין פלא שהחובה של ספירת העומר חומקת מזכרונם כתינוק הבורח מבית-הספר. וכבר היו דברים מעולם בקהילתנו הקדושה כי חברים יראי שמים שכחו לספור לאחר שחזרו הביתה. הספירה בבין השמשות, על

---

[26] ר׳ שלמה לוריא, שו״ת מהרש״ל, סימן יג.

[27] ר׳ משה מפרעמסלא, מטה משה, חלק חמישי, סימן תרסד—המחבר, שהיה תלמידו של המהרש״ל, כותב: "ואדוני מורי מהר״ש ז״ל לא היה אוכל עד צאת הכוכבים כי אמר פן ישכח הספירה בטרדת הסעודה, וקודם צאת הכוכבים לא היה רוצה לספור".

[28] ר׳ יואל סירקיס, בית חדש, אורח חיים סימן תפט.

[29] ר׳ שניאור זלמן מליאדי, שולחן ערוך, אורח חיים, סימן תפט, סעיף יב.

[30] ספר המנהגים לרבינו אייזיק טירנא, לעיל הערה 65; ר׳ יוסף ב״ר משה, לקט יושר, חלק א, עמ׳ 97 —ככל הנראה כך נהגו בבניאושטט, ואולי אפילו הקדימו לפני צאת הכוכבים. לפני בין השמשות, ואכמ״ל; ר׳ יחיאל מיכל הלוי עפשטיין, ערוך השולחן, אורח חיים, סימן תפט, סעיף ז: "ואין אנו סומכין לספור בבין השמשות רק משום דמצוה לקבל שבת מבעוד יום". כך גם עולה מדברי ר׳ שלום מקוידינוב, לעיל הערה 61.

[31] ר׳ יוסף תאומים, פרי מגדים, משבצת זהב, סק״ה: "ובערב שבת בציבור המאחרין יותר טוב, ולא כאותן המקדימים ואומרים כבר לילה, ורגע מקודם אומרים יום גדול לקבל שבת, וקורא אני שָׂמִים חֹשֶׁךְ לְאוֹר (ישעיה ה, כ), ואותו האור במעט רגע לחשך, על כן ראוי למנוע זה, וישראל קדושים שומעים ומקבלים תוכחה ומוסר, על כן לקבלת שבת מקדימין ולספירה מאחרין".

ועיינו הערתו של ר׳ יעקב מולין בתשובה (תשובות מהרי״ל החדשות, יורה דעה, סוף סימן צה)—לדידו חרף הדין של תוספת שבת, אין להוספה דין של לילה לעניין ספירת העומר ומצוות התלויות בלילה האחרות.

בכיוון דומה, המהרש״ל (לעיל הערה 66) לא ראה את תוספת שבת בתור סיבה להקדים את הספירה, אך כאמור לעיל הוא הכיר במנהג לספור בבין השמשות.

חובתו, למרות שלכתחילה ראוי לספור לאחר צאת הכוכבים.[19] [20]

יש הסוברים כי למרות שהסופר בבין השמשות יצא, ראוי שיחזור ויספור ללא ברכה לאחר צאת הכוכבים, מפאת החשש שמא ספירת העומר בזמן הזה מדאורייתא.[21] לפי זה, ראוי לעשות סימן כדי שהסופר בבין השמשות לא ישכח לספור שוב ללא ברכה לאחר צאת הכוכבים.[22]

כיצד נוהגים?

בספרו בית יוסף,[23] מציין המחבר כי "מנהג העולם" הוא לספור לאחר צאת הכוכבים, כפי שנהגו המדקדקים בתקופתו של הרשב"א.

לאור מסקנה זו, היו חכמים אשר הציעו דרך לוודא כי הקהל יספור לאחר צאת הכוכבים: "ומה טוב ומה נעים המנהג שנוהגים בכמה קהילות מישראל שבימי הספירה בין מנחה לערבית הקהל יושבים, ותלמיד חכם שבקהל עומד ודורש להם בדברי אגדה ומוסר השכל עד שיגיע זמן הספירה, והוא בכלל מצוה גוררת מצוה.".[24]

למרות הפסק הברור המצדד בספירה לאחר צאת הכוכבים ודברי ר' יוסף קארו כי נהגו כך, קיימות עדויות בספרי מנהגים מקהילות באשכנז כי אכן נהגו לספור בבין השמשות.[25]

---

[19] ר' אברהם אבלי גומבינר, מגן אברהם, על אתר, סק"ו; משנה ברורה, על אתר, סק"ו. ואולי אף הר"ן (לעיל הערה 44) היה מסכים למסקנה זו, שהרי הוא כתב "ואין זה נכון שיכניס עצמו בספק לכת-חלה" ומדיוק לשונו ניתן להסיק כי הספירה בבין השמשות לכתחילה אינה ראויה, אך בדיעבד מי שספר בפרק זמן זה יצא ידי חובתו.

[20] שאלה הנושקת לנדון הנ"ל היא באדם ששכח לספור בלילה שכידוע עליו לספור ביום שלמחרת, ובכך יכול להמשיך בלילה הבא לספור בברכה. אם לא זכר במשך היום להשלים ולספור ללא ברכה, והגיע בין השמשות— האם הוא רשאי לספור בבין השמשות ללא ברכה ולאחר צאת הכוכבים להמשיך לספור בברכה? בבסיס השאלה עומדת ההנחה כי בין השמשות הוא ספק יום (כפי שהוא ספק לילה). היות ומצב דברים זה אינו שכיח לא נאריך כאן. למתעניינים בשאלה נציין את המקורות הבאים: ר' חיים יוסף דוד אזולאי (החיד"א), ברכי יוסף, סימן תפט, סעיף יז (הובאו דבריו אצל ר' חיים מרגליות, שערי תשובה, סימן תפט, סק"כ); ר' אברהם דוד ורמן מבוטשאטש, אשל אברהם, סימן תפט—שהסתפקו בכך. ר' יוסף באב"ד, מנחת חינוך, מצווה שו, אות ח—אשר תלה את השאלה במחלוקת האם ספירת העומר בזמן הזה היא דאורייתא או דרבנן (לעיל הערות 44, 47 ו-52). והשווה: בית דוד, סימן רסח; שו"ת מהרי"א הלוי, חלק א, סימן קנה—שכתבו שימשיך ללא ברכה. ואילו: ר' יוסף שאול נתנזון, שו"ת שואל ומשיב, מהדורה ד, חלק ג, סימן קכז; ר' שלמה מסקאהל, שו"ת בית שלמה, אורח חיים, סימן קב—כתבו שניתן להמשיך לספור בברכה. ר' עובדיה יוסף, שו"ת יביע אומר, חלק ק, אורח חיים, סימן מג; ילקוט יוסף, להלן הערה 64, סעיף כ—מסכים כי ניתן להמשיך לספור בברכה, אלא שהוא מוסיף "ונכון שבבגון זה יזהר שלא יספור יותר ספירת העומר אלא אחר צאת הכוכבים" וזאת כדי שלא יהיה מצב של תרתי דסתרי.

[21] ר' אליה שפירא מטיקטין, אליה רבה, על הלבוש, סימן תפט, סק"י; ר' יוסף תאומים, פרי מגדים, משבצות זהב, אורח חיים, סימן תפט, סק"ה; ר' שניאור זלמן מליאדי, שולחן ערוך, אורח חיים, סימן תפט, סעיפים יב-יג; ר' שלום מקוידינוב, משמרת שלום, סימן לו, אות ו. וע. ו. להעיר שלפי כמה מגדולי האחרונים, כשהמחבר פוסק בסימן תפ"ט סעיף ג—"המתפלל עם הציבור מבעוד יום מונה עמהם בלא ברכה ואם יזכור בלילה יספור בלא ברכה." כוונתו לציבור הסופר בזמן בין השמשות, ולא בזמן פלג המנחה כדעת רוב האחרונים. לפי הבנה זו, הציע המשנה ברורה שם: "דהוא ימנה עמהם פן ישכח אחר כך, יחשוב בדעתו אם אזכור אחר כך בלילה למנות, אין אני רוצה לצאת בספירה זו...ועל כן כשיגיע הזמן אחר כך יברך ויספור."

[22] ר' חיים יוסף דוד אזולאי, מורה באצבע, סימן ז, אות ריז.

[23] ר' יוסף קארו, בית יוסף, אורח חיים, סימן תפט.

[24] ר' יצחק יוסף, ילקוט יוסף—פסקי הר' עובדיה יוסף, ירושלים, תשמ"ח, הלכות ספירת העומר, סעיף יד. וכך גם הציע האדמו"ר מקליוזינבורג, לעיל הערה 52.

[25] ספר המנהגים לרבינו אברהם קלויזנר, מהדורת ירושלים, תשל"ח, סימן קכא, אות ג; ספר המנהגים לרבינו אייזיק טירנא, מהדורת ירושלים, תשל"ט, עמ' סא.

שנית, גם בין הסוברים כי ספירת העומר היום היא דרבנן, היו מחכמי ספרד אשר שללו את האפשרות של ספירה בבין השמשות, כפי שנראה עתה.

הרשב"א[13] נשאל על צבור אשר ביום מעונן חשב כי היום כבר פנה, ומשום כך התפלל תפילת ערבית וספר את העומר. העננים התפזרו והצבור גילה כי עוד היום גדול. האם עליהם לשוב ולספור את העומר? הרשב"א השיב כי עליהם לחזור ולספור, שהרי ספירתם הראשונה היתה בטעות "דהיכי לימא 'היום עשרה ימים לעומר' ואינו אלא תשעה!? כי אותו יום תשיעי הוא ולא עשירי עד צאת הכוכבים". מדברי הרשב"א משמע כי אין לספור עד צאת הכוכבים.

הרשב"א סיים את תשובתו בהוספה: "והמדקדקים אינם סופרים בימי הספירה עד צאת הכוכבים, וכן ראוי לעשות". מילים אלו יוצרות אי-בהירות בשיטת הרשב"א. לדעתו, אם ספר בבין השמשות—האם עליו לחזור "כי אותו יום תשיעי הוא ולא עשירי עד צאת הכוכבים", או שמא רק "המדקדקים אינם סופרים בימי הספירה עד צאת הכוכבים וכן ראוי לעשות" אך בדיעבד הסופר בבין השמשות יצא? אין פתרון לשאלה זו. מכל מקום ברור כי לדעת הרשב"א, ספירה בבין השמשות אינה ראויה.

בצורה ברורה יותר חולק הר"ן[14] על האפשרות של ספירת העומר בבין השמשות. הר"ן כותב כי למרות שחובת הספירה היום היא מדרבנן, אין זה ראוי להכניס את עצמנו לספק לכתחילה על ידי ספירה בבין השמשות.

כיצד נפסקה ההלכה?

הפוסקים נוקטים כי לכתחילה אין לספור בבין השמשות, וראוי להמתין עד צאת הכוכבים.[15] בכך דחו הפוסקים את הטענה שיש עדיפות לספירה בבין השמשות.[16]

השולחן ערוך[17] מעתיק את תשובת הרשב"א בשינוי לשון. במקום לנקוט כי היום ממשיך "עד צאת הכוכבים", כתב המחבר כי "חוזרים לספור כשתחשך", ורק המדקדקים מחכים עד צאת הכוכבים. משינוי קל זה, הסיק המשנה ברורה[18] "דמן הדין היה אפשר להקל לספור משתחשך אף קודם צאת הכוכבים... אלא דמכל מקום אינו נכון להכניס עצמו לספק לכתחילה, ועל כן המדקדקים ממתינים עד צאת הכוכבים שהיא ודאי לילה. מכאן שהסופר בבין השמשות יצא ידי

יוסף קארו, בית יוסף, אורח חיים, סימן תפ"ט. וכך כתבו האחרונים: ר' יעקב עמדין, מור וקציעה, סימן תפ"ט; הנ"ל, סידור שערי שמים; ר' יוסף דב הלוי סולובייצ'יק, שו"ת בית הלוי, חלק א, סימן לט; ר' מאיר שמחה הכהן מדווינסק, אור שמח, הלכות תמידין ומוספין ז, כב, ועיינו דברי הגר"ח בחידושי הגרי"ז למנחות. ויש להוסיף כי כך משמע מהנוסח של לשם יחוד וכו' הנאמר בקהילות רבות לפני ספירת העומר. אולם, עיינו דברי האדמו"ר מקלויזנבורג-צאנז, ר' יקותיאל יהודה האלברשטאם, שפע חיים—מכתבי תורה, כרך ב, נתניה, תשמ"ח, סימן קלה. שם העיד על עצמו שהוא שינה את הנוסח ובמקום "לקיים מצות עשה של ספירת העומר כמו שכתוב בתורה", אמר "לקיים מצות ספירת העומר וכתוב בתורה" מאחר שרוב הפוסקים נוקטים שספירת העומר בזמן הזה היא מדרבנן. להשלמת התמונה יש לעיין בשיטתו האמצעית של רבינו ירוחם, לעיל הערה 47.

13 שו"ת הרשב"א, חלק א, סימן קנד.
14 ר"ן, לעיל הערה 44.
15 ר' מרדכי יפה, לבוש, הלכות פסח, סימן תפט, סעיף ב; ואחרים.
16 לעיל הערה 48 וטקסט הסמוך לה.
17 ר' יוסף קארו, שולחן ערוך, אורח חיים, סימן תפט, סעיף ב.
18 ר' ישראל הכהן מראדין, משנה ברורה, על אתר, סק"י"ד ושער הציון, על אתר, סק"ח.

שבין ודאי יום לבין ודאי לילה.

קיימת מחלוקת גדולה אודות תחילת בין השמשות וסופו. בארץ ישראל, המנהג המקובל הוא כי בין השמשות מתחיל משקיעת שפתה העליונה של החמה ונמשך עד צאת ג' כוכבים בינוניים. במציאות, פרק הזמן הזה משתנה מקו-רוחב אחד לקו-רוחב אחר. בארץ ישראל בין השמשות, לפי המנהג המקובל, נמשך פחות מעשרים דקות.

מבחינה הלכתית פרק הזמן של בין השמשות מוגדר בתור ספק יום וספק לילה.

זכר למקדש בבין השמשות—מהי הנפקות ההלכתית של הגדרות אלו?

צירוף שני המרכיבים הנזכרים: סיווג מצוות ספירת העומר בתור זכר למקדש, והגדרת בין השמשות בתור ספק יום ספק לילה—הביא חלק מרבותינו הראשונים להציע נפקא מינה הלכתית אודות עיתוי הספירה. לדידם, הסופר בבין השמשות יצא ידי חובתו ואינו צריך לספור שוב.

מקור השיטה הזאת היא מתקופת בעלי התוספות באשכנז, והיא מובאת על ידי ראשונים רבים.[7]

לצד דעה זו הסוברת כי יש אפשרות לספור בבין השמשות, קיימת אפילו סיבה להעדיף את הספירה בבין השמשות. בתורה נאמר שֶׁבַע שַׁבָּתוֹת תְּמִימֹת תִּהְיֶינָה (ויקרא כג, טו), וכדי להבטיח שעד זמן הבאת העומר יהיו שבעה שבועות תמימים, הרי יש להקדים את הספירה לפני רדת החשיכה, דהיינו יש לספור בבין השמשות.[8] הצעה זו לא התקבלה והיא נדחית להלכה.[9] יש לציין כי רק העדיפות לספירה בבין השמשות נדחית, ולא עצם האפשרות של ספירה בפרק זמן זה.[10]

"כמה ימי הספירה הלילה?"

מהאפשרות לספור בבין השמשות עולה נפקא מינה הלכתית מעניינת. מי שנשאל בבין השמשות "כמה ימי הספירה הלילה?" עליו להשיב "אתמול היה כך וכך", שהרי אם יאמר "היום כך וכך" הרי הוא יצא ידי חובתו ולא יוכל לחזור ולספור בברכה.[11]

האם ספירת העומר בבין השמשות מקובלת על כולם?

ספירת העומר בבין השמשות לא התקבלה על ידי כל הראשונים. ראשית, יש לציין כי שקיבל את ההנחה שספירת העומר היום הינה מדאורייתא, לא ראה כאן שני מרכיבים להקל—דין דרבנן וספק לילה.[12]

---

[7] תוספות, מנחות סו, א ד"ה זכר למקדש הוא; פסקי תוספות, מנחות, אות קצב; ר' שמשון ב"ר צדוק, תשב"ץ קטן, סימן שצד; רא"ש, פסחים, פרק עשירי, סימן מ; רבינו ירוחם, תולדות אדם וחוה, נתיב ה, חלק ד; טור, אורח חיים, סימן תפט; ר' דוד אבודרהם, ספר אבודרהם, תפלות הפסח; ר' אהרן הכהן מנרבונה, ארחות חיים, הלכות ספירת העומר, אות ה; ספר כלבו, סימן נה; ר' יצחק מקורבייל, ספר מצוות קטן, מצוה קמה—בשם הר"ש משאנץ; ועוד.

[8] רא"ש; רבינו ירוחם—לעיל הערה 47.

[9] תוספות, לעיל הערה 47. ועיין, ר"ן, לעיל הערה 44: "ואי משום תמימות אין להחמיר בתמימות בזמן הזה שהוא מדרבנן טפי מספירה דאורייתא אלא כל שסופר בליל תמימות קרינן ביה".

[10] לא כך הבינו חלק מן האחרונים—ר' יוסף קארו, בית יוסף, אורח חיים, סימן תפט; ר' יואל סירקיס, בית חדש, אורח חיים, סימן תפט. אולם מריבוי ההבאות של האפשרות של ספירה בבין השמשות ללא העדיפות לספירה בפרק זמן זה, ברור כי האפשרות התקבלה למרות שהעדיפות נדחית.

[11] כך נוקטים הפוסקים, עיינו לדוגמא: ר' שניאור זלמן מליאדי, שולחן ערוך, אורח חיים, סימן תפט, סעיפים יד-טו.

[12] בין הראשונים הסוברים כי ספירת העומר היום היא דאורייתא, ראו: מרדכי, מגילה סימן תתג; תשובות מהר"ם מרוטנבורג, דפוס פראג, סימן תרמ"ה, ועוד. כך לכאורה גם דעת הרמב"ם—עיינו: ר"ן, פסחים כח, א באלפס; ר'

- **לצורכי חינוך**—במשפחות בהן מחנכים את הילדים לספור את העומר, אך שוכבים לישון לפני צאת הכוכבים;
- **ספירה לפני צאת הכוכבים בדיעבד**—כאשר סופרים את העומר, ורק לאחר מכן שמים לב כי טרם הגיעה שעת צאת הכוכבים.

הדיון בסוגיה זו מתחלק לשני סעיפים:

1. ספירת העומר לאחר פלג המנחה[2] ולפני השקיעה;
2. ספירת העומר בין השמשות, דהיינו לאחר השקיעה ולפני צאת הכוכבים.

במאמר זה ננסה להציע בפני הקוראים את עיקרי ההלכות אשר נאמרו לגבי ספירת העומר לפני צאת הכוכבים. נעסוק בסעיף השני בלבד—ספירת העומר בין השמשות—שהרי לא ניתן לשאת ולתן בספירת העומר לפני השקיעה, אם אין כל אפשרות של ספירת העומר לפני צאת הכוכבים. זאת ועוד: בקהילתנו, ספירת העומר בין השמשות שכיחה יותר, ועל כן ראוי שנתייחס אל התדיר לפני הנדיר.

ספירת העומר – זכר למקדש

הגמרא[3] מצטטת את דברי אביי כי מצוות ספירת העומר כוללת חובה למנות את הימים ואת השבועות. הגמרא מביאה עדות אודות קבוצת חכמים—רבנן דבי רב אשי—שאכן מנו ימים ומנו שבועות. הפסקה מסתיימת בהבאת מסורת של אמימר אשר מנה רק מנה ימים ולא מנה שבועות. הגמרא מביאה נימוק למנהגו של אמימר שאמר "זכר למקדש הוא". כוונת הנימוק "זכר למקדש" היא כי במציאות ללא בית המקדש שאין מקריבים את העומר, הרי אין למצוות ספירת העומר תוקף של דין מן התורה. היום, אם כן, לספירת העומר יש ערך סמלי, המזכירה לנו כיצד נהגו בזמן שבית המקדש היה קיים. משום כך די לספור ימים ללא שבועות.

גישתו של אמימר התקבלה למחצה. מצד אחד, נפסק כי סופרים גם ימים וגם שבועות בהתאם למסורת אביי ודבי רב אשי. מצד שני, רוב חכמינו קיבלו את הקביעה כי ספירת העומר היום היא זכר למקדש. משמעות קביעה זו היא שאין למצוות ספירת העומר תוקף של דין תורה, אלא החיוב לספור את העומר הוא מדברי סופרים.[4]

"בין השמשות"—ספק יום ספק לילה

קצרה היריעה מלהתייחס לעומק הסוגיה הסבוכה של הגדרת "בין השמשות".[5] לצורכי הדיון כאן, די אם נזכיר כי בין השמשות הוא פרק הזמן ש"ספק חשיכה ספק אינו חשיכה",[6] והוא הזמן

---

[2] פלג המנחה הוא שעה זמנית ורבע מסוף היום ההלכתי, ואין כאן המקום להאריך בהגדרה מדויקת של זמן זה. בבלי מנחות סו, א.

[3] בבלי מנחות סו, א.

[4] ר"ן, פסחים, כח, א באלפס: "... ורוב המפרשים מסכימים דספירת העומר עכשיו דליכא הבאה ולא קרבן אינה אלא מדרבנן בעלמא זכר למקדש, כדאמר אמימר התם זכר למקדש בעלמא הוא. ובהגדה גם כן אמרו—בשעה שאמר להם משה תעבדון את הא-להים על ההר הזה, אמרו לו ישראל: משה רבינו, אימתי עבודה זו? אמר להם: לסוף חמשים יום. והיו מונין כל אחד ואחד לעצמו מכאן קבעו חכמים לספירת העומר כלומר בזמן הזה שאין אנו מביאין קרבן ולא עומר אלא מחשבין ג' יום לשמחת התורה כמו שמנו ישראל באותו זמן וזה ודאי דרך מדרש הוא דעיקרא דמילתא זכר למקדש כדאמר אמימר. אבל מ"מ כל זה מוכיח שאין הספירה עכשיו אלא מדרבנן."

[5] הרוצים להשכיל בסוגיה נכבדת זו ייטיבו לעיין בספרו של ר' חיים פ' בניש, הזמנים להלכה, בני-ברק, תשנ"ו, עמ' שכה-תען; תקמה-תקנה. ובעניין הנדון כאן—ספירת העומר בין השמשות, עיינו: עמ' תקמח-תקמט; תקסט-תקעא.

[6] משנה, שבת, פרק ב, משנה ז; בבלי מנחות לו, ב.

רב לוי יצחק קופר רב קהילת הצור והצהר, צור הדסה.
הרב מלמד תלמוד, פילוסופיה של ההלכה, תנ״ך וחסידות
במכון פרדס בירושלים.

ספירת העומר בבין השמשות
הרב לוי יצחק קופר

הקדמה

היישוב צור הדסה, השוכן בהרי ירושלים, נוסד בשנת 1960. בעשור האחרון, זכה היישוב
לשגשוג ולהרחבה משמעותית. כיום אוכלוסיית היישוב מונה כאלף משפחות.

מרבית תושבי היישוב אינם שומרים על אורח חיים דתי, אך לרבים מהם הערכה וכבוד למסורת
היהודית. רבים מהתושבים נוטלים חלק בחיים הדתיים ביישוב בצורה זו או אחרת. בשנים האחרונות
אנו עדים לתנופה דתית והתפתחות המוסדות הדתיים, כגון: פתיחת גן דתי, שיעורי תורה לרבים,
בניית בתי כנסת וכו'.

לקראת ראש השנה תשס״ה החליטה קבוצת אנשים, נשים ונוער על יסוד "קהילת הצור והצהר".
מאז הקמתה, נדרשה הקהילה לתת מענה לשאלות רבות של סדרי הקהילה, נוהלי בית הכנסת,
ארגון התפילה והיחסים בין באי הבית הכנסת לבין כלל אוכלוסיית היישוב.

כידוע, קיימות דרכים מגוונות לפתרון שאלות אלו, העולות כדבר שבשבגרה בכל קהילה, ובמיוחד
בעת ייסוד קהילה חדשה. הדוגמא להלן משקפת דגם לפתרון אשר יושם בקהילת הצור והצהר.
המיוחד בפתרון זה הוא השמירה על נאמנות להלכה מחד, ומאידך כבוד הציבור ושיתוף המתפללים
בשיקולים ההלכתיים המולידים את הנוהל.

הדברים הבאים, אשר הופצו בעלון "הדס שיטה" (גליון 3),[1] הוצעו בפני חברי הקהילה בימי
ספירת העומר אשתקד. הרשימה לא נכתבה בתור תשובה לשאלה, ואף לא נוסחה בתור פסק
הלכה מחייב. לפני חברי וחברות הקהילה הוצעו הדברים בתור הרצאת מסכת הלכתית שנועדה
ליצור בסיס לדיון הלכתי מעמיק בקהילה. מטרתי היתה שחברי וחברות הקהילה ירגישו שותפות
בקביעת הנוהל, ובכך ליצור תחושה של שייכות ואחריות. בחרתי לפרסם את מאמר המוגש להלן
מפאת עניינו לציבור שוחר תורה ומפאת שכיחות הנסיבות המתוארות.

הצגת הבעיה

מידי שנה בבואנו לספור את העומר, קהילתנו הקדושה, כקהילות רבות, עומדת בפני בעיה.
לעתים התפילה מסתיימת לפני צאת הכוכבים, ועולה השאלה האם ניתן לספור את העומר לפני
צאת הכוכבים, או שמא יש לחכות עד שתחשך כדי לספור? לשון אחרת: מה הדין של ספירת
העומר בבין השמשות? שאלה זאת עולה בשלוש נסיבות:

- **תפילת ערבית המסתיימת לפני צאת הכוכבים**—כגון: מקומות שמתפללים ערבית
  מוקדם.

---

[1] הרשימה הוקדשה לצעירי המתפללים שעלו לכתה א'. תפילתי שנזכה לחנך את הדור הצעיר על ברכי המסורת
ויהי חשק בתורה ובמצוות. אני אסיר תודה לידיד-נפשי, אמיר גוטל אשר קרא את הגליון רב והציע הערות
והארות מועילות.

מעתה ענוותנותו של כמעגתוצ״ה תרבני לבקש מלפניו להטיב עמדי ולהודיעני
את דעתו הגדולה והרחבה, דעת תורה א[ו]דות שלש התלונות שלמעלה שכנגד
פסק דינו של דיין עד כמה צודקות הן עפ״י דין, ואם הן צודקות וההוראה היא
מוטעה אם יש הרשות לעבור עלי׳ מבלי כל חשש ופקפוק ולהטיל פתקא לבנה
ולומר גם לאחרים לעשות כן. מצוה גדולה יעשה כמעגת״ה בתשובתו זו, כי
אנכי העומד במקום המעשה ויודע ומכיר גם את השרטוטים היותר דקים שבתוך
הענין, דומה בעיני למי שרואה בירה דולקת ולבו בוער בקרבו על אבדן הקהלה.
ככה גם אנכי רואה כי אש פרצה בתוך קהלת ישרון שבפה, אש המחלוקת,
וח״ו עד אבדון תאכל אם לא יקומו לה עוזרים מבחוץ, ואם לא יבואו הגדולים
אשר בארץ לכבות את אש המחלקה [!] במי הדעת של תורה ולהשיב את
השלו׳ על כנו בדבר ה׳ אשר בפיהם כדרך שעשו מעולם הגדולים אנשי השם,
ולא די שכל המזכה אינו מפסיד כ״א גם שכרו יגדל עד אין קץ לפענ״ד מפני
שהביא ברכה ושלו׳ בעולם.
דברי עבדו המתאבק בעפר רלגיו ושותה בצמא את דבריו, משתחוה מול
כמעגתוצ״ה מרחוק ומחכה לתשובתו הרמה כאל מלקוש,

בן ציון ראכעלזאהן

הנני כעת בבאד נאוהיים ובדעתי להתעכב עוד פה אי״ה כ״ה כ״א יום וע״כ ייטיב
נא לכתוב לי על אדריסתי שבפה

Herrn B. Rachelsohn
z. Zt. Bad-Nauheim
Frankfurterstr. 40
Deuschland

ג) אין ההוראה מתקבלת על הלב, שהמחילה של הבן על זכות חזקתו תועיל רק לחצאין, היינו רק להעמיד עוד קאנדידאט אבל לא לבחור. ואדרבה הדבר ידוע שאף להסוברים שיש חזקה ברבנות וגם החזקה היא מצוה—המוטלת על הציבור—ולא ירושה, בכל זאת מועלת מחילה לבטל את זכות המוחזק לגמרי וגם בלא שום קנין כמו כל מחילה שאינה צריכה קנין.

אך כשם שהצד שכנגד מתלונן על הדין ומחזיק את הבחירה לדבר בלתי אפשר כל זמן שהדיין מחזיק באזהרתו ואוסר בחירת רב אחר כן מתרעם הצד שבעד על הצד שכנגד ואומר כי הוא מחריב את הקהלה במה שהוא מעכב את הבחירה וגורם שהקהלה תהי' בלא רב זה שנתים. אבל להצד שכנגד קשה לעשות הבחירה גם מטעם אחד. כי לאחר שנתפרסם מכתב הדיין הנ"ל חזר הד"ר קליין מנירנבערג מדעתו ואינו רוצה להעמיד עצמו בתור קאנדידאט מפני שאינו רוצה שיתחלל שמו ושיאמרו עליו כי לפי דעת הדיין השיג כמעט גבול בן הרב. ובכן אין לשני הצדדים עתה כי אם קאנדידאט אחד והוא בן הרב, ואם יעמידו את בן הרב לבדו ואזהרת הדיין תשאר בתקפה הלא תגדל החשש פי עשר פן יבחרו בהבן הזה. ובכן פעל הצד שכנגד על לב הצד בעד, שהד"ר מונק מבערלין יבחור מרצונו בי"ד של שלשה מטובי המורים שבארץ אשכנז והם יעיינו בפסק דינו של הדיין אם נכון הוא ויגישו את משפטם הם לפני גדולים אחרים מארצות המזרח וככל אשר יאמרו אלה הגדולים כן יקום. הד"ר מונק השתדל לבחור בי"ד—והוא נקרא בפי כל הבי"ד הבערליני מבלי שיודעים הפראנקפורטיים מי הוא ומי הם חביריו ורק מונק לבדו ידוע זאת—אבל זה הבי"ד לא מצא לנכון להתערב בעניניו של דיין מעיר אחרת ולבקר את פסק דינו. הצד שבעד הציג את מאונו של הבי"ד הבערליני להתערב בדבר בתור הסכמה רשמית על פסק הדין וע"כ כאשר הציע אח"כ הצד שכנגד לבחור בבי"ד אחר מארצות המזרח והיה כדאי להציע לפניו את הדבר, מאן הצד שבעד בהההצעה הזאת, באמרם כי הדיין שאנו סומכים עליו בכל ענינים איסור והיתר כדאי הוא שנסמוך עליו גם בדבר הרבנות ואין אנו צריכים לדיינים אחרים. או אז שלחו, עפ"י הסכמת שני הצדדים, לפני שבועות אחדים אחרי הד"ר מונק הנ"ל שיבוא לפראנקפורט לדבר על לב הדיין ולהשיבו מדעתו כדי שיוכלו לעשות בחירה—איינע וואהל—מחדש. אבל דברי הד"ר מ. לא פעלו על לב הדיין מאומה. הוא עומד על דעתו הראשונה כי עפ"י תורה מחויב כל אחד לבחור בבן הרב אף שמחל על חזקתו, ורק הנחה אחת עשה: הוא נתן רשות להפרנסים לכתוב בשמו אל כל הקהל, כי אף שלפי פסק דינו מחויב כל אחד לבחור בבן הרב בכל זאת מי שהוא חושב שיש טעות בדין הזה הרשות בידו לבחור באופן כמו זה שהוא חושב לצאת בו ידי רגש המוסרי שלו וידי חובתו לשמים, היינו או לבחור בבן הרב—שהוא הקאנדידאט היחידי—או למאן בו ולהטיל לאות מאונו פתקא לבנה, כלומר חלקה לתוך הקלפי.

כשראה הצד שכנגד שאפסה כל תקוה להשיב את הדין מדעתו ושמצד אחר הקהלה באמת יורדת מטה מטה לרגלי[17] חסרון רב, בחר את הרע במיעוטו והסכים לעשות בחירה מחדש לאחר תשעה באב למרות היות בן הרב הקאנדידאט היחידי ולמרות פסק הדין שעומד בתקפו. אך לבו מלא דאגה, כמובן, כי לא בנקל כ"כ ירהיב חבר הקהלה—שרובה ככולה כמעט אינו מבין מעצמו ללמוד אף סעיף קיצור שו"ע כראוי—עוז בנפשו לומר שהדיין טעה בדין ולהטיל בשביל כך פתקא לבנה לתוך הקלפי. ואף הלומדים החרדים על דבר ה' מפקפקים בדבר כל עוד שלא ישמעו מפי גדול מפורסם ומומחה לרבים שמותרים הם עפ"י דין להחזיק את הוראת הדיין למוטעה ולהטיל בשביל זה פתקא לבנה לתוך הקלפי.

---

[17] מלה זאת מופיעה בתחלת עמוד חדש. בראש העמוד כתוב: "ב"ה יום ד' דברים, ר"ח מנחם אב, תפרח. כעת בבאד נאוהיים."

עשו הפרנסים. ומכיון שעפ״י מחילתו של בן נפלה טענת החזקה התרצו שני הצדדים להעמיד את שני הקנדידאטען שלהם—בן הרב והרב ד״ר קלין מנירנבערג—ולהגביל את יום הבחירה על יום 22 מאי, הוא יום א׳ במדבר בשנה העברה והי׳ כבר הכל ערוך ומתוקן להבחירה וגם הבחירה היתה כבר נשתכחת אלמלא קרה מקרה אחד ברגע האחרון אשר הפך את כל ההחלטות לתהו ובהו. וזה הדבר: ביום השבת בבקר, השבת שביום א׳ שלמחרתו היתה צריכה להיות הבחירה, קבל כל הקהל מכתב ארוך מודפס מאת דיין הקהלה, הרב הישיש מר גרשום [צ״ל גרשון] פאזען שליט״א[16]—הוא שימש בתור דיין הקהלה כל ימי רבו המובהק, הרב ברייער המנוח ז״ל וגם הי׳ כבר דיין אצל הרב ר׳ שמשון רפאל הירש זצ״ל מיסד הקהלה—בתוך המכתב הוא מתאונן מרה על כבודו המחולל במה שלא שאלו הפרנסים את דעתו במשך כל ימי המחלקה [!] א[ו]דות דבר הרבנות ונבחרי׳—ומה שלא שאלו אותו הוא, הוא מפני שהוא ידוע לבעל פירוד קיצוני בטבע בנוגע לשיטת הפירוד מן המתקנים וגם מפני שכל ימיו היה בעיניו אסקופה הנדרסת תחת רגלי הרב המנוח ז״ל ולא נשאו לבו להרים ראש כנגדו ולחלוק על דבריו אפילו אם אמר לו על שמאל שהוא ימין ובכן ידעו הפרנסים מראש נאמנה, כי לא יטה כמלא השערה מדברי הרב, רבו, המנוח ז״ל, אשר גם בעודו בחיים ברור מללו במכתביו אל פרנסי הקהלה, כי בנו ראוי למלאות מקומו וביקש גם כי יבחרו בו בעודו בחיים להיות לו לסגן. ומטעם זה חשבו גם את הדין לנוגע בדבר, כי הלא הרב החדש יהי׳ ממונה גם עליו—ומתאמץ גם להקטין את אשמת הפירוש על שיר השירים מבן הרב. בנוגע לחזקה הוא כותב כי כבר הלכה רווחת היא בישראל לילך גם ברבנות אחר חזקה. ומוסיף עוד לומר, כי אף לאחר מחילתו של בן החובה על כי שמחזיק את הבן לירא חטא להקדים אותו על פני הקאנדידאט שכנגדו ולתת לו משפט הבחירה, כי המחילה לא מהני—כן הוא כותב במכתבו—כי אם שיהי׳ הרשות ביד הפרנסים להעמיד עוד קאנדידאט מלבד בן הרב—מה שלא היו רשאים לעשות בלא המחילה—אבל לא שיהי׳ הברירה ביד הבוחר במי שירצה משני הקאדידאטין כל זמן שאין הקאנדידאט השני ידוע למופלג בחכמה יותר מן הבן.

המכתב הזה פעל את פעולתו והבחירה של יום המחרת נתבטלה, כי הצד שכנגד הבן אמר כי במקום שהשמו״ץ עומד ומזהיר בפומבי עפ״י חוקי התורה: את זה תבחרו ואת זה לא תבחרו! לא שייך בחירה. הבחירה אמנם נתבטלה אבל המריבה קמה וגם נצבה ורק שנתה צורתה. כי בעוד אשר מתחילה היתה המריבה בין שני הצדדים וע״כ פרצה אש המחלוקת מבחוץ ע״י פרסום טענותיהם ברבים, הנה עתה הצדדים אינם מתקוטטים זע״ז וכל תלונות הצד שכנגד הם רק כנגד הדיין מבלי שישמיע דבר ברבים מפני כבודו של זקן. ואלה הן התלונות שכנגד הדיין מן הצד שכנגד.

א) מאחר שהדיין ראה כי אין ברצון הקהל לשאול את פיו בדבר הרבנות הי׳ לו להמנע מלכוף אותו ולאסור עליו בחירת רב אחר בעל כרחו—של קהל—מאחר שלפי דעתו—של הצד שכנגד —אין בהאיסור הזה שום מיגדרא מילתא, יען כי בחירת הרב קלין מנירנבערג הידוע ג״כ למחזיק בשיטת הפירוד רק שאינו מזלזל בכבוד המתנגדים לשיטתו, בחירתו הוא [!] יותר טובה בעד הקהלה וקיומה מבחירת בן הרב.

ב) לא הי׳ לו להדיין להשתמש בהוראתו בתור אמצעי של רֶקלָמה [מודעה] ולפרסמה ברגע האחרון בשעה שעומדים כבר לפני הבחירה ואי אפשר לנטות ימין ושמאל כי אין זה כבוד התורה.

---

16 טופס של מכתב זה נמצא בארכיון של ה׳מכון לחקר תפוצות ישראל בעת החדשה׳ אשר באוניברסיטת בר-אילן, תיק 105/16-ו. בדעתי היה לתרגם את מכתב זה ולכלול אותו במאמר הנוכחי, אלא שדוחק השעה, ודופק העורך, מנענוני מהפיק חפצי, ועוד חזון למועד. וראה את מכתבו בספר קרן ישראל, לונדון תש״ס, עמ׳ צט-ק.

של רעייתי תחי' הייתי טרוד גדול ולא היו עתותי בידי להשיב, ואנא הסליחה. אולם לא אכחד כי גם התשובה מצד עצמה היתה קשה עלי מאד עד כה. כמעגתוצ"ה שאל ממני שני דברים במכתבו: א) אם שקטה המריבה ב) מי נתקבל לרב, וביקש לתת לו תשובה ע"ז. על הפרט השני יכולתי אמנם להשיב בקצרה, כי עדיין לא נתקבל שום רב אבל על הפרט הראשון לא ידעתי באמת מה להשיב, כי כלפי חוץ אמנם שקטה המריבה אבל כלפי פנים התלקחה התבערה עוד יותר ולא הי' אפשר להציל [!] דבר ברור עד כה. והשנוי מחוץ לפנים בא לרגלי השנוי בעצם המחלקה [!].

מתחילה לחמו שני צדדים מתוך הקהלה. הללו חפצים בבן הרב מפני כח ההטפה שלו ואומץ רוחו להגן על שיטת הפירוד—מן המתקנים—אשר היא לו מורשת אבות, [13] והללו ממאנים בו א) מפני פירושו הנתעב על שיר השירים, ב) מפני שהי' מזלזל בכבוד אנשים גדולים ממנו בתורה ובמע"ט אם אך אינם הולכים בשיטתו שיטת הפירוד, ג) מפני שבעירו אין מחיצה ראוי' מפסקת בתוך הבית הכנסת בין עזרת נשים לאנשים[14]—ולפיכך לא התפלל אביו המנוח ז"ל בבית הכנסת הזאת כשבקר את בנו שמה, אף שהתיר לו לקבל את הרבנות שם במצב כמו זה—בגלל הטעמים האלה אין מדת יראת שמיותו [!] [15] מספקת בעיני הצד שכנגדו להיות ממלא מקום אביו ביראת חטא וגם מפחדים כי בהתקבלו לרב תרד הקהלה מטה מטה ויושפל כבודה כלפי חוץ מפני שהוא כמעט שנאוי למרבית היראים שבארץ אשכנז ובאבדן כבוד קהל עדת ישרון שבפראנקפורט יאבד טובה הרבה מן היהדות החרדיית בכלל. נוסף על הטעמים הנ"ל תמך הצד שבעד את יתדותיו על דין החזקה ברבנות בעוד אשר הצד שכנגדו מפקפק בעיקר הדין וגם מוכיח כי בפראנקפורט המנהג שלא לילך אחר חזקה ולאחר ווכוחים רבים הסכימו פרנסי הקהלה העומדים בראש שני הצדדים (כי גם בין הפרנסים עצמם ישנם שני צדדים) להגיש את הדבר לפני גדולי תורה וככל אשר יורו אלה הגדולים כן יעשו.

כשמוע בן הרב החלטה זו פנה במכתב אל הפרנסים וכתב להם שהוא מוחל על כל הזכיות המסתעפות מן דין החזקה מפני שהוא חס על כבוד אביו ז"ל ואינו רוצה שהפסק דין שלו יובא בכור המבחן לפני גדולים אחרים וגם כתב שהרשות ביד הפרנסים לפרסם מחילתו זו לפני כל הקהל. וכן

[13] בפירוש זה הוא באר את המגלה על דרך הפשט. ראה ספרי Between the Yeshiva World and Modern Orthodoxy (London, 1999); p. 83.

[14] אין הכוונה שאנשים ונשים ישבו בערבוביא, הס מלהזכיר ולהעלות כזאת על הדעת, אלא שהמחיצה היתה נמוכה באופן שהאנשים יכלו לראות את הנשים—כמו המחיצות הנמצאות לרוב בימינו. צורת המחיצה היא מחלוקת ישנה ובאסיפה הגדולה במיכאלוביץ בשנת תרכ"ו תקנו הרבה הרבה מגדולי הונגריה ש"אסור לעשות המחיצה המבדלת בין עזרת נשים ואנשים רק באופן אשר לא יוכלו להסתכל אנשים בנשים, וכן אם כבר נעשה לא יכנסו שם". (כל התקנות נמצאות בחלק ב' מספר "לב העיברי" מהמקנאי הגדול לוחם מלחמות ה' הג"ר עקיבא יוסף שלעזינגר). וראה עוד בשו"ת מהר"ם שיק, או"ח סי' עו. והיה זה המנהג גם כן בהרבה מקומות בגרמניה, שהמחיצה היתה באופן שאי אפשר היה לראות את הנשים כלל. ראה הגר"ע הילדסהיימר, Gesammelte Aufsätze, (Frankfurt, 192)3, pp. 20, 26.

[15] = ה"יראת השם" שלו, או אולי ה"יראת שמים" שלו.

מכוונים כנגד הרבנים שעמדו בראש הקהלה האורתודוקסית, שהיתה חלק מהעדה הגדולה, הג״ר
מרדכי הורוביץ, מח״ס מטה לוי, ולאחרי פטירתו, הג״ר נחמיה נובל. בעיני הגרש״ר הירש וחתנו כל
מי שהעיז לקבל על עצמו משרת רב בקהלה הגדולה, קהלה שבתוכה נמצא גם בית כנסת רפורמי,
התיר את השרץ ונתן גושפנקא למפירי התורה. ובעטיו של מעשה זה נחשבו רבנים אלו בעיניהם
כחוטאים ומחטיאים את הרבים. ולא רק את הרבנים עצמם הוציאו חוץ למחנה אלא גם את כל
הקשור אתם. אפילו בית הכנסת שלהם נחשב כמקום מוחרם, שלא ידרוך בו כף רגל.9

אבל, דא עקא, שרוב חברי הקהלה הפורשת, למרות הזדהותם עם שיטת הפירוד של הגרשר״ה
והבאים אחריו, לא יכלו לעכל לעצל קיצוניות זו ולהשלים עמה. ויעיד על זה מש״כ אחד מחשובי קהלה
זו, ר׳ יעקב רוזנהיים, בהספדו על הגר״מ הורוביץ, שם הצהיר ש״תלמיד חכם שמת הכל קרוביו".10
ובזכרונותיו העיד על הרהורי לבו: "הנני מודה בגלוי שנרתעתי מהרגע הראשון מפני קיצוניות זו
במלחמה נגד אנשים שהיו מדקדקים במצוות ולומדי תורה לשמה ושאף בעניני אמונה אי-אפשר
היה למצוא בהם כל פגם".11

ולא ללמד על עצמו בלבד יצא, כי מן המפורסמות הוא שהיו רבים ושלמים בתוך הקהלה
הפורשת שדעותיהם היו שוות עם זו של רוזנהיים, והוקירו מאד את הגר״מ הורוביץ על אף הבדלי
הגישות ביניהם. רוזנהיים אפילו חשב שמן הנכון היה שרבו—הרב של ק״ק עדת ישורון—והרב
הורוביץ ישבו ביחד וידונו בעניינים שעמדו אז על הפרק. ואין זה מן התימה שהצעה זו נדחתה בשתי
ידים ע״י הרב ברויאר, שבעיניו להפגש ולשוחח עם הרב הורוביץ כאשר ידבר איש אל רעהו—
כמוה כסטיה מדרך ה'. ואכן בנו ותלמידו של הרב ברויאר, ההוגה הגדול ד״ר יצחק ברויאר, מסר
לנו שאביו "לא שהה בכל ימי חייו באותו חדר בו נמצא הרב השמרני [הרב הורוביץ] של קהילת
פרנקפורט הרפורמית".12

לאחר הקדמה קצרה זו ניגש אל דברי האגרת כאשר יעדנו למעלה.

ב״ה יום ד׳ פנחס ט״ז תמוז תפר״ח פפד״מ יצ״ו

אל הוד כבוד שר התורה, גאון נורא, רשכבה״ג כו׳ כו׳, כקש״ת מורנו ורבנו
הרב ר׳ יוסף ראזין שליט״א אב״ד דק״ק דווינסק יצ״ו.
אחד״ש כבוד מעלת גאון תורתו וצדקתו הרמה ברגשי יראה וכבוד כראוי.
בהגישי את תודתי הרבה לכמעגתוצ״ה על תשובתו הרמה מן יום כ״ו אייר
העבר, עלי לבקש מקודם את סליחתו על איחור תשובתי על המכתב ההוא. סיבת
הדבר הוא כי לרגלי חמותי החולנית תחי׳ אשר בביתי וגם לרגלי אי בריאותה

9 ראה יצחק ברויאר, דרכי, ירושלים תשמ״ח, פרקים א-ב, Jacob Rosenheim, Erinnerungen (Frankfurt,
1970), p. 38
10 Aufsätze und Ansprachen (Frankfurt, 1930), vol. 2 pp. 449-453. וראה עוד שם עמ׳ 478-480,
הספדו על הרב נחמיה נובל, ובספרו 86ff. ,37ff .Erinnerungen (Frankfurt, 1970), pp
11 Erinnerungen, p. 38 (תרגום ב׳זכרונות׳, תל אביב תשט״ז, עמ׳ 34). וראה את מכתבו בספר מכתבים ואגרות
קודש, בעריכת דוד אברהם מנדלבוים, ניו יורק תשס״ג, עמ׳ 712.
12 דרכי, עמ׳ 10; .Matthias Morgenstern, Von Frankfurt nach Jerusalem (Tübingen, 1995), pp
41-45. ראה יעקב כ״ץ, הקרע שלא נתאחה, ירושלים תשנ״ה, עמ׳ 335 הערה 64: "מפיו של מרדכי ברויאר אני
למד על המסורת המשפחתית, שבבוא הורוביץ לפרנקפורט ביקר אצל הירש אך לא נתקבל על ידו. המסורת
תואמת את הידוע על אופיים של שני האישים ועל עמדותיהם".

טרם אציג לפני הקורא את המכתב של הרב ראכעלזאהן אעיר בקצרה בענין ירושה ברבנות. כתב הרמב"ם בהלכות כלי המקדש פרק ד הלכה כ: "כשימות המלך או כהן גדול או אחד משאר הממונים מעמידין תחתיו בנו או הראוי ליורשו, וכל הקודם לנחלה קודם לשררות המת, והוא שיהיה ממלא מקומו בחכמה או ביראה אע"פ שאינו כמותו בחכמה שנאמר במלך הוא ובניו בקרב ישראל, מלמד שהמלכות ירושה והוא הדין לכל שררה שבקרב ישראל שהזוכה לה זוכה לעצמו ולזרעו." וכך גם בהלכות מלכים פ"א ה"ז, ובספר החינוך בסימן תצ"ז. הרמ"א ביו"ד סי' רמה סע' כב פוסק כדברי הרמב"ם, אלא שהוסיף בשם הכל בו ש"במקום שיש מנהג לקבל רב על זמן קצוב, או שמנהג לבחור במי שירצו, הרשות בידם." ואכן כך היה המנהג בגרמניה בעידן החדש. ואין צורך להאריך כאן בענין זה, ולדון במחלוקת הפוסקים אם יש ירושה ברבנות כלל, ואם כן, האם היא דאורייתא או רק מדרבנן, כי כבר האריך כיד ה' הטובה עליו הגאון מבראשוב בשו"ת אפרקסתא דעניא, חלק ד חו"מ סי' שד, ולא הניח פנה וזוית אשר לא דרך בה, והרוצה לעמוד בשרשי הדברים יעיין שם וירוה את צמאונו.[7]

אמנם למרות חלוקי הדעות בנידון זה, כל הפוסקים מסכימים ומודים שאין ירושה ברבנות אלא אם כן הבן ראוי לאותו איצטלא. הדיון על הירושה של כסא הרבנות הוה את הציר המרכזי שעליו סבבה המחלוקת בפרנקפורט. בעיני רבים היו אנשי משפחת ברוויאר קיצוניים יותר מדי ולא רצו שהקיצוניות תקנה שביתה ושליטה כ"כ חזקה בקהלה. הם התנגדו למינויו של ברוויאר —הבן—לא (כ"כ) בגלל אישיותו הפרטית כי אם בגלל שבעיניהם היה הוא המייצג את שיטת הפורשים הקיצוניים. הללו לא רצו למסור את ההנהלה הרוחנית של הקהלה בידי משפחת רבנים שהיו מיועדים להוליכה שולל אחרי קנאות מופלגת וקיצוניות מוגזמת.

יתכן ויתמהו קוראים רבים וישאלו: "מה היתה טיבה של התנגדות זו ועל מה הוטבעו אדניה"? הלא ברור שרבני משפחת ברוויאר לא היו מבודדים ומסוגרים בתוך ארבע אמותיהם, אלא היו אנשים בעלי השכלה, מורגלים בנימוס, מעורבים בדעת עם אנשי קהלתם ותרבותם משוכללת. איך זה, איפוא, שנוצר פער בין השקפת משפחת ברוויאר לבין הרבה מחברי הקהלה עד שנחשבו הראשונים כאנשים קיצוניים שעברו את הגבול? אך בין תבין שתרבות לחוד וקיצוניות לחוד, ומי שסבור שאי אפשר לתרבות וקיצוניות לגור בכפיפה אחת אינו אלא טועה. ובאמת מצינו לא פעם שתרבות וקיצוניות הינם ממשפחה אחת ובני דודים אחד לשני. וכך היה המצב אצל משפחת ברוויאר. אמנם משפחת ברוויאר היתה מעוגנת היטב בתרבות הקהלה היהודית-גרמנית אורתודוקסית, אבל ביחד עם זאת הם נקטו בשיטות קיצוניות של התבדלות.[8] עיקר חציצתם היו

[7] ראה גם Jeffrey I. Roth, "*Inheriting the Crown in Jewish Law : The Struggle for Rabbinic Compensation, Tenure, and Inheritance Rights* (Columbia, S. C., 2006); Simon Schwarzfuchs, "The Inheritance of the Rabbinate Reconsidered," Jewish History 13 (1999), pp. 25-33; Shaul Stampfer, "Inheritance of the Rabbinate in Eastern Europe in the Modern Period – Causes, Factors and Development over Time," Ibid., pp. 35-57.

[8] כדאי לצטט כאן את דבריו של מרן הרב קוק, «שאין לנו אפילו מדה אחת בעולם שלא תהי' הקצוניות מזיקתה" (אגרות הראי"ה, ח"א עמ' יט). וכן אמר ש"דרך ד' הישרה היא דרך המיצוע" (שם, סי' רנא). לעומת זאת כתב הגאון החזון איש, "כשם שהפשטות והאמת הם שמות נפרדות, כן הקיצוניות והגדלות שמות נפרדות. הקיצוניות היא ההשתלמות של הנושא. הדוגל בהבינוניות ומואס בקיצוניות, חלקו עם הזייפנים, או עם חדלי-תבונה. אם אין קיצוניות—אין שלמות, ואם אין שלמות—אין התחלה... הבינוניות שיש לה זכות הקיום היא מידת הבינונים האוהבים את הקיצוניות ושואפים אליה בכל משאת נפשם, ומחנכים את צאצאיהם לפסגת הקיצוניות, אבל מה עלובה הבינוניות הסואנת בוז לקיצוניות. חובת חינוכנו לקיצוניות!" (קובץ אגרות חלק ג סי' סא). ואין כאן המקום לדון בדבריהם הקדושים, איש איש על דגלו, איש איש לפי תפיסתו.

דומני שהמחלוקת על דבר הרבנות בק"ק עדת ישרון בפרנקפורט בשנות העשרים של המאה
העשרים—נושא מאמרינו—נופלת בסוג הראשון. אין מן הצורך לחזור על כל הפרשה היות וסקירה
על המחלוקת כבר סוכמה ע"י אחד החוקרים בימינו,[4] והרב בן ציון ראקעלזאהן,[5] מחבר האגרת
שאנו מפרסמים פה לראשונה, מאריך בפרטי פרטים ומגלה לנו כמה סתומות בפרשה זו. ואין עלי
אלא לסכם במלים ספורות על מה סבב העניין.

עם הסתלקותו של הג"ר שלמה זלמן ברויאר זצ"ל (בשנת תרפ"ו), רב הקהילה וחתנא דבי
נשיאה של מייסדה, הג"ר שמשון רפאל הירש זצ"ל, פרצה המחלוקת. השאלה היתה: מי יבוא
אחרי המלך? היה בדעתו של הרב ברויאר המנוח שבנו הרב רפאל, רבה של אשפנבורג, יירש את
הרבנות כמנהג הרבה מקומות, אלא שגדולים וטובים בקהילה לא הסכימו לזה. ונעשה פרץ בבית
הכנסת וצוחה ברחובות. פרופ' יעקב כ"ץ שהיה בפרנקפורט בתקופה זו, כתב בזכרונותיו:

> רבים . . . מצאו פגמים בבן—בין השאר טענו כנגדו שבנעוריו פירסם פירוש
> לשיר השירים על פי פשוטו, כשיחת גומלין בין אוהב ואהובתו, דבר שהוציא
> אותו מכלל מועמד מעיקרו. הנהלת הקהילה דחתה את הבחירות שנועדו
> להתקיים למחרת היום. כתוצאה מהתערבות הדיין [פאזען] החליט המועמד
> הנגדי, הרב [אברהם יצחק] קליין להסתלק מן התחרות . . . רפאל ברויאר
> נשאר מועמד יחיד. אך בחירתו היתה עדיין תלויה בהצבעת רוב הבוחרים
> למענו. ואולם מתנגדיו עמדו במרדם. הם מוכנים היו לא רק להעדיף מועמד
> אחר כנגדו, אלא אף לדחות אותו בהשראת מנהיגם יעקב רוזנהיים בהיותו
> מועמד יחיד. הבחירות השניות נתקיימו לאחר בואי לפרנקפורט בשנת 1928,
> והייתי נוכח באסיפת המתנגדים שרוזנהיים כינסה ערב הבחירות. הוא מנה את
> הסיבות למניעת המשרה מבן הרב, שחשובה שבהן היתה אימת ההישתלטות
> של משפחת ברויאר על חיי הקהילה, משפחה שלפי דברי הנואם דבקה בה
> פסיכוזה דינאסטית.[6]

שידוע שהוא עבירה לעשות מחלוקת או לרדוף אדם מישראל, מכל מקום מחשב שהוא עבירה לשמה היינו לשם
מצוה ויקבל שכרה . . . אף אנו נאמר שהשורף את העיר ח"ו אינו מאבד אותם אלא לשנה או שנתים עד שישיבו
למעמדם, והעושה מחלוקת בעיר אין דבר עבירה שעומד בפני אש הנצוח אשר תוקד עד שאול תחתית . . . היוצא
מכל זה דמי שהוא בעל נפש ודעת ישרה אין לפניו לפשוט נבלתא ולא יקפוץ ליורה
רותחת מאש הנצוח של שני צדדים.' וכבר בדורו, דור דעה, כתב הנודע ביהודה (שו"ת מהדו"ק יו"ד ס"א) ש"אין
לך גרוע מהמחלוקת ובזמננו לא שכיח מחלוקת לשם שמים והשטן מרקד." ותלמידו בעל תשובה מאהבה (חלק א
סי' סא) כתב :"ורגיל אני לומר מה דאז"ל איזו היא מחלוקת שהיא לש"ש זו מחלוקת הלל ושמאי ושאינה לש"ש
זו מחלוקת' קרח וכל עדתו ר"ל איזהי מחלוקת שהיא כלה לש"ש בלי שום פני' אחרת זו מחלוקת הלל ושמאי שכל
מחשבותם לשמים וישרים בלבות ושאינה לש"ש שלא היתה בה מחשבה טובה לש"ש זו מחלוקת קרח כו' אבל זולת
שתי כתות האל מחשבת פיגול איכא ביניהו לא נמצאת מחלוקת שהיא כלה לש"ש פגמים
ותערובות גופי' מחולקי' ומחשבת חוץ לש"ש שלא כלה לש"ש בלתי תערובות קודש מחשבת
פנים ויצאה הפסדה בשכרה ותועבת ה' גם שניהם דרך כלל אם לבנות מקדש על במחלוקת מוטב שלא תבנה."

[4] יהודה בן-אבנר, "לפולמוס על הרבנות בעדת ישרון דק"ק פפד"ם בשנות העשרים," סיני, קו (תש"נ) עמ' 79-
72.

[5] חפשתי בחיפוש מחופש ולא עלה בידי למצוא שום ידיעות עליו, זולת מה ששמעתי מפרופ' מרדכי ברויאר ז"ל
כי היה תלמיד חכם ממזרח אירופה שבא לפרנקפורט והיה חבר בקהילה הפרושת, ושם נתן שיעורים. עצם שייכותו
לקהילה זו היא מעניינת כי רובם של המהגרים מהמזרח היו חברים בקהילה הגדולה.

[6] במו עיני: אוטוביוגרפיה של היסטוריון, ירושלים תשמ"ט, עמ' 67.

ד"ר מלך שפירא פרופסור באוניברסיטת סקראנטון,
פנסלווניה, ומרצה בישיבת חובבי תורה.

המחלוקת על הרבנות בפרנקפורט: מבט מבפנים[1]
ד"ר מלך שפירא

דור דור ורבניו, דור דור ומחלוקתיו. לצערנו המחלוקת ממשיכה עד היום, ועד בכלל. אולם,
למרות המחירים הכבירים שכלל ישראל משלם עבור השיקוע בבוץ המחלוקת, ועם כל הכאב
לאנשים ישרים ותמימים הרואים את רבניהם לוחמים זה עם זה ונלכדים בסבך המחלוקת עד חרמה
(וכ"ז בנוסף למדנים ה'בלתי נעימים' בין הקהלות ורבניהן), אין לכחד שמחלוקת מסוג זה מהווה
פרק נכבד בתולדות ימי עמנו. ויש ללמוד הרבה מהן ומהשלכותיהן לגבי העניינים העומדים ברומו
של עולם והעולים על שולחן מלכים, מאן מלכי רבנן, בימינו אנו. צא ובדוק את פרטי המחלוקות
מסביב לספרי הרמב"ם, הקבלה, הציונות, העירובין וכו' ותוכח על אמיתות הדברים. אלו הן
המחלוקות שהיו, ועדיין ישנן, שאינן מעוגנות בדגמות אישיות של כסף וכבוד וכדומה, אלא
מחלוקות שנוצרו, במישרין או בעקיפין, על ידי מבקשי אמת ושונאי בצע. במרכז מחלוקות אלו
עמדו עניינים חשובים הנוגעים למהותה של היהדות: עיקריה, איכותיה ויעדיה. באלו המחלוקות
יש לנו ללמוד הרבה, גם בהיסטוריה וגם בהלכה, וכבר אמרו חכמינו זכרונם לברכה שכל מחלוקת
שהיא לשם שמים סופה להתקיים.[2]

מאידך גיסא, האמת ניתנת להאמר שבתולדות ימי עמנו היו לא פעם מחלוקות שקשה למצוא
בהן את ה'לשם שמים'. בהרבה מחלוקות מסוג זה הוצתה אש המחלוקת על ידי מחרחרי ריב
למיניהם, אנשים הדיוטיים ושפלים שקפצו לראש הקהלה והדליקו את מדורת המדנים שהתפשטה
כאש בנעורת. אמנם לאחר שננעץ חרב המחלוקת בקהלה, החריבה המחלוקת כל חלקה טובה.
ואפילו הגדולים והישרים שבקהלה נתפסו במריבתה ונלכדו בשחיתותה. למחלוקת כזו—חיים
משל עצמה. היא אינה מוגבלת ואינה מרוסנת; וככל שיגוזים צד אחד בהתקפות חסירי רסן כנגד
יריבו, הנה, לא נשאר הצד השני חייב, וגם הוא אינו מהסס מלשפוך על הצד שכנגד קיתונות
מלאות בוז ולדונו ברותחין ובחמי חמין.[3]

---

ments of the fundamental nature of these obligations and an assertion that a marriage could not properly exist—and should probably be terminated by divorce—in their absence.

כתובה שיש בו ענין רומנטי במיוחד היא מעיר צוֹר, נכתב בכ"ד סיון (פריידמן, חלק ב #20):

...ואמר: מדעתי ומרעותי ומטבותי ומצבויוני נפשי,

ד[ל]א אנ[יס] ודל[א] כעיס ודלא כפיף ודלא... רווי חמר אלא בהון מלא ובממלל חלי

ל[מכ]נוש ית הדא מבא[רכה כלתא בתו]לה ברת מ נתן סט בן ישועה... חברתי ואשת בריתי[23],

[ו]עלי למוק[רה...] ול[פ]רנסה ולעמוד בסיפוקה כהלכת גוברין כשירין [יהודאין]...

ומיקרין ומפ[רנסין]... ית נשיהון בטהרה ובקדושה...

פעם נוספת אנו רואים את הדגש על רצון הבעל, כמה הוא באמת רוצה לשאת את האישה הזאת. אבל מה שמרשים ביותר בכתובה הזאת הוא השימוש בפסוק ממלאכי שמדבר על האישה כחברה ואשת ברית.

האם אינו אפשרי שהמחלוקת רבא ור' יוחנן, מחלוקת אמורא בבלי ואמורא ארץ ישראלי, תלויה בתפיסות שונות של אישות? אם נדגיש ונעריך את החשיבות בנוכחות הבעל בתוך ביתו, דבר התלוי במידה רבה בחשיבות שיש באישות לאהבה ולמודל של "ויקרא את שמם אדם" היוצא מתוך "וידבק באשתו". ובמקביל, השאלה האם מסתבר להתחיל מנקודת ראות של האישה או שרק מסתבר להתחיל מנקודת ראות של הבעל, לכאורה תלויה במידה לא קטנה בשאלת מעמד האישה באישות—האם יש מושג של הדדיות או אין? האם היא שותפה או לא?

ו. סיכום

בסופו של דבר, ניווט המתח בין אישות לתלמוד תורה תלוי גם בהערכת הכח של תלמוד תורה לפטור אדם (אדם רגיל / תלמיד חכם / מי שתורתו אומנתו) מחיוביו האחרים וגם בהערכת המשמעות שנותנים לאישות ולנוכחות האיש עם אשתו. אנו, בזמננו, מחזקים את ההבנה של אישות כשותפות, וזה מחדד עלינו את העמות. ולכן, במסגרת האישות, המתח הזה בין חיוב אדם לעצמו ולתורותו וחיוב אדם כלפי בן או בת זוגו וכלפי משפחתו עומדת בעינה. ככל שמדובר בסידור שבא מתוך הסכם של כל הצדדים, בעסק של שותפות ממש, העמות נפתר מאליו. אבל, ברוב המקרים, העימות קיים, וחובתנו לשים לב תמיד לשתי הדרישות גם יחד, ולהתמודד עם חובתנו ההלכתיים, הדתיים והמוסריים לאורך ימינו.

---

23 מלאכי ב:יד

וכן ענת פ' בתולתא כלתא ואמרת וקבילת עלה
שתהא פלחא ומשמשא ומוקרא ומיקרא ית ר' פ' החתן
כנימוסי נשיא דבנתהון דישראל דפלחן ומוקרן ומיקרן ית בעליהון בנקיו
ובדכיו.

השימוש במינוח "וכן ענת... ואמרת" גורם לנו לחשוב שזה מה שקרה בטקס הנישואין.
ביחס לכל הנושא הזה, מרדכי פריידמן בספרו *Jewish Marriage in Palestine*, בחלק
א כותב (דף 19):

Mutuality of the contract.—Most Palestinian-style *ketubbot*
contain a number of elements which appear to convey to the
document the form of a mutual contract between two parties.
The wife's status seems, almost, to be approaching equality
with the husband's. This contrasts sharply with the Babylonian
ketubba which essentially may be characterized as a testimony
of unilateral obligations undertaken by the husband to the wife.
Granted, there probably were few fundamental differences between Babylonia and Eretz Israel, if any, as to the actual legal
status of a married woman. We are speaking, rather, of the style
and form of the *ketubba*.

Most conspicuous in the Palestinian tradition is the provi-
sion which entitled both parties to initiate divorce proceed-
ings. The very term for marriage in that stipulation is שותפות
"partnership."

וגם בחלק א, דפים 181-186:

In formulating the bride's acceptance of the proposal, no
ketubbot contain a direct quote of her words. But some specifically indicate that, in agreeing to marry the groom, she did
speak; and her acceptance was not by silent consent... More
significant than these occasional phrases is the regular inclusion,
in the Palestinian marriage deeds, of an explicit statement of
obligations undertaken by the bride, to serve and respect her
husband... The wife's undertakings aptly depict the reciproc-
ity of the marital arrangements and the active role played by
the bride in contracting the "partnership"... One can hardly
imagines that these stipulations ever rendered the *qiddushin*
conditional in the technical sense, so that the marriage would
be considered automatically null and void were these martial
obligations not fulfilled. Rather, they could be seen as state-

יהווי משלם לה כל מה ד[כתיב בהדן שטר] פרנא מן שלם.

ואן הדה רחל כלתא תשנא להדן נתן בעלה, ולא תרצי בש[ותפתיה—

תהוי מאבד]ה מאוחר מהרה, ותיסוב מה דאעלת.

ולא תהוה נפקא אלא על פי בית [דינא].

בכתובה זו, שזמנה סוף תקופת הגאונים, אנחנו רואים את הדברים החשובים לזוג: לא רק חיים
ומוות, אבל גם אהבה ושנאה, והיחסים ביניהם הינם מוגדרים כשותפות.
ההדדיות הזאת גם נמצאת בכתובה שנכתב בטבריה, ביום חמישי, י״ב סיון, תשצ״ה לאלף
הרביעי (פרידמן חלק ב 19#):

אנא יצחק במ׳ אברהם נ״נ אמרית מן דעתי ומן רעותי ומ[ן צביוני נפשי],

ואנא לא אניס ולא כעיס ולא רעיץ ולא עציב ולא כפוף ולא משדל [ולא רוי
חמר,

אלא בלב של[ם] ובדיעה שלמא צבית למכנוש לה[דא] קירא נאעמה פניתה
ברת [מרי משה חזנא,

ואנא א[הוי זאיין ומפרנס ומלבש ומוקר ומיק[ר יתה,

כ]הלכת גובריין יהודאין [דזאיינין ומפרנסין ומ[לבשין ומוקרין ומיקרין ית נשיהון
בקושטא.

וכן הי[א ש]מעת וקבלת [על נפשה דתהוי פלח]ה ומשמשה ומוקרא מיקרא
ית בעלה,

כהלכת נשייה כ[ש]ירתה בנתה[ון דישראל

דפלחן ומ[שמשן ומוקרן ומיקרן ית בעליהון בטהרה ובדכיו.

ורצ[ת] והוות לה לא[נתו ולאמהון דבנין הי]ך די צ[ב]א [ו]בעא, כדת משה
ויהודאי.

בולט בכתובה הזאת הוא הכבוד שהחתן מראה לכלתו. פעמיים הוא מבטיח שהוא יכבד אותה.
אבל בנוסף אפשר לראות את ההדדיות, שהכלה מקבלת על עצמה לכבד אותו. דבר אחד בולט
בכתובה והוא מאמרה, שהוא בעצם תגובה לחתן, שהיא מוכנה להיות אשתו ואם ילדיו "כמו
שהוא רצה".
אפשר להבין את התגובה הזאת לא רק כסגנון, אבל כמיצג טקס ריאלי שהאישה דיברה בפה
וקיבלה על עצמה את החיובים האלו.[21] דוגמא שממחישה זאת טוב יותר הוא כתובה לימודית[21]
משנת 1081/2 למניינם, (פרידמן חלק ב מספר 4)[22]:

פ׳ בן פ׳ אמר לה למרת פ׳ בת ר׳ פ׳ בתולתא:

הוי לי לאנתו כדת משה נביא וישראל בחירא,

ואנא אפלח ואיזון ואיסובר ואפרנס ואכלכל ומיקר יתך,

כהלכת גוברין יהודאין דזנין <ומלבשין> ומוקרין ית נשיהון בקושטא...

---

[21] הכתובה הזאת בעצם שבלונא, כנראה בשביל סופרים לצטט ממנה.

[22] ראה גם מספר 16 לניסוח דומה.

קיים".

ובקשר להלכה הזאת יש את הסיפור הבא (כתובות ז:ו):

מעשה באחד [שאינו בעלה] שראו אותו נותן את פיו על פיה שלה,
אתא עובדא קומי רבי יוסי, אמר: "[תיסב פלג][17] פרן".[18]
והויין קריביה עררין ואמרין: "אין שוטה [= אם סוטה] היא—תיפוק בלא
פרן,
ואין לית שוטה היא—תיסב פרן שלים".
אמר לון רבי מנא: "אייתון פרנא ניקריניה".
אייתון פרנה ואשכחון כתוב בגווה: "אין הדא פלנית תס[נ]י להדין פלוני
בעלה,
ולא תיצבי בשו[ת]פותיה—תהוי נסבה פלגות פרן".
אמר רבי אבון: "מכיון שקיבלה עליה שיתן את פיו על פיה של[ה]—
כמאן דשנאת, ולית לה אלא פלגות פרן".

ועל זה כתב המאירי (כתובות, פרק ששי, המשנה הששית, דף 270):

והם[19] כתבו על זה שחדשו הגאונים הוא מפני שהיו רגילים לכתוב בכתבותיהם
שאם תשנאהו תטול כתבתה ותצא, ולא יהא רשאי לדונה במורדת, ומאחר
שנתפשט המנהג—קבעוהו לעשותו אף בזמן שלא נכתב כאלו נכתב, כשאר
תנאי כתובה...

מכל זה אפשר לראות עד כמה היה נפוץ בארץ ישראל לכתוב תנאי על השנאה, ואיך האישות
צריכה להיות מבוססת על תשתית של אהבה. זאת אומרת, בארץ ישראל היה תנאי כתובה
לכשהאישה לא תרצה עוד בבעלה, היא יכולה לתבוע גט וליטול חצי כתובתה. ולפי המאירי,
התנאי היה מובן, ולא היה צורך אפילו לכתוב אותו כבר בתקופת הגאונים.

דבר שני שאפשר לראות מניסוח הכתובה הוא ההדדיות ביניהם. כבר במימרא של רבי יוסי אנו
רואים שהוא סובר שהם חייבים להתגרש אם הוא שונא אותה או אם היא שונאת אותו. ההדדיות
הזאת מתחזקת משימוש במונח "שותפות" שאנו רואים בכתובה המצוטטת בירושלמי. דוגמא
לכתובה כזאת היא הכתובה מהעיר צור, שנכתבה בה ג' כסלו תשפ"ד לאלף הרביעי[20]:

ואתנון ביניהון על עסק שנתא ורחמתא וחייא ומיתותא:
אן הדן נת[ן] חתנא ישנא להדא] רחל אינתתיה ולא ירצה בשותפתה שנאת
מגן—

[17] כך הוא בהלכות ירושלמי של הרמב"ם, ומוכרח להיות על פי ההקשר, ועיין בהערת ליברמן על המקום, אות צ'.
[18] מילה נרדפת לכתובה.
[19] לפי אברהם סופר ושאול ליברמן מדובר על "רבותיהם של רבותיו".
[20] מובא ב מ.ע. פריידמן, *Jewish Marriage in Palestine*, כרך ב #2, וכרך א דף 329.

לרעיון של שותפות, האישה נחשבת כסוביקט מלא בעסק. לעומת זאת, אם יש אפשרות של אישות של בעל עם הרבה נשים, אז מודל כזה מוביל לרעיון של אי-שוויון ואי שותפות, מודל עם הבעל במרכז ועם האישה בפריפריה.

עוד מקום שאפשר לראות את ההבדל בהדגש באישות הוא בספר החילוקים בין בני מזרח ומערב (סימן כה):

אנשי מזרח אין רואין טבעת קידושין, ובני ארץ ישראל רואין טבעת קידושין גמורין.

ומפרש הרב ראובן מרגליות בהערה:

המובן הפשוט ביותר הוא, שבני ארץ ישראל היו מקדשין בטבעת ובני בבל לא נהגו לקדש בטבעת... יש לפרש שמתוך שהורגלו בני ארץ ישראל לקדש בטבעת, נחשב להם נתינת טבעת מהחתן לכלה לקידושין גמורין, אף על פי שלא פירש שנותן לה לשם קידושין אבל לבני בבל, שלא היו רגילים לקדש בטבעת, אין נתינת טבעת נחשבת לקידושין.

המנהג לקדש בטבעת דווקא—אינו עתיק ביותר. במשנה ובתלמוד אין אנו מוצאים זכר לטבעת קידושין, ומכמה עובדות אנו לומדים שקידשו בכל מיני חפצים שונים משונים, ובלבד שיהא בדבר שמקדשים בו פרוטה או שוה פרוטה. המנהג הזה הוא איפה יציר תקופת הגאונים ונובע כנראה מתוך זה, שבני ארץ ישראל נהגו על פי רוב, שהאישה עצמה מקבלת קידושיה ולא היו רגילים לקדש את האישה על ידי אביה, כפי שנהגו לרוב בבבל, כי גיל הנשואין היה גבוה בארץ ישראל מאשר בבבל, ומתוך כך נהגו לתת לה תכשיט, והמצוי ביותר: טבעת. [ואפשר שיש כאן השפעה חיצונית שלמדו מהרומים, דנהגו לארס בטבעת – הערת הרר"מ]. אבל בבבל שלרוב האב קיבל קידושי בתו לא נקבע שם המנהג לקדש בטבעת.

תכשיטים בכלל, וטבעות בפרט, הם חפצים רומנטים, שנתינתם לאישה מהווה מעשה רומנטי והצהרת אהבה. מההערה של רב מרגליות, אנו רואים לא רק שבני ארץ ישראל קדשו בטבעת ובני בבל לא, אבל שבני בבל קדשו על ידי אבי הכלה כשהיא היתה עדיין נערה, אבל בארץ ישראל קדשו את האישה עצמה, כשהיא כבר בוגרת. אפשר לראות בזה יחס אחרת לגמרי מבחינת מקומה של אישה בנשואיה, ויחס הבעל לאישה המיועדת לו כרעיה.

ההבדלים האלו נמצאים אפילו בדברים הלכתיים יותר, כניסוח כתובות. לדוגמא, בכתובות ישראליות, יש שימוש במינוח "שנא", שהוא יותר מניסוח טכני. בירושלמי כתובות (פ"ה ה"ח, ל ע"ב) איתא:

<u>אמר רבי יוסה</u>: "אילין דכתבין 'אין שנא' 'אין שנאת'—תני ממון ותניין

התאווה המיני שמנקה מחשבותיו של הגבר, יש להביא הסיפור של אותו רב שאשתו היה מצער לו בסוגייתינו. בבבלי ברכות (סב.) איתא:

רב כהנא על, גנא תותיה פורייה דרב. שמעיה דשח ושחק ועשה צרכיו.
אמר ליה: "דמי פומיה דאבא כדלא שריף תבשילא!"
אמר לו: "כהנא, הכא את? פוק, דלאו ארח ארעא."
אמר לו: "תורה היא וללמוד אני צריך."

רואים פה שלמרות הבעיות שהיו בינו ובינה, היה להם חיים מיניים תקינים ביותר—דבר העומד במרכז הנשואין לאמוראי בבל.

מאד מסתבר שמחלוקת רב ורבי יוחנן בנויה על הבנות שונות של אישות. אם עיקר הערך של האישות הוא להציל הגבר מהרהורי עבירה, מאד מסתבר שלא נדגיש כל כך את חיוביו כלפי אשתו ובניו כשהם עומדים נגד רצונו ללמוד תורה. לעומת זאת, אם אישות נותן לו חיים ועשה אותו לאדם שלם, הרי יש ערך רב לו ולאשתו[15] בהיותו נוכח עם אשתו. ולכן קשה להתיר לו לעזוב את אשתו, אפילו לצורך גדול של תלמוד תורה. זאת היא שיטת רבי יוחנן לעומת שיטת רב.

ה. איסור ריבוי נשים, טקסי נישואין וניסוח כתובות בארץ ישראל

אחד מהההבדלים הבולטים בין ארץ ישראל ובבל הוא הנושא של ריבוי נשים. בארץ ישראל הסתכלו על ריבוי נשים כפגיעה באישה, אפילו כבגידה, במובן מסויים, כשבבבל ראו אותו כדבר רגיל. בבבלי יבמות (סה.), בהקשר של בעיות לידה, איתא:

הוא אמר מינה, והיא אמרה מיניה? אמר רבי אמי: "דברים שבינו לבינה—נאמנת."
וטעמא מאי? היא קיימא לה ביורה כחץ, הוא לא קים ליה ביורה כחץ.
אמר איהו: 'איזיל אינסיב איתתא ואיבדוק נפשאי?'
אמר רבי אמי: "אף בזו—יוציא ויתן כתובה,
שאני אומר: כל הנושא אישה על אשתו—יוציא ויתן כתובה."
רבא אמר: "נושא אדם כמה נשים על אשתו; והוא, דאית ליה למיזייננהי."

לרבי אמי ורבא יש תגובות שונות לחלוטין להצעת הבעל שהוא יבדוק את כשרונותיו המיניים על ידי מישהו אחרת. רבי אמי, אמורא ארץ ישראלי, טוען שלקיחת אישה שנייה מוגדרת כפגיעה באשתו הראשונה, והיא יכולה לתבוע ממנו גירושין וכתובה. רבא אומר להפך, שאין בעיא עקרונית בלקיחת אישה שנייה אם לאיש יכולה כספית לפרנס שתי נשים. והרי ידוע שבבבל נהגו כרב, והתירו ריבוי נשים, ובארץ ישראל נהגו כרבי אמי, ולא נשאו יותר מאישה אחת[16].

חשוב להדגיש שבתרבות האוסרת ריבוי נשים משמעות האישות שונה לגמרי מתרבות המתירה ריבוי נשים. אם יחסי האישות צריכים להיות רק בעל אחד ואישה אחת, אז מדובר במודל שמוביל

---

[15] ברור שהמדרש בבראשית רבה כולה מנקודת ראות של הגבר. אבל מהסוגיא אצלנו בכתובות משתקפת נקודת הראות של האישה.

[16] ראה, למשל, ריבוי נשים בישראל: מקורות חדשים מגניזת קהיר, מאת מרדכי עקיבא פרידמן.

האשה וגו' (קהלת ז:כו).

רב הוה קא מצערא ליה דביתהו,

כי אמר לה עבידי לי טלופחי—עבדא ליה חימצי, חימצי—עבדא ליה טלופחי.

כי גדל חייא בריה, אפיך לה.

אמר ליה: איעליא לך אמך!

אמר ליה: אנא הוא דקא אפיכנא לה.

אמר ליה: "היינו דקא אמרי אינשי: 'דנפיק מינך טעמא מלפך',

את לא תעביד הכי, שנאמר: 'למדו לשונם דבר שקר העוה וגו' (ירמיה ט:ד)'.

רבי חייא הוה קא מצערא ליה דביתהו, כי הוה משכח מידי, צייר ליה בסודריה ומייתי ניהלה.

אמר ליה רב: "והא קא מצערא ליה למר!"

אמר ליה: "דיינו שמגדלות בנינו, ומצילות אותנו מן החטא."

מקרי ליה רב יהודה לרב יצחק בריה: "ומוצא אני מר ממות את האשה."

אמר ליה: "כגון מאן?" "כגון אמך."

והא מתני ליה רב יהודה לרב יצחק בריה: "אין אדם מוצא קורת רוח אלא מאשתו ראשונה, שנאמר: 'יהי מקורך ברוך ושמח מאשת נעוריך'(משלי ה:יח)"?

ואמר ליה: "כגון מאן?" "כגון אמך!"

מתקיף תקיפא, ועבורי מיעברא במלה.

היכי דמי אישה רעה?

אמר אביי: "מקשטא ליה תכא ומקשטא ליה פומא."

רבא אמר: "מקשטא ליה תכא ומהדרא ליה גבא."

אמר רבי חמא בר חנינא: "כיון שנשא אדם אישה—עונותיו מתפקקין,

שנאמר: 'מצא אשה מצא טוב ויפק רצון מה' (משלי יח:כב)."

במערבא כי נסיב אינש איתתא, אמרי ליה הכי: "מצא או מוצא?"

מצא—דכתיב: 'מצא אשה מצא טוב',

מוצא—דכתיב: 'ומוצא אני מר ממות את האשה'.

יש לנו רשימה של אמוראים שרבו עם נשותיהם, ואפילו ראו את האישות כמר ממוות. חוץ מרבי חייא, כולם בני בבל. ואפילו ביחס לרבי חייא, למרות שהוא תנא וגר בארץ ישראל, הסיפור מובא רק במקור בבלי. מעניין גם שהאופציה של "מצא" רק מובא כפתגם ישראלי.

מיותר להעיר שמה שמובא פה הוא ההפך של רומנטיות ושל שותפות בין איש לאשתו. אין מקור דומה לזה בתלמוד ירושלמי או המדרש ארץ ישראלי הקדום.

להדגיש את הנקודה שהטוב באישות בעיני חכמי בבל היה בשמירתם מהרהורים וסיפוק

"אף בלא חיים, שנאמר: 'ראה חיים עם האשה אשר אהבת' (קהלת ט:ט)."

<u>רבי חייא בר גמדא אמר:</u>

"אף אינו אדם שלם, שנאמר: 'ויברך אותם ויקרא את שמם אדם'
(בראשית ה:ב)—שניהם כאחד קרויים אדם."

<u>ויש אומרים:</u>

"אף ממעט את הדמות, שנאמר: 'כי בצלם אלהים עשה את האדם' (בראשית
ט:ו), מה כתיב אחריו? 'ואתם פרו ורבו'."

ודומה לזה בבבלי יבמות (סב:):

<u>אמר רבי תנחום אמר רבי חנילאי:</u>

"כל אדם שאין לו אישה—שרוי בלא שמחה, בלא ברכה, בלא טובה;

בלא שמחה—דכתיב: 'ושמחת אתה וביתך',

בלא ברכה—דכתיב: 'להניח ברכה אל ביתך',

בלא טובה—דכתיב: 'לא טוב היות האדם לבדו'."

<u>במערבא אמרי:</u> "בלא תורה, בלא חומה.

בלא תורה—דכתיב: 'האם אין עזרתי בי ותושיה נדחה ממני' (איוב ו:יג).

בלא חומה—דכתיב: 'נקבה תסובב גבר' (ירמיה לא:כא).

<u>רבא בר עולא אמר:</u>

בלא שלום, דכתיב: 'וידעת כי שלום אהלך ופקדת נוך ולא תחטא.'
(איוב ה:כד)

חוץ מרבא בר עולא, כל אחד מהאומראים בבראשית רבה והגמרא הם אמוראים ארץ ישראליים.
ברור מהביטויים החזקים ביותר על חשיבות האישה והאישות שהערך של אישות בעיני חכמי ארץ
ישראל אינו רק להציל את הגבר מהרהורי עבירה. אלא שהאישה היא טובה וברכה והיא אפילו
חלק אינטגרלי מהגדרתו כאדם.

מצד שני, עלינו להודות שהסוגיא הבבלית המקבילה (יבמות סב:) מסבכת את התמונה במקצת.
למרות שרבי תנחם בר חנילאי הינו אמורא ארץ ישראלי, הסתם מבין את מאמרו כמייצג דעת
בבלית, ומצטט מימרא אחרת להציג את העמדה בישראלית, והמימרא הזאת מבינה את הטובה
של האישות כעזרה ללימוד תורה, וחומה להגן עליו מהרהורים ואיסורים, מה שעד עכשיו ראינו
כמייצג הסתכלות בבלית דווקא. בכל אופן, ברור מבראשית רבה שזה לא הדרך שחכמי ארץ ישראל
מציגים את עצמם. בכל אופן, חשוב להעיר שאפילו כשהבבלי כותב במילים יפות על האישות,
הם עושים את זה בשימוש במאמר של אמורא ישראלי.

אפשר לראות ברוח המקור הזה ניגוד מוחלט לרוח מקור הבבלי הבא (יבמות סג.–סג:):

<u>רב הוה מיפטר מרבי חייא,</u> אמר ליה: "רחמנא ליצלך ממידי דקשה
ממותא."

ומי איכא מידי דקשה ממותא? נפק דק ואשכח: 'ומוצא אני מר ממות את

לעיל, שתלמיד חכם צעיר אמור להתחתן לפני שהוא יוצא ללמוד כדי למנוע מעצמו ההרהורי עבירה. ולכן, אפילו מישהו שפטור מפריה ורביה יכול לחטוא בהרהורי עבירה וחייב לשמור על עצמו בדרך היחידה שיש. וכן הבין הרמב"ם את שיטת שמואל:

> וכן מצות חכמים היא שלא ישב אדם בלא אישה שלא יבא לידי הרהור...
> (רמב"ם הלכות אישות, ט"ו:ט"ז)

מקור אחד מפתיע ביותר ביחס למשמעות האישות נמצא בבבלי יומא (יח):

> רב כי מקלע לדרשיש מכריז: מאן הויא ליומא.
> רב נחמן כד מקלע לשכנציב מכריז: מאן הויא ליומא.

רש"י מפרש:

> כי מיקלע לדרשיש—שם היה רגיל לילך.
> מאן הויא ליומא—יש אישה שתנשא לי ליומא, שאתעכב כאן, ותצא לאחר מכאן?

כנראה מפירוש רש"י, לא רק שריבוי נשים היה מותר, אבל החכמים עצמם נהגו לשאת נשים מרובות, ואפילו נשואים ארעיים[14].

כל זה אפשר להסביר על רקע היחס של חכמי בבל לאישות. כמו שהסברנו לעיל, עיקר החשיבות לאישות לפי חכמי בבל היה בהצלת הגבר מהרהורי עבירה. כשרב ורב נחמן היו מחוץ לעירם, ודאגו על האפשרות שיכשלו בהרהורים, החליטו לשאת נשים לתקופת ביקורם בעיר.

אחרת היא יחסם של בני ארץ ישראל לאישות. בבראשית רבה (וילנא, פרשה יז) כתוב:

> 'לא טוב' (בראשית ב:יח):
> תני רבי יעקב:
> "כל שאין לו אישה שרוי בלא טובה, בלא עזר, בלא שמחה, בלא ברכה, בלא כפרה.
> בלא טובה—'לא טוב היות האדם לבדו',
> בלא עזר—'אעשה לו עזר כנגדו',
> בלא שמחה—שנאמר: 'ושמחת אתה וביתך' (דברים יד:כו)
> בלא כפרה—'וכפר בעדו ובעד ביתו' (ויקרא טז:ו),
> בלא ברכה—'להניח ברכה אל ביתך' (יחזקאל מד:ל)."
> רבי סימון בשם רבי יהושע בן לוי אמר:
> "אף בלא שלום—שנאמר: 'ואתה שלום וביתך שלום' (א שמואל כה:ו)."
> רבי יהושע דסכנין בשם רבי לוי אמר:

---

[14] אפילו לפי ההסבר שהגמ' נותנת לסיפור, הדאגה להרהורים ולחשיבות של נישואין עדיין עומדים במ – כז.

אמר ליה: "מאי טעמא לא פריסת סודרא?"

אמר ליה: "דלא נסיבנא."

אהדרינהו לאפיה מיניה,

אמר ליה: "חזי, דלא חזית להו לאפי עד דנסבת."

רב הונא לטעמיה, דאמר: "בן עשרים שנה ולא נשא אישה—כל ימיו בעבירה."

בעבירה סלקא דעתך? אלא אימא: כל ימיו בהרהור עבירה.

אמר רבא, וכן תנא דבי ר' ישמעאל: "עד כ' שנה, יושב הקב"ה ומצפה לאדם מתי ישא אישה,

כיון שהגיע כ' ולא נשא, אומר: תיפח עצמותיו."

אמר רב חסדא: "האי דעדיפנא מחבראי—דנסיבנא בשיתסר,

ואי הוה נסיבנא בארביסר, הוה אמינא לשטן גירא בעיניך."

אפשר לראות פה שני דברים מנוגדים. קודם כל, אנו רואים את חשיבותו של מוסד האישות, עד שרב הונא לא מוכן אפילו לדבר עם תלמיד חכם שאינו נשוי. מצד שני, הגמרא מסבירה שהסיבה לחשיבותו של האישות נמצאת בעובדא שמי שאין לו אישה טמוע בתוך תאווה.

הטענה של הגמרא היא שנשואין מצילים את האיש מהרהורי עבירה, וככל שאדם מתחתן יותר צעיר יותר טוב לו, כפי שרב חסדא אומר בפירוש. רב חסדא אפילו מאמין שנשואין בגיל מאוד צעיר יצילו את האדם מהרהורי עבירה לעולם. אפשר לראות את זה ברור מפירוש רש"י על המקום:

הוה אמינא ליה לשטן גירא בעיניך—כלומר, הייתי מתגרה בו, ושטן הוא יצר הרע, ולא אירא שיחטיאני.

רב חסדא טוען שהסיבה היחידה שיש ליצר הרע שלו שליטה כל שהוא עליו, הודות לאיחור נשואיו; בן שש עשרה, ולא בן ארבע עשרה.

אפשר לראות את חשיבות הנשואין בעיני חכמי בבל גם בסוגיא של פרו ורבו (בבלי יבמות סא:):

מתני'. לא יבטל אדם מפריה ורביה—אלא א"כ יש לו בנים. ב"ש אומרים: שני זכרים, וב"ה אומרים: זכר ונקבה, שנאמר: 'זכר ונקבה בראם' (בראשית ה:ב).

גמ'. הא יש לו בנים—מפריה ורביה בטיל, מאישה לא בטיל. מסייעא ליה לרב נחמן אמר שמואל, דאמר: "אע"פ שיש לו לאדם כמה בנים, אסור לעמוד בלא אישה, שנאמר: 'לא טוב היות האדם לבדו' (בראשית ב:יח)."

הגמרא מדייקת פה שישנו חיוב להיות נשוי, וזאת מחוץ למסגרת פריה ורביה. שמואל אפילו טוען שאסור להיות בלי אישה. אפשר היה להבין ששמואל מעריך את האישות כדבר משמעותי כשלעצמו ("לא טוב היות האדם לבדו"), אבל יותר נראה ששמואל הולך לפי שיטתו שהבאנו

ובטלים מפריה ורביה, שנקל בעיניהם ילדים וילדות.

למה רש״י פרש את המאמר על הילדים כמתיחס לביטול פריה ורביה ולא כהרעבת ילדיו? כנראה היה מאד קשה לרש״י להאמין שבני בבל באמת עזבו את ילדיהן, והיה יותר פשוט להאמין שהם עזבו את הבית לפני שנולד להם ילדים. אבל גם לרש״י וגם לתוס׳, יש כאן ביקורת על הנוהג של בני בבל העוזבים את נשותיהם, ובטלים מפריה ורביה (רש״י) ו/או מרעיבים את ילדיהם (תוס׳).

ענין הביקורת עולה גם מהתוספות בקדושין (כט: ד״ה הא לן):

הא לן והא להו—פי׳ בקונטרס... וקשה לר״ת... ועוד קשה, אחר שנשא אישה, היאך יצא חוץ למקומו ללמוד? והלא הוא צריך לחזור אחר מזונות אשתו ובניו!

ובפרק קמא דגיטין אשכחן... על כן נראה לרבינו תם איפכא, דר׳ יוחנן, דאמר "ריחים בצוארו ויעסוק בתורה"—לבני בבל דיבר, שאינו יכול להניח אשתו וילך וילמוד תורה, ועוד שהם עניים.

ושמואל, דאמר "נושא אישה תחלה"—לבני ארץ ישראל אמר, שיכולים ללמוד במקומם,

וגם הם עשירים, וטוב לו שישא אישה וילמוד תורה בטהרה.

רבינו תם מפרש את הסוגיא בצורה הפוכה מהפשט הפשוט. הוא הרגיש שהוא חייב לפרש כך מכיוון שפירוש הפשוט של הסוגיא הינו קבלת הנוהג הבבלי כנוהג ליגיטימי. הוא מעדיף להבין את מאמרו של רבי יוחנן כפסק הלכה נגד עזיבת המשפחה, ומאמרו של שמואל כעידוד לחיים משפחתיים. לדידו חיים משפחתיים עושים את תקופת הלימוד של התלמיד חכם יותר שמחים וטהורים.

ראינו שבעירובין, בדרשות על הפסוק "שחורות כעורב", שהמצב בבבל (רבא ורב אדא בר מתנה) הוא בדיוק כמו שמתואר בסוגיות בקדושין וגיטין, שעזבו את נשותיהם וילדיהם, וכנראה זאת היתה המציאות ואפילו האידיאל, של החכמים הבבליים. ועל הנוהג הזה קבלו ביקורת מבני א״י.

היה, אולי, מקום להסביר שכל הסיבה שבני א״י נהגו אחרת יוצא מתוך פסיקה שונה של בני בבל ביחס לתלמוד תורה. הם פסקו בדומה לשיטת רבי יוחנן בשבת (יא.) שראינו לעיל, שתלמוד תורה אינו פוטר אדם מחיובים אחרים.

אבל באמת אינו נראה כך. הביקורת של רב אביתר מתיחסת לדאגה לטובת האישה והילדים. וכשנחקור את השקפותיהם של בני בבל ובני ארץ ישראל על אישות, יתברר שהדגש על החשיבות של אישות שונה לגמרי. כבר ראינו למעלה שבני בבל מדגישים את שמירת הגברים מהרהור עבירה. לדוגמא, בבבלי קידושין (כט:-ל., ההמשך הישיר לגמרא שציטטנו למעלה) איתא:

משתבח ליה רב חסדא לרב הונא בדרב המנונא דאדם גדול הוא, אמר ליה: "כשיבא לידך הביאהו לידי."

כי אתא, חזייה דלא פריס סודרא,

ת״ר: ללמוד תורה ולישא אישה—ילמוד תורה ואחר כך ישא אישה,
ואם אי אפשר לו בלא אישה—ישא אישה ואחר כך ילמוד תורה.
<u>אמר רב יהודה אמר שמואל</u>: "הלכה: נושא אישה ואחר כך ילמוד תורה."
<u>ר׳ יוחנן אמר</u>: "ריחיים בצוארו ויעסוק בתורה?!"
ולא פליגי: הא לן, והא להו.

אנחנו רואים פה מחלוקת בסיסית בין בבל וארץ ישראל שמיצגיה הם שמואל ורבי יוחנן. בבבל
נושאים אישה ואחר כך לומדים, ובארץ ישראל הפוך. לפום ריהטא, היינו יכולים להגיד שזה מראה
לנו את גודל מסירותם של בני ארץ ישראל ללמוד תורה, או שהחשששות לתאוות והרהורים היו יותר
חזקות בבבל. אבל, באמת, הנושא פה אחר לגמרי. כדי להבין זאת היטב, נעיין ברש״י במקום:

הא לן הא להו—בני בבל היו הולכין וגורסין משניות התנאים בארץ ישראל,
ומתוך שלומדים חוץ למקומם אין צרכי הבית מוטלים עליו.
להו—לבני ארץ ישראל הלומדים במקומם, אם נושא אישה יהו צרכי הבית
מוטלין עליו ויבטלוהו.

לפי רש״י, בני בבל היו יוצאים מביתם ללמוד תורה בארץ ישראל, ולא היו דואגים על נשותיהם
העגונות ובניהם הרעבים, אלא היו לומדים בשקט ושלווה.[13] מצד שני, בני ארץ ישראל היו גרים
בבית עם משפחותיהם, ולוקחים על עצמם את האחריות לפרנס אותם, והיה על צואריהם "רחיים",
היה קשה להם ללמוד.
האם מדובר כאן רק במנהגים שונים, או האם זה מלמד על גישות שונות לאישות? בבבלי גיטין
(ו.), אפשר לראות את תגובת בני ארץ ישראל על נוהג זה:

הא איהו (ר׳ אביתר) דשלח ליה לרב יהודה: "בני אדם העולין משם לכאן הן
קיימו בעצמן: 'ויתנו (את) הילד בזונה והילדה מכרו ביין וישתו' (יואל ד:ג).

ברור שיש פה תוכחה גלויה של בני ארץ ישראל על התנהגותם של אחיהם בבבל. אפשר
לראות את זה באופן הפשוט ביותר בפרוש התוספות לסוגיא בקדושין (כט:):

פירוש שצריכין בניו ובנותיו להתמשכן בעבור מזונותיהן, משמע שאין עושים
יפה שהולכים ללמוד חוץ למקומן.

רש״י מסביר קצת אחרת:

ויתנו (את) הילד כו׳—שהיו משתהין בארץ ישראל ומניחין נשותיהן עגונות

---

[13] תוספות על המקום (ד״ה הא לן) מקשה על פירושו של רש״י: "וקשה לרבינו תם, דמשמע דקאמר שמואל דנושא
אישה תחלה כדי להיות בלא הרהור, ומוקי לה למילתיה בבני בבל, אם כן אכתי איכא הרהור, כיון שהולכים ללמוד
חוץ למקומן!" אפשר לטעון שרש״י מבין את ההרהור לא כהרהור מיני, אבל כדאגה על העתיד שלו, שנפטר
בנשואין מטעם פת בסלו.

ואנשי חיל הם אבירי הלב בשלימות הבטחון כולו לעשות מצות תמיד ולהגות
בתורה יום ולילה, אף שבביתו אין לחם ושמלה, ובניו ובני ביתו יצעקו לו:
"הבה לנו מחיה להחיינו ולפרנסנו!" ואינו משגיח עליהם כלל, ולקולם לא
יחת כמו שאמרו שחורותו כעורב במי אתה מוצאן כו' במי שמשים עצמו
אכזרי על בניו ועל בני ביתו כעורב... והוא כי בטלו כל אהבותיו נגד אהבת ה'
ותורתו ומצותיו.
(ביאור הגר"א – משלי כג:ל)

המקור שבו הגר"א משתמש הוא דווקא הגמרא בעירובין שציטטנו לעיל. לפיכך אפשר לראות
בגר"א דוגמא למופת בפתרון המתח — בחירת הערך של תלמוד תורה והמשך רוחני של רב אדא
בר אהבא ורב אדא בר מתנא בר מתנא באופן מוחלט.[10]
בכל זאת, בסופו של הדבר, הגר"א צמצם את דבריו לאלו שהוגים "בתורה יום ולילה", לאלו
שתורתן אומנתן ולא לכל תלמיד חכם. ולכן אנו מוצאים שבביאור הגר"א על שולחן ערוך[11] הוא
חולק על הרמ"א שהרחיב את ההיתר לכל תלמיד חכם ומביא דווקא את שיטת הראב"ד להלכה,
שמותר רק למי שתורתו אומנתו לעזוב את הבית לזמן שאינו מוקצב.
לאנשים כאלו, ליחידי סגולה, ייתכן שזו היא ההכרעה הנכונה. אלו שתורתן אומנתם הם בבחינת
כהן גדול, שאינו יוצא מהמקדש לשום דבר של העולם הזה, אפילו כשמת אביו ואמו. אבל, כשמדובר
בתלמיד חכם רגיל, באלו שהם בבחינת כהן רגיל, העובד במקדש אבל גם יוצא ממנו לפרקים, האם
ההכרעה הזאת צודקת? האם מותר לתלמיד חכם רגיל לוותר על החיוב לביתו כדי ללמוד תורה?
לשיטת הרמ"א—כן, אבל היא עומדת בניגוד לשיטת הראב"ד והגר"א.[12]
לסיכום, ביחס למתח בין תפילה לת"ת, ראינו שבסוגיא במסכת שבת ר' יוחנן מצמצם את
הכח של לימוד תורה לפטור אדם מחיוביו. בנוסף, ראינו שבסוגיא בעירובין רבא (וגם רב אדא
בר אהבה, לפי נוסחאת הר"ח) מדגיש את החיוב ללמוד תורה ולוותר על החיוב לביתו. אם כן,
אולי כל המחלוקת בין האמוראים תלויה בחשיבות שנותנים לתלמוד תורה כנגד שאר החיובים
של האדם.
לדעתי, אכן זה כך, אך זהו רק חלק אחד של המטבע. החלק השני הוא לא ביחס לתלמוד תורה
אלא ביחס לאישות—איזה חשיבות נותנים לאישות ולנוכחות הבעל בתוך הבית.

ד. הערך של האישות בכלל בבבל וארץ ישראל

אפשר לראות שרב, רבא ורבי יוחנן לא חולקים—או לא רק חולקים—ביחס לתלמוד תורה,
אלא ביחס לאישות. ובזה, הם לא רק מייצגים את דעתם הפרטיות, אבל בעצם, הם מייצגים את
השקפת מקום המגורים שלהם, בבל וארץ ישראל. נעיין בכמה סוגיות כדי להבהיר זאת.
בבבלי קידושין (כט:) איתא:

---

[10] באמת יש הבדל אחד עצום, והוא שלהגר"א היה תמיכה כספית מלאה מהציבור בווילנא, לפחות בבגרותו.
[11] אבן העזר עו: ס"ק ד.
[12] אפשר, כמובן, לפסוק עקרוני כהראב"ד, ובכל זאת להגדיר הרבה תלמידי חכמים כ"תורתן אומנתן." כמובן,
השאלה בהגדרת הקטגוריה של "תורתן אומנתן" דומה לשאלה של הגדרת הקטגוריה של הנשים שנותנים רשות
בלב מלא.

היותר קיצוני בעניין הזה הוא הגר"א מווילנא. וכך כותב ר' יהודה ליב ור' אברהם בני הגר"א על אביהם[9]:

הן בהיותו בן י"ג שנה ויום א' קבל תוקף חסידותו ופרישותו... מאז לא הסתכל עד יום מותו בד' אמותיו חוצה, שלא להנות מעולם הזה רצה. אכל לחם צר צנומה שרויה במים שיעור ב' זיתים, יאכל אותן ערב ובקר, ולא טעמן בחכו רק בלען שלימות...

במה מסר נפשו להרחיק מחברת ביתו בניו ובנותיו, רק יראת ה' טהורה... עד שמימיו לא שאל את בניו ובנותיו בעסק פרנסתם ומהות מצבם. מימיו לא כתב אליהם איגרות לשאול בשלומם. ואם בא א' מבניו לגבולו, גם כי הגדיל השמחה, כי לא ראו אותו שנה או שנתים, אפס לא שאל אותו על עסקי שלום בניו וביתו וענין פרנסתו, וכאשר נח מדרכו שיעור שעה אחת, מהר ימהרנו שוב לקבוע סדר לימודו...

אחי הרב הגדול... שלמה זלמן ז"ל, בהיותו בן חמש שנים או כבן שש היה רך ויחיד לאביו, ואבי אהבו שעשועיו בכל עת, כי הכיר בו מדת טובו וצדקתו. פעם אחת נפל למשכב, טרם שב לאיתנו הסכים מר אבא הגאון ז"ל בדעתו לנסוע אל מקום אשר הכין להתבודד... הבוקר אור ויסע אל המקום ההוא להתבודד כפעם בפעם... עד ששכח ביתו ובניו יותר מחודש ימים. פעם אחת הלך לבית הרחיצה. גלוי וידוע שאסור להרהר שם בדברי תורה, התחיל לעיין בענייניו ונזכר כי בדרך זו הלך מביתו יותר מחודש ימים, ובנו חביבו מתהלך בתומו נעשב ממנו מושכב על ערש דוי, ונכמרו רחמיו וצוה לאסור רכבו לשוב לביתו לפקוד שלומו לדעת מה יעשה לו...

כשנשים לב אל כל המעשים אשר עשאם... תראה שכלם באו בתכלית החריצות והשלימות. אם במה שעבר עליו בהסתכנותו במלחמתו עם כחות גופו, ואם בכובד העבודה שקיים וקבל על עצמו כל ימיו שלא לישן יותר מב' שעות במעת לעת, ומימיו לא ישן יותר מחצי שעה רצופה... וגם תחבולותיו נגד היצר מה שהיה לבו חפץ גזר עליה אומר שאינו טובה אמיתית, והתרחק ממנה, ויט שכמו לסבול הצער של רעבון והדחק של קיצור שינה... רוב פקחותו והשתדלותו בעבודת ה' היא שעמדה לו נגד כל מעיק לו, והיא שהסיר כל דאגה וכל עצב לעבוד את ה' בשמחה ובטוב לב כל הימים.

הדברים האלו מדברים על עצמם. הגר"א, הוא האידיאל של תורתו אומנתו, הוא העמיד כל רגע של לימוד תורתו מעל לכל דבר אחר. הגר"א לא ראה שזוהי דרך חיים ששייכת רק לו, אלא כדרך שכל תלמיד חכם צריך לשאוף אליה. וכך כותב בפירושו למשלי:

---

[9] הקדמת בני הגר"א לביאור הגר"א על השלחן ערוך.

הראשון דורש התמדה. רבה דורש חיי עוני בשביל הלומד. רבא דורש אכזריות על בניו,והגמרא
מביאה אמורא,רב אדא בר מתנא, שחי את הדרישה הזאת. כדאי לזכור שזה אותו רבא שפוסק
בסוגיא בכתובות שמותר לעזוב את המשפחה לזמן ממושך, בלא רשות. וכדאי להעיר שגירסת
רבינו חננאל בסוגיא, האיש שעוזב את המשפחה, אינו רב אדא בר מתנא אלא רב אדא בר
אהבה, האמורא שהביא את שיטת החכמים בפעם הראשונה, ושרבא פסק כמותו! אנו מוצאים
שלאמוראים אלו האידאל הוא שתלמוד תורה עומד כנגד כולם ומתיר למי שתורתו אומנתו לעזוב
את ביתו ואת משפחתו בעבור תורתו.

דברי הראב"ד הובאו ברמ"א, אבל בצורה אחרת:

ואם נותנת לו רשות, ת"ח יכול לילך בכל מה שתתן לו רשות [טור בשם
הראב"ד]. (רמ"א, אבן העזר, ס' ע"ו סע' ה')

והרי תלמיד חכם אינו בהכרח מי שתורתו אומנתו. ולראייה, כשהשו"ע פוסק את הדין שמי
שתורתו אומנתו פטור מתפילה הוא כותב שהדין אינו שייך לנו, שאין אף אחד ממנו שתורתו
אומנתו:

מי שתורתו אומנתו,כגון רשב"י וחביריו, מפסיק לק"ש, ולא לתפלה; אבל אנו,
מפסיקים בין לק"ש בין לתפלה. (שולחן ערוך אורח חיים קו:ב)

אם כן, איך פסק הרמ"א שברשות מותר ואין צריך לדאוג לאורחא דמילתא? על זה עונה הבית
שמואל:

בטור בשם הראב"ד כ' ת"ח שתורתו אומנתו לא חשו לאורחא דמילתא
משמע כגון אנן צריכין לחוש
מיהו הרב רמ"א סבר למה דקי"ל אפי' בלא רשות יוצאים ב' וג' שנים
משום הכי אם נתנה לו רשות יכול לילך כל מה שתתן לו רשות. (בית שמואל
אבן העזר סימן עו ס"ק יא)

כלומר, כדי שתלמוד תורה יבטל חיוב הלכתי—חיוב תפילה—צריך להגיע למדרגה של מי
שתורתו אומנתו. אבל כדי לבטל את החיוב המוסרי של "אורחא דמילתא", חיוב נחות כששיש לו
איזשהו רשות מאשתו[7], לזה מספיק להיות תלמיד חכם רגיל. משקל לימוד תורה של כל תלמיד
חכם הוא יותר מהחיוב המוסרי של בעל כלפי אשתו.

אנחנו מוצאים במשך הדורות שבעולם התורה הביעואת הגישה שתלמוד תורה עומדת כנגד כולם—
ובודאי כשמדובר בתלמידי חכמים. וכשהיא עומדת מול ערכים אחרים, היא תמיד מנצחת[8]. הדגם

---

[7] אפשר שכוונת הב"ש—וכוונת הרמ"א—היא שהיות שהיא נתנה רשות ושמדובר בתלמיד חכם—אנחנו מגדירים
את רשותה כרצונה המלאה. אם זה הוא פירוש הדברים, אז זה מעין שיטת תוס', אבל זה מדברי הרמ"א ומדברי הב"ש
לא נראה ככה.
[8] מאמר מעניין על איך הגישה הזאת התבטא בתוך המאה התשע עשרה הוא:
"Marriage and Torah Study Among the *Lomdim* in Lithuania in the Nineteenth Century,"
Immanuel Etkes, in *The Jewish Family*, ed. David Kramer (Oxford University Press: New York:
1989)

אפשר שהדיון בערך תלמוד תורה לעומת צרכי אשתו, קשור ביחס למי מדובר. הרא"ש בשם הראב"ד מתרץ את הסתירה בין שתי הסוגיות כך:

והני רבנן דנפקי טובא כתב הראב"ד ז"ל לפי שהיתה תורתן אומנתן ולא חשו לאורחא דמילתא.
(רא"ש מסכת כתובות ה:כ"ט)

כלומר, מי שתורתו אומנתו, תלמוד תורה שלו דוחה כל ערך אחר. ולו מותר להתעלם מהחיוב המוסרי כלפי אשתו. שיטת הראב"ד לקוחה, כנראה, מהסוגיא בשבת (י"א) הפוסקת שאלו שלומדים תורה פטורים מתפילה:

דתניא: חברים שהיו עוסקין בתורה—מפסיקין לקריאת שמע, ואין מפסיקין לתפלה.
אמר רבי יוחנן: לא שנו אלא כגון רבי שמעון בן יוחי וחביריו, שתורתן אומנתן.
אבל כגון אנו—מפסיקין לקריאת שמע ולתפלה.

למרות פשטות הברייתא, ר' יוחנן סובר שלא כל אדם העוסק בתלמוד תורה רשאי לבטל תפי־לה, אלא רק מי שתורתן אומנתן. בכך ר' יוחנן דומה לשיטתו אצלנו, שתלמוד תורה לא תמיד מנצח, ויש דברים—תפילה, חיוב הבעל לאשתו, וכדו'—שבעבורם צריכים לוותר על תלמוד תורה המלאה. ורק מי שתורתו אומנתו מותר לוותר על חיובו לאחרים.

יותר מזה, ר' יוחנן מדגיש שהקטגוריה הזאת של "תורתו אומנתו" מצומצמת מאד, ואפילו האמוראים, כולל ר' יוחנן עצמו, אינו נחשב לאלו שתורתן אומנתן. ולכן, היה מקום לומר שלר' יוחנן הקטגוריה הזאת של "תורתו אומנתו" היא פחות או יותר פיקטיבית, ואינה שייכת לשום אדם בזמן הזה. ובכל זאת, לפי הראב"ד[6] הקטגוריה ההיא נשארת הלכתית, ומי שבאמת תורתו אומנתו פטור מתפילה, ולכן ק"ו שיפטר מהחיובים של "אורחא דמילתא."

אפשר לראות סימנים לשיטת הראב"ד, מהגמ' בעירובין, שמשבחת את אלו שעוזבים ביתם וילדיהם לצורך תלמוד תורה, ובפשטות מדובר —בניגוד לשיטת תוס'—שנהגו ככה בלא רשות נשותיהם:

'שחרות כעורב'—במי אתה מוצאן? במי שמשכים ומעריב עליהן לבית המדרש.
רבה אמר: "במי שמשחיר פניו עליהן כעורב."
רבא אמר: "במי שמשים עצמו אכזרי על בניו ועל בני ביתו כעורב."
כי הא דרב אדא בר מתנא הוה קאזיל לבי רב,
אמרה ליה דביתהו: "ינוקי דידך מai אעביד להו?"
אמר לה: "מי שלימו קורמי באגמא?!" (בבלי עירובין כא:-כב.)

הגמרא מונה את הדרישות המתבקשות מן התלמיד חכם כדי לרשת את התורה. המאמר

---
6 וכן לפי הרמב"ם, הל' תפילה ו:ח'; בניגוד לפסק השו"ע, או"ח ק"ו:ב'

אלא אורחא דמילתא כמה—פי' בקונטרס שלא ישא עליו חטא ואפי' הוא
יכול לפתותה.
ואם תאמר: והיאך יצא רבי עקיבא וכל הנהו דלקמן?
ויש לומר דהתם בלא פתוי היו שמחות שהיו בעליהן הולכין ללמוד תורה, ולהיות
תלמידי חכמים, ואדרבה, אדעתא דהכי נשאו שילכו ללמוד תורה.
(תוס' סב. ד"ה 'אלא אורחא דמילתא כמה')

לפי התוספות, על אף שרב ורבי יוחנן חלקו כשהאישה נתנה רשות, בכל זאת, לא כל ההסכמות
ניתנות במידה שווה. כידוע, אפשר לשכנע את בן או בת הזוג להסכים למשהו שבאמת הוא או
היא לא רוצים לעשות. ולכן, במקרה כזה חייב אדם להתנהג כפי הנורמות המוסריות—ה"אורחא
דמילתא"—ולא כפי הרשות שבאה רק על ידי פיתוי. ובמילים של הרא"ש (ה:כ"ט): "שלא ישאל
ממנה דבר של צער, דשמא אף על פי שנותנת לו רשות על ידי פיוסו או על ידי שמתביישה ממנו
לבה מצטערת." לעומת זה, אם הרשות ניתנת משום שהאישה והבעל הם תמימי דעות בדבר, אז אינו
מדובר ברשות אלא בעסק משותף, וכשהמצב כך, מותר ונכון לו לעזוב את הבית ללמוד תורה.

למעשה, אף רש"י מוכרח להודות שיש מקרים שהאישה מסכימה לגמרי בעזיבת הבעל את
הבית לצורך תלמוד תורה. שהרי שורת הסיפורים בגמרא מסתיימים בסיפור המפורסם על רבי
עקיבא שהלך ביוזמת אשתו ללמוד תורה כ"ד שנים, והכריז לתלמידיו ש"שלי ושלכם שלה הוא".
האם רש"י יאמר שרבי עקיבא עשה שלא כהוגן? הרי אין שום צליל של ביקורת בסיפור הזה,
וברור שהסיפור הוא כולו שבח על ר' עקיבא ורחל אשתו.

אלא מחלוקת רש"י ותוס' היא בזאת—איך מבדילים בין מקרה של פיתוי בלי רצון אמיתי
למקרה של הסכמה, שותפות ורצון אמיתי? תוס' יותר אופטימי ויותר מוכן להגדיר מקרה צפיציפי
של רצון האישה. רש"י, לעומתו, יותר סקפטי, וחושש תמיד שיש בכל מקרה מידה של פיתוי
ואי-רצון, ושצריך לדאוג לחיוב המוסרי והנימוסי שבדבר. אמנם קיימים מקרים כמו של רחל אשת
ר' עקיבא—מקרה שבו האישה היא היוזמת ומסכימה במלא רצונה—אבל מקרים כאלה נדירים
ביותר, וצריך זהירות רבה לפני שאומרים לאדם שאין לו לדאוג ל"אורחא דמילתא".

נמצאנו למדים שרש"י ותוס' חולקים בהערכת המצבים המסובכים הנ"ל בהם האישה אומרת
שרצונה שהבעל יעזוב ביתו ללמוד תורה. האם זה באמת רצונה, האם פיה ולבה שווים? כנראה
מה שעומד מאחורי מחלוקת רש"י והתוספות הוא בדומה למה שפירשנו במחלוקת רב ורבי יוחנן
ביחס ל"אנחה שוברת חצי/כל גופו של אדם". המחלוקת בהערכת המציאות עצמה יכולה להיות
מושפעת מאחת משתי השאלות האלו:
איך שוקלים תלמוד תורה לעומת דיכאון האישה?
והאם מתחילים מנקודת ראות של הבעל או זו של האישה?
במידה שמעריכים יותר תלמוד תורה של הבעל, דואגים לצרכיו יותר, אנו מוכנים לראות את
הסכמת האישה כמקרה של רצון של ממש. לעומת זאת, במידה שאנו דואגים יותר לטובת האישה,
נהיה מוכנים לחשוש שהבעת ההסכמתה אינו משקף את רצונה האמיתי.

ג. הערך של תלמוד תורה כנגד שאר החיובים

שמותר לפי הלכה לצאת מהבית יותר מחדש אחד. ובאמת, לפי שיטת החכמים, היה מותר לרב
רחומי להישאר במחוזא לכמה שנים רצופות, בלי לחזור כל ערב יום כפור. אבל אם נוהג כזה הוגן,
למה רב רחומי מת בסוף הסיפור?

כנראה שהסיפור נמצא פה כדי להדגיש את הבעייתיות בגישה שמתייחס רק לפסק ההלכתי
של הדברים—שההלכה כחכמים—ומתעלם מהמחלוקת של רב ורב יוחנן, מהשאלה של "אורחא
דמילתא כמה?" בלי להתווכח על עצם העובדא שכך נהגו רבנן, הסיפור מראה לנו את הקושי
שנגרם לאישה בגלל הנוהג הזה.

אמת היא, שמבחינה הלכתית אפשר לנהוג כפי הדין ולא כפי הנימוס. אבל מי שנוהג רק לפי
הדין, הקב"ה מתייחס אליו במידת הדין ומדקדק עמו כחוט השערה, ואפילו איחור קטן על הנהוג
אצלו אולי גורם מיתה. וכך כותב הרא"ש בשם הרמ"ה:

> והרמ"ה פסק כרב אדא בר אהבה מדקאמר סמכי רבנן אדרב אדא בר אהבה
> וקא עבדי עובדא בנפשייהו ואע"ג[5] דהלכתא הכי לא מיבעי לעגוני לנפשייהו
> כולי האי דמתוך שדעתה מצויה אונאתה קרובה ודמיא להא דאמרי' לעיל
> דאורחא דמילתא בכמה דאע"ג דיהבא ליה רשותא עצה טובה קמ"ל שלא
> יעגנה אע"פ שהוא ברשותו. (רא"ש מסכת כתובות ה:כ:ט)

יש לציין שהרמ"ה, בדומה לשיטתו לעיל, דואג לרגישות האישה ולחיוב המוסרי של הבעל
מעבר לחיובו ההלכתי.

אפשר להוסיף שהסיפור מרמז לדיון של "אנחה" ששוברת את גופו של אדם. הרי במצב
שהבעל עוזב לזמן מרובה החיים של האישה הם במתח מתמיד, ומצבה הרגשי כל כך עדין, שהתסכול
שהיא מרגישה כאשר בעלה שכח לחזור הביתה הופך את המצב קשה שבעתיים, וגורם סבל מרובה
לאישה. במלים אחרות, אפילו אם בדרך כלל "אנחה שוברת חצי גופו של אדם", במצב כל כך
עדין, במי שלא שם לב ל"אורחא דמילתא" בכלל, אז "אנחה שוברת כל גופו של אדם." הפתרון
שהסיפור מציע, הוא שבמקום לתת לאנחתה של האישה לשבור את גופה, הקב"ה גורם לשבור
את גופו של רב רחומי, בנפילת הגג של הבית מדרש מתחתיו.

הסיפור בגמרא בא ללמד על הבעייתיות בהסתמכות על שיטת חכמים והתעלמות מהחיוב
המוסרי. וכפי שרש"י לעיל הדגיש את החיוב המוסרי והדתי שקיים מעל לחיוב ההלכתי, כך הוא
מדגיש את הבעייתיות בסיפורים המופיעים בגמרא. בפירוש רש"י לאמרו של רבא של רב כתב (סב):

> בנפשייהו—והוא בא להם ליטול מהם נפשות שנענשים ומתים.

רש"י סובר שהמעשה של עזיבת האישה הינו כל כך אכזרי ובלתי-מוסרי, שעשייתו מהווה סכנת
נפשות ממש. זאת אומרת, התלמיד חכם שעוזב ביתו פותח לעצמו אפשרות של נקמה ועונש
מהקב"ה. והכל בגלל אנחת אשתו, ששוברת את כל גופה.

לעומת רש"י, כשהתוספות רואה את הסתירה בין המשנה והסוגיא הראשונה מצד אחד,
והתנהגות הרבנים בסיפורים מצד שני, הוא מתרץ את הסתירה לא בביקורת על הרבנים אלא
בהרמונזציה בין שתי הסוגיות:

---
[5] לפי גירסת הב"ח.

כעת נעבור ונראה גישה שלישית להבנת המחלוקת רב ורבי יוחנן. לגישה זו, המחלוקת הנה מחלוקת בערכים—מה המשקל של החיוב המוסרי/דתי של בעל כלפי אשתו לעומת החשיבות של תלמוד תורה?

ב. אישות ותלמוד תורה—שיטת חכמים והסיפור של רב רחומי

כעת נעיין בסוגית ההמשך (סב:) שמתחילה בפסק ומסיימת במעשים של בעלים, תלמידי חכמים, שעזבו את ביתם כדי ללמוד תורה:

> אמר רב אדא בר אהבה אמר רב: "זו דברי רבי אליעזר [שהתלמידים יוצאים
> שלשים יום שלא ברשות] , אבל חכמים אומרים: 'התלמידים יוצאין לתלמוד
> תורה ב' וג' שנים שלא ברשות'."
>
> אמר רבא: סמכו רבנן אדרב אדא בר אהבה ועבדי עובדא בנפשייהו. כי הא
> דרב רחומי הוה שכיח קמיה דרבא במחוזא, הוה רגיל דהוה אתי לביתיה כל
> מעלי יומא דכיפורי. יומא חד משכתיה שמעתא, הוה מסכיא דביתהו 'השתא
> אתי' 'השתא אתי'. לא אתא. חלש דעתה, אחית דמעתא מעינה, הוה יתיב
> באיגרא, אפחית איגרא מתותיה ונח נפשיה.

בסוגיא זו אנו רואים שיש גם את שיטתם של רב אדא בר אהבה בשם רב ושיטת רבא, שפוסקים כשיטת חכמים, ואומרים שמותר לתלמידים לצאת אפילו לכמה שנים בלא רשות. במחלוקתו עם ר' יוחנן, רב, לכל הפחות, מנווט את המתח, אבל רב אדא בר אהבה בשמו של רב מביא את שיטת חכמים הפוסקים בזכות לימוד התורה בהתעלמות מוחלטת מהחיוב המוסרי/דתי כלפי האישה. רבא מספר ש"רבנן" פסקו כחכמים, וההוכחה שכך נהגו, הגמרא מביאה את המעשה ברב רחומי שנהג למעשה כך.

אחרי פסיקת רב אדא בר אהבה בשם רב וכן דברי רבא האם מבחינה מעשית אפשר להתעלם משיטת רב ורבי יוחנן? ראוי לשים לב שמחלוקת רבי אליעזר וחכמים היא מחלוקת הלכתית, ולכן היא אינה שייכת, בעיקרון, למחלוקת רב ורבי יוחנן. לשיטתם של רב ורבי יוחנן, אפילו אם מבחינה הלכתית יש לבעל רשות לעזוב את ביתו ב' וג' שנים בלי רשות אשתו, עדיין יש לשאול "אורחא דמילתא כמה"? ישנו חיוב של נימוס ודרך ארץ למרות שהאישה נתנה רשותה, אז קל וחומר שחיוב זה הוא במקומו כשהאישה לא נתנה רשות.

העובדא שדברי רב אדא בר אהבה בשם רב, אותו רב שהובא לעיל שאדם צריך לחלק את זמנו בשווה בין הבית לתלמוד תורה, מדגישה שיש שני סוגי חיובים. הראשון מתיחס לחיוב הלכתי, והשני מתיחס לחיוב מוסרי-ערכי.

לכן, ה"רבנן" ש"עבדי עובדא בנפשייהו" עשו לפי שורת הדין, אבל בכל זאת יש לשאול, האם הם עשו כהוגן? כשנעיין בסיפור של רב רחומי ובשאר הסיפורים הדומים שבאים לאחר מכן בגמרא, יתברר שכמה מהם נסתיימו, או שכמעט נסתיימו, באסון.[4] לצורכינו, נתמקד בסיפור של רב רחומי. הסיפור מספר על תלמיד חכם שסמך על פסיקת רב אדא בר אהבה, וסופו היה למות. יש לשאול: מה הסיפור בא ללמד? מצד אחד הסיפור מביא ראייה לרבא ורב אדא בר אהבה

---

[4] לדיון יפה בסיפורים אלו, ראה שולמית ולר, "נשים ונשיות בסיפורי התלמוד," ספריית הילל בן-חיים, פרק ד, "עזיבת הבית לצורך תלמוד תורה".

היות שאינו ברור להיפך (החיוב לאשתו הוא "רק" חיוב מוסרי), המוציא מחבירו עליו הראייה, ויש להקל כרב.

ראינו עד כה שמחלוקת רב ורבי יוחנן, וכן מחלוקת הרא"ש והרמ"ה, תלויה בנקודת המוצא— נקודת הראות של הבעל או נקודת ראות של האישה. לעומת זאת, מהמשך הסוגיא יוצא אפשרות אחרת—שרב ורבי יוחנן לא חולקים בקריטריונים של עימות המתח אלא בהערכת העובדות. הגמרא ממשיכה במחלוקת אחרת של רב ורבי יוחנן, שלפי פשט הדברים אינה שייכת לסוגייתנו:

אמר רב: "אנחה שוברת חצי גופו של אדם,
שנאמר: 'ואתה בן אדם האנח בשברון מתנים ובמרירות תאנח'
(יחזקאל כא, יא)."
ורבי יוחנן אמר: "אף כל גופו של אדם,
שנאמר: 'והיה כי יאמרו אליך על מה אתה נאנח,
ואמרת אל שמועה כי באה ונמס כל לב ורפו כל ידים וכהתה כל רוח וכל ברכים
תלכנה מים' (יחזקאל כא, יב)."

ברמה הפשוטה, סוגיא זו הובאת דרך גררא, ואינה שייכת לסוגיא הקודמת. ובכל זה, דומני שאפשר לראות במחלוקת הזאת, בין רב ורבי יוחנן, קשר למחלוקתם הראשונה. מחלוקתם היא ביחס לאנחה המרומזת לאנחת האישה שאותה הבעל עזב כדי ללמוד תורה.

רבי יוחנן מאמין שאנחה, שפירושו בהקשר שלנו דיכאון, שוברת את כל גופו של האדם. זאת אומרת, עזיבת האישה לעתים קרובות הורסת את חייה לגמרי. אם כן, כמובן שאי אפשר לתת לבעל את האופציה לצאת ללמוד תורה ליותר מדי זמן, שאנו חייבים להיות מוסריים כלפי האישה.

מצד שני, רב מאמין שהאנחה רק שוברת את חצי גופו של האדם. בתדירות ודאי שהיא קשה, אבל היא לא הורסת את חייה לחלוטין. ומכוון שלימוד התורה דבר חשוב והכרחי, אנו מתפשרים עם האישה חצי-חצי. כך אנו לא לוחצים עליה יותר מדי, או ליתר דיוק, יותר ממה שאפשר לה לסבול.

לכן, מחלוקת רב ורבי יוחנן ביחס ל"אורחא דמילתא מאי" היא תוצאה מהבנתם את כובד הקושי שסובלת האישה בהעדרות הבעל.

אבל, אפשר להסביר את הדברים דווקא בכיוון הפוך. לא שמחלוקתם מתחילה במחלוקת של כמה קשה לאישה היעדרות הבעל, אלא שנקודת המחלוקת היא איך לאזן את הערכים המנוגדים. ומחלוקתם ביחס להבנת המציאות היא תוצאה ממחלוקת זו. רב המשווה מבחינה מעשית את חיוב הבעל לתלמוד תורה עם חיובו כלפי אשתו, כשבא לשקול את דיכאון האישה, רואה את מעשה הבעל כחצי-נורא. רבי יוחנן, שמעדיף את חובת הבעל לאשתו, כשבא לשקול את המשמעות של העדרות הבעל, רואה אותה כדבר נורא ועצום.

לסיכום-ביניים, ראינו שתי גישות בהבנת מחלוקת רב ורבי יוחנן ביחס ל"אורחא דמילתא כמה":

1) מחלוקת מאיזה מבט מתחילים—מנקודת ראות של הבעל או של האישה? מחויב אדם לעצמו או מחויבו לאחרים?

2) מחלוקת בעובדות—מה הן ההשלכות המעשיות של העדרות הבעל מהבית?

חובתו המינימלית (ק"ש שחרית וערבית)?[3] וכן, איזה משקל יש לחיוב מוסרי/דתי שאינו חיוב
הלכתי? ובפרט, איזה משקל יש לחיוב מוסרי/דתי של הבעל כלפי אשתו ומשפחתו?

יתכן שאין לדעת איזה ערך שוקל יותר. השאלה היא מאיזה צד מתחילים—הבעל או האישה?
המוציא מחבירו עליו הראיה, אבל מי המוציא ומי המוחזק? האם ההנחה הבסיסית-הראשונית
היא שיש לבעל חיוב ללמוד תורה בצורה האופטמלית ואשתו באה לדרוש ממנו להיות בבית, או
ההנחה הבסיסית היא שיש לו חיוב להיות בבית והוא בא להפטר ממנו ללכת ללמוד תורה?

כעת נעיין ברא"ש והרמ"ה, ונראה כיצד הם פירשו את המחלוקת בין רב ורבי יוחנן. המתח
בין חיוביו שלו וחובותיו כלפי אחרים, כפי שהסברנו, באים על ידי ביטוי במקורות אלו.
ביחס ל"פסק" הסוגיא, כתב הרא"ש (כתובות ה:כ"ט):

> וכתב הר' מאיר הלוי ז"ל דמסתברא כרבי יוחנן דגמר מבנין בית המקדש. ולי
> נראה כיון דלית כאן אלא אורחא דמילתא והיא קא יהבי רשות, עבדינן להקל
> כרב.

מה הפירוש בדברי הרמ"ה "דגמר מבנין בית המקדש"? למה הראיה ממקדש יותר משמעותית
מהראייה מעבודת המלך? כנראה, שכוונת הרמ"ה היא שאם בעבודת המקדש צריך הבעל להיות
בבית יותר מחצי הזמן, כך גם ההולך לתלמוד תורה—דינו כך. אבל זוהי בדיוק שיטת רבי יוחנן,
עליה חולק רב—אם כן מה חידש הרמ"ה?! אין מנוס מלומר, שכוונת הרמ"ה היא ששיטת רבי
יוחנן יותר מקובלת עליו משיטת רב. הראייה מעבודת המקדש משכנעת יותר מהדחייה ש"אפשר
על ידי אחרים". אבל מדוע הנימוק "עבודת המקדש" יותר משכנע? הלא מבחינת הבעל, תלמוד
תורתו אינו אפשרי על ידי אחרים! אך הגישה שלנו היא מנקודת הראות של הבעל, ולא מנקודת
ראות של האישה, ומבחינתה, עזיבת הבעל—לא משנה למטרת איזה הישגים, בנין המקדש או
תלמוד תורה—פוגע בה באותה מידה. לפיכך הרמ"ה פוסק כר' יוחנן—שמבחינה עקרונית הוא
מתחיל מנקודת הראות של האישה.

הרא"ש אינו מסכים לשיטת הרמ"ה ומשיב שני דברים:

1. "דלית כאן אלא אורחא דמילתא"—דהיינו, שמדובר בענין מוסרי, ולא הלכתי טהור.

2. ולכן, "עבדינן להקל כרב"—שאפשר להקל ביחס לחיוב הלא-הלכתי הזה, ולהתיר לאיש
   להשקיע יותר בתלמוד תורתו.

ההנחות האלו אינן פשוטות. אמנם, מדובר בענין מוסרי, אבל מי אמר שזהו אינו חיוב משמעותי?
ברור, לפחות, שלפי שיטת רש"י "נשיאות חטא" במי שלא שומר על כך בדקדוק הדרוש.

לגבי הטענה השנייה—שיש להקל כרב—קשה להבין איזה מין קולא היא זאת. נכון שזו קולא
לבעל שרוצה להיות פטור מן הבית ולהשקיע את עצמו בתלמודו, אבל היא חומרא כלפי אשתו,
שמחמיר עליה ביחס לצרכי הבית ומכביד את דיכויה.

אלא, כמו שהרמ"ה ראה את הדברים מנקודת ראות של האישה, באותה מידה הרא"ש ראה
אותם מנקודת ראות של הבעל. לבעל יש קיום/חיוב תלמוד תורה שאי אפשר לעשות על ידי
אחרים, וזה מנצח את חיובו המוסרי כלפי אשתו וביתו. לא מפני שברור שהאיש יותר חשוב, אלא

---

[3] שאלה זאת שייכת לסוגית חיוב תלמוד תורה כנגד שאר מצוות שאפשר ושאי אפשר לעשותן ע"י אחרים. ע' שבת
יא., ירושלמי ברכות א:ב, מאירי שבת שם ט., רמב"ם הל' תפילה ו:ח, והל' אישות טו:ב, ובנו"כ שם, ובפרט בשולחן
ערוך הרב, הל' תלמוד תורה, קונטרס אחרון, פרק ג', אות א', ועיין בהמשך.

את ההלכה בצורה קפדנית ומדוייקת, אבל לא מספק את חובתו לאשתו ולמשפחתו[2], וכן לא רגיש מספיק לתחושתה של האישה—לא רק שזהו חיסרון מוסרי, אלא האיש חוטא ממש.

לכן, לפי רש"י השאלה אינה שאלה של הלכה, אלא שאלה של מוסר וערכים דתיים, ובתשובת הגמרא מצינו מחלוקת בין רב ור' יוחנן:

<u>אמר רב</u>: "חדש כאן וחדש בבית,

שנאמר: 'לכל דבר המחלוקת הבאה והיוצאת חדש בחדש לכל חדשי השנה' (דברי הימים א כז, ב)."

<u>ור' יוחנן אמר</u>: "חדש כאן ושנים בביתו,

שנאמר: 'חדש יהיו בלבנון שנים חדשים בביתו' (מלכים א ה, כח)."

ורב נמי, מאי טעמא לא אמר מההיא? שאני בנין בית המקדש, דאפשר על ידי אחרים.

ורבי יוחנן, מאי טעמא לא אמר מההיא? שאני התם, דאית ליה הרווחה.

במרכז הסוגיה עומד המתח בין תלמוד תורה שהוא כידוע "כנגד כולם", לערך הדתי לדאוג לטובת אשתו, ולספק את צרכיה הרגשיים והמעשים.

מחלוקת זו יכולה להתפרש כמחלוקת במסגרת רחבה יותר. קיים מתח בין אחריות האדם כלפי עצמו, פיתוחו הרוחני מצד אחד, לאחריותו כלפי אחרים מצד שני. רב מדגיש שתלמוד תורה דומה לעבודת המלך שאינה יכולה להעשות על ידי אחרים. לדעתו, האדם אינו רשאי להתפשר עם חובתו לתלמוד תורה מעבר לנקודה מסוימת. לכן הלומד תורה צריך להיות חדש בבית וחדש בבית המדרש—כשויון באחריותיו. לעומתו, רבי יוחנן מדגיש שלאדם ישנה אחריות רחבה כלפי אחרים. לדעתו, עבודת בית המקדש דומה לתלמוד תורה, שהעובד לבד נהנה משניהם. לאור האינטרס עצמי-דתי שיש בהבנת תלמוד תורה שלו, רבי יוחנן גם דוחה הדמיון לעבודת המלך, שיש לה אינטרס גם למשפחתו כרווח כספי, וגם פוסק שצריכים לכפל זמנו בבית שצרכי משפחתו דורשים התחייבותו יותר גדולה.

וכך מסביר רש"י את ההבדל בין העבודה בעבור ביתו לעבודה בעבור עצמו:

<u>שאני התם דאית ליה הרווחה—שהיו נהנים מבית המלך ואיכא רווח ביתא</u>,

לפיכך מקבלת עליה שיהי' בבית המלך [חדש] אחד משני חדשים, שכיון שיש לו

שכר יש לה מזונות מרווחים ותכשיטין, <u>אבל תלמוד תורה מצוה דיליה הוא</u>.

לסיכום, המחלוקת בין רב ור' יוחנן מתפרשת כמחלוקת עקרונית בין אחריות האדם כלפי עצמו למחויבותו כלפי אחרים—העימות של "אם אין אני לי מי לי, וכשאני לעצמי מה אני." נכון, שבדרך כלל ש"חייך וחיי חבירך—חייך קודמים," אבל כאן הרי ישנו חיוב ספיציפי וקונקרטי כלפי אשתו, ולכן אפשר שבמקרה זה חיובו לאחרים קודם.

מצד שני, אפשר שהמחלוקת בין רב ורבי יוחנן מתמקדת בתלמוד תורה, נשואין, והחיוב המוסרי, לא הלכתי, לאדם כלפי אשתו. למשל, מהו הערך של קיום/חיוב תלמוד תורה למי שכבר יצא ידי

---

[2] למרות שהמשנה דנה בענין עונה, ולא בחיוב הבעל למשפחה כולה, מתשובת ר' יוחנן "שאני התם דאית ליה רווחא," והסברו של רש"י שם, נראה שמדובר כאן בחיוב הבעל לכל צרכי אשתו וכלפי המשפחה כולה.

אישות ותלמוד תורה – ניווט המתח[1]
הרב דב לינזר

ובפרק קמא דגיטין אשכחן דשלח רבי אביתר בני העולין משם הן קיימו
עצמם: 'ויתנו (את) הילד בזונה והילדה מכרו ביין.' פירוש שצריכין בניו ובנותיו
להתמשכן בעבור מזונותיהן, משמע שאין יפה עושים שהולכים ללמוד חוץ
למקומן.
(תוס' קדושין (כ"ט:) ד"ה הא לו)

ואנשי חיל הם אבירי הלב בשלימות הבטחון כולו לעשות מצות תמיד ולהגות בתורה
יום ולילה, אף שביתתו אין לחם ושמלה, ובניו ובני ביתו יצעקו לו: "הבה לנו מחיה
להחיינו ולפרנסנו!" ואינו משגיח עליהם כלל, ולקולם לא יחת... והוא כי בטלו כל
אהבותיו נגד אהבת ה' ותורתו ומצותיו.
(ביאור הגר"א – משלי כג:ל)

מאמר זה יעסוק בשאלה משמעותית המתיחסת לשתי אהבותיו ומשיכותיו של האדם—אחת,
ביתו ומשפחתו, והשניה, בית מדרשו ותורתו. בסקירת הסוגיות נעסוק בערכים שונים הבאים לידי
ביטוי בהתנגשות בין שתי משיכות אלה, והמסקנות הנלמדות מכך.

א. אישות ותלמוד תורה – מחלוקת רב ורבי יוחנן

המשנה בכתובות (פ"ה מ"ו) פוסקת:

התלמידים יוצאין לתלמוד תורה שלא ברשות שלשים יום, הפועלים—שבת
אחת.

הגמרא על המקום (דף ס"א:-ס"ב.) מציעה שאלה המתבקשת מלשון המשנה:

ברשות כמה? כמה דבעי.

הגמרא מתחילה בנקיטת עמדה שברשות האישה, הבעל יכול לצאת כמה זמן שהוא רוצה.
לכאורה, עמדה זו סבירה, אבל הגמרא לא מסתפקת בכך, אלא שואלת: אורחא דמילתא כמה?
כפי שנראה מתשובת הגמרא (להלן), השאלה איננה מה היה נהוג בפועל, אלא מה הנוהג הנכון,
המוסרי. וכן מפרש רש"י: "אורחא דמילתא—דרך ארץ שלא ישא עליו חטא, ואפילו הוא יכול
לפתותה שתתן לו רשות." לפי רש"י, המשנה נוקטת את ההלכה—את שורת הדין. אבל מי שבא
לחיות את חייו כפי הדרישה המוסרית והדתית המלאה, שורת הדין אינה מספקת. אדם השומר

---

[1] מאמר זה הינו עיבוד שיעור הפתיחה להלכות נידה ואישות שניתן בחורף ה'תשס"ז. אני מודה להר' זאב פרבר
על עזרתו בעריכת המאמר.

ג

תוכן המאמרים שבעברית

מילין חביבין

שנתון המוקדש לעניני תורה, חברה, ורבנות

יוצא לאור ע״י תלמידי ישיבת חובבי תורה

ניו יורק

כרך ג׳
כסלו תשס״ז

⤳⤳⤳⤳⤳⤳⤳⤳⤳⤳

עורכים ראשיים:

עקיבא דוד וייס, בנימין שילר

צוות עורכים:

יהודה האזמאן, דוד וואלקענפעלד, מיימון ויאריאל, אסף וינברג, מייקל כצמאן, דרו קפלן

מדריך הפרויקט:

הרב נתנאל הלפגוט